THE PLAN

A novel

By

J. Richard Wright

The Plan is a work of fiction. Names, characters, places and incidents are the products of the author's imagination or are used fictitiously. Any resemblance to actual events, locales or persons living or dead is purely and entirely coincidental.

However, having said that, in this work and some others by this author, there may be one or more events which happened personally to the author but did not involve other individuals.

Copyright © 2013 by J. Richard Wright

All rights reserved

Visit **jrichardwright.com** or **jrichardwright.ca**

ISBN – 978-1484891940

Book cover creation and design by Sherron Moorhead
www.motivationgraphics.ca
Offering custom and creative quality web site and eBook cover design to maximize your marketing efforts and enhance organizational exposure.

*For Sandi, my love,
Who watched the good times from afar
And when they ended,
Picked me up and made me whole again*

ACKNOWLEDGEMENTS:

I wish to thank a number of people who were kind enough to encourage and support me during my lengthy journey to transform from a long-time television and radio writer into a novelist. First among many is Lorna Stone who read early bits and pieces of this novel over many, many years and who encouraged me initially and along the way with her positive feedback, bright outlook and unwavering confidence. Then there were my other readers including: Sandi Johnston, Sue Rautenberg, Nancy Denise, Bob Moorhead, Heinz Rautenberg and Diane Underwood who read the manuscript and offered insightful and helpful comments. I also apologize to Sandi for the many prolonged and spirited debates we had (Okay, okay… arguments!) over portions of the manuscript that she felt needed to be changed or did change as a result. Also, thank you Sandi for your medical and story input.

Also, many thanks to Nicole Rautenberg for her help in marketing and promoting *The Plan* and her donation of hosting services.

I also wish to thank Captain Bob Ferguson (Retired) Air Canada pilot who spent time vetting the aircraft landing and takeoff sequences to make them true to life. Bob, who has served as a consulting pilot for some high-profile feature movies was amazingly patient throughout the process. However, any and all errors or omissions that may have occurred are totally mine.

Thank you to my children Matthew and Sarah who always had faith.

Finally, I wish to thank my dear friend Sherron Moorhead who tirelessly, generously and graciously created, designed and executed a perfect cover for *The Plan* as well as a beautiful and very effective website – `jrichardwright.com` – and who had to wait and wait for copy. While patience is a virtue, sometimes a whip works better.

Thanks so much everybody.

6

PROLOGUE

"THE BEGINNING"

In the beginning, God created
the heaven and the earth. And
the earth was without form, and
void; and darkness was upon the
face of the deep. And the spirit
of God moved upon the face of the
waters. And God said, "Let there
be light; and there was light...."

Genesis 1; 3

Rather than the popular theory of a single moment of creation 14 billion years ago, some biblical scholars believe that the earth was created not once, but twice. Its first appearance was during the Ante-Chaotic Age when God created Heaven for His angelic beings. Here the Dispensation of Angels was complete and they ruled the planets under His light of eternity and peace. But during this time of great joy, one archangel, the Light-Bearer, a favorite and more beautiful than the others, was not content to be one among many. Lucifer thirsted for knowledge and power.

And so, eons before earth saw light and before the salvific birth to save mankind from the torment of the everlasting damnation of sin, Lucifer the Accuser screamed blasphemy at a loving God and questioned His right to rule. For a time, God's perfect love quieted Lucifer; his ambitions fell victim to God's will. But finally he again thirsted for what he could not have, all-knowledge and all-power. He again challenged the Divinity and union of God – The Trinity.

But as the Heavens split asunder with his jealousy, rage and covetousness, Lucifer learned that his loving God was also a just God. The Holy Trinity summoned the Nine Orders of Angelic Beings; the Seraphims, Cherubims, Thrones, Dominations, Virtues, Powers, Principalities, Archangels and Angels stood in council before the Most High.

Archangel Lucifer stood boldly aside. In a cunning oratory ripe with promises, lies and deceit, he swayed legions of angels to join him in revolt.

And as Lucifer viciously attacked the justness of The Order, it soon became apparent that the irrevocable lines of conflict were being drawn. The word was set and there was no retreat from the blasphemy.

Sadly God mourned the loss of perfection as it lay at the feet of The Trinity – the first victim of His servant's malicious goals. He knew that other, more terrible ordeals would follow though they were neither of His choice nor making. A challenge was issued by the traitor in a fiery proclamation of individuality and hate. He and his would turn out The Trinity and seize the power.

And it came to pass that God's sadness soon turned to anger. He called to a new lieutenant to champion the cause of goodness. Preparations for war followed.

Soon Archangel Michael led God's angels against the usurpers in a celestial and eschatological conflict where solar systems served as marshalling points for the multitudes of warriors and universes as the bloody battlegrounds.

Epic, unimaginable destruction followed as the battle raged. Bloody, smoldering weapons and powers of such intensity as to melt the Heavens were employed. When the last trumpet sounded, Lucifer's forces were found to be no match for the Sons of Light; the Trinity triumphed.

Banished in disgrace from the Light forever, the new Keeper of Hell screamed foul and echoed forth that so-called righteousness would again be truly tested. He and a full third of God's angels became embodiments of evil and slunk into the blackness of space vowing to seek revenge.

God walked the planets, now dark and void of those angels who had been banished. Though He had triumphed, the calm emptiness was not a sign to rejoice. He knew that while perfection was the first casualty of the battle, innocence was the second victim of Lucifer's ambitions. Now a spectrum of good and evil existed where only goodness had reigned before. The evil blackened even the night and God was troubled.

God looked at the dark, wasted earth – the former planet of Lucifer – and said: "Let there be light."

And there was light. And God saw the light and that it was good. And He separated the light from the darkness.

For five days God created a second incarnation of earth adding the waters, the beasts, fishes and fowl. On the sixth He created man and He called him Adam; and from Adam, He created Eve. Together He gave them dominion over every living thing on the earth.

On the seventh day He rested and watched their pleasure in His garden. He was well pleased with His creations.

But from the shadows Lucifer also watched and yearned to test the power of this goodness. After all, God had bestowed upon Adam and Eve a free will, the will to choose their personal destiny.

The dark one, now believed to have taken the name Satan, approached God and from the safety of the shadows taunted Him. If He believed goodness without evil could exist, then make earth the arena and mankind the gladiators. Let free will be tested.

And God had faith in His creatures.

But as Adam found happiness with Eve in the Garden of Eden, Satan created his own advocate, a black champion to second evil's presence and tempt God's creatures – an arch demon in the infernal satanic hierarchy: Adramelech.

And so a serpent was indeed loosed upon the earth; not just a mere reptile – but a serpent of evil taking many forms over the ages. The first incarnation was a snake.

And as the Scriptures recorded, malevolence in the form of the Beast led God's children to fall from initial grace and to be banished from the Garden. Hell's leaders Satan, Belial and Leviathan rejoiced and commanded their champion to continue his evil torment on earth, to sway mankind from God's path whenever possible and point them on the path to hell.

God saw this and vowed to help His creatures. He would send His son to renew hope even as the Beast brought more followers to evil. Though earth spurned Jesus, His teachings lived on.

And so, through the ages, Adramelech lived: when Moses led the Jews out of Egypt under Jehovah's charter, he cursed and thirsted in the hills; when Jesus of Nazareth went into the desert to fast, he tried to turn Him from the Father; when Roman General Gaius Marius waged wars against Jugurtha, he fed quietly on the battlefield wounded; and when Charlemagne restored Leo III to the Holy See and was crowned Emperor by him in Rome on Christmas Eve in 800 A.D., the Beast slunk in the shadows of a stone passageway and cursed the seed of the Holy Roman Emperor.

As the Beast moved on the mists of time and performed his black deeds, he became legend and was known by many names and personifications: in Romania people whispered of the blood-sucking Vampira; in Denmark, the savagery of a wolf-like man called the Vaerulf; and in other cultures, as he seized women and spirited them away, he was known as an Incubus, a male demon who copulated with human women to produce devil children known as Cambions.

In his many forms he watched the Ch'in dynasty begin building the Great Wall of China, the blood flow during the Crusades and the rise of modern monsters such as Hitler and Ceausescu.

And now, slightly less than half a century after he had haunted the Nazi death camps and from there journeyed to Central America where he was found out and put into the Deathsleep, the Beast was awakening again to begin anew the work for which he had been created.

With a cumulative and inherent cunning born of billions of years in spirit and millenniums in flesh, he would rip into the very bowels of humanity and force the pitiful wretches to confront their own mortality and see the inevitability of eternal damnation.

* * * *

PART ONE

THE AWAKENING

…But thou art cast out of thy grave like an abominable branch and as the raiment of those that are slain, thrust through with a sword, that go down to the stones of the pit; as a carcase trodden under feet. Thou shalt not be joined with them in burial…

ISAIAH 14:19; 20

12

~ 1 ~

PANAMA JUNGLE – SOMEWHERE SOUTH OF THE RIO CHAGRES RIVER

DECEMBER 1989

It was time.

Six feet down in the damp earth, shadows stirred where stillness had reigned for almost half a century. A manlike shape, a creature of the night entombed in the remnants of an old wooden vessel emblazoned with a fractured silver cross, shuddered in a damp hollow pocket in the earth as the inky blackness of the grave witnessed catatonic slumber surrender to a greater, primitive urge.

Starvation yanked the Beast through a fog-shrouded haze of oblivion towards the sanctity of conscious life as a pulsing hunger raced urgently through his body. Cobwebs of sleep were swept aside, and ravaged muscles rippled and contracted. Fingers curled in agony and the creature's back arched upwards to where a mortal's spine would have snapped with the tinder of a dry twig.

But this creature was not mortal.

Nor had he ever floated peacefully in a loving womb, a product of a sacred union. The Beast, an arch demon of hell – having taken the name Adramelech – had been conceived from hate and born of fire when only time and space existed. He was a supernatural challenge to all that was blessed and privileged, the Beast Master's answer to goodness and an antithesis of righteousness. This was evil incarnate sent to irrevocably seal the fate of the near-damned while further seducing pure innocence to enter its fiery mouth and experience the raptures of hell; he had always done his work well.

He groaned....

Suddenly Adramelech was fully conscious; nerve endings danced and screamed for relief from the dreaded hunger gnawing painfully at his congealed insides.

Frigid blood, previously dried and crusted, began to ooze sluggishly through long-collapsed veins. Vessels and arteries ballooned into new life as an unholy power created, healed and rejuvenated long decayed tissue that for a mortal would have turned to dust.

Aware of his awakening, he tried to roll over but found no strength. His impotency and an arrogance born of his inherent supremacy over the earth's beings brought angry indignation.

He bawled weakly....

The surprising and frightfully pitiful sound of his own mewling filled him with despair at first, and then with rage. In desperation, one twisted, talon-like hand lashed violently out and burst through the side of the rotted coffin to plunge into the damp earth. Cracked and dried lips screamed for sustenance but only a rasping croak emerged.

Two encrusted eyelids peeled open and dried orbs, shrunken and yellowed by time and rot, blinked unseeingly at the roughened wood of the vessel that trapped him.

He tried to roll over again. This time a powerful shoulder crashed into the lid of the casket tearing the beaten metal and splintering the remaining wood. He began to move.

Above, the grass rippled and parted; fresh, moist dirt forced its way upward and squeezed through the earth's wound like a stream of black blood. The tear rapidly widened as small rocks, roots and rotted vegetation appeared and spilled over. The hole grew larger.

Yellowed eyes blazing with anger, the Beast pulled himself swiftly through the shadows of the earth. He burst upward from the bowels of his grave in an explosion of mud and squatted trembling on the turf like a shadowy, giant grasshopper, spent and exhausted.

Sapped by the exertion, his head lolled from side to side as he sniffed the air. With his body temperature near freezing, the humid tropical air misted and steamed about the creature. An answering wisp of frost escaped from the depths of the hole and lost itself against the twinkling stars in the night sky. The Beast's eyes followed the wisp as a misshapen, pointed tongue lolled from his mouth.

The Central American jungle was strangely silent now, the quiet broken only by the low, snarling rumble of a nocturnal predator. He swung drunkenly towards the sound. After a moment, a black panther, warned by some primeval instinct, beat a hasty retreat from the area and vanished into the safety of the underbrush.

As he moved clear of the hole, the last few pieces of a rotted, wooden stake dropped from his chest to the ground. Though still weak, he seized the moment of triumph and with mouth open in a soundless scream, leaped defiantly upward to his full height of almost seven feet.

Though he had the head, torso, appendages and general shape of a human being, the resemblance to any of nature's creations ended there. He lifted his head in the hazy light of the full moon and took in his surroundings.

Dried morsels of rotted meat were dropping from his cheeks and forehead. But as he drew his first shuddering breath in decades, these rotted pieces were replaced by spider-veined, milk-white skin and flesh growing magically to cover the gleaming bone of his skull.

Slanted eyes shone with the pale, yellow, reflective light of an animal as perfectly preserved white fangs gaped from the black hole that served as a mouth. Above the mouth, cartilage and mottled flesh were reforming a semblance of a nose which had surrendered to the ravages of the grave. A wrinkled, hairless dome topped by two bony protuberances over a squat triangular head looked up and hungrily drank in the pale light of the moon. Except for the tattered remains of a coarsely-woven, black cloak hanging from his shoulders, the Beast stood naked. The shawl, fastened by an intricately-carved iron clasp, was draped over unnaturally wide shoulders which grew into arms, long and powerful, and ended in hands which more resembled talons. The fingernails had grown long, black and curled. From his shoulder blades, two bone-ribbed skin wings protruded; a reptilian spider webbing of moist, pink veins throbbed with newfound life within them.

His bulk, supported by long, muscular legs, swelled ever so slightly as he felt his strength returning. His male sex, long, hard and gnarled, swayed as the creature, no longer unsure, now betrayed the savage energy of a coiled snake.

As the Power returned, the Beast vowed never to sleep the Deathsleep again. He would eviscerate all of humanity rather than allow the pitiful innocents of this planet to again drive a missile through his pulsing heart and reduce it to a busted, bloody, deflated mass unable to mend itself around the stake cursed with the blessing of the Hated One.

A new contest for possession of the Hated One's chosen masses had now begun. It was time to feed, grow stronger and reap what had been sown so long ago. As foretold, Lucifer would seek to dominate the earth, and for his good work, the Beast would sit at the right hand of the true Chosen One – the antithesis of that incarnation whom man called The Savior, The Father or The Holy Spirit.

The constant need for food, an ancient covenant inherent in the genetic make-up of the creature, had awakened him hundreds of times before to grasp new life in a grim paradox: to suck the blood of his prey for life-giving nourishment while his victims became cold and eternally still. Suddenly he grew quiet and listened.

The rip of a burst of automatic rifle fire echoed from some distance away. Adramelech sniffed the air. War? Images of wounded soldiers lying helplessly on the battlefields with great, gaping, bleeding wounds immediately flooded into his head.

If there was a battle, he fervently hoped for living among the causalities. Though he could feed on the dead, he ached for a victim with a pulsing heart to drive coursing rivulets of warm, sweet blood down his throat; to allow him to benignly nurse at a well-opened artery like a contented babe. Once satiated, healed and rested, he would regain his powers of shape-shifting and move undetected among mankind as he continued his work.

The horror rose and moved swiftly through the tropical ferns and palm fronds of the Panamanian jungle, an unholy expectation surging through ice-cold veins.

The Awakening heralded the coming of a remorseless aberration – a spawn of hell had risen to lay siege once more to the Forces of Light. Soon even the Hated One would be forced to acknowledge that evil had triumphed over goodness and Satan would retake the name Lucifer and begin his rightful ascension into the Light.

As the Beast moved, he could taste the sweetness of life. Humanity would soon taste the bitterness of death.

~ 2 ~

Tonight, Clay Montague knew he might die.

But as a U.S. Lieutenant with the 3rd Ranger Battalion of the 75th Ranger Regiment out of Fort Benning, Georgia, now engaged in nightly missions against Panamanian Hunter Platoons along the Panamanian coast, he also admitted to himself that this feeling wasn't particularly unusual. Operation *Just Cause* was in full swing. U.S. forces poured into the small Central American country to oust and capture dictator and strongmen Manuel Noriega. Panama City had already fallen to American forces as well as the airport, areas near the Panama Canal and Rio Hato. But though the majority of the 16,000 member Panamanian Defense Force (PDFs) had been defeated, there were still pockets scattered throughout the countryside in small garrisons called "cuartels."

To avoid needless killings, U.S. Forces had created "capitulation missions" and sent Special Forces' elements with Spanish-speaking liaison officers, to arrange and coordinate the PDF surrender. While most garrisons quickly laid down their arms, contingents of hard core resistance fighters had also fled and night missions had become extremely dangerous. With the PDFs showing unexpected resilience and their Hunter Platoons not to be trifled with on their own turf, Clay's orders were to find them, coordinate their surrender or neutralize them.

As a fairly serious Catholic, the 24-year-old prepared for his patrols by confronting his own mortality and expressing contrition for his sins; his faith always gave him comfort.

From his crouched position by a scrub palm somewhere deep in the jungle near the Atlantic side of the Panama Canal, Clay straightened his six-foot frame. He wiped sweat from the corners of a wide, handsome mouth. Flint-grey eyes peered from his grease-darkened face and raked the darkened jungle. He brushed dirt off his jungle battle dress.

Not a leaf stirred, not a bush moved.

Removing his M-1 steel helmet, he ran fingers through his thick brown hair now soaked with sweat and bog-tainted humidity. He waited a moment longer before finally shouldering the M249 Squad Automatic Weapon, a SAW light machine gun capable of delivering a devastating volume of 5.56 mm slugs at the rate of 725 rounds per minute. He signaled his ten men to get ready to move out from the protective cover of the Mangrove thicket.

SOMETHING ISN'T RIGHT....

A small inner voice nagged him, challenging his professional confidence. He ignored it. After all, they merely had to cross a small, unprotected clearing. No big deal...maybe.

He looked up.

The silvery disc of a bloated full moon slipped silently behind a thick cloud and a grey shroud settled over the jungle like a huge, humid blanket. He waved his arm and one-by-one his men moved like phantoms in the night, shadowy, furtive, hunched-over gnomes scurrying frantically for fresh cover in a jungle ripe with hidden peril. Quickly he followed them. Reaching the other side of the clearing, they again concealed themselves amongst the ferns, sedge, and mangrove forest; all motion ceased and they turned to hushed figures of stone.

Silently they waited.

He scanned the area....

Nothing moved.

Grinning inwardly at his own angst, he tried to shrug off the unsettled feeling gnawing at him. His point men were out, the jungle was alive with sounds and there were no fresh traces of the enemy. Every sign indicated they were secure for the moment.

Still the feeling refused to leave. It whispered that somehow, tonight, tragedy was poised to strike. Perhaps in the form of a stray enemy patrol, the deadly bite of a bushmaster or copperhead, or a bunch of coarsely-woven, grass-mat-covered punji pits housing upright, sharpened stakes ready to impale some poor soldier like a hapless butterfly crucified by an entomologist's straight pin.

Clay was grateful for one advantage. As a prior Panamanian ally, their U.S. unit had availed itself of American jungle warfare training facilities at Fort Sherman Military Reservation and the Pina Range Complex right in Panama. They had trained throughout 2,300 acres of both single and double canopy jungle, now enabling them to read their surroundings like natives.

WATCH OUT...!

Goddamnit, he was being as careful as he could. He shrugged off the inner voice and glanced down the barely visible overgrown pathway stretching into the night mist.

The motionless air steamed with humidity. Beads of sweat ran down Clay's face. The moon finally slipped from behind the cloud and bathed the area in a blue-white wash casting deep, fragmented shadows along the jungle trail.

The sounds of feeders seeking their prey suddenly exploded in death screams as the hunted squirmed helplessly in the jaws of a predator. Its life was quickly snuffed out in a squealing, savage tearing of flesh and crunching of bone. Clay felt a momentary sympathy as the screams gurgled shrilly in mid-note and went silent. The hush uttered a finality that only death could bring.

The night scene was beautiful, Clay thought. Possibly more alluring if every patch of black didn't have the potential to hide death. He glanced up at a break in the leafy forest canopy at the mass of stars winking silently in the black sky. The jungle was alive.

Time to move out.

Clay lifted his hand and the patrol rose as one and made ready to trudge on. Cursing the heat, and nervously swinging their weapons to the left and right to cover the shadows, the men made their way cautiously down the trail. Adrenaline levels surged at the slightest noise or the barest glimmer of movement; restless eyes probed every leafy nook and cranny of the jungle. Silently, they bore the stress of knowing that at any moment an enemy ambush could send a withering hail of fire into their ranks and literally cut them to pieces.

Ahead, Clay held up a hand.

The gesture was repeated down the line of ten men, bone weary in their heavy battle gear. Warily they came to a halt, teeth and eyes shining like beacons amidst the camouflage grease.

Looking back Clay whispered: "We look like a damn traveling minstrel show." His half-hearted attempt to ease the tension caused a few men to grin; others made no sign they'd heard. Edgy, Clay thought.

His disquiet lingered.

SOMETHING IS TERRIBLY WRONG....

A quick burst of machine gun fire echoed in the distance. *What the hell...?*

The jungle immediately grew silent again but his suspicions were confirmed. The enemy was obviously on the move. A few more distant shots rang out. Time to trust those instincts alright, to pay heed to the tiny, visceral voice from his gut that warned of subliminal changes in jungle and animal patterns.

The hair on Clay's neck prickled upward....

The jungle maintained its deadly quiet! *How close were they?*

Not a bird, not a cricket, not an animal stirred in a jungle that, moments before, had pulsed with a cacophony of life.

Breathlessly the patrol waited, listened, aching, straining to penetrate the sudden silence, to pick up the slightest snap of a branch whipping back on a uniform, the rustle of leaves, or the careful tread of a combat boot on the move.

The hairs on the back of Clay's neck were literally at attention now....

SOMETHING IS NEAR....

The ten men tensed; uneasy and sweating, they waited....

After five minutes of remaining motionless Clay could feel the strain in every muscle and bone. Nerves were strung as taunt as bow strings.

They waited another two minutes....

Still nothing, not a whisper.

The resumption of the jungle sounds began almost as abruptly as they had ceased. The incessant babble of night predators running, slithering, or winging their way through the moist air mixed with the squawk of prey being run to the ground. Insects buzzed madly. A few howler monkeys screamed their rage at being awakened by the distant shooting and their personal instinct for danger; a sudden, heavenly cool breeze wafted through the trees.

Clay breathed a sigh of relief and slapped at an insect whining around his ear. The jungle was telling him there was nothing nearby. Perhaps the fire came from a nervous sentry at a jungle outpost. He checked his map; they were heading for a valley.

He dismissed the persistent little voice warning of doom and gloom.

Still, it nattered on.

~ 3 ~

FOOD!

Adramelech moved swiftly through the jungle, scales of lifeless tissue continuing to drop from a grotesque body as cells magically divided and multiplied to replace the aged and worn features. But the replacements, while functional, seemed lifeless and misshapen, ugly, mutated caricatures of reality; genetics somehow gone terribly amiss.

In his frantic evolution, this creature of darkness had passed oddity and even monstrosity to become a living nightmare – one that would send most humans screaming into the night. Later, however, when he was at full strength, he would be able to shape-shift into a form more acceptable to humanity, a useful and diabolical camouflage.

But now he cared not, intent only on the desperation of the hunt, the expectation of filling his belly with thick, soupy blood and the wildness of stalking his prey. Running a close second to the need for food, was a crazed desire for revenge, a burning need to kill, to avenge himself for the indignity of the Deathsleep.

Bred for the challenge, this champion of evil knew neither remorse nor conscience. Hunger drove the Beast to conform to the way of the jungle – hunt, kill and eat. Once fed, a diabolical, satanic intellect would awaken and pedagogy – not instinct – would rule his course.

He was a fearsome sight plunging through the night, now almost three hundred pounds of death, glowering eyes scanning the thick, tropical vegetation and long arms ripping leafy fern plants and young trees from his path as he moved. Small and large animals scurried for cover as the rampage quickened. Explosive grunts of effort hissed from his nostrils.

He could smell the blood of fresh kills.

~ 4 ~

Clay squinted at the glowing numerals of his watch: 0200 hours.

After searching most of the valley, they hadn't found any signs of a PDF outpost. At a brief nod from him, the men shrugged out of their ammo-laden belts and backpacks, rested their weapons and dropped quietly to the left and right of the trail in exhaustion.

Clay waved a rifleman out to relieve the point man.

Strange how a kid from the green hills of Vermont could wind up in such a tropical hellhole. Lately he almost wished he'd finished veterinary school and taken over his father's small animal hospital in Newport. Instead, as a young man he had been cursed with itchy feet – a longing to see what was over the next hill. His sense for adventure eventually led him to an army recruiting office.

It was only after trading stories with men from his platoon, many who had come from the New York, Boston or Philadelphia projects that Clay realized what a privileged life he'd led in Newport. His youth had been one of a father and mother devoted to him and his sister, Holly. He had graduated from stickball to baseball, cubs to scouts and, as a young boy resisting the company of girls, to adolescence when he desired their company more than anything else on earth. And, as a good-looking, personable young man with New England manners and a healthy respect for the rights and needs of others, he'd never been short of dates either at Sacred

Heart High or at the University of Vermont. In fact, his teen-age years were a blur of drive-in movies, bowling, afternoons at the malt shop, swimming in Lake Memphremagog, and backseat adventures with his girl friends. Now, he carried a weapon for his country.

Not that the army had turned out to be half bad for an officer. The recruiting office was only too glad to pick up a fit young fellow with his education. After fourteen weeks at Officer Candidate School at West Point, and then attending the Officer Basic Course, he received his commission as a 2nd Lieutenant. He volunteered for Ranger School and graduated three months later.

Two weeks after graduation, he'd been at his mother's bedside as she prepared for surgery for invasive carcinoma highlighted by two lumps in her throat. Over the next six month, she'd endured repeated surgeries, and radiation and chemotherapy until her small body was a mere walking skeleton.

In turn, Clay found himself spending more and more time in chapels begging God to spare her; she didn't deserve this hell. Instead, though the statues of Jesus, Mary and Joseph stared down on him with carefully crafted, plaster-cast looks of benevolence, there was but a cold, empty silence that emanated from them.

Ironically, as though sensing his anger and disappointment with his Catholicism, his mother's words to him in a thin, reedy, pain-filled voice that was not hers were: "Don't give up your faith, Clay. God hears. He just sometimes says no...."

Later, with his father and Holly out of the room taking a well-deserved break for a coffee in the hospital cafeteria, Clay felt her pressing her long-worn golden Crucifix into his hands with a request for him not to be sad. "Remember: All that matters in life is love and it *never* dies; it simply changes." Moments later, exhausted by a life no longer tolerable, she slipped away. Clay silently left the room, angry with a God that abandoned a harmless, loving woman to such a horrible death.

After a week of compassionate leave spent with his father and Holly, he'd returned to a variety of postings including providing covert support for DEA agents in Colombia, and finally, action in Panama. His father, heartbroken over their mother's death, sold his Newport veterinarian practice and moved in with Holly in Portsmouth, New Hampshire. Four months later, Clay attended his father's funeral. The doctor's unofficial diagnosis: his father died of a broken heart.

Clay clicked the safety on the M249. He looked up at his men quietly kneading tired muscles, re-lacing boots and putting on fresh DEET insect repellent. Though prepared for combat, there was a sense of relief in knowing that U.S. forces had overwhelmed the PDFs loyal to General Noriega and that the action had a definitive life measured in days. It was strange how one dictator could make thousands pay for his personal ambitions.

General Noriega was such a man in a banana republic sort of way. But when the general had tried to cling to power by voiding election results and having his irregular paramilitary units called "Dignity Battalions" (DIG BATs) beat up political opposition leaders, it ran afoul of the United States of America. His other mistake was that his regime's paranoia made daily existence for U.S. forces and other U.S. citizens unsafe. For instance, when the government declared a state of war existed with the U.S., and Americans were harassed culminating with a marine lieutenant being killed, the general assumed his past relationship with the U.S. would ensure everything would be handled diplomatically. Instead the U.S. State Department decided he had stepped over the line this time. The abrupt departure of U.S. noncombatants signaled the ultimate arrival of a U.S. invasion force.

A low whistle sounded from farther down the path and the point men came back in, nodding quietly to Clay as they passed and slumped down beside the others.

"God, I need a weed," Sergeant Rufus Token hissed from down the line.

"This is the no smoking section, Sarge," Corporal Figaro whispered with a grin from the other side of the trail. No one smoked on patrol.

Token, a huge black man of about 30 from Detroit, looked over at the small Italian from Brooklyn. His white teeth glistened in the dark. "I'm gonna whup your ass if you don't show me no respect, white boy."

The corporal responded with a crooked grin and threw Token a can of bourbon-flavored Copenhagen chewing tobacco. The man nodded, popped a generous chaw into his cheek and threw the can back.

Clay slapped at another mosquito and cursed as perspiration ran down between his shoulder blades making him itch. He could take the enemy, the dirt and even the insects but the eternal heat and unrelenting humidity sapped his strength and endurance. Yanking his Ka-Bar combat knife out of a scabbard attached to his leg, he probed at a maddening itch on his back.

No doubt about it, when his hitch was finished, there was no way he'd re-up.

~ 5 ~

Adramelech stopped. Gently he tested the air with his nostrils and cursed his dependency on the human nourishment he needed to give him life. Just as the Hated One had shed the sacred blood of His Son to give humanity eternal life, Satan had decreed that Adramelech must rely on human blood to also give him life – an irony ensuring he would wreak havoc on God's pitiful creations. Blood for blood.

Instinctively he pulled the coarse cloak close as insects tried to feast on his new flesh. The jungle moon revealed a thickly vegetated forest full of bamboo, palm trees and heavy fauna. But what time was this? And, where was Miguel, that miserable familiar who was supposed to guard his resting place with his life? His brain no longer spun madly now but exercised the full powers of a sophistication and cunning based on the cumulative knowledge and wisdom of his life of many millennia. He focused on remembering the time just before he entered the Deathsleep.

He had slaughtered a sizable portion of a small Central American village. Satisfied, he traveled for two days before finding another village where a pious priest ruled supreme from his small Catholic church. A monastery also sat near the village and each day monks would come to teach the village children or work alongside the villagers in fields laboriously carved from the jungle.

First he had found a place of safety for the days, deep in the cellar of an abandoned building well outside of the village. Satisfied with his lair, the first night he dined on a young man named Miguel and made him his own. Miguel would thereafter be his link to the happenings in the sun.

After that, each night he quietly bled the villagers as they slept. Sometimes he took but a little...sometimes too much. Panic had followed the discoveries of the mutilated dead, and more and more wounded, weakened and anemic villagers moaned of monsters in the night. Prayers were said by some, and sacrifices made by others to try to stop the mysterious killings. It seemed God ignored them as Adramelech continue to feed, his deeds fit only for the shadows.

Occasionally, when he captured a young woman and the urge took him, a mad, savage rape would follow battering the poor victim into insensibility. And when finished, Adramelech would tear her legs open and bite into the femoral artery of her groin for a sticky, sweet meal pumped into his mouth compliments of a heart frantically beating in terror. In less than two minutes, he would drain her dry, collapse her vessels and leave a bloodless, stiff husk of a corpse, huge dead eyes pleading for salvation while mirroring her final moments of fear and despair.

For a time, Adramelech had been content to prey upon the peasants of the small Latin American community, but later he had grown increasingly bold and stalked the holy man as he sat in meditation near a stream.

The priest had left his church that evening and come to pray in nature's garden. Unmindful of the recent slaughters in other villages, or possibly believing his devotions protected him from the evils of the world, he barely noticed when the sun began to set. Night descended swiftly but his religious dedications continued to bind him in rapt and divine contemplation. His meditations were only interrupted when he heard something heavy land on the earth behind him. A chill, much colder than any night should be, caused him to shiver.

Slowly the priest had turned, his cowl pulled high against the coolness of the evening. He barely had time to gape, much less run, before the creature had sliced his throat wide with one quick swipe of a fingered nail. The hooded man's eyes bugged and he collapsed to the ground thrashing aimlessly and trying to staunch the blood coming in great ripping bursts from his throat. Within seconds his eyes rolled up in his head as he drowned, sucking blood into his lungs.

Adramelech had sunk over him, fastened his mouth securely about the hemorrhaging wound and passionately inhaled the life-giving liquid. He held the holy man in an iron grip and sucked lovingly, rapturously on the throat, squirming against his victim and groaning in delicious ecstasy as the warm, sugary blood slipped into his belly. He had then returned to his tomb, fat and satiated.

But something had gone wrong.

Frightened over his Master's increasing boldness, Miguel had found the strength to betray the Sacred Trust. Somehow that miserable piece of dog meat had led the heathen to where Adramelech rested in his vessel awaiting the night, a final, futile attempt to save his immortal soul through betrayal of his Master.

Slowly Adramelech allowed the rest of the bitter memories to return: the discovery of his resting place near the monastery; the screaming fury of the monks and the maddening slap of hundreds of sandals as they poured out of their monastery gate and burst into his crypt; the arousal and the chase by the holy men into the forest in the early dawn; being burned and weakened again and again with sacred water; and, the curdling effect of their unceasing monastic chanting of holy verses.

Finally, as the sun began to paint a pale, golden glow in the eastern sky, his strength gone, his fear intensifying by the second, the monks dragged him like a bag of animal feces back to the church. On the cold, stone floor, in front of the merciless stare of the Virgin Mary and under an intricately carved Crucifix hanging over the alter, they had surrounded his weakened, burned body. He remembered their bronze faces and frenzied onyx eyes gleaming like hundreds of black coals in the flickering firelight of their torches.

As Adramelech had snarled defiance, he saw with sudden dread the huge, sharpened and blessed wooden stake raised high above his heart.

He tried to rise up and fight but the prayers turned his arms to jelly, his resolve to confusion, and he sank back, weakened beyond redemption.

A fat monk, his robes billowing, eyes red with anger, swung the stake high in two beefy hands. Suddenly, with a whispered prayer, and in the name of Jesus, he drove it downward with all the strength and fury of his collectives' fear and rage.

The Beast screamed at the memory of the pain....

~ 6 ~

"What the hell was that?!" It was Token, his voice edgy as the scream died away. It came from some distance but its tenor and strength made it seem much nearer.

Clay, his heart also racing, shrugged but said nothing. Something was wrong; he could feel it in his bones. There had been a ghostly, almost alien quality to the scream.

YOU'RE NOT ALONE....

He cursed the inner voice and listened intently to the night. Token sat up as they all reached for weapons and stared down the shadowy jungle path. Leafy tropical ferns and the crab-clawed shapes of the heliconias competed in the half-light of the moon to become ghostly squadrons of marching enemy soldiers.

Clay blinked, sweat running freely into his eyes; the salt stung and tears sprang to flush the hurt away. His men were already shrugging into back packs and ammo belts, snatching up their weapons and making ready to dive into the underbrush. Their nervousness was palatable.

"I don't hear anything any more," PFC Danny Osborne said, much too loudly, his voice innocent and full of hope. He barely had time to catch the patrol's glares before Token had his hand over the boy's mouth and his lips pressed against his ear.

"That's the problem, kid, there ain't no friggen sound," Token whispered. "Something's comin'!" He was right.

Suddenly the shriek of a shell arcing through the night air was followed by a muffled crump shaking the earth. It was quickly followed by a series of consecutive and multiple detonations racing towards the men. Mortar attack!

"Incoming," Clay screamed, grabbing his weapon and rolling off the path. His men did the same. They pulled helmets tight and tried to burrow into the earth. A split second later Clay's world erupted into a steaming orange fire mixed with flying dirt and vegetation.

For a second he was lifted skyward and then slammed heavily into a thick clump of cunna grass. Another nearby concussion immediately picked him up again. It flung him a full 20 feet sideways where he landed with a grunt and skidded madly into a grove of young saplings that bent and snapped.

Half-blinded, his ears ringing, he tried to scramble to his feet. Losing his balance, he pitched forward into a merciful black void. He was falling, tumbling madly, end-over-end. Somehow he knew it was useless to struggle so he relaxed. Accepting his fate served as a powerful narcotic, stripping away all cares and worries.

DYING ISN'T SO BAD...IT'S JUST YOUR TIME, the little voice whispered before finally fading into nothing.

~ 7 ~

Clay sat up and spat soil and leafs out of his mouth.

A black velvet night sky, brilliant with firecracker stars, whirled like a mad carousel above his head. He closed his eyes, held his breath and opened them a second time. The display in the sky gradually stopped its rotation; the stars changed from exploding pinwheels of color to twinkling points of light. Still, he continued to feel off balance.

Taking stock of himself and his surroundings, he realized his SAW and helmet were gone, and his skull was one massive ache. Instinctively he touched the back of his head. Finding it wet and sticky, he examined his fingers. A dark smear dripped slowly from them. Blood, thick, oily and partly-congealed, showed like black tar in the moonlight.

Tenderly he explored the wound and pricked his finger on a quarter-sized, jagged piece of sharp metal sticking straight out the back of his skull.

Shrapnel!

Jesus, it must be embedded in his brain! His breath exploded in quick gasps as the realities of his wound brought him to near panic. He fought to regain control.

Forget the shrapnel....

But cripes, it hurt!

Tenderly he explored the wound again.

A three-inch, partially crusted scab surrounded the large metallic protrusion. It was clotting up nicely. If he didn't disturb it, he wouldn't lose any more blood.

Reassured and grateful he was still able to think and function, his thoughts returned to his men. Where the hell were they? Grabbing a small tree, he dragged himself upward but immediately fell back on one knee. Finally he got his footing. A burst of pain shot through his head but he resisted the urge to touch the wound. His dizziness said he couldn't afford to loose more blood. Nausea overwhelmed him momentarily; he fought to avoid throwing up as he looked at his surroundings.

Where the hell was his weapon? A quick search of the surrounding vegetation turned up nothing. How long had he been unconscious? Where were his men? What about the PDFs?

He crouched low and staggered deeper into the shadows of the trees. The stench of cordite still burned in his nostrils and his ears rang from the explosions. After a few minutes, he pushed the thick growth aside and found the spot on the trail where his patrol had rested.

Thanks to a break in the canopy, a full moon momentarily lit up the area quite well and he could make out at least ten smoking holes scarring the pathway; they'd suffered direct hits. How did the PDFs know their location? Was anyone else alive?

He scanned the trail.

No movement.

Clay moved on and stumbled over something glinting in the moonlight. Bending to retrieve the object he recoiled in horror. It was a stainless steel watchband on a bloody severed arm, the upper part still clothed in the remaining few inches of a shirt. The corporal's stripes on the sleeve told him the arm belonged to Figaro. Beside the arm he found and donned a Night Vision Device.

As had become his habit in times of danger, Clay fingered the small, golden Crucifix which he kept hanging alongside his dog tags on a brass chain around his neck. He moved on. Moments later, he found the rest of Figaro's body. Pausing only briefly, he felt tears stinging his eyes; he was supposed to bring his patrol home safe and sound. He adjusted his NVD and continued.

Next he found Token sprawled against a tree. His eyes were wide open, his chest a mass of oozing red meat through which a thick, broken branch and an accordion of shattered ribs protruded.

Clay looked closer. The man's throat had also been slit from ear to ear. His neck gaped open exposing a pink, sinewy windpipe resembling a bloody sliced-off garden hose. Trapped air and latent bowel sounds gurgled up through the esophageal passageway. Little blood issued from the cavernous wound. Mercifully the moon slid behind another cloud again.

Clay remembered his Beretta M9 sidearm, drew the automatic and chambered a round. He hated the damn thing but it was the only weapon he had. Though, prior to adoption by the military the year before, the weapon had tested out at 35,000 MRBF – mean rounds between failure – Clay had personally had miss-feeds occur with its 9x19 mm Parabellum ammunition. It was also as heavy as sin despite its aluminum frame. This was something he noticed in particular in his weakened state. The main advantage was that he had 15 rounds in its clip and one in the chamber, if desired. At 41 ounces fully loaded, it also made a formidable club for close quarter combat.

Staying in the foliage and moving parallel to the path, he found other members of his patrol. Uniformly, they consisted of bloodied bodies, some with only stumps where heads should have been. Strangely the bodies were well out of the kill range of the mortars. *So what happened*!?

He swiped at another mosquito whining about his ear and moved further through the jungle. After first checking to ensure it wasn't a hanging snake, Clay pulled aside a vine and moved a huge palm leaf to find himself staring at a uniformed PDF soldier less than three feet away. The man looked back, wide-eyed in fright.

Heart pounding wildly, Clay yanked up his weapon and squeezed the trigger. The M9 bucked and the 9 mm slug took the man in the left shoulder jerking him backward. As the sharp report cracked through the jungle, Clay was astounded that the man didn't fall. He instinctively crouched low, waiting for hidden weapons to open up on him.

Nothing happened!

He stared at the man he'd just shot. The soldier stared back, still wide-eyed in fright but not moving a muscle. Finally, Clay realized he was looking at another dead man. In fact, he had been dead before he fired.

He moved forward for closer scrutiny.

The enemy soldier was hanging a foot off the ground, impaled below the sternum on a savaged branch, his stare vacant. A mixture of blood and body sewage flowed slowly from the wound down along the errant branch and dripped from the end with a rhythmic slop. The stench of the man's open bowels made Clay quickly cover his nose and mouth with his hand. He staggered on, now worried the shot might have alerted the enemy.

Moving forward in a half-crouch, his weapon at the ready, he soon discovered the scattered remains of an enemy patrol, all dead. The bodies of the PDF were strewn about as though some giant had taken them on, hand-to-hand, leaving behind a shadowy carnage of severed limbs and headless torsos. He checked a few more bodies;

his blood chilled at what he didn't find. There were no bullet holes or shrapnel wounds. *What had killed these men?*

They also weren't within the kill range of the shell holes he'd found. He looked for hidden tell-tale craters.

Nothing.

At first he thought the sound was merely his imagination. Then he heard it a second time, a low moan wafting towards him on the night breeze. It came from his right. Clay froze and slowly sank to his haunches, ready to dive prone. He waited a few minutes and then, with all the stealth derived from his extensive training, he rose and melted into the jungle.

After carefully traveling a few feet, he stopped, held his breath and listened. Something rustled leaves nearby. Sweat dribbled freely into his eyes as he tried to calm his labored breathing and drumming heart. His palms were greasy with sweat. Fearing he'd lose his hold on the weapon, he gripped the M9 with almost fanatical strength. His NVD chose that moment to quit. He shook it a few times and finally discarded it.

There it was again....

Another moan, slightly louder. Someone in pain...just ahead.

Pistol extended towards the sound, Clay moved cautiously forward, his dripping index finger curled tensely on the trigger, eyes probing the shadows.

He could make out a small field as the moon slipped from behind a cloud again; the area was now awash in a pale, milk-white light showing the grass in the clearing as being unnaturally short. Perhaps he was close to a village? That would make sense. By day, the local livestock likely grazed here where sparse grass had grown out of the shadow of the jungle canopy.

He took in the trees bordering the clearing and, at one end, the black bulk of a steep ridge. Almost directly in the center a solid-looking shadow seemed somehow out of place. It was too well defined, too dark to match the surroundings. Puzzled, he watched it for a moment, then decided it was probably a rock.

LEAVE THIS PLACE - RUN! The voice was back.

The moon chose that moment to disappear, leaving only the wan light emanating from around a silver-bordered cloud behind which it vanished. The entire area was plunged back into semi-darkness again.

Another moan sounded and Clay knew it came from near – or maybe behind – the shadow in the field. He studied it more carefully this time.

It appeared to be solid, a curious half-round shape, but almost too rounded for a work of nature. As Clay watched, he was sure it moved...ever-so-slightly.

Sweat stung his eyes again. He silently cursed and hurriedly wiped it away with his fist. Had it moved, or was it his imagination?

Maybe his eyes were just playing tricks on him?

He watched the object for another minute.

What in the hell was it? He was no longer sure it was a rock.

Clay shook more droplets of water from his face and fought a continual urge to swallow; his mouth was dry, his tongue felt like a piece of sandpaper.

GODDAMN THE HEAT....

Clay faced a choice. Listen to the voice, withdraw and come back with reinforcements or stay and possibly be killed. But if there was a wounded man in the field, it could be one of his own. And despite the popular misconception that soldiers fought for country and honor, he and every other active soldier knew they fought for their buddies.

Still, he cursed his sense of honor, his sense of military ethics, his morality and his inbred sense of fair play; he cursed his coaches, his teachers, his military instructors and even inwardly regaled his parents for their teachings. All the personal codes and morality drilled into him throughout his life might very well be responsible for ending it in a few seconds. Though admirable in a perfect world, fair play and loyalty were definite liabilities in war.

Another weak sigh of agony drifted across the clearing. Clay took a deep breath and moved forward keeping his pistol trained on the shadow.

As he inched closer across the grass, he became even more perplexed. It looked like a black tent pitched dead center in the field.

He covered more ground quickly, closing with the shadow, barely breathing as he carefully placed one boot in front of the other, setting each down with the care of a wild animal stalking its prey. He licked dry lips and worked hard to steady his arm and keep his weapon's muzzle trained directly on the center of his target.

The moan was now continuous; undulating in tone, it rose momentarily in intensity and then subsided into a hopeless whimper of miserable suffering. Whoever the man was, there was little doubt he was mortally wounded.

GET AWAY!
RUN!
HIDE!

Inside, the small voice continued to urge him to forget his duty, to turn and run as fast as his legs would carry him from this place. His effort might be for nothing, the voice whispered. The PDF could be watching him from the jungle; he would be killed and the wounded soldier would die anyway.

FLEE...!

Clay ignored the voice, feeling an immense sympathy welling up inside him for the wounded soldier. Though he knew he was following the only moral course of action open to him, his sense of rightness smashed solidly against a deeper instinct, a genetically-based, primitive safety net dedicated to his own survival. It seemed to scream that it was HE who needed saving; the sufferer in the shadow was doomed.

A mere thirty feet from the black mass now, he inched forward in a low crouch, the pistol at arms length. The distance between him and the shadow lessened.

It was a tent!

He could make out the thick folds of heavy, black material that seemed to stir slightly in a light, cool wind which sprung from nowhere. Suddenly a foul stench wafted towards him on the breeze; it invaded his nostrils, a suffocating blanket of pus-like particulate, and a smell so pervasive, so repulsive that he gagged. Hot bile stung the back of his throat as he felt his stomach churning. There was no mistaking what it was; he'd smelled death often, but never with such intensity!

He swallowed, blinked back tears of effort and tried to block the smell as he continued to move cautiously forward. Another sound now displaced the moaning, a hungry, greedy sucking sound. *What the hell was going on?*

As he drew closer, the stench became so powerful, so unbearable that it smothered him, soaking him in a vile haze of rotted fog until he was loath to draw another breath.

Still he moved forward, the 23rd Psalm running through his mind. *Yea, though I walk through the valley of the shadow of death....!*

He had to breathe, had to breathe, had to breathe...!

He took a tentative breath but the putrid fumes stung his lungs once more. His head spun. Then the breeze shifted and the odor dissipated somewhat. Clean air flooded his lungs and his mind cleared.

Barely twenty feet from the object he realized that whatever it was, it wasn't like any tent he'd ever seen. The material lay flat against an under-surface which rippled and throbbed like a living cell.

With hot sweat running freely down Clay's face, he suddenly began to shiver.

Damn, he thought, now I'm freezing. The cold was coming from the tent, a nipping arctic-like chill that set Clay's teeth chattering.

IT'S NOT HUMAN....LOOK OUT!!

The voice inside screamed its warning. Angrily Clay tuned it out.

His breath was coming in shallow pants now, frosting in the frigid air before him. He couldn't believe what he was seeing.

The tent was moving...the whole thing was lifting, expanding, growing, and becoming HUGE...!

The silvery moon chose that moment to slide out from behind grey clouds and expose the body of PFC Osborne lying at the foot of the rising shadow. The boy was on his back in the grass, mouth wide open, arms out-flung like a ritual sacrifice awaiting the knife. From his sallow, ghostly face, a whimper of terminal suffering rose as his body involuntarily jerked in the final throes of mortal shock.

Meanwhile the shadow over the boy was rising like a giant black pillar into the night sky. Instinctively Clay recoiled at the immensity of the figure as it spun, threw back its cloak, and snarled a rasping hiss. Red hot, menacing eyes glared at Clay who tore his gaze from the young soldier on the ground and stared uncomprehendingly at the reality of the horror before him.

TIME TO PAY THE PIPER....

The face was malevolence personified, every horror movie he'd ever seen come to life.

WELCOME INTO THE PRESENCE OF THE LORD OF ALL EVIL....

The eyes gleamed like twin, fiery torches above the creature's blood-soaked hole of a mouth. Black, viscous liquid dribbled unheeded down his chin as Adramelech issued another rasping hiss growing in bass intensity until it became thunder in Clay's ears, knifing into his brain, and shaking him to the core.

Two white dagger shapes dropped from the roof of the creature's mouth and Clay realized he was looking at shining, razor-sharp, incisor teeth.

Three things happened simultaneously.

Clay triggered his weapon. The M9 exploded and belched a foot-long orange flame. The heavy slug crashed into the Beast and rocked it back on its heels. And then, faster than any eye could follow, an arm snaked out from the huge creature with the fiery eyes and crashed into his skull flipping him over backwards.

The blow set Clay adrift in a sea of indigo and though he struggled to make out some light, to be able to fight the good fight, in a far off corner of his brain he welcomed the reprieve as he sank back into another bleak pool of darkness. His last bizarre thought was: This is getting to be a habit.

Adramelech looked down at the supine mortal, so close, so tempting, white throat exposed less than ten feet away in the tall grass. Blood covered the side of the man's face and head and the arch demon lifted a claw-like hand to taste a red smear on one nail. Again he felt the familiar burning thirst, the unquenchable craving that drove him to kill and drink from his victims.

The other miserable human, almost used up, convulsed and moaned behind him. Without turning Adramelech stepped back and placed a foot on the young soldier's throat. With a crunch of bone, he ground the neck, spine and esophageal tissue into a bloody jelly.

The boy shuddered and lay still.

At that moment, among the million points of light in the night sky, a shooting star moved purposely across the heavens. Just as purposely, it stopped dead. Then, ever so slowly, it grew in size as it descended rapidly towards the Panamanian jungle.

The creature approached Clay lying spread-eagled on the ground, his open shirt exposing his dog tags. A small gold Crucifix on a chain lay askew at the base of his throat. It shone dully in the moonlight.

From a thousand feet up, a pencil-thin, silvery blue beam shot from the arc-white ball of Light. It pierced the wetness of the jungle haze, slid between tree overhangs surrounding the clearing, and focused on the small Crucifix.

The golden cross began to glow, growing brighter by the second.

The Beast stopped his forward motion. Slowly he lifted his head and gazed heavenward feeling despair mixed with undying hatred. He looked back down at the soldier.

The Crucifix stood out bright and shining against his tanned skin....

THE HATED SIGN OF REDEMPTION....

The power of His presence was too near, too omnipresent for comfort. The creatures shrank from the gleaming cross which now seemed to throb with light, life and warning. He knew fear again as Clay stirred.

The golden cross pulsed, its metal almost white hot....

HOLY...HOLY...HOLY....

Adramelech screamed in frustration, the taste of human blood still on his lips. Angrily he shook himself to dispense the coppery weakness that rushed through his core muscles as he viewed the Savior's cross.

Though disappointed, he knew the mortal's survival was merely a temporary state. Like the other humans who had seen him in the past, he would eventually dispatch him to hell and mute a witness to his presence on earth.

Right now he would find his favorite familiar, Rosalita, and make her wake once more to serve his needs. Though merely a child, his undead servant would give him the allegiance he needed and be his passport to the world of the sun. Then, at a time of his own choosing, he would find and joyously dispatch this soldier into the eternal blackness of hell.

On the jungle floor, Clay groaned and stirred.

The Light in the sky remained like a guardian over the fallen soldier, its beam focused on the Crucifix which continued to glow as it pulsed like a living entity....

HOLY...HOLY...HOLY....

The Beast knew better than to defy an Emissary and tempt it to do battle. Better to retreat and strike when it had the advantage. It spun from the living soldier and crashed into the blackness of the jungle.

~ 8 ~

VETERAN AFFAIRS HOSPITAL
UPSTATE NEW YORK
SPRING, 1990

Father Benito Gallo answered the phone on the second ring. "Father Gallo."

A young female voice was on the other end. "Father, it's Amy Pruett, the duty nurse on the second floor. I'm afraid Lieutenant Montague is critical. His kidneys are failing and we don't expect him to last the night. His sister is on her way up from New Hampshire but it's unlikely she'll make it in time."

"I'll be over directly to administer the sacraments," Gallo answered. He paused for a moment. "There's no hope at all?"

"The doctors say no; right now we're just keeping him comfortable."

"Very well, Nurse. About twenty minutes."

"Thank you, Father." The phone went dead.

Twenty minutes later Gallo shuffled down the corridor of the Veteran Affairs hospital towards room 218. He sighed as he passed a recent arrival lying asleep on a gurney in the corridor. A plastic IV bag hung over the man and a urine bag was clipped to the side of his sheets.

A pretty, young dark-haired nurse carrying a tray of medication smiled at the priest as she hurried past. Gallo paused by the sleeping soldier and watched her turn into one of the rooms, unable to help noticing the tightness of the green scrubs on her lithe figure and the firm roundness of her bottom.

The familiar stirring was quickly followed by the familiar guilt. Though celibacy was a cross which Gallo had successfully managed to bear throughout his priesthood, he knew he was forever damned with impure thoughts. In fact, he resented the Almighty for saddling His servants with sexual urges. Right now, he thought, he wouldn't mind saddling that nurse. He said a quick Hail Mary asking for forgiveness.

The elderly priest realized his thoughts merely reflected a personal crisis of faith. His years as an Army Chaplain in Vietnam had sorely damaged his beliefs. As the war progressed, he had found it harder and harder to pass out benign platitudes to soldiers laying out their fears of death to him. And, even as he spoke liberally of a heavenly afterlife, he wondered if he was selling snake oil. Had he chosen the wrong vocation? Was he wasting his life in a thankless calling of sacrifice and self-denial destined to accomplish little and reward him with a cold grave and the nothingness of death; a black plum similar to that earned by an adulterer or murderer? In the final analysis, was there no cosmic difference between saints and sinners?

Regretfully, his doubts had extended far beyond either his moral or his dogmatic concerns. He found himself posing the same questions many parishioners routinely dumped in his lap. Was there really a loving and merciful Being who had sent His own Son to suffer the indignities and pain of Crucifixion, to die in a predestined ritual of sacrifice to atone for the sins of mankind? If so, who was the object of the atonement? The Father? Wasn't that like cutting off one's nose to spite one's face?

And, if God was all-knowing, all-good, and all-powerful, why was He content to allow wholesale slaughters such as the Crusades, two World Wars, or Vietnam? How could He stomach the eternal global hypocrisy and inherent cruelty of the human race; a race supposedly created in His own image?

Last, but not least, why didn't He show Himself rather than hide in the shadows of faith, hoping for perfect contrition for the wrongs perpetrated by humanity, all the while knowing His creations were only capable of, at best, imperfect contrition for their sins?

Gallo felt his ulcer begin to throb and abandoned the introspection. After all, he wasn't about to solve the pandemic puzzle of man's God-given right to exist any more than the billions who had pondered it before him, and the billions who would probably ponder it long after his tired old body had been shoveled into a hole. The only thing the priest knew for certain was that he had sacrificed a helluva lot to follow in the footsteps of someone who might have been no more than the son of a Galilean carpenter, a man with a gift of gab and no obvious desire for pecuniary rewards.

As a boy he dreamed of glory, and with the proper coaching, was led to enlist in God's army – the priesthood. The harsh realities of his decision came in adulthood, as he suffocated under a series of disappointing diocesan appointments while being ruled by the stuffiness of ecclesiastical doctrine.

Forty-five years ago, he had been certain he'd made the right choice. His mother and father had wept for joy at his announced vocation and reaped new respect and honor in their village when he'd finally been ordained.

Now he wondered if his motivations had been based on a love of God or on an adolescent yearning to belong to a collective that would accept him for who and what he was, a simple man looking for answers to the riddle of existence.

His thoughts swept back to his youth; the choice, back then, had seemed simple.

As a young boy in a poor Italian village, he'd been very lonely. Fortuna, his older sister, had shunned him with disdain because of their seven-year age difference. His mother and father, working hard to keep a roof over their heads and food on the table, seemed only interested in having young Benito help in the vegetable store or do other chores to earn extra money to help the family.

After school each day, there was no time to play. He'd sweep out the village carpenter's shop, clean and polish boots at the bootmaker's store and then run home to work in their own little store until supper. After that he did his lessons.

Not that he regretted being unable to form many friendships; he'd never been comfortable with his peers. Their simplistic and foolish pranks and hi-jinks had both distressed and unnerved him. He preferred a much simpler, orderly life of contemplation while discovering the wonders of literature, science and mathematics. His studies were his recreation and he looked forward to finishing his jobs, bolting down his food and attacking his books.

Ultimately, his hard work paid off.

His teachers, impressed by his quick grasp of lessons and his love of study and scholastic exploration, had pronounced little Benito exceptionally bright. In fact, he heard them whispering that he was *gifted*.

The boy was elated; he was someone special. But, if he was so smart, how come he didn't have any friends? How come he didn't have one school chum?

His school counselor patiently explained that, intellectually, Benito was light years ahead in intelligence and maturity. He further urged the boy to forget the ninnies, assume a responsible air and apply himself even harder to his studies.

The counselor resolved his gift must not be wasted.

Though it was doubtful Benito's parents would have the money or the inclination to allow him to fulfill his full educational capabilities and ultimately progress into university, the counselor told Benito there were other ways.

Upon hearing of Benito's extraordinary gift, the village priest, Father Vocelli, had taken a keen interest in the boy. After meeting him, he felt sure that a boy of Benito's intelligence would positively flourish in an atmosphere of learning, of rigid and studied discipline. He would make an excellent candidate for the seminary.

Secretly, he also believed that given the right training, the youngster would climb to great heights in the church hierarchy. He made it his mission to secure a new recruit for the Roman Catholic Church and lured Benito with the possibilities the clergy had to offer: education, security, opportunities for travel and advancement, and the honor of doing God's work. His family didn't take too much convincing. As for Benito, well…he'd always listened to his parents.

The course was set, and at nine years of age and throughout Benito's subsequent schooling, his chosen vocation was well-known.

He became a favorite of Father Vocelli. On visiting day at the school, the priest never failed to slip little Benito a piece of candy or gum, rarities in their village.

But, while he was thrilled by the attention and the exclusivity of his position, there were times as he grew older when he found himself wishing that his father or *someone* would volunteer to act as a counterbalance to the priest's persuasive indoctrinations; that a friend or confidant would encourage him to determine his own wants from life. Benito himself was a timid lad, too frightened to disappoint those who held out such high hopes for him. And, the public knowledge of his calling, and the focus of the village priest on Benito, helped discourage any other friendships. He became known as the "holy boy" and as far as the rest of the students were concerned, Benito was going to be a priest and that was that.

The result was the boy led a solitary life of study and hard work. Now, his parents encouraged his studies. After all, Benito had been called by God to take on an onerous responsibility and he must be ready. There was little time for enjoying boyhood in his youth.

Another, equally pretty nurse passed Father Gallo in the hospital corridor. This one was tall and leggy with blond hair drawn into a tight bun at the back of her neck. He wondered what it would look like spread out on a pillow, a golden halo about her perfect features and startling blue eyes.

Angry at his own thoughts, the priest thought back to his ordination, the day he had taken his final vows and become a priest. Triumphant in having attained his goal, in the back of Benito's mind, doubt still festered like a hidden cancer.

Before long, however, he found himself embarked on a busy schedule of assisting at various parishes around Rome and quickly fell into the mindless routine of self-denial, service to God and attempting to sustain piety. Once in the rut, he found it really was quite easy to serve and comply.

But over time, contrary to Father Vocelli's predictions, Benito Gallo did not distinguish himself by rocketing up the ecclesiastical ladder to attain exalted status in the sanctum sanctorum of Vatican City.

The reason for his failure was the same as the reason for his success – his intellect. His mentors had quickly seen that, though his grasp of theological implications and dogma was complete and far reaching, his personal renderings and implementations of local programs for his various dioceses based on the church's inherent beliefs, and a variety of pontifical pronouncements, were generally flawed in ways sympathetic to his own interpretations. And, these interpretations brought dissention to his calling.

In fact, whenever he spoke on church matters such as reform, he inevitably seized the moment to make his opinions known. Sadly, at the time, his ideas on church reform were thought to lightly skirt the mists of heresy.

It was obvious that this Father Gallo was too much of a free-thinker for a system based on slavish compliance, said those who ruled the Vatican. Though he obviously had the qualifications, the brain power and the talent, if he were transferred into a department such as the Curia Romana or the "Segretario di Stato" (Secretariat of State) in the Vatican, he would, no doubt, be the rotten apple in the barrel, the odd man out. Anyhow, with his manifested and sometimes brutal honesty, it was doubtful he would progress up the ladder of ecclesiastical responsibility. And the word went silently forth; they were not denying a future leader, they were heading off a giant pain in the ass.

In a convoluted but telling way, they were right. He was most certainly lacking in the manipulative and self-preservation instincts needed to thrive in any highly competitive organizational jungle where a mere a word in the right ear, or an arched eyebrow at the mention of a name, could prevent an appointment or a reward and banish the subject to a form of career purgatory. He would never be a star – more like an "also ran."

But to be fair, Gallo also accepted the fact that he had neither the stomach nor the inclination for bickering, lobbying or politicking. In short, he preferred to serve rather than seek to be served.

Though he never really knew for certain, he'd have been an utter fool not to suspect that he'd been silently damned by his superiors. Of course, he never learned of opportunities denied him for the simple reason that, after consideration, they were never offered.

But this Benito was not the ignorant youth of a small village; he was a man of learning and discipline, a man of opinion. He began to speak out, to comment on a need for reform and to criticize the inner workings of the Curia and the Church.

The Italian press shunned him at first, honoring a long-standing, unspoken, agreement between them – the supposed guardians of free speech – and the cloistered and repressive members of the Vatican politico. To Gallo, the press and the Vatican made strange bedfellows indeed but the power of the Holy See was not to be underestimated; he soon came to expect very little in the way of acknowledgement or publicity from the Italian press.

Finally, however, a few younger, daring journalists, eager to make a name for themselves, began to see that Gallo's opinions had merit. They listened and wrote about his ideas on church reformation. For instance: about making the Mass less mystical to help parishioners reconnect with their beliefs; his cautious but straightforward views on birth control in a world with millions already starving; and, his beliefs that celibacy should be optional in the priesthood.

Though he was years ahead in his thinking, they began to print the daring views of this young revolutionary; some even went so far as to agree with him. Soon he began receiving the full attention of the Vatican again, including the direct attention of Pope Pious XII.

In addition, he garnered the attention of the Congregation for the Doctrine of the Faith and then, within a few months, he was summoned before a special gathering of the College of Cardinals and asked to account for his actions. His answer was simple and straightforward: among Christ's many teachings was an understood plea for honesty and openness. To silence free speech would be to silence the voice of prophecy, which is the voice of God – that from which ultimately came God's laws and the scriptures.

The esteemed members of the College were neither impressed nor amused at his simple but logical deductions. There were, among some, even angry mutterings of excommunication.

Instead, he was transferred as far from Rome as possible, to America where, over the next fifteen years, he assumed the role of parish priest in various small towns.

At first he was too busy to get into any mischief, but once routine had set in, he began to air his views publicly again. Happily he found the American press eager to listen to a priest with new ideas.

Soon his name surfaced in Rome again. A tired sigh was heard from the Holy See as disciplinary actions were discussed and discarded. Perhaps he could be persuaded to join a Monastic Holy Order with a vow of silence? This was discarded with concerns expressed that the press would see this as a gag order to muzzle the young idealist; he might become a form of martyr that, undoubtedly, would be eagerly supported by the paper and electronic media.

But then a more creative idea surfaced and was wholeheartedly endorsed by the secret commission set up to see to the problem of Father Benito Gallo.

He was *asked* to assume a pastor's role in the U.S. Army. His Bishop smiled and said that they desperately needed spiritual help and Gallo was being nominated. The cards were on the table now. Of course, their prodigal son would be happy to serve where needed.

Soon after, he found himself in a variety of warring hot spots around the world. With wry amusement, he sometimes wondered if Rome was secretly in league with the army executive in choosing his postings in the hope that a stray bullet would someday end their frustrations with Gallo.

Slowly his thoughts returned to the present, and the nurse he'd just seen with the bum you could crack eggs on. Gallo continued his journey in the hospital corridor towards room 218 clutching his small black purse in hand. However, it wasn't only the wars and death he'd seen that made him experience doubt in the wisdom of his faith, his belief in the sanctity of the Mass, and the infallibility of the Pope. Parish posting after parish posting had also insidiously eaten away at his beliefs as he was fully exposed to the realities of life, the temptations, the fears, the battles and the defeats of so many.

He'd been privy to the innermost terrors and misdeeds of his parishioners and watched them come back week-after-week to confess the same sins, take his absolution like a hot shower, and then eagerly race out to screw, steal and gossip again.

From his pseudo-omnipotent view in the confessional, there appeared to be no accountability, no learning process and certainly no improvement in their spiritual or moral lives. Obviously they felt they weren't on earth for a long time, so they chose a form of moral turpitude from which they could recover through the sacrament of confession. So what was the point? What was his purpose on earth?

Of course, during his parish days, there had been temporary joy in certain duties, though, it would also ultimately become a source of frustration too.

As parish priest, one of his responsibilities was to visit the schools. Here he enjoyed the respect and adoration of the small children of his parish. He loved visiting the classrooms and watching the awe on their little faces as he strode in, his black skirts swishing and his beads clacking as they swung from his belt.

He enjoyed telling the little ones stories from the scriptures and reinforcing the message of the special love of Christ for children. He had no problem with this message at all. He also loved leading them through the halting recitations of their first confessions and marveled at their purity, innocence and unquestioning acceptance. Suffer the little children to come unto me, indeed. When the stories of sexual interference had first surfaced in the Church, his anger knew no bounds as reflected in his sermons. He felt that boiling in oil was too good for these so-called priests and his letters to the Vatican stressed the need for immediate defrocking and public prosecution. Forgiveness wasn't a strong suit of Gallo's when it came to children.

His second disappointment came as he'd watch the children grow up, make their First Communion and finally be received fully into the church at their Confirmation ceremony. It was then puberty brought new challenges. The boys would discover cigarettes, liquor and sex. After that it was just a matter of time before they stopped coming to church.

The girls, on the other hand, kept coming, victims of the guilt heaped on them by their mothers for being female and enjoying the secret sins of youth. Tearful confessions of their first sexual experience, their second, third, fourth, fifth, sixth...would follow until ultimately they grew as tired as he of the recitations. He could understand the power of the hormones but he couldn't very well condone them ad infinitum. When he asked them to get a handle on their sexual impulses or he would refuse them absolution, boys and girls alike inevitably abandoned the sacrament of confession in favour of the sanctity of the rear seat of an automobile.

There had also been times during Mass when he'd looked up at the raised, beatific faces of the parishioners and wanted to put down the chalice, cross to the pulpit and ask them if, as free-thinking adults, they believed all the mumbo jumbo?

But he knew that his torment merely reflected his own angst. He ached for confirmation, for a sign, for *anything* that would tell him he hadn't been living a lie. But heavenly communications remained mute. There had never been a sign. Until now, at least. Until he entered room 218 more than a month ago. As a local priest, serving the VA hospital for years, he was now convinced he had finally stumbled on some proof of a supernatural presence. The nature of his find, however, continued to puzzle him.

~ 9 ~

Father Gallo stopped outside 218, and then slowly pushed open the door for what was likely his last visit. The soldier on the bed looked pale and deathly still with an oxygen feed in place. The familiar restraints had been removed. Sitting on the side of the bed, a nurse was holding his hand. Multiple plastic tubes festooned his body and disappeared under the blankets. The priest now had a final duty to perform for the man; God only knew if it would do him any good, especially if he'd been exposed to the devil's work as he claimed in his ravings.

"Good evening, Father," Nurse Pruett said, carefully tucking the soldier's hand back under the blanket and standing up. I wanted to spend some time with him during his last..." She trailed off, quite aware that supposedly comatose patients often reported that they could hear and even remember bedside comments. "It's so awful not to have anyone with him."

"Of course," Gallo said, gently. "I'll stay with him for a while."

The nurse smiled her thanks and slipped from the room.

The priest was both saddened and disappointed the soldier was now close to death, for he had almost become convinced that Lieutenant Clay Montague might be the sign he'd so desperately yearned for throughout his priestly life – a sign of someone having encountered a supernatural presence, even if it was something from the underworld.

When the wounded officer had been brought in, he'd been in a strange post-op coma running a low-grade fever and obviously delirious as he ranted about devils and omnipresent evil.

Like all new arrivals, Gallo had paid him a visit to deliver his blessing. Because of the nature of his head wound, he had been flown from Panama to Fort Bragg, North Carolina, and then to the University of Rochester Medical Center for specialized surgery

In a three-hour, highly complex operation, the doctors had removed a second, previously hidden, piece of shrapnel resting against his brain stem, installed a metal clip on a potential aneurysm, and delivered an optimistic prognosis of a full recovery. In post-op, however, and later back in his room, the soldier had failed to awaken. The nurses rubbed his sternum, shouted at him, and even cruelly twisted the nipples on his chest but he continued to sleep the unblemished sleep of the innocent. An EEG surprisingly revealed normal brain activity.

Eventually, he was transferred to the chronic care neurology ward of the Finger Lakes VA Hospital. There, he thrashed about and cried out in the language of Ancient Latin: "Daemon excitavit" which translated into the warning: *A demon has awakened.* More than once he also cried out: "Adramelech."

The priest spent days at the lieutenant's bed as the young man muttered warnings in Latin to: "Beware of the demon." As time progressed, he had become increasingly violent until doctors ordered him placed in restraints. Though patients in comas could not physically speak, this young soldier was routinely muttering, shouting and even crying. Several consulting neurologists viewed this anomaly, examined him, and deduced he was in a deep sleep rather than a coma. And yet, they could not awaken him. They clucked, shook their heads and went back to business they understood.

Nightly, Gallo had visited the young man in hope of easing his torment but each night the patient merely fought the straps and muttered in terror about Ball-Zebub's disciple until, exhausted, he slept. Slowly, the priest became more and more certain that somewhere, somehow, this man had been touched by a profound evil.

In fact, after seven weeks, Gallo had convinced himself that Clay was part of a puzzle that might have undertones of the supernatural. For instance, where and how had the soldier learned a Latin dialect that was indigenous to the ancient Roman region of *Latium*? And, how did he come up with the name Adramelech, an arch demon in the hierarchy of hell? In fact, the more Father Gallo listened to the ranting, the more he became convinced that it was more than a hallucination. Indeed, that the soldier was reacting to something he had seen. Possibly something irrational in a supposedly rational world? The priest learned that the lieutenant had been the sole survivor of a night patrol killed and horribly mutilated in curious fashion. Reportedly, not one had been shot. They all died from major traumatic injuries – injuries not even consistent with a mortar attack. And some had been virtually exsanguinated.

But there was something else.

When Gallo had visited Lieutenant Montague and it first happened, he'd been puzzled and put it down as coincidence. But after the third time, coincidence wouldn't wash. And there was no rationalizing something he'd personally experienced.

It first occurred when he stopped by the lieutenant's bed to say a quiet Lord's Prayer over the soldier. Though sound asleep, and without hearing a spoken word from the priest, the moment the prayer ended with the word *Amen*, the soldier's hand had somehow extracted itself from the straps, unerringly found his own, and gripped it with a strength that was almost frightening. He sensed he was being thanked for the prayer. Then, in a trembling whisper, the soldier would whisper weakly about hell's disciple and fall back to sleep.

And visit-after-visit gave him the same result. When Father Gallo repeated the sequence of prayer, at the exact moment he would silently whisper *Amen* in his mind, the hand would come up, seize his robes or hand and the young soldier would plead for salvation from the rage of the Beast.

How the lieutenant knew the exact moment he was saying *Amen*, when, in fact, he was praying inwardly, fascinated the priest. He tried to fool him several times; for instance by pretending to pray but deliberately keeping his mind blank.

Nothing happened.

Next he muttered gibberish.

Nothing happened.

But when he silently said the *Our Father*, the lieutenant's hand grabbed him and whispered fevered warnings of an evil loosed upon the earth.

In truth, the warnings stirred at vague, uncomfortable memories and Father Gallo asked himself: Was this a sign? Was it a warning that a spiritual evil had taken secular form on earth? Or, was it the utterances of a man with brains so scrambled, he was seeing flashbacks of every horror movies he'd seen as a kid?

Then, two nights ago, he heard something else – something that made his blood run cold. The soldier's voice had suddenly changed its timber to a hoarse, broken rasp as he whispered in an ancient Latin dialect: "I have loosed my Beast upon the world; the *Hellspawn* shall take the blood of the innocent…and with all the fury of hell…make them mine!"

Shivers ran up the priest's spine at the word *Hellspawn*. He'd swallowed and stared at the pale, now silent soldier, on the bed. A distant memory of a story he'd heard as a young seminarian surfaced. The story concerned the Great Battle between Lucifer and God.

Though never included in the official teachings of the Church, the story was that as Lucifer was being banished to hell for questioning God's right to rule, he had chosen a black champion to serve him, an arch demon named Adramelech who he decreed would roam time and space until the earth was reformed. Also, that there had been an understanding between the two powers that evil would battle righteousness and earth would be the arena. Lucifer mandated that Adramelech would spread hate, confusion and fear, and serve as a time-master to determine when the Antichrist would rise.

The story said that Lucifer's champion, through shape-shifting, often took the form of humans as well as legendary supernatural beasts. But, in fact, this creature was not a legend. It was a living, breathing *spawn of hell*, a direct descendant of evil that throughout history had initiated chaos and had been hunted, found, stabbed with blessed stakes in its heart, and buried…only to rise again from the grave upon the decay of its instrument of death.

Gallo remembered asking some older priests about the story. He expected to be smiled at and told not to be so foolish. They neither smiled nor made jokes. In fact, one older priest actually glared at Benito and placed a finger against his lips in a warning as he whispered: "Omerta." Another one had quietly said for him to leave it alone lest it awaken – whatever that meant.

He heard from others that deep in the secret archives of the Vatican was the full story of the *Hellspawn*, a tale so disturbing that the Church refused to allow it to be made public. Still, as young people are wont to do, Father Gallo inevitably wrote it off as the seminary students' equivalent of a good ghost story.

The same night Clay Montague used the word *Hellspawn*, Father Gallo had placed a long distance call to Rome to one of the few friends he had left in the Vatican. A Jesuit scholar and a man on the fast-track to becoming a cardinal with an order in council to exempt him from the usual Episcopalian consecration, Father Mustavias Malachi was a church veteran and a man on the move. The reason Gallo called him was that, in conversation, his friend Malachi had once mentioned the legend of the *Hellspawn*, a legend he had also said was best left alone.

After initial pleasantries on the trans-Atlantic call, Father Gallo had congratulated his friend on his coming appointment to Cardinal. Father Malachi, a distinct Boston twang in his accent, had brushed it aside with some, but not too much modesty.

Finally Gallo brought up the matter of the soldier and his ravings about the *Hellspawn*. The Jesuit paused. "Wasn't that an old wives' tale? Some sort of *John the Baptist* of hell preceding the Antichrist looking to doom hope and turn the righteous from the Father?"

Gallo agreed and enlightened him a bit more saying: "I have a comatose soldier in a VA hospital here who should be incapable of any speech and he's ranting in Ancient Latin, Mustavias. Not high school Latin, but a dialect that is surely from Ancient Rome. And, from what I can make out – you know I majored in Latin studies – he's warning us that the *Hellspawn* has awakened again." Gallo thought he might have imagined it but he noted a guarded tone in Malachi's voice as he spoke.

"Where did *he* hear of it, Benito?"

"I don't know. We ourselves spoke of it in Rome, as seminary students."

"But we were young and foolish, willing to believe anything that confirmed our choice to become men of the cloth, were we not? Surely we've grown beyond ghost stories, my friend?"

"Hardly a ghost story if he saw something," Gallo muttered, disappointed.

"No offense…" Malachi hastened to add, taking the sting out of his words. There'd been silence at the other end of the phone and so he asked: "What would you like me to do, Benito?"

"There *is* something going on here," Gallo said. Surprisingly he found his own voice tight and angry.

"Alright. What do you think is going on, Father?" Malachi asked, getting serious again.

"I don't know but it's something…something –"

"Supernatural?"

"Yes…and don't laugh at me."

"Never, my friend. I have too much respect for your intellect to ever take you lightly. In fact, I'd say that was eminently true about most of your brethren here in Rome." They both chuckled at the joke. It was Father Malachi who had often warned Benito when he was treading on thin ice and disciplinary measures were afoot.

Finally, Malachi said: "I confess I've heard of the *Hellspawn* from time-to-time Benito, so, for you I shall make some inquiries. Covertly, of course so they don't lock me up." Father Malachi said he'd pray for the soldier and asked Benito to keep him informed of any further developments.

But further developments did not come. Clay Montague had remained lost in his "coma" for months, a mute prisoner in his brain that, from periodic EEG readings was rapidly deteriorating in function; his vital signs began to fluctuate and signal that his time was growing nigh. The doctors, while mystified by the cause, had resigned themselves to the likely outcome.

After an extended conference call with the patient's sister in New Hampshire and a leading neurologist, the woman had finally agreed to a *Do Not Resuscitate* order. The last tests mirrored brain activity rivaling what might be expected in a turnip and a fever that resolutely crept up a tenth of a degree at a time.

The priest stood over the soldier and unzipped his small purse. He uncapped the oil blessed by his bishop, lit a candle, kissed the stole and placed it about his shoulders to administer the sacrament of Extreme Unction – the Last Rites. He used the oil to anoint the soldier in six places as he quietly spoke: "Through this Holy Unction and His most tender mercy, may the Lord pardon thee of whatever sins or faults thou hast committed…by sight…by hearing…by taste…by smell…by touch…by carnal delectation – ."

Suddenly the man moved. His right leg jumped followed by a harsh protest, as he wantonly thrashed about. This time he spoke in English: "Malachi…the Beast!" Abruptly he slipped back into unconsciousness.

Gallo stared at the ashen soldier, goose bumps rising on his neck and the back of his arms. Had the soldier said *Malachi*? How could he know that name?

For some reason the priest found himself making the sign of the cross. Then he recoiled slightly in surprise.

The soldier gazed silently up at him from the bed.

He was awake.

~ 10 ~

As Clay returned to the land of the living in upstate York State, less than three hundred miles away in Beebe, Quebec, directly on the Vermont border not far from where Clay grew up, 16-year-old Maria Michelle Lapierre gave her chestnut-colored hair one final brush and examined its shine in her bedroom mirror. She sighed. The time was coming when she had to start making choices. In her final year as a senior attending Sacred Heart High in Newport, Vermont, just across the border from her Canadian home, she was approaching a cross-road in her young life. Would she move on to university, accept a retail dead-end job in Rock Island or Derby Line, or choose another, less traditional path in life – one that had been occupying her thoughts for some time?

She knew she was privileged to live in Beebe Plain, a quintessential, crime-free small Quebec town where the main street was canopied by stately elms and maples setting off the pristine white wooden houses buffered by perfectly manicured green lawns. The weekly trips to Monsieur Boisvert, the butcher, and to Monsieur LeClair, the green grocer, and to the picture-perfect white, wooden Catholic Church, had delivered a predictability and security that was good for any maturing, young adolescent. And, Maria had some prestige in that her father, Ben Lapierre, was the Canadian Immigration Officer in Charge in nearby Stanstead.

Because there was no readily available secondary school in Beebe, each day she and other friends boarded the bus for the cross-border trip to Sacred Heart High. Friday nights were spent at the Beebe Curling Club watching her parents in their favorite pass time, or in summer, going for a ride to pick up custard cones and play five-pin bowling.

Still, her favorite day was Saturday when she hitch-hiked with best friends Sandra Couture, Joanie Steward and Abby Langford to Stanstead and the Haskell Free Library and Opera House where she selected three books for the week. She had always been a voracious reader graduating from Nancy Drew, the Hardy Boys and the Mercer Brothers, to Douglas Coupland, Joyce Carol Oates and Kurt Vonnegut. These she would devour during the week, and then dutifully return them for new ones the following Saturday.

The library, half in Rock Island, Quebec, and half in Derby Line, Vermont, was also unique in that it was a shared library between Canada and the U.S. with the international boundary marked by a single painted, black line on the hardwood floor.

Saturday night was Roxy Theatre night in Rock Island where she had previously attended Our Lady of Mercy grade school run by the nuns. She continued to drop in and see Sister Alice of the Immaculate Order, her former teacher and favorite nun.

This year had been an exciting time for Maria as she had come to believe that her reputation for being "weird" mattered less every day. More and more boys were throwing longing glances her way at school.

Anyhow, it wasn't her fault that the French tabloid press in the form of Montreal's *Allo Police* newspaper had jumped on her reported precognitive ability six years ago.

Maria had been innocently playing near a frozen-over stream with her friend Monique when the girl broke through the ice and disappeared. Maria ran to the girl's nearby house for help. Her mother frantically ran back in her slippers only to find her daughter playing safely on the ice. As she turned to scold Maria, there was a sharp crack and Monique splashed into the water, was seized by the current and carried away under the ice. Firemen found her lifeless body 30 minutes later. All resuscitation attempts failed.

After the accident was reported in its entirety, Maria had been sought out by the press and interviewed at school without her parents' knowledge; it was then widely reported that the child from Beebe had a strange ability to sense future danger or tragedy.

As a young girl wanting to please an adult, she remembered how innocent and forthcoming she had been telling the reporter, exactly what she had seen in advance of her girlfriend's death as well as her own role in the tragedy. And, she made the mistake of admitting to having *visions* since she could first remember. The reporter busily scribbled in his notebook. Unfortunately, the visions were always of bad things. When the article was picked up by international news agencies, Maria's "coming out" was not welcomed by her parents. And, for good reason.

More and more, she was viewed as an oddity in the small town. Upset, her mother made her promise never to reveal any extraordinary knowledge she might possess, no matter what the incentive or circumstance.

If only it was so easy to turn off, Maria thought. And why, she wondered for the umpteenth time, were the visions or feelings mostly centered on something evil or tragic? Why couldn't she predict good things?

Later in years Maria finally decided that the best and most effective way to deal with her gift or curse – depending on your view – was to refuse to acknowledge these precognitive visions. She firmly placed them in her psyche as the silly and idle wanderings of a teen-age mind. And, as for her occasional glimpses into what people were thinking, albeit, infrequently, she labeled them as lucky guesses.

And, it worked.

For instance, she had managed to push aside the ridiculous image of a fellow student (in the process of showing off his new yellow Mustang) when a picture of him lying crumpled and lifeless beside twisted yellow metal obscenely compacted against a telephone pole flashed into view. She had managed to suppress, as just plain silly, the notion of her Uncle Fred putting a black revolver to his temple and seeing blood and brains vomit out the opposite side of his head to smack onto the green tiled wall of the bathroom like so much spaghetti sauce as he slipped backwards into the tub. And, she resolved as totally nonsensical the picture of her friend Margaret Beaumont pushing her boy friend Claude Champagne down the cellar stairs of their house to break his neck an hour after he'd charmingly had his way with her younger sister.

Yes, it worked well, Maria decided. By viewing these events as what she called "imaginary speculation" she was able to ignore her visions and get on with her life. The fact that all these people had died pretty much in the way she had foreseen wasn't her fault. So she'd worked hard to push her guilt deep into the recesses of her mind. After all, who could account for coincidence?

Maria wiped away a smudge of lipstick and her thoughts turned to the dance she was about to attend and the boys who would invariably ask her out. She was as thrilled by their attention as any young girl would be, but something seemed to hold her back. Officially allowed by her parents to start dating at 16, her sole experience so far had not been the best. She had spent most of the date fighting off a very good looking boy with more arms than an octopus in the front seat of his Oldsmobile Cutlass Cruiser at the drive-in movie. She was, after all, a good Catholic girl skilled in the art of saying no. And though she also felt guilt because the boy so obviously liked her, she could not bring herself to weaken and possibly compromise her virtue.

She sighed and put one last crimp in her full, dark eyelashes and lifted her chin for a final inspection in the mirror. The pixie-like face framed by the short brown hair curling under her chin, and her large brown eyes gave her a vulnerable, doe-like quality that turned most boys' knees to mush. One boy had assessed her as having that quality that made men want to care for and protect her – dynamite when it came to arousing the paternal instincts of the male animal. But this, he asserted, was attractively offset by a perky sexiness that excited and thrilled the hormone-ruled young men. She had laughed at his analysis.

The school dance was featuring *The Cobras*, a popular local band specializing in 60s and 70s music by artists such as The Ventures and Duane Eddy. They usually offset their instrumentals with British Invasion pop including the Beatles, Cliff Richards, the Dave Clark Five and the Rolling Stones. Maria was looking forward to a strenuous night of dancing. Quickly she bent down and inhaled the heady fragrance from a single, long-stemmed yellow rose she'd bought on the way home from school. It was her favorite flower and she faithfully purchased one a week.

Finally she wriggled her way into her blue leotards and pulled them up under her red, tartan skirt. Her Dad, who was to drive her across the border to Sacred Heart High School, would be relieved she was finally ready. She twirled once in front of the mirror, her skirt rising up but not immodestly. She certainly didn't want to be a tease, but she loved to dance. Perhaps there was one boy there who would be content to be her friend. That was all she needed right now.

~ 11 ~

The eyes were old but wise, Clay decided as the heavily lined face of an elderly man weaved into smoky focus. For a moment, he did not see the white Roman collar peaking from under the dark shirt. He blinked rapidly to clear away the fog in his eyes and sucked in a deep breath at the same time.

A ragged pain flashed through his chest but then disappeared almost as quickly as it had come. Cautiously he filled his lungs with air again and watched the man; for the first time he realized that he was a civilian priest.

There was sadness in the priest's face and a hint of resignation in his movements as he automatically undertook to perform some sort of ceremony. Clay watched as he mumbled softly in Latin and took a dab of something from a small silver container.

Abruptly the expression on the priest's face gave way to surprise as he realized Clay was watching him.

The priest hurriedly set aside the metal container of oil and awkwardly removed a purple stole from around his neck. He turned and called frantically for a nurse.

Long forgotten Catechism lessons slowly seeped into Clay's mind and he made sense of the ritual of the oil, the stole and those words; the priest was administering the Last Rites.

Great, he thought. I wake up and I'm dying. He tried to speak: "W-Water...?" His voice cracked dryly. He pulled the oxygen cannula aside.

"Lieutenant...my heavens...you're awake! Wait, I'll get water...! I'm Father Gallo."

He disappeared from view and Clay moved his hand weakly up to his face. Some sort of lubricating grease seemed to have been smeared around his eyes, nose and mouth. The priest reappeared with a white paper cup from which angled a plastic, bendy straw.

Clay sipped weakly. He cleared his throat and was rewarded with a mouthful of thick mucus. The priest held a tissue to his mouth. Awkwardly he spat. Father Gallo wiped the excess from his lips and smiled at him.

A moment later another face appeared above Clay.

"I'm Doctor Amond," the man said in a professional, clipped voice as he snapped on a penlight and flashed it into Clay's pupils.

Next he held up three fingers and asked Clay how many fingers he was holding up?

Clay gave him a tired grin and croaked a whisper: "Twenty-four?"

"Close enough," Amond said, and returned the grin. "Now Lieutenant...can you move your fingers and toes?"

Clay complied and the doctor spun about to a nurse and fired off orders for a barrage of tests.

A blood pressure cuff was already being wrapped around Clay's arm by a pretty, blond nurse who silently appeared from somewhere; another was checking a urine bag hanging by the side of his bed for fluids; and a third was slipping a thermometer under his tongue while taking his pulse

The doctor barked orders at the nurses and demanded the patient's vitals, stat.

The nurses called out their results.

"Pulse 68..."

"Respiration 16...

"BP 110 over 70..."

"Temperature 98.1..."

"We have output ..."

A pretty brunette nurse appeared over Clay, twisted a rubber tourniquet around his arm, and slapped a vein with her fingers; he felt the sharp stab of a needle. A sudden thought hit him. "M-My men! What about my men?"

"Forget about your men for now, Lieutenant," Amond replied. "You've been in a coma of sorts for more than four months, my friend."

"Four months?" Clay's mind whirled.

The doctor continued speaking. "This morning you started slipping away from us. An hour ago you had the brain wave activity of a two-by-four, your kidneys were failing and your blood pressure was competing with your other vitals to see which could check out first. Next thing we know, you decide to wake up...all by your lonesome! You're one lucky puppy."

"W-Where am I?" Clay's voice was still hoarse, weak and shaky.

"You're in a veterans' hospital in upstate New York." He answered a question from a nurse, and then turned back. "Now you hang in there, soldier, I'll be back in a few minutes."

The doctor disappeared from view and Father Gallo's face reappeared almost instantly. Clay saw that this time he was holding a black notebook and pen.

"Lieutenant," he said in a whisper, "You spoke of the *Hellspawn*. How do you know of it?"

"What...?" Clay felt his pulse racing at the memory of a dark shadow squatting over PFC Osborne's convulsing body. An alarm went off on the cardiac monitor somewhere over Clay's head.

"You said many things while you were unconscious. The doctors thought you were hallucinating but I think I know what you saw. I must have information for Rome –."

"Something dark...something evil...." Clay finally whispered, struggling to remember.

"You said it was coming...?"

Clay shook his head and regretted it as he realized he had a giant headache. "I-I'm sorry ...."

Somewhat desperate, Gallo pleaded with him. "Think Lieutenant, think! *What* was coming?"

"Excuse us, Father...." Dr. Amond was back with a gurney. "This man's going to ICU."

Gallo was politely elbowed aside as three nurses untied Clay's urine bag from the bed, moved his intravenous bottle, switched off the monitor alarm and lifted him onto the gurney.

"Lieutenant, I must see you..." began Father Gallo, but the doc laid a gentle hand on his arm.

"Sorry Father, no more visitors for a few days at least."

"But I must..." the priest began and his voice trailed off as he was pulled aside.

The doctor had put an arm around his shoulder and led him away. "Padre, a few hours ago this man was dying. Luckily, he woke up. Now, brain injuries are tricky things and any excitement could send him back into the coma. Just let us get him to an ICU and stabilize him...okay Father?"

Gallo saw Clay watching quietly from the bed as Amond's team readied him for the move. The priest nodded silently. Amond clapped him on the back, moved to the foot of Clay's bed, and snapped up and studied the soldier's chart. Miracles did happen.

The look of distress on the priest's face saddened Clay. The man looked beaten, almost haggard as he bit his lip and reluctantly put away his pen and notebook.

As Clay was wheeled out of the room, he felt himself lazily drifting off to sleep. Silently he prayed there wouldn't be any more nightmares.

~ 12 ~

Father Gallo watched the gurney disappear as the medical team rolled it quickly out of the room. The extra-wide door slowly closed and he was alone; not a whisper of sound disturbed the stillness of the empty hospital room despite the flurry of activity only moments earlier.

Gingerly he sat down on the bed. He felt old and tired, and disappointed in not being allowed to question the lieutenant. He also found himself experiencing a slight guilt for his preoccupation with his theory in the face of the soldier's amazing awakening. After all, before his very eyes, he had witnessed the return of a man who had been on a one-way journey to his final reward.

Reaching deep in his cassock, he extracted a small metal flask and downed a healthy swig of rye. It warmed his belly feeling familiar and good. Quickly he took another swig, capped the flask and furtively returned it to his inner pocket. He crossed to the hospital window and looked out at the town ablaze in the night.

The main street, a continuation of the street that wound down the small hill on which the hospital was perched, allowed him to survey the commercial part of town. It was unseasonably warm for May and had rained again, a short-lived torrent. The pavement was still shining with the fresh moisture and the streets looked rejuvenated and clean.

As far as he could see, the town was bright and alive, the Saturday night spring crowd flowing through the streets. It was a pulsing, breathing entity proudly flaunting a small collection of colorful neon signs of blinking and flowing light. The signs bubbled, winked, and snapped on and off, garishly depicting a variety of boutiques, bars, billiard parlors, cafes and laundromats – a tacky, urban mosaic of modernism throbbing to the beat of brash rock and country music blasting from dozens of car radios. Farmhands and tourists alike flooded the Finger Lakes' town for their Saturday night festivities.

As the moisture evaporated from the roads, it rose in wispy clouds of steam, each cloud taking on the colored hues of the neon signs nearby and becoming playful rainbows dancing and swaying, and finally rising to disappear into the night sky.

Unmindful of the spectacle, the crowd poured busily through the avenues on foot, bicycles or cars in their never-ending quest for food, drink and later, the pleasures of the flesh. Father Gallo knew if the window was open he'd hear music and war whoops from the crowds dancing on outdoor pavilions. A particularly bright star glowed almost directly overhead; he craned his neck to see it.

As a popular Finger Lakes' resort town, the area was dead in winter but became party central in summer for the flatlanders arriving from New York and Boston to swim and sunbathe by day and raise hell by night. Idly he wondered if the permanent citizenry cared about the disappearance of their small town culture as well as its implied and inherent morale character. Inevitably small town virtues were sublimated by a crass commercialism that appeared whenever and wherever the well-heeled chose to land. Truth be told – money bred drugs, drunkenness and debauchery.

He watched the crowd below for another few minutes. Ants, decided Father Gallo. Maybe earth is just one giant ant farm to God. Maybe there is no grandiose scheme for the world, no plausible or lasting course for humanity. Perhaps we're merely pets and when God tires of his ant farm, he'll empty it into his equivalent of a toilet.

He chuckled to himself: now wouldn't that be a surprise? Imagine if earth ended, not with some great apocalyptic atomic war fulfilling the Prophesies of Armageddon, but with the sound of a cosmic flush? The flask reappeared. He took another swig.

After inquiring as to the condition of the soldier and being told he'd remain in the Critical Care Unit that night, he picked up what he called his "implement case" and Bible and left the hospital to walk back to his rectory.

As he walked through the warm night air, he remembered Lieutenant Montague's words: Tell Rome, he'd begged. Tell Rome what? About a mythological Beast that was supposedly again loosed upon the earth? Indeed, this would be a gift to the Vatican. Instant justification to have Father Gallo committed to the funny farm where they'd tranquilize and neutralize him all in one foul swoop.

He decided to cut across a residential section of town and turned down a quiet street, moved past a low-rise apartment building and then into a housing area filled with Victorian homes mixed with the occasional repossessed and empty house. He could smell the scent of freshly mowed grass as he cut between some houses via a breezeway. Once he crossed the park, he'd be home in ten minutes. He looked up again at what appeared to be a particularly bright star high in the heavens. For a second he thought he saw a pencil thin ray of light shining down from it towards the hospital he had just left. Then a low lying mist from the lake drifted in, obscuring his vision of the sky. Some sort of atmospheric anomaly, he decided.

A lone dog barked forlornly off in the distance and the night grew increasingly still as he trudged on. Nearby a twig snapped. Was someone following him?

"Who's there?" he called out.

There was no answer. Even a priest had to be careful, he thought. He should have waited and hitched a ride with one of the nurses or doctors finishing their evening shift.

Gravel again crunched off to his right and he peered toward the shadows of a darkened house and ram shackled shed beside it. Was that a person standing under a giant oak tree at the rear of the lot? It couldn't be a man, he thought. Unless he was a giant.

The priest stopped walking and stared at the shadow under the collection of grotesquely twisted oak limbs, still half bare of leaves. Something touched his hand and he jumped: "What the--?" He found himself staring at a small, barefoot waif of a girl in a torn and dirty dress. She couldn't be more than eight or nine he decided, his attention taken off the shadow. What was she doing outside without shoes or socks?

The child smiled innocently up at him. For a moment, however, a tiny glint of light seemed to make her eyes flash with a strange luminescence.

"Who are you little girl? Where is your Mommy and Daddy?"

Wordlessly she took his hand and attempted to lead him towards the empty lot.

"What is it? Something you want me to see?" Her tiny hand felt like a frozen stone. This is disgraceful, he thought. Where are her parents?

She smiled at him again as he gazed down at her upturned eyes. For a split second they seemed to roll back in her head exposing two sickening egg whites. Startled, he blinked and they were back to normal – fully dilated black pupils drawing him into their depths as he stumbled on the uneven surface of the cracked and broken asphalt of the driveway. She continued to lead him across it towards the oak tree.

Gallo stared hard at her as an inner consciousness sent out increasingly dire warnings. This feeling of danger was juxtaposed against a new and strange feeling of calmness that was rapidly overtaking him like a powerful narcotic; he felt so sleepy. He looked up again. Was that a man under the tree, he wondered again? Glancing back down at the child, the calmness abruptly vanished and he grew cold with fright. The little girl's eyes had again caught the glint of a faraway street lamp only now they glowed inhumanly greenish yellow in the dark. Suddenly they were no longer innocent child-like eyes, but the cunning eyes of an animal on the hunt.

Something crunched heavily in the gravel ahead and he looked up at the monster waiting for him. Gallo began to tremble in terror as he squeezed his personal Bible in desperation, nails marking the leather cover even as he struggled to control his bladder. The child continued to draw him closer. Unable to resist her pull on his hand, he became acutely aware of the peril he faced and summoned the strength to pray aloud for the redemption of his soul. "The Lord is my shepherd...I-I shall not want...."

The thing under the tree responded with a cavernous snarl.

~ 13 ~

For the next few weeks Clay rested and very gradually progressed from chicken broths to some thin, light, solid foods and drank gallons of water. He'd lost 35 pounds but the doctors assured him he wouldn't be long regaining the weight. Every muscle and joint had stiffened and he'd been told he'd have to undergo physical therapy to restore lost muscle tissue and regain flexibility. His sister had paid him a brief tear-filled visit, and then, because he insisted, had returned home to wait for him after his hospital discharge.

As soon as he was able, he sent a message back to his unit thanking the patrol who rescued him from the jungle, and expressing his sadness over the deaths of the fine men who had died beside him that night. He had already started work on his report explaining the sequence of events and was soon handing it for delivery to a regular army captain. They exchanged salutes and the officer departed.

He received a brief telegram of good-luck back from his colonel who said he was proud to have had him in his command. Further, he understood Clay would be staying back home and he expected their entire unit to be posted back to the States for some well-deserved R & R.

Clay had had a few dizzy spells since waking up but other than that he felt fine. Dr. Amond told him he expected a full recovery but only time would tell for sure; the spells initially worried the doctors who said there was no way he could return to active duty. He was told that when they operated, they found the beginning of a potential aneurism and had clipped it. While he would likely lead a normal life, it wouldn't allow for him to continue in the army.

Then the rehabilitation processes began – physical and mental.

For the next three weeks he was probed, stuck, CAT-scanned, X-Rayed and prodded by a variety of neurologists and other specialists. The dizziness had faded away and for that he was grateful. He spent about a dozen half-hour sessions with an army psychologist helping him get over what they called "survivor guilt" due to the loss of his patrol. After intense counseling he acknowledged an unfortunate fact: his men, his comrades were tragic casualties of war.

Finally, after some thought, Clay had mentioned the monstrosity he'd seen bending over Private Osborne in the jungle. After listening to its description the doctor had smiled sympathetically and convinced him that it was merely a case of transference; he'd created a personification of the enemy that had been responsible for the death of his friends in the shape of something cruel, unusual and vile. In reality, there was no "monster" except the enemy soldiers.

To deal with the decline of easy mobility in his limbs, he was assigned a grey-haired, battle-axe of a physiotherapist with breath that would take the paint off a brick wall. Margie, the rehabilitative therapist, had worked with him to correct the impairment and limitations of his left hand and leg. Her relentless and demanding schedule of daily exercises made Clay think she was determined to finish what the PDF had started. Less than a month later the doctor informed Clay that he was well enough to be processed. He received an honorable discharge for medical reasons and could return to civilian life; his health was good, but not good enough for the army.

Over the next few weeks, papers were signed, options exercised and pretty soon he was released to rejoin the world. Doctor Amond shook his hand and wished him well. Then he handed Clay a small brown manila envelope. His dog tags and his Crucifix fell into the palm of his hand. He looped the Crucifix over his head, looked at the dog tags for a moment and finally slipped them into his pocket.

Amond pointed to his throat and said: "One thing we were curious about, Lieutenant – that burn?"

Clay's hand went instinctively to the base of his Adam's apple. He'd seen the cross-shaped burn mark as soon as he'd become well enough to start shaving.

"Your Crucifix seems to fit that burn scar on your throat," Amond pressed. "Know how it happened?"

Clay professed ignorance; he could only assume that as he lay in the jungle, at some point he'd been in direct sunlight and it heated the tiny cross to where it burned a permanent mark on his throat.

"Strange," observed Amond. "I thought you and your patrol were found the same night."

Clay shrugged. He shook hands with the doctor and thanked him. Then he paid a final visit to Margie the physiotherapist as she ate in the cafeteria. He thanked her for not killing him and dodged a good-natured, meaty-pawed swipe. For a moment, as he said goodbye, he even thought he saw her eyes mist up a bit. But he quickly realized that the tears were more likely due to the onion and garlic sandwich she was in the process of devouring.

As he packed his meager belongings, Clay remembered the priest who had been with him when he awakened. He asked Helen, a pretty blond nurse who spent more than her share of time tending on him, where he could locate the elderly cleric.

Helen smiled sadly. "The Padre – Father Gallo – is not with us any longer."

"Oh?" Clay said, and asked if he'd been transferred.

"We don't know what happened to him. The night you woke up, he left the hospital and never showed up at his rectory. He vanished into thin air."

"No sign of him at all?"

"None." She paused and then added: "Pretty unusual. There's an on-going police investigation. Unfortunately, nothing so far. It's pretty bad when even a priest isn't safe in a small town like this."

Clay's felt a flash of guilt as he remembered how desperate the priest had been to question him about something that night.

For a fleeting second a dark image flashed into memory but he quickly banished the image; it was his personal nightmare, nothing more.

Helen sighed and continued: "I liked Father Gallo."

There was a knock at the door to his room and a tall, distinguished-looking, handsome man with black hair liberally speckled with grey and a square, handsome face entered. Though he seemed to be about 50-years-old, from the way his dark suit and turtleneck hung on his frame, Clay could see he was in excellent physical condition. The man stuck out his hand. "I just thought I would wish you well, Lieutenant. Good luck in civilian life." He accent was a curious mix of cultured English tempered with a ripe Bostonian twang characterized by its non-rhotic quality.

Clay smiled, accepted the hand. "Thank you. And you are Doctor…?"

"My name is Malachi," the man said, without disclosing rank or title. "Mustavias Malachi. We had a friend in common, Father Gallo."

"The priest," Clay said, letting go of the man's hand. "I really didn't know Father Gallo but I was told he was here for me throughout my illness. I hope he's okay."

Malachi nodded: "So do I. Well, I'm sure the police will find something soon."

"Yes," Clay said. "I hope so."

Malachi paused and looked at him a little closer. "You are well?"

"Nobody is offering me the Last Rites these days," he responded, with a smile.

Malachi returned the smile. "Father Gallo mentioned that you'd had…" he glanced over at the departing nurse and waited till she exited the room. "...an extraordinary experience during your final patrol?"

Clay shook his head: "Just a typical patrol with a brutal end."

"I see," Malachi said. "Nothing out of the ordinary occurred. Apart from the ambush?"

Clay slowly shook his head and waited for the man to expand on what he meant.

Instead, Malachi merely stuck out his hand again. "Well I wish you Godspeed in your recovery." As he went to turn, he stopped and stared intently at the burn mark on Clay's throat. "That mark on your throat? Have you always had it?"

Clay put his hand to his throat and shook his head. "It matches perfectly the small Crucifix I wear. Not sure how this happened. I didn't have the burn when we went on patrol that night. Had it when I woke up here."

Malachi nodded, shrugged and without further hesitation turned on his heel and left the room.

Puzzled, Clay crossed to the window and absentmindedly toyed with the Crucifix round his neck. He wondered why his visitor hadn't identified himself beyond his name. As for Father Gallo being a common friend? Not really. So who was this man? One thing, however, was abundantly clear. His demeanor and confidence were unmistakable – he belonged to some powerful organization. And, though Malachi was an odd name, it sounded familiar.

Abruptly a cold shiver ran up Clay's back – the sort of chill associated with the irrational belief that someone had just walked over the site of one's future grave.

~14~

Malachi exited the room and began walking down the hospital corridor where he was immediately joined in step by two U.S. Army officers, one bearing the silver eagles of a bird colonel on his epaulets, and the other man proudly displaying his captain's bars.

"Satisfied, Father Malachi?"

"Yes," the priest said, as they all strode down the corridor, their heels cracking with hollow echoes.

"What's this about, if I may?" the colonel asked. Malachi gave him an appraising look. He was a well conditioned man of about forty, threads of iron grey hair already showing at his temples.

"You had your orders?" Malachi asked.

"Yes Father...."

"And, what were they?" Malachi persisted, not unkindly.

"To get you in to see the lieutenant before he was discharged...and not to ask any questions."

"There's your answer, my good man."

"Sorry sir...Father," the colonel said quickly, his face reddening.

"Any news on Father Gallo?"

"No sir. But the New York State Police are working closely with the town police, the Sheriff's department and our own MPs to try to find him."

"How does a man just vanish?" Malachi shook his head.

The colonel shrugged. "The FBI tells us that on any given day, there are 100,000 active missing person cases being investigated in the country."

"Who would harm a priest," Malachi grated, though he knew he was being intentionally naive. He continued. "If he was murdered, police should have found something by now?"

"He could have been kidnapped and removed from New York State," the colonel said. "The feds also tell us that in evidence rooms around the country there are partial remains of more than 40,000 people they can't identify. Can you give me a hint of what the hell...pardon me, sir....is going on? If we knew more, perhaps we could help more?"

As they turned a corner, Malachi stopped abruptly and the two soldiers did likewise. "I'm sorry Colonel Rutlege. If I could tell you, I would. Suffice to say that your lieutenant is a very lucky man, and I'm looking into what made him so lucky. That's about it."

"And our part-time Chaplin? How does he fit into this?" The colonel was suspicious.

"He was...is... an old friend," Malachi answered. A partial truth at best.

"Do you need us anymore, Father?" the captain asked, much younger than the colonel but with a certain hardness and directness that said he didn't appreciate being kept out of the loop any more than the colonel did.

"No...that's everything I needed, gentlemen. I can find my own way out."

Both men stepped back and for some reason saluted. "Very well," Colonel Rutlege said. "If there is anything else we can do for you, please just let us know. You have our cards."

"You've been most kind, truly," Malachi said. He shook both their hands exuding a warm smile that both intrigued and captivated the men who suddenly felt a kinship for the priest which they couldn't readily explain. By way of apology for any abruptness they might have perceived, he threw them a nugget. "If it puts your mind at ease, this is strictly church business…nothing to do with the army."

"Thank you Father," they answered, almost in unison, and smiled back at him.

"Good! Now you gentlemen, be at peace and stay out of harm's way. I'm going to get a coffee in the cafeteria and do a little thinking."

"Good-bye, sir," they said, again almost together, and marched off.

Malachi sat in the cafeteria sipping a sour-tasting, acidic liquid claiming to be freshly brewed coffee out of a state-of-the-art vending machine. He watched the comings and goings of nurses, doctors and orderlies as they juggled food trays and kibitzed with each other. A familiar shakiness throughout his body signaled low blood sugar, and he took another bite of a doughnut. He should be eating crackers and cheese he realized but this would have to do. In a few minutes he would return to two priests sitting outside the hospital in their rented automobile and give them their orders. Having met Clay briefly, he had pegged him as a serious young man and not one likely to make up tales. He wished he'd been able to press him further on what happened the night of the ambush but confidentiality was paramount at this point in his investigation. He had settled for a quick meeting where he was able to assess the man.

The previous month, before Gallo called, Malachi had received news that he was one of 44 candidates appointed to the College of Cardinals and would soon officially become a Prince of the Catholic Church. He'd sent an email to a few of his church brethren, including Father Gallo, telling them of his upcoming appointment. Congratulations flowed in, all saying it was well deserved. As a member of the Romana Curia, he would be appointed a Cardinal Deacon. In fact, his appointment meant he would be by-passing the usual hierarchical route of becoming a bishop first, courtesy of a special dispensation. Malachi felt he had certainly earned it. He had paid his dues and his reputation had survived intact despite some controversies over the years.

When his old friend Gallo had called from America, he felt obligated to make some inquiries about the legend of the *Hellspawn*. Rather than being treated with amusement, contempt or benign neglect, he had been surprised at the reactions he received. In fact, it seemed that his questions had served as a catalyst, and galvanized some inner church workings since it hadn't been long before he'd been summoned to the *Chamber*. When he found out the reason for the summons, it didn't take a rocket scientist to deduce that his questions led to the summons.

On his first visit, Malachi had been accompanied by Brother Fagan, a serious looking and well-fed Christian Brother who moved surprisingly fast for his bulk. The man led him through a series of concealed entranceways and low tunnels which, his ample-girthed guide had needlessly explained, were secret passageways constructed for ancient Popes who often had to flee from potential assassins in the Vatican buildings. After they traversed a final brick-lined corridor and reached a well-hidden anti-chamber that appeared to be an ex-dungeon of sorts, the brother vanished; he was left staring at a group of six clerics clustered around a heavy oak table. One tall man welcomed him and said with tongue in cheek that they were known as "*The Seven.*" When, with a hint of humor Malachi pointed out the mathematical discrepancy, he was informed there was none since they hoped he would become number seven replacing one Cardinal Cal Brott, a 70-year-old member suffering from terminal cancer and unable to attend.

Rather presumptuous, Malachi had thought, puzzled but interested. Still, to their credit, when he pressed them as to their mandate, they hadn't hesitated. The tall man with a squared off crew cut introduced himself as Monsignor Heinz Rautenberg. He had looked Malachi in the eye and said that it was their collective, sworn and holy duty to track down and kill for all time an earth-bound demon known as the *Hellspawn*.

At first, Malachi had been somewhat amused by the obvious link between his inquiries and the summons. But as one-by-one they spoke to him about the seriousness of their purpose, individual duties and specializations, as well as their need for new leadership, he had also become intrigued.

And now, here he was, smack dab in the middle of it all. Somehow he had been *recommended* as one who could provide leadership, no less. Not that he wasn't up to the task. Rather he had seen it as a chance to clarify things, to put an end to wild speculation and rumor, and reveal this *Hellspawn* for what it really was – a series of evil men throughout history who had been mistakenly lumped together as one and attributed with "devilish" powers.

Malachi felt he was getting a little long in the tooth to believe otherwise. After, all, he was an educated man having studied at the Catholic University of Louvain in Belgium where he received doctorates both in Semitic Languages and Middle East History. Not to mention the numerous seminars and auxiliary courses he had attended, and the impressive number of papers he had authored including: *The Church and Modern Man; Vatican II: An Appeal to Modernity;* and, *Living Saints of the Catholic Church*, a dissertation that had caused some concern within the Vatican since it was "they" who would decide who was a saint and who was not.

He reached over to try to cut the acidity of his coffee by dumping more whitener in it as he marveled that an English lad such as himself, who had come through the orphanage system when his parents died in an automotive crash, had come so far in life.

His family had been living in the small English village of Bath when the motoring accident happened and his life changed forever. Because he was an only child, and authorities could not find any living relatives, he was ultimately consigned to the British orphanage system with his parent's assets put into a trust for him. An independent spirit, he couldn't wait to grow up and be free. But then fortune smiled on him when he was thirteen-years-old.

An aunt, whose husband had recently died, had looked into her husband's family tree and found that, contrary to his assertions, he did indeed have a sister in England. From what she could determine, because of a family squabble, they were estranged and he had told his wife that his entire family was deceased. However, she now had proof that her husband did indeed have a living relative. But when his Aunt Helen, who was living in Boston, found that her husband's sister and her husband had been killed, and had a living son, she immediately sought custody. That was how young Mustavias Malachi originally came to America to live in Boston, Massachusetts.

In fact, it turned out to be an extremely good life for him. His aunt had inherited a considerable fortune from her husband who purchased substantial stock in a popular bank and other start-up companies such as Apple, Microsoft and some unknown called Wal-Mart. She both loved young Mustavias to a fault, and devoted her life to seeing to his welfare and education. In fact, she had used her financial influence to get him into England's famous University of Oxford, and despite her loneliness, had suffered stoically through his absences looking forward to the holidays each year with great expectation. In turn, Malachi had grown to love this charitable and upstanding woman who had taken him into her heart and home. At the same time, however, he was noticing a change in himself during his university years. No longer was he playing rugby, interested in films or even trips into London to go clubbing. Rather he was becoming more introspective all the time. And, one small event in his life began to assume a renewed importance and a strange significance.

As a lad in Bath, before his mother and father's death, he'd been playing on a soccer field with his friends most of the day. The sun was gold and low in the sky, the sweet scent of newly mown hay in the air, when he heard his mother calling across the field that his tea was on. As he made ready to head home, he felt a hole in his pocket and realized he'd lost his prized pocketknife. Despair flooded his young being: how could he possibly find it on such a vast field? He began to wander in an aimless grid of sorts, desperately searching the grass. His mother's voice drifted across the green once more, a note of finality in her tone. His father would soon come searching for him.

Close to tears, young Malachi asked the only one he could ask at the time for help – God. He'd closed his eyes, stuck his hands in his pocket and whispering prayers, allowed himself to continue to wander about the field. He moved far and wide, stumbling now and again, his eyes remaining tightly closed, saying to himself that when he stopped and opened them, the knife would be there. Again, his mother's voice shouted for him, her irritation at his continuing absence and perhaps a small hint of concern growing. Malachi stopped, opened his eyes and looked down. The green shell-sided pocketknife lay directly between his two running shoes.

Heart pounding in joy, he scooped up the knife, said a thank you to God, and bounded home to supper. He was now a youngster who knew there was a God in Heaven, a God who took a moment to answer a cry for help from a small boy.

When, in his final year of Oxford, it was time to pick a vocation, he knew with certainty that his calling was not necessarily in the business, arts or scientific world. His interests were more spiritual. Indeed, as Malachi's fascination with his Catholic faith had blossomed, his Aunt Helen had fully supported him there too. Later, she financed his post-graduate studies at Louvain and was immensely proud of his choice to enter the priesthood. Her hope was that he would one day be assigned to a diocese in Boston. For Malachi, however, his focus was on serving God wherever he was needed. And while he had not always been a scholarly sort, and more a person with a healthy skepticism for many of life's mysteries, doubt did not extend to his faith. Somehow, he knew there was a God in Heaven, a tangible, reasonable being who gloried in the good deeds of His people and experienced tremendous sorrow when they transgressed. How he knew it, he didn't know. He just knew.

After his graduation and ordination, however, he had been assigned to the Holy See in Rome. It was an opportunity, his aunt agreed, that he could not turn down. As personal secretary to a number of Cardinals at different times, he worked in a variety of departments of the Romana Curia for many years. He made it a point, however, to travel back to Boston to see his Aunt Helen every three months, and have her come to Rome each June when they would explore the marvels of the ancient city and the Italian vineyards and countryside, enjoying the sun and the better vintages.

Unfortunately, this lasted only for a few years. Aunt Helen had passed in her sleep of a brain aneurism. Malachi soon found that she had placed her fortune in a trust for him in case he left the priesthood early or retired. While he had full access at any time, she knew that due to his vows of poverty and obedience he would not use the money during his tenure.

As a Jesuit, he had learned sacrifice and discipline that served him well in the Vatican. And, as his experience and knowledge increased exponentially, he had been repeatedly sought out for his wisdom and perspective on many practical, ecclesiastical and even philosophical matters. His reputation had grown and, in truth, he wasn't surprised that his appointment had come by way of a dispensation. Only that it *now* appeared to have come with a price – an appointment to the *Chamber*.

His thoughts returned to the present and the course of action he must now choose after having met the ex-lieutenant. The problem with his current challenge was that after some initial research and counsel with his dying predecessor, who had largely held this "demon-hunting" duty as a ceremonial post, he finally believed there might be something to it. Without knowing it, Father Gallo's call to Malachi had initiated a defined protocol that necessitated *The Seven* exploring the validity of the news. And so here he was in upstate New York.

He sighed, finished his coffee and consigned the cardboard cup to the proper green waste bin on his way out of the veteran's hospital.

A few minutes later, he sat in the backseat of a dark blue Mercury Marquis while two middle-aged priests sat in the front. Father Dermott Murphy and Father Ronald Langevin were on special assignment, and charged with keeping watch over Lieutenant Clay Montague. They would become part of a group of *Watchmen* managing his surveillance.

"He remembers nothing," Malachi said to the priests who sat staring straight ahead.

Without turning, Father Murphy asked, "So what now?"

"We watch him. Like a hawk. Day and night. Sooner or later it will come."

According to Malachi's predecessor, it was unusual to have a *live* victim of the *Hellspawn* and if this was indeed true, they might have been handed an extraordinary opportunity to bait and kill it.

~ 15 ~

The wailing began again.

Father Gallo sat up on his mattress and began to tremble; he looked in fear towards the five slits in the curved stone wall of his cell. The sounds of suffering erupted periodically only to fade away after a few moments. They were filtering in through the openings where he could see a few twinkling stars and a crescent moon against a mauve evening sky. The window slits were too high for him to access even if he had the will or the strength to hoist himself up. He still had no idea where he was, only that he had been confined in a small cell for an outrageous amount of time. And, that he could smell salt air, hear the shrieks of sea gulls and occasionally the sound of waves breaking on a shoreline; he was certainly near the sea.

He looked at the wall in the faint moonlight and again counted off the days he'd been held prisoner – 104. More than three months. And yet, no contact with his captors, and no attempts at rescue. Whoever had kidnapped him had done a good job of making him vanish and keeping their identity secret. Whenever he slept, his jailors crept into his cell. He would invariably awaken to find a tray of non-descript food that resembled pig swill and some hunks of bread beside the door. Still he was grateful for it and ate every sop.

Occasionally, when needed, he also found rolls of toilet paper beside the tray, a bar of soap and a metal safety razor welded shut so he couldn't use the blade on himself. And though he stayed awake for up to 24-hours at a time, and even faked sleep, he had never glimpsed the steel door open or the faces of his jailors.

His space consisted of an 18-by-18-foot stone cell furnished with a foam mattress and a few worn and putrid smelling blankets. In one corner was a stainless steel toilet. There were no facilities for cleaning, even a basic sink, so he washed and shaved as best he could over the toilet. Other than his daily tray of food and two liters of water in a plastic jug, nothing else entered his cell. He had been using a piece of black candle wax he'd found in an unused iron sconce bolted to the wall to make marks on the stone and count the days. From the stone and the curve of the wall, he wondered if he was in some sort of turret, possibly in a castle-like building. But where in upstate New York would you find a castle and salt air, he mused? There was Boldt Castle in the Thousand Islands, but it was a tourist attraction. And, then there was the smell of the ocean. There was also the possibility he was no longer in New York State.

Gallo passed the time in prayer and meditation; there was nothing else to do. The days and nights proceeded endlessly. His last conscious memory before he had awakened in his cell, was standing in the lieutenant's hospital room about to give him Extreme Unction. Though he tried diligently to remember what had happened after the soldier awakened, everything was blank.

Unfortunately for Gallo, his memory loss was only temporary. When he finally managed to obtain a reaction from one of his jailors, it somehow lifted the veil from his amnesia; it also proved to be the dawn of a terror he fervently wished he had avoided.

It happened on day 125, even though, by that time he had stopped counting. Gallo had again begun his regular campaign of shouting, banging and otherwise making noise to try to attract his captors. This night, however, he succeeded.

He'd been yelling for more than ten minutes because a low wattage overhead light, a good 20 feet up and riveted to a wooden crossbeams in the ceiling, had been turned off plunging him into total darkness. The bulb had been on since his capture and he wondered if this was an escalation of deprivation. Would he lose his food, bedding or water next? He decided he wouldn't take it lying down. Whoever they were, they'd soon find that there was still spunk in the old man, he thought letting loose another bellow of protest.

He'd screamed challenging obscenities, finally yelling that they would all be consigned to hell for his imprisonment. It was then he heard a distinct scratching at the steel door. It resembled the sound of four or five nails being slowly pulled across the metal on the outside. The sound was repeated.

The old priest rose from his mattress and crossed to the steel door where he cautiously placed his ear against it. When he heard nothing, he again shouted that his captors would be spending eternity with the devil for treating a man of God in this way. The scraping on the door came again and he'd held his breath, pressed his ear close and listened.

On the other side of the door, he could now hear labored breathing. Finally, a low, rasping and gravelly baritone whispered "W-We want...you ...!" It was barely loud enough for him to hear. The words were stilted and hesitant as though the person wasn't used to speaking. Still he got the message when the voice continued: "Don't...curse the devil...Gallo...or one night...he'll be sure to answer." This was followed by a low, nasty hiccupping that passed for a laugh. And then something scuttled away followed by... silence!

For some reason the words had hit the old priest hard. A split second later the cobwebs in his mind cleared as though someone had shoved smelling salts under his nose. He remembered everything that had happened after he'd left the hospital: How the little girl with the hellish eyes led him to the giant figure near the tree; how he'd panicked; and, how the monster had reached for him.

Now, in the cell, his heart had begun to race and sweat poured from his forehead. Revulsion, terror and despair returned anew as memories flooded back in a jumbled ménage of flash pictures that bloomed and faded, swept into focus and abruptly dropped from the sight of his mind's eye to be replaced by even more disturbing visions.

He remembered how, on seeing the creature, his legs had begun to tremble and his breath had shortened until he was puffing like a wasted animal. He remembered being frozen, unable to move or run despite being relatively near the hospital and safety. He remembered the blackened countenance that passed for a face with the two protrusions on its head beckoning him forward. He remembered how powerless he had been to resist. And, finally, as the being had pulled him close and enfolded him into his cloak, he remembered being smothered by what he knew to be the wicked stench of mortal sin. Screaming, his mind had retreated into the blackness to hide. The next thing he remembered was waking up in his cell.

After first contact, Gallo retreated from the door, trembling in fright, fighting nausea and trying to pray. But he was incapable of reciting his prayers, even by rote. He merely mumbled sounds that he hoped were prayers.

Thereafter, he made no more protests or challenges. He meekly accepted the food that was offered and kept silent. He prayed continuously for salvation through deliverance or death – either was preferable to this torturous limbo of meaningless existence devoid of purpose or control.

Now, barely a month later, the nightly keening began again sending chills up his spine and setting goose bumps alive on his arms and legs. One thing was certain: whatever was making those sounds – he wasn't even sure if they were human or not – was slowly being murdered.

Because of prolonged inactivity, the old priest's bones constantly ached and his joints had stiffened. He rolled onto his knees and used his hands as leverage to stand upright. Shuffling to the steel door, he pressed his ear against it. The screams were definitely coming from somewhere distant, though loud enough to also be heard through the small, stone openings of his cell. Why didn't someone else hear them, he wondered? Surely they were loud enough that any passer-bys would alert the police. But, he also understood the possibility that he was in a rural area since, despite the nightly weeping and pleas for mercy, nothing happened. At these times, there was little Gallo could do other than to say a prayer for the souls of those sufferers.

Despite frequent awakenings from the shrieks of victims in the night, his routine continued unaltered for days. It was about a week later that the nightmares began. These dreams held vivid and monstrous scenes that sickened him to the point of physically throwing up after awakening.

Night after night he would dream that he was being roused, led out of his cell, and dragged down some stone steps to a giant rocky cavern where he would see the naked bodies of hundreds of terrified men, women and children being tortured.

Some were hanging by chains from stone walls, their flesh pierced by iron meat hooks slicing into their backs and holding them a few feet from the floor. Unable to escape, they would kick, cry and plead as small orange and red gnome-like creatures scuttled up to them, retreated, and scuttled up again as though testing the waters to see if they were a danger in any way.

The creatures were only three feet tall and yet had overgrown adult-sized heads complete with the mythical horns of devils. They were naked and seemed to be almost androgynous since he couldn't make out any defined genitalia. Their sole intent seemed to be to torture their terrified prisoners, pretending at times to be afraid of them and retreating.

After a number of forays by the creatures towards their victims, who screamed in terror at their approach, they would retreat a few more times sporting sadistic grins. Ultimately they would end the game by returning a last time with scythe-like knives in their misshapen claw-like appendages. With heads cocked to the side as though puzzled over what to do, they would suddenly arrive at a decision en mass and scurry up to their victims to slit the bottom of their bellies open. Then they would drop their knives, dig their claws inside the hemorrhaging wounds and drag out the victims' entrails to stuff them in their mouths. They would chew frantically, pulling their heads back to extract more intestines with their teeth as the victims heaved and screamed, and blood pulsed in scarlet gushes from their wounds and mouths. Gallo would very soon throw up.

And, there were more games from hell.

Once he was made to watch as dozens of the creatures seized chains attached to a number of naked victims' limbs. The chains were pulled in different directions until the arms and legs made great fleshy pops, soon following by meaty ripping sounds as the limbs were torn from the body trunks leaving four streaming, gaping holes from which the screaming victims quickly bled out.

Other nights he dreamed that he was led to the same cavern where he'd see hundreds of people hanging by chains around their wrists above individual fires set in molten seas of crimson lava which flared, subsided, and then surged higher causing them to scream and to try to pull their legs up from the flesh-scorching heat. There was no lighting in the rocky cavern, though none was needed with so many fires. The red hot flames, which uniformly seemed to rise higher and higher over the minutes, would cast the orange macabre, dancing shadows of the victims on the surrounding rock walls as hanging bodies jerked and twisted in agony. Gallo was forced to watch as each one was slowly roasted to death from the feet up.

The end would come when the blistering heat caused their internal cavity organs to burst into steak-sizzling masses of jelly, frying and popping in their bellies while seared flesh sloughed off their feet and legs into the fires. They screamed and screamed but never seemed to lose consciousness until the very last moments of their lives. Then their heads dropped and their bodies emptied themselves into the fires sending up a hissing, steaming stench. Finally, they would recover, sickened and confused, and the games became again. In short: endless death.

Gallo knew this could only be a rendition of hell and he was being made privy to the tortures of the eternally damned. But were these events real or mere nightmares? He began to suspect that they were real after awakening several times with his knuckles skinned and bleeding, his lips bitten through, his pulse racing, and his body drenched in sour sweat. The pork-like aromas of the smoldering flesh of the human sacrifices were often still in his nostrils and the pitiful screams of the victims resonated in his ears.

Sometimes he would remember being dragged by the small horned creatures close to the cooking bodies and having a long pike shoved into his hands. He was urged to prod and turn the bodies of the young men and women. If he failed to do so, he was thrust ever closer to the fires himself until he complied. The priest would never forget the sweating, terrified face of one young girl who couldn't have been more than eighteen and who stared down at him from where she hung above the fire and begged: "Father! Father, for the love of God, please save me! I beg you! Save my soul."

He felt the small creatures near his knees beginning to push him towards the edge of the sea of fire. To save himself he pushed the pike into her side and turned her face from him as she died. Indeed, what could she have done to deserve this cycle of torture?

Each morning after the horrific dreams, he desperately worked to erase them from an increasingly numbed mind, to forget the horrible deaths of the people and the small, reptilian creatures that forced him to do unspeakable things. Sometimes, in an attempt to avoid what he hoped were dreams, he would try to remain awake. Eventually, however, he would fall asleep and it would happen all over again. He valiantly fought thoughts of suicide.

Then one night, everything changed.

Gallo had vowed to himself he wouldn't sleep; he wouldn't be coerced back into the fire pits, real or not. Suddenly the steel door had swung open with a metallic crash and a huge, umbrageous figure stood silhouetted in the doorway. Terrified, the priest squeezed his eyes shut feigning sleep, desperately trying to wish his visitor away.

Trembling, he heard what sounded like a chuckle or perhaps even a small growl from the figure in the doorway.

Bow to the King of Fire.

The old priest's terror was great as the figure in the doorway began to speak in a soft, modulated and hypnotic voice. "Oh Father, Father, Father...what is to become of you cowering there in fear? Where is your faith now? Where is your trust in The Trinity? Where is your *hope*, old man?"

Gallo tried to keep his breathing steady. Retreating into the innocence of a child, he desperately pleaded in his mind: Go away...go away...go away!

"Have you lost all courage, Father Gallo? Can you not face me? What happened to all those threats you voiced so clearly over these last months? Were they hollow? Was your faith - that you professed so vehemently - nothing but a lie? Do you not continue to believe in the Son of the Wood Worker's death and resurrection? What about the infallibility of the Church?" He laughed, a deep roar that seemed to shake the stone walls of Gallo's cell. "Ah...so many questions, so little fucking time."

The figure then suddenly advanced and stood over the quaking old man, knowing full well he wasn't asleep. Gallo knew, with every fiber of his body, that this could only be Adramelech, the arch demon himself. Though he kept his eyes shut, he could feel an overpowering sense of evil growing in strength and proximity as the demon leaned close and whispered in his ear.

"Perhaps you'd like a turn in the pit? How would you like to feel your innards roasting like a fat, young pig, your outer flesh sizzling like crispy bacon?" He chuckled again.

The priest's heart hammered in his chest. Had the demon truly come for him? Was it his time to be tortured like the others? Visions of himself being slowly roasted to a screaming death forced him to abandon any charade of sleeping. Terrified, he scrambled off his mattress and flung himself away from the demon to where he huddled against the far wall. He was still too fearful to look at the Beast. With his blanket clutched in his hand, his mind reeled and snapped in and out of reality as madness tore into his brain; his beliefs, intellect and rationality surrendered to a single, primal desire – to survive. All he wanted to do was live. At any cost.

As Father Benito Gallo of the one, holy, catholic and apostolic church began to croon in baby-like sounds to comfort himself and block out the horror, the silhouetted form stood up and laughed again. "Don't worry Priest. Be of good cheer. You have much work to do."

The monster moved closer to explain how the old man could save himself. "There is no hope, no redemption, Priest. You are nothing but human meat. But you may live out your miserable years if you follow orders. So be a good boy and start by simply disavowing any belief in the Father, the Son of God and His whore mother."

* * * *

PART TWO

"THE COMING"

By the pricking of my thumbs,
Something wicked this way comes,
Open locks,
Whoever knocks…?

William Shakespeare
MACBETH

~ 1 ~

WOODSTROM, VERMONT – 2003

As they headed west on Route 4, Sheriff Clay Montague slowed the patrol car on the Ottauquechee River Bridge and carefully maneuvered across it before picking up speed on the other side. Like most bridges in the area, this one spanning the 165-foot Quechee Gorge froze rapidly and regularly featured some of the most treacherous black ice he'd ever encountered.

Though the National Weather Service out of Burlington had promised a clear day for tomorrow, it was snowing lightly now, huge flakes dancing in the sky with the promise of at least three inches of light powder. He could imagine the slopes of Suicide Six the next day bobbing with happy skiers cutting trails through the virgin snow under a wintry blue sky.

Clay hoped that he and his deputy, Bob Hitchcock, aka Hitch could make it back to Woodstrom before darkness closed in. Vermont winter weather was unpredictable and unforgiving, particularly in December.

"What the hell are we looking for again, Clay?" Hitch asked, sitting beside him carefully sipping coffee from a steaming Styrofoam cup.

Clay glanced over, his gaze sliding past the Ithaca 37 12-gauge pump and the .30-30 Winchester clamped, barrels upright, against the dashboard between them. The deputy's six-foot-four-inch frame was uncomfortably wedged in the front seat, his Stetson cocked on the back of his head and hazel eyes thoughtful. He blew steam off his coffee and cautiously took a sip.

"Damned if I know, Hitch," Clay said, cautiously watching an oncoming SUV as it approached. "Mrs. Jackson claims she saw lights at the old Baker place."

Slush from the other vehicle splattered the windshield so Clay hit the wiper button.

"Mrs. Jackson sees lights all the time," Hitchcock muttered, swallowing another mouthful. "It's those damn UFO books she keeps reading. Probably just someone with a hankering for venison up there jacking deer."

"Maybe...but we'd better have a look. That place has been rotting away for years. If it's kids fooling around, they could go through a floorboard and break their necks."

They drove in silence for a few more minutes.

The highway unwound before them, a silent ribbon of dirty grey slush and snow marked only by twin black tracks where another car had made its way minutes before. The rest of the valley was blanketed in banks of soft, white crystals which now whirled lazily in the light wind and settled across the highway in sweeping mounds. He glanced up through the thick flakes at the mountains looming on either side of the road, awesome guardians of the valley. The car periodically hesitated, bumping through the small drifts of snow before surging ahead to pick up speed again.

Bordering the highway were crowded stands of spruce and pine trees staggering under the loads of snow on their branches. Their soft beauty reminded him of gauze-swathed angels perched on the Christmas trees of his youth.

Hitchcock said: "A virtual winter wonderland, eh Clay?"

Keeping his eyes on the road, Clay nodded in agreement. Like Hitch, he had grown up in Vermont, and was well used to the winters.

The car slowed and staggered as it hit another drift and slewed sideways. Clay spun the wheel into the skid; the automobile responded beautifully. It was instantly arrow-straight again.

The flakes were huge and fluffy now, making it harder to see. They were also beginning to stick to the windshield. The warm air from the car's vent melted the snow as it hit the glass and it puddled, ran, and froze on the wiper blades. In turn, the wipers lay twin smears of ice across the glass. Clay cursed and hit his washer button. The fluid sprinkled half-heartedly onto the windshield. The wiper cleared the slush for a minute, and then the window iced up again, worse than before.

"I wouldn't use the washer," Hitchcock ventured, hesitantly.

"You want to drive?" Clay shot back. He didn't tolerate additional drivers, front or back seat.

Hitchcock grinned: "Naw, you're havin' too much fun."

Clay smiled in spite of himself and was grateful for Hitch's easy-going good humor. He'd worked with the man for four years now and he'd become a close personal friend as well as partner.

Martha Hitchcock, Hitch's wife, had also become best friends with Clay's wife, Jody.

The deputy was a great back-up in a scrap as Clay had found when he had to face down a half-dozen drunken, good-ole-boys outside the Loose Moose Bar & Grill one night two years before. The six men had just finished a free-for-all in the Moose and trashed it in the process. Clay chuckled at the memory of Hitch using a .12 gauge to make the rowdies understand they weren't in charge any longer.

He carefully slowed the car and then gently accelerated around a curve.

There wasn't a day that went by that he didn't thank his lucky stars for his job as County Sheriff. And, he was still amazed at the fantastic streak of coincidences that had given him his wife, his job and his happiness.

After his release from the Veteran's hospital, he'd accepted an honorable discharge and headed down to Florida, where a friend had guaranteed him a job on one of his charter fishing boats.

Arriving in Gulf Breeze, he met up with his friend who had a Hatteras 48 Fly-Bridge waiting for him. He acquired his U.S. Power Squadron Certification and studied and then wrote the exam to become a licensed charter skipper. For the next year he hauled a cadre of cigar-smoking tourists into the Gulf of Mexico where he supplied them with cold beer and encouragement as they happily reeled in sailfish, marlin and tuna.

Deciding he was heading nowhere fast, Clay answered a newspaper recruiting ad and soon found himself completing the 26-week basic training course at the Florida Highway Patrol Training Academy in Tallahassee. After ten weeks riding with a Field Training Officer, he was a fully accredited state trooper. And, there was little doubt that he'd found his niche in life.

He liked law enforcement with the excitement and challenge of dealing with human situations day in and day out, with no two days alike. But though he'd been judged an exemplary officer by his superiors, it had been observed in evaluation sessions that he seemed almost too fearless in the line of duty. In fact, at times, he showed a reckless disregard for his own safety. His fellow officers noted that whenever they gave aid in takedown situations, he was always first through the door. He charged gun-wielding felons as though he was invulnerable. But he had also received two commendations and the

Florida Highway Patrol's Medal of Valor for saving other officer's lives through courageous initiatives that placed him at considerable personal risk.

After one particularly dangerous incident where he'd disarmed a pistol-wielding young woman attempting to take her own life, he suffered a gunshot wound in his arm. While congratulations were definitely in order, his captain also showed concern. He was asked to see the police psychiatrist for an all-round discussion.

It wasn't long before the doctor had zeroed in on the fact that he could be suffering from a post traumatic form of guilt because his army patrol had died and he had lived. Though the word's "death wish" had never been spoken, Clay soon found himself on daytime traffic patrol; it was this transfer that ultimately changed his life.

He could still remember the day it happened as clearly as though it was last week. There'd been a three-car pileup on the southbound lanes of Interstate 75 near Ocala. As he skidded to a stop, light bar flashing and siren dying, he spotted a light green Chevy SUV lying upside down on a partially crushed roof. Flames roared into the air from its undercarriage. Two other automobiles with crumpled fronts and rears were off to the side of the road. He was already on the radio requesting fire and ambulance services before his siren died.

A grey-haired man and a middle-aged lady were lying on the shoulder of the highway being tended by other motorists. The man was trying to stand on an obviously broken leg and yelling that his daughter was inside the burning Chevy. Three men were dashing about trying to get near the overturned vehicle but being driven back by the relentless heat and flames.

Clay grabbed his highway patrol car fire extinguisher and hit the fire with it as he ran in close. The flames dampened slightly, enough for him to throw the empty extinguisher to the side, kick in the remains of the back window of the overturned vehicle and squirm his way inside.

Lying on his belly, with his feet sticking out the rear window, he searched desperately with his hands for the girl. Above, the gas tank exploded and he felt the car rock violently and the heat intensify.

Bystanders were screaming at him to get out! Flames shot skyward from the bottom of the automobile in ever-larger, orange mushrooms. More small explosions rocked the vehicle as fumes from gas puddles trapped in the undercarriage ignited.

Inside, thick, oily, black smoke seeped into the cab. Hot cinders dropped onto Clay's back, burning through his uniform as the fire reached down to consume the upholstery. He began coughing and tried to shield his nose and mouth with his arm. It didn't work; he sucked in more smoke and fumes.

Decision time: either he got out now, alone, or he stayed until he freed the victim; the chances they'd both survive – slim. Clay had always been someone who did the right thing; he wasn't about to quit now. Besides, there was that survivor guilt to feed.

He heard the girl cough.

She was alive!

He steeled himself against the pain on his back as more flaming cinders fell and his shirt began to smolder.

The girl was thrashing about in the back seat, moaning and coughing as he reached forward and felt a thick tangle of long hair. Gently he touched her face to let her know he was there.

She screamed in fright.

Clay yelled: "Easy...easy...I'll get you out."

"Oh God...!" she gasped, went into a coughing fit and then reached back. "Please…help me. My Mom and Dad…"

"They're out," Clay said. He felt her hand touch his face but instead of grabbing him in a panic reflex, his presence seemed to calm her and she relaxed. Gently she cupped his face with her hand as though to reassure herself that he was not going anyplace. His own hands traveled down over her chest and to her waist.

Just as he suspected, her seat belt was holding her fast. Eyes streaming from the smoke, he held his breath, and worked at freeing her from the belt. Acrid fumes filled his lungs; he struggled to breathe as he worked at the buckle.

It was bent and jammed!

Another flaming piece of upholstery dropped and seared the exposed back of his neck; he groaned in pain. He couldn't take the time to lift his hands and brush it away.

Somehow, sensing his hurt, one of the girl's hands left his face and magically he felt it brushing the fire from his neck; he continued to punch the button on the seat belt. It refused to open. He grabbed his clasp knife from his pocket.

Twenty seconds later, he wormed his way back out of the car dragging the girl with him to the applause of the crowd. They were immediately surrounded and Clay gratefully accepted the ministration of a bystander who dumped a thermos of cold coffee on the back of his smoldering uniform. The burning momentarily subsided.

Clay never forgot the look on the faces of the girl's mother and father as they sobbed and tearfully hugged their daughter. Miraculously, though bruised and cut, she was otherwise unhurt.

As her father hugged her, she met Clay's eyes over his shoulder, studying him intently as she murmured reassurances into her father's ear.

Two bystanders helped Clay sit on the pavement. The smoke he'd inhaled was finally taking its toll. His head swam and he coughed repeatedly. Other patrol cars and a fire truck were arriving. Suddenly the girl, Jody Mathers, left her parents and limped to where Clay sat on the asphalt.

Her face was blackened by soot, her thick, raven-colored hair was a tangled mess and her clothes filthy and ripped. Yet, Clay found himself forgetting all of that and gazing into what must surely be the deepest and bluest eyes on earth.

He swallowed nervously and his heart raced. He guessed her to be in her mid-twenties and noted that her face was a perfect oval with high cheekbones setting off those magnificent eyes. A model's sculpted nose ended above the fullest, most desirable-looking lips Clay had ever imagined. As she moved towards him he couldn't help taking in the sway of her full, denim-clad hips, tiny waist and the swell of her breasts straining against a yellow plaid shirt. Even at her worst, Clay decided she was the most beautiful girl he had ever seen.

She stood before him and, for a moment, they lost themselves in a world that seemed to exist only for them. In one tiny nanosecond they exchanged messages of wonder, happiness, and promise. Then she reached down and gently kissed him on the lips. He found himself responding and then hurriedly broke it off when he realized grinning bystanders were applauding again. His face went beet red as she smiled down at him.

"I'm a nurse…let's see that back, mister," she said with authority, moving behind him. He felt his burned shirt being ripped apart as another motorist ran up with a small first-aid kit in hand. In moments, Jody was smoothing a salve over his blistered back.

She coughed and spoke, "You married or engaged, copper?"

Clay tried to look round at her in amazement but she gently pushed his face forward again as she worked on his burns.

"Married?" he asked in surprise.

"Yes...married, hitched, betrothed, promised, a legal ceremony joining man and women, a physically-consummated, paper-approved relationship...notice anything like that in your life?"

Clay couldn't help smiling even as he winched at her gentle touch. "Afraid not, miss."

"Good. Then you won't mind taking me to dinner."

Without another word she finished taping two ointment-gauze pads over the most severe burns on his back. As two ambulances pulled up and Emergency Medical Technicians appeared, she patted him on the head and made her way back to her parents.

"Excuse me ma'am...but I don't even know you." Any sting in his words was negated by a good-natured and somewhat silly grin that he knew was plastered across his features. The wail of more sirens came closer.

She smiled back at him: "We'll work on that too, hero."

He lost himself in the blue eyes again as she tossed him an impish grin, and with a confidence born of those who know the power of their beauty, she brushed back her long, thick hair, turned and re-joined her parents as EMTs loaded her father onto a stretcher.

In fact, her father turned out to be Sheriff Bill Mathers of Woodstrom, Vermont. He and his wife Nancy, and Jody had been heading for Orlando on a two-week vacation when they'd been cut off by a Chinese Food Supply delivery truck entering the Interstate. Mathers tried to avoid the truck but the SUV hit the gravel and slewed sideways, causing two other cars to have minor collisions. The SUV rolled as the delivery van increased speed and continued down the highway. Clay had been five miles north of them in a southbound lane when he'd received the call.

In the end, Jody's instincts had been right. One year later, to the day, after an impatient, long-distance courtship, she became Clay's bride. The same year he finally accepted a job as a Deputy Sheriff of Winder County from Jody's father and moved himself back to his home state.

Bill and Nancy treated Clay like a son and when Mathers had retired the year before, he'd encouraged Clay to run for his position as Winder County Sheriff.

Clay was liked by the citizens, his fellow officers and had his father-in-law campaigning for him before he'd even made up his mind to accept the nomination. His campaign was treated with more enthusiasm by his campaign team than by Clay himself. He felt guilty, sensing he was, in effect, riding on Mather's coattails.

Still, he won by a landslide. He couldn't argue with the voters and reconciled himself to his new position. He knew he was, as a military doctor once called him, one lucky puppy. And right now he had the love of his life waiting for him at home.

"There it is, on the right," Hitchcock said, breaking into his thoughts and using the patrol car's spotlight to illuminate the broken shingle with the word "Baker" on it dangling from a weathered, disintegrating and crooked, cedar post beside the highway.

Clay slowed and turned onto a barely visible road leading up a steep hill towards the house. He lowered the window and listened to the corn starch crunch of the tires on the snow as cool snowflakes melted on his face. He knew that the building was more than a mile up the side of the mountain but the slope and the depth of the snow had their tires spinning within a minute.

"Looks like we go in on foot," Clay said, picking up the radio microphone. He punched the transmit button. "Dispatch...Unit One...10-23 Baker Estate." Silence. "Base...do you read me, over?" He let up on the button and was rewarded with a burst of static but no acknowledgement from the dispatcher.

He tried twice more and shrugged: "Damn the mountains. We might as well use smoke signals for all the good these radios are up here. Got to get a satellite-based system."

Hitch chuckled and pulled the upright .30-30 Winchester carbine from its clamp.

"What do we need that for?" Clay asked.

"Squirrels," Hitch replied with a grin.

"Squirrels!?" he grunted. "How big are *your* damn squirrels?"

"The two-legged kind," Hitchcock mused, checking the tube magazine to ensure it was loaded. "Seth Borden said he heard some jackers took a shot at a game warden last autumn."

"Anybody takes a shot at us, they better make it a good one," Clay said, his annoyance with the call evident. He slammed his door.

Snow flakes landed on the back of his neck and he shivered, zipped up his parka, pulled his Stetson low and his collar up. He glanced at his watch. Five o'clock. The light was fading fast. "Let's get moving. Jody wants me home for supper on time tonight."

Wordless they trudged up the darkening, spruce tree-bordered road through the blowing snow.

~ 2 ~

The child tensed.

Something was nearby; danger for her Master. Rosalita must guard him for he would sleep until the last rays of twilight faded and shadows covered the earth. Only then would he rise.

Another sound!

Though she did not know worry...she still retained a sense of fear. The Master slept and would not help her. Still, she must fulfill her mandate to preserve his safety.

She shuddered at the prospect of failure and his resultant anger; the insane rage, which brought bludgeoning attacks and the terrible shame she would feel for having betrayed his trust. If only he would release her from her immortal existence. If only he would let her sleep.

Outside, the winter wind increased, a mournful howl of protest weeping through trees.

The sound came again.

Intruders!

She rose from where she huddled in the corner of the cold, dark bedroom, her shift pulled over her bare feet. She did not know why she covered her feet with her dress since she no longer felt cold or heat. Perhaps, covering her feet, was a habit from before.

The child debated lighting the rusted, coal-oil lamp sitting on the floorboards beside her. If it were darker, she knew she would see as well as any animal, but the twilight, a time of transition, made sight difficult.

She stood upright and looked around. Once again, the bedroom, devoid of furniture, but with faded wall paper showing cartoon woodland animals, stirred distant, confusing memories; these memories had originally made her choose it as her lair when she and the Master had come to this refuge.

Deep in her still heart, the child knew that she was not like other beings. Yet sometimes in the night, there were images of long ago, ghosts playing across her mind of a childhood filled with happiness and security, picnics in the sun, dolls and a gaily painted rocking horse in an upper room in a large white adobe house. Best of all, however, a mother and father who held her, loved her and made her feel safe.

Occasionally she would see an image of a buckboard wagon filled with ore bearing down on her pitiful small body as she innocently crossed the deeply rutted road. She heard the frantic shout of the driver, felt herself recoiling in terror from the scream of the horses, and suddenly...she was no more.

Until the Master came.

These images would sweep in and out of her consciousness like pernicious mists only to finally slip away like phantoms leaving behind nothing but the mocking music of a child's laughter or a child's scream. Then her mind would numb again, and the memories, rootless in any form of reality, would fade into oblivion until the next time. When the memories left she felt a longing together with a deep sense of loss, but she knew not what she missed nor why.

She knew only of Adramelech and his needs, needs at rest now as he slumbered in a quasi-sleep deep in the root cellar beside the house. A bloody goat, drained and hanging in the tree outside, served as a warning to those who might stray nearby.

Sometimes, in the still of the night, he would stroke her fevered face and whisper in fetid breath of how he had snatched her back before she reached the Light; how she was now immortal and need not think of death though she might wish for it. Adramelech said he left her with the sense of pain because pain brought obedience and fear; both indigenous to her compliance and self-preservation.

At these times, enraptured by the Master's power and hypnotic stare, she would forget the fear. Wincing at what was to come, she would spread herself for the pain which was perceived rather than experienced physically while deep in some cobwebbed corner of her mind, she wailed in despair at the loss of her mortality.

The night was descending fast. Outside, the wind, rather than calming, was increasing in ferocity. It moaned as if in agony as it sailed through the mountains and swept down into the valleys.

There would be no need for light, she thought as she moved towards the bedroom door to deal with the intruders.

~ 3 ~

Clay and Hitch waded resolutely through the two-foot deep snow. Progress was slow as they slipped and slid their way upward. Most of the time the wind moaned softly through the trees, but periodically, with renewed vigor, it would suddenly gust and send sweeps of snow down on them from above, clouding their vision and making both shiver. After a few minutes, Clay held up his hand.

They paused for a moment and listened in the stillness of the twilight. He thought he'd heard a sound, possibly the wail of a child.

"You hear something?" he asked Hitch.

The deputy shook his head. "Just my stomach growling for Martha's cooking."

"Must be the wind," Clay said, moving forward.

As they drew near the house, he carefully looked for tracks in the snow. It was a virgin crust, unblemished by man or beast. Beside him Hitchcock stopped.

The formidable, multi-turreted, cedar-shingled house loomed above them in the shadows like some charcoal medieval castle. It featured a main section, topped by a cupola, and two building wings which angled forward; each crowned at the end with a windowless tower. Though, at first glance the building looked merely fashionably weathered, closer inspection revealed the decay and rot brought on by years of neglect.

The house, built more than one hundred years before, had been purchased and totally renovated by multi-millionaire Jerome Baker into a stately Vermont home complete with in-ground pool and detached garage. Now, it resembled a haunted house from some movie: hardly a downstairs window pane remained intact; broken shutters dangled from windows; half the porch had fallen in – its roof tilted at a drunken angle; creepers, sprouting a few dead, frozen leaves, curled up over windows and walls; and, the porch railing was missing dozens of spindles like some gape-toothed Halloween pumpkin. Finally, the shingles had grayed, cracked and finally blackened from the harsh weather.

The owner had died half a decade ago and his will had been before the courts for more than four years now as a half dozen relatives vied like vultures for the spoils of the estate.

The house was only one of four the man had owned, and from what Clay had heard, there was close to a total of $25 million at stake in the dispersal of his assets. He knew that people would do some pretty funny things to get their mitts on major portions of that kind of money. The court battle had become a maze of judgments and appeals, suits and counter-suits...each relative hoping to wear the other down for the lion's share of the fortune as the Vermont house slowly went to wrack and ruin.

At first he tried to contact the relatives to let them know that, as they fought, the house was becoming next to worthless, but the one brother whom he'd managed to find and telephone in Boston had sneered that he didn't give a damn about the place and it could drop into its own basement for all he cared. Clay never wasted another taxpayer dollar on long distance calls after that. The property taxes were automatically paid on time and so the authorities had no quarrel with the court-focused heirs.

"Well, looks like there's nobody here," Hitch drawled, casually draping the Winchester in the crook of his left arm as he brushed snow from his face. He looked westward. "Besides, that woman lives more than a mile away on the next ridge. How could she see somebody or spot lights in this weather?" He leaned over, clasped his hands together and tried to breathe life into frigid fingers while balancing the rifle in his arms. He straightened, paused and stared off to the right towards a broken limbed, lifeless tree in the front yard.

Clay followed his gaze to a stark and broken upper branch where a dead goat hung upside down, its rear feet tethered and a massive dark stain running from its neck down over its head obliterating all features except for sightless eyes magnified in a ball of gore. Its throat had been savagely slit and its head hung from its body by a few strands of muscle and skin.

"Charming," Clay said. "It's dripping blood, obviously a fresh kill. Let's check the front door and round back." He trudged towards the front steps.

Hitch shrugged and headed round towards the back of the house.

"It's amazing how fast a place can go downhill," Clay commented, but found he was talking to himself. He avoided a rotted plank on the stairs as he stepped up onto the main porch. He'd been by a few times over the years and had watched its decline as weeds, flaking paint and untreated wood slowly surrendered to the ravages of the weather. His boots sounded hollow on the plank floor of the porch as he clumped up to the front door, stopped and stared.

There were signs of a recent entry.

The screen door had been opened and part of a small drift had been swept back while another drift against the inner door had obviously collapsed inward.

Clay thought: In a wind like this, the drift should have repaired itself in about ten to 20 minutes, so the door must have been opened fairly recently.

He felt an ever-so-slight rise in his adrenaline; a little more caution was warranted. Complacency got more police officers killed in the line of duty than any other single factor. He continued to stare at the broken mounds of snow for a moment longer. If there was anyone inside, his footsteps on the porch would have warned them he was here. That is, if he and his deputy hadn't already been observed approaching the house.

He decided to circle the building and warn Hitch before going inside. Carefully he made his way along the porch extending round the wing to where it ran along the left side of the house. He moved quickly by each window. It's probably kids, he thought, but once again: Complacency...!

To his chagrin, the porch didn't continue all the way around to the back of the house. It ended against a solid wall that jutted out to form one wing of the building. A head-high fence extended from the porch into the woods with no sign of an opening so Clay retraced his steps to the front door.

To avoid the rotting stairs, he jumped to the ground and proceeded to follow Hitch's tracks around the right side. As he rounded the corner of the house, the northwest wind sent a whirling cloud of snow at him.

He could feel the temperature dropping as night approached and he hunched his shoulders, shielded his face from the biting cold, and squinted at the ground. Hitchcock's footprints were already filling with snow. If they didn't get back home soon, they'd find it hard going on the roads.

He cursed the kids under his breath. They needed a lesson after what they'd done to that goat. He trudged on. The footprints near the back of the house had all but vanished, almost filled with snow. Was Hitch inside or checking the woods?

Clay looked into the back yard and surveyed the tangle of an overgrown garden populated by two-foot-high frozen weeds. A half-filled, swimming pool, also frozen and cluttered with dead branches and debris stood empty save for an assortment of Grecian stone statues surrounding it, most with heads and limbs missing. The vandalism confirmed his suspicion that the place was probably a regular haunt for local teenagers.

"Hitch!" Clay called out.

There was no answer.

Clay stopped and narrowed his eyes against stinging bits of snow and ice that swirled about in miniature tornadoes. They had to get back soon or possibly be trapped in this blizzard. It was getting harder to see as the snowstorm increased in intensity. They were also losing their daylight.

He called again: "Hitch!"

No response except for the banshee-like howl of the wind. He cursed silently: Where the hell had the man gone? He lost Hitch's tracks where they mounted the steps to the patio.

If he stayed round back, whoever was inside could high-tail it out the front door and get halfway down to the highway before they were even aware he'd been there. He tried to remember if he'd locked their patrol car. Probably not.

Clay decided that the deputy could take care of himself and waded back through the gathering snowdrifts to the front door once again. On the porch, he pulled the screen door wide open. The old spring creaked and moaned and gamely tried to pull the door closed again. Clay used his boot to pile some snow against the bottom. It held.

Until he knew he was dealing with kids for sure he had to be cautious. Carefully he drew his .45 caliber Glock pistol, jacked the slide and tried the rusted handle of the main door. Fashioned of stout-looking oak beams, it would make a formidable barrier if it was locked.

Instead, it swung easily inward. He peered inside letting his eyes adjust to the gloom. The room wasn't quite pitch black but it was dark enough for a quiet man to remain out of sight in the shadows.

Clay took out his flashlight and manhandled it round the doorjamb keeping it well away from his body while he worked it around the inside of a pentagram-shaped foyer. He probed each corner with the beam.

Empty.

Nothing stirred.

"This is Sheriff Montague. Is there anyone in here?" He used his most authoritative tone. If it were kids, they'd probably speak up rather than risk his wrath when he cornered them. Still no response. He moved quickly into the house with the light held low and to the left.

He was immediately struck by the size of the entrance hall. Five-sided, it had a complement of ionic pillars around it supporting a second story banister-edged walkway which served the upper floor. Clay could see bedroom doors branching off the upper hallway as he played his light almost vertical. The shadows jumped, grew in length and disappeared as the beam cut a swathe through the darkness. If there was any movement up there, it would be hard to pick it up in the dancing shadows.

Moving the beam higher, he realized that the ceiling extended right up to the top of the cupola he had seen from outside. Three stories up, two eight-inch square beams intersected to form crossbars from which dangled a large, rustic iron chandelier via a formidable length of heavy chain.

On the main floor, an assortment of rooms faced the foyer with a hall to the left of a wide curving staircase bordered by a broken railing sweeping majestically to the main floor. Down the long hallway Clay could also make out twilight peeping through a distant back window. This was quite the house in its day, he thought.

Something crashed behind him and he spun about bringing the pistol up as his heart leapt into his mouth.

"Hell's bells," he muttered aloud, realizing that the snow he'd piled against the screen door had dislodged and its spring had slammed it shut.

He swallowed, felt foolish at his jumpiness and eased his finger off the trigger. He was grateful Hitchcock hadn't been around to witness his fright. Grinning ruefully, he wondered again where the deputy had disappeared. Perhaps he was waiting for Clay to chase someone out through the back.

He decided to work his way through the lower level towards the back of the house. Once he connected with Hitch, they'd search upstairs together.

Clay walked carefully into the center of the foyer shivering slightly as his breath steamed into the frosty air in the flashlight's beam. It seemed colder *inside* the house than outside.

He quickly checked the living room, family room and den off the foyer. They were all paneled in mahogany and walnut, expensive as hell but dark and unfriendly. Not a stick of furniture remained in any of them. Satisfied nobody would be coming at his back unless they came from upstairs, he tip-toed slowly down the hallway. He'd hear anyone on those broken stairs.

Other hallways led into the wings off to his left and right but he would have to save them for later. He continued down the main hall reminding himself that, based on the dislodged snow he'd encountered at the front door, someone had been in here fairly recently.

A room opened to his left and he shone his light inside. Bookcase-shelved walls gaped at him with just a few volumes of dust-covered books remaining. At one time it would have been a showcase library, he thought.

Moving further down the hall to the end of the house, he made out a sunroom to his left and a large kitchen off to his right.

The kitchen was bigger than Clay's own living room at home and he noted the long, pine harvest table in the center surrounded by ladder-back chairs. Why hadn't the movers taken the table, he wondered? He stared around the kitchen; something wasn't quite right. It didn't take long to figure it out.

In a far corner, nestled against a set of pine cupboards, stood a shiny new refrigerator. It gleamed white in the light from the window, but more surprising, it was running. Even from ten feet away, Clay could hear the whine of the electric motor despite the fact he was certain there was no power coming into the house.

He looked down the hall behind him. Satisfied that he was alone he entered the kitchen and crossed to the appliance. It was a General Electric and seemed to be the only thing in the house that wasn't covered with a thick layer of dust. He stepped on something, lifted his foot and shone the light down on a plug with an electric cord running under the refrigerator. He reached down and yanked at the cord. The refrigerator couldn't be running if it wasn't plugged in, he reasoned; the motor continued to purr contentedly in the appliance.

He pulled open the fridge door and jumped slightly as the small lamp inside flooded the kitchen with light casting more shadows about the room. Clay stared fixedly at the contents.

Every nook and cranny of the refrigerator was filled with stacks of plastic sacks of some kind. There were dozens of them piled on top of each other, jammed end-to-end in the milk, meat and vegetable compartments. Some were even squeezed into the juice compartments inside the door.

He pulled out one of the bags and squinted at it in disbelief though he already knew what it contained. Made from a heavy plastic with tubes at one end and filled with a thick, dark brownie-red liquid that moved under his fingers and oozed in a thick flood towards the end of the bag opposite to where he squeezed, he saw he was holding a sample of the river of life – whole blood.

He read the paper label sticking on the side of the bag; he'd handled dozens like them before.

CPDA-1 Anticoagulant...

O...

Rh POS...

Human Whole Blood....

Blood! Bags of blood much like he'd held high above wounded soldiers' heads as he'd run alongside stretchers towards medivac choppers evacuating wounded during his army days.

The familiar Red Cross symbol stared bleakly up at him. The entire refrigerator was filled with Red Cross blood donor bags. Full bags! And the refrigerator was running without benefit of electricity? What the hell was going on!?

"Hitch..." he yelled, stuffing the bag back into the refrigerator. His voice seemed muted in the confines of the room, almost as though he had hollered into a vacuum. He was about to close the door when he sensed movement behind him.

Clay turned, expecting to find his deputy there. Instead he found himself staring at a small, barefooted girl. Impassively she stared back at him.

Her face was filthy, her hair a disheveled tangle of thick, oily, snake-like strands. She was about eight or nine years old, frail looking, but somehow also exuding an aura of strength which Clay found hard to fathom. What struck him most were her eyes; they were not the eyes of a child! They were old eyes, haunted eyes, eyes that had seen too much for a child; eyes that were dulled by a hard life and ringed with bluish circles from lack of sleep; eyes that mirrored a potpourri of sadness, anger, hurt and despair. There was also a hint of something else. He struggled to put a name to it. All he could come up with was the word: *madness.*

    He broke off his gaze and took in the rest of her. The child looked emaciated and he felt immediate anger at whoever was responsible for the neglect. He tried to smile so as not to alarm her. She looked back at him, unblinking, resolute, and dour.

    "Hi there," he said, as nonchalantly as possible and extended a hand as he moved forward.

    She retreated a step.

    Clay froze. The hair on the back of his neck stood up. The light from the interior of the refrigerator had fallen fully across the child's face. Her eyes shone like hot coals in the night; a reflective sheen emanating from them like twin phosphorescent beams. She had the eyes of an animal!

    He swallowed and tried not to notice as he spoke again.

    "Who are you, little girl?"

    He looked behind her expecting her parents to appear at any moment; in fact, he found himself hoping they would. For some unfathomable reason he felt distinctively uneasy with this child.

    She failed to answer him for the second time. Was she too traumatized to speak? But what was she doing here? How had she gotten here? Could she be part of a family of squatters? If so, they were going to have to do better for this child or lose her to the authorities.

    Likely that was it. She was part of a family of squatters who'd camped out in the house, he thought. Perhaps they were hiding, afraid to come out. He listened for sounds of stirring.

    Silence.

    She didn't move.

    Though he found it difficult to believe that she was alone, he'd seen plenty of abandoned children before. Still she seemed too young to be able to survive on her own. Besides, she wasn't dressed for the weather, she must be freezing.

    The little girl stared sullenly at him.

He tried again: "Where's your Mommy and Daddy, sweetheart?"

Silence. She watched him with a furtive, almost calculating glare.

Realizing he was still clutching his pistol, and feeling somewhat foolish, he swept back his parka to holster it in a show of good faith. Maybe that's why she was mute.

"I won't hurt you little girl," he said, and moved a foot closer. "I'm a policeman."

She merely stared up at him. He crouched to bring himself to her level and appear less threatening.

He tried to smile again but found it damn difficult when the light from the refrigerator made her eyes light up like car headlights cutting through a foggy night. His skin crawling, he cursed himself for feeling frightened. He was letting himself be spooked by a child.

Suddenly the little girl began backing up. She was out of the kitchen and heading down the hall, before he realized it. Quickly he followed, using his flashlight to light her way and his own.

"Come here, child...I won't hurt you," he said again, his mind alive with questions. It must be ten below zero in the house and the little girl was barefoot and wearing only a rag and yet she didn't appear to notice the cold. He had on long johns, his uniform and a parka and he was shivering.

She was backing up rapidly now, staring at him with the same calculating but listless look. Together they moved down the hall towards the foyer. If she made it outside, she might make a run for it and escape. If so, she'd freeze to death inside an hour. Clay decided he'd better grab her and worry about scaring her later.

They'd almost reached the foyer. Rapidly he moved forward to clutch her arm. She stopped dead. Clay put on the brakes and a thin sheen of frost on the floor made his feet fly out from under him. He fell back and hit the floor with a grunt. Gasping for breath, he sat up quickly and shone the light on the girl to make sure she was still there.

She was....

...but something was different now.

Deep in his bones he felt as though the tide had turned, as though their positions had suddenly been reversed and *he* should be the one looking to escape.

Nonsense, he thought angrily as he realized she was now grinning at him. She must think it's funny that I fell on my ass.

He started to grin back to put her at ease. Just as quickly his smile faded and he sobered. The child's grin wasn't the good humored smile of an innocent. It was a malicious grin saying she hoped he'd hurt himself – hurt himself bad!

She shuddered, then spasmed in seeming ecstasy and her eyes rolled back in her head to become white orbs; a low growl came from her wide open mouth. She opened her mouth and vomited a clear, stinking fluid onto the floor.

Quite suddenly Clay felt afraid.

He looked down at the steaming puddle at her feet as another low, nasal, half-growl escaped from her lips. Leaving steaming wet footprints on the tiled floor, she moved towards him.

He tried to scramble to his feet but he didn't make it in time.

The waif reached up and grabbed him by his biceps and squeezed until the pain drove tears from the corners of his eyes and made him cry out. Her grip was like an iron vise, tightening, squeezing his arms until he thought his bones would snap. Paralyzed with pain, he suddenly felt himself being turned sideways. He struggled to escape but now her grip had changed as one hand lifted him from under his arm and the other grabbed him by the flesh of his hip. He was being hoisted horizontally and bodily off the floor, balance maintained by hands that grown in size, hands that had become vicious pinchers scissoring into his flesh.

It was impossible!

No child could have this much strength...!

The pain washed over him in red waves and the sound of his heart pounded like thunder in his ears. Her holds shifted and suddenly one hand was now clutching his neck while the other grabbed his thigh in an iron grip. She seemed to have grown larger.

But his right arm was free!

He stared wildly down at the child, suddenly becoming aware of a putrescent odor, an unforgettable stench he'd only encountered once before....

...PANAMA!

He'd smelled it the night he'd seen something hunched over the dying soldier in the field. Suddenly he knew he was in more danger than he'd ever been at any time in his life. Jesus help me, he thought, and used his free hand to claw desperately for his holstered weapon.

~ 4 ~

Hitch slogged his way through the snow around the side of the house. He looked at the gathering twilight and shook his head. He wanted to get home just as much as Clay, maybe more so since he was pretty sure this was all a wild-goose chase.

Reaching the back garden he paused and surveyed the swimming pool. It had been left half-filled and froze, he surmised. Yard litter and dead branches poked up through the snow.

Decapitated stone statues of ancient Greek gods, victims of wanton vandalism, stood as grim guards at the four corners of the pool flanked by a broken Italian marble balustrade ringing the entire back yard. Hitch was well versed in Italian marbles having explored them at an import company when building a new kitchen a few years back. The fence alone must have cost a fortune he realized moving up some stone steps towards the patio.

Four marble benches, also hammered by vandals until they snapped in two, littered the raised, marble-floored patio. The entire surface, swept clean of snow, revealed cracked and chipped tiles sporting a thin sheen of ice, a serious invitation to break a leg or hip.

This must have been some place in its heyday, Hitch thought. Of course, he could never have hoped for an invitation to the place; deputy sheriffs earning $35,000 a year weren't exactly in the right financial bracket to hobnob with the Bakers.

He snorted and stepped gingerly onto the first level of the patio. He crossed to another set of steps, mounted them and peered through a window in one of the dirty, weather-proof, multi-paned doors. Strangely the panes remained unbroken, a rather fickle display of respect for property. The deputy cupped his hands to shut out the reflection of the silver clouds in the twilight sky and peered inside.

He could barely make out a table, chairs and a blob of white in the far corner of the room. It must be the kitchen, he decided, unable to see much detail through the grime. Hitch slung the Winchester over his shoulder and stepped back off the patio. He carefully checked the snow for footprints at the perimeter of the property. Other than his own, now rapidly filling with snow, there were none. Well, somebody butchered that goat, he thought. Looking back at the house, he noticed a set of wooden doors set at a forty-five degree angle into a frame on a raised pile of earth near the right corner of the building. He plowed his way towards it.

It must be the entrance to an old root cellar, he thought, spotting the heavy timbered doors and the rusted iron hinges. Probably hasn't been opened in years. Still, if it connected to the house underground, it could be a way in – and therefore a way *out*. If there were vandals hiding about and they tried to escape from Clay through here, they'd be in for a surprise.

Leaning the Winchester carefully against a pile of snow, Hitch leaned down and tugged at one of the iron handles. The door moved slightly but the rusted hinges creaked in protest.

He set one foot flat on the left door to brace himself and put all his weight into pulling the right door upward and open. If he put his back out again doing something deliberately stupid, Martha wouldn't be exactly overflowing with compassion. He'd have to return to work to get sympathy.

Rust bits flaked off the hinges as they shrieked with the intensity of someone drawing a dozen nails over a chalk board; Hitch felt his teeth being set on edge.

"C'mon you son-of-a-gun," he grunted. "Open or I'll come back here with some WD-40 and really put you in your place."

Veins swelled on his forehead. Gritting his teeth, Hitch slowly gained ground as, inch-by-inch, the rusted hinges gave way. The door finally yawned open. It stood fully upright, balanced precariously on its edge and held fast by the rusted hinges. Winded, he gasped for air, straightened and rubbed his aching back.

The door was made of four-inch thick oak boards, formidable and heavy as sin. Probably meant to discourage thievery by animals or humans. He deciding not to pull the door past the point in the arc where it would crash wide open; he'd just be setting himself up for the challenge of closing it. He looked admiringly at his handiwork.

"There my man," he said, happily. "Now I can close you with one finger."

He peered into the black opening. Rickety stairs led down to what appeared to be an earthen floor gloomily soaking up the glow of the vanishing light.

Hitch tested the steps with one foot. Assured they'd take his weight, he grabbed the carbine and made his way down until he stood safely on the dirt floor. It was packed hard and he could make out frozen puddles of water off to his left and right. The air was stale, smelling mostly of mold and dampness, but also containing another underlying smell of something foul. An animal must have crawled down here and died, he mused, looking around in the dim light.

At least, being out of the wind made him feel warmer–!

Suddenly the light vanished plunging him into total blackness as a deafening crash made him leap in fright. The heavy door above slammed shut sending clouds of dust whirling into the air to rapidly fill his nostrils and mouth. Caught unaware, Hitch rendered two explosive sneezes and then coughed into his hand.

Something tugged at his pant leg!

"Cripes!" he yelled, stumbling back. His foot caught in the cellar steps and down he went in an awkward heap, the Winchester spinning from his grasp. Unable to see the ground coming up, he grunted in surprise when he hit.

"Damn...damn...damn," he cursed, half in anger, half in frustration. Hitch sat there taking stock of himself, making sure there were no broken bones. Finally, satisfied he hadn't done any great damage, he put a hand down on the dirt floor to help himself up.

Something small and furry scampered across it.

"Whoa!" he yelped, pulling his hand back. He laughed out loud. Rats! This whole adventure was turning out to be a black comedy and he had landed the starring role. He chuckled again, took a deep breath, got to his feet and bent down to begin feeling about for the carbine. The darkness was absolute; black as pitch and not a glimmer of light from anywhere. At that moment he thought he heard someone call his name, but it was a far-off sound, distant and muffled to the point where he wasn't sure if he actually heard or imagined it.

In case it was Clay, Hitch decided to answer: "Clay! I'm down here...I'm in the root cellar."

He waited for a response.

Nothing. Only the deadened call of the wind whispered from above. Either he couldn't be heard or he was replying to some wishful thinking. He shrugged and went back to looking for the Winchester.

So this is how it feels to be blind, he thought getting down on his hands and knees. He travelled his hands over the floor in ever-increasing circles. The weapon couldn't have gotten that far away. He hoped there were no rats in his path; he wasn't crazy about getting his fingers nipped.

Suddenly he became aware of a foul odor growing in intensity. It was all-encompassing and invaded his lungs. He wretched at its rankness and gasped aloud, "What the hell is THAT?"

He gave voice to his alarm because something made him want to hear the sound of his own voice, to bring a semblance of normalcy to a situation rapidly declining into dark surrealism. He knew that speaking out was akin to the false bravado of whistling in a graveyard to stave off imaginary spirits. Still, he didn't care.

Trying to ignore the smell by breathing mainly through his mouth, Hitch decided to explore slightly to his right. If I don't find the rifle, perhaps I can find the stairs and get the hell out of here, he thought. Turning slightly, his fingers encountered something solid on the ground.

At last – the carbine.

He breathed a sigh of relief even as a momentary suspicion flitted across his consciousness; he was sure he'd checked the area moments before.

Still, as his fingers probed, trying to find the familiarity of the stock or barrel, he realized with dreadful certainty that what he was touching wasn't the carbine.

It was flat, cold and mucky!

His fingers instinctively recoiled and he stared desperately towards the floor. He was on his knees but couldn't make out any contrast whatsoever in the perfect darkness.

He was virtually blind down here.

Slowly he drew back, repulsed by the presence of some invader who had entered his psychic space – that few feet or so out from the body that most people mentally claim as their own.

Hitch swallowed and berated himself.

He was acting like a child.

What the hell was it?

Since he couldn't see, there was only one way to find out. Tentatively he put out his hand again and touched the cool object. It was about five inches wide, and angled slightly upwards. It felt fleshy and Hitch imagined a giant, fat slug, its pink body undulating towards him as he steeled himself against pulling his hand back.

Through sheer force of will, he kept exploring and felt a skeletal-like structure supporting a clammy, slimy covering.

A dead and decaying animal, he ventured in disgust, drawing back. That would account for the smell.

Hitch tensed, ready to retreat at the slightest movement. He could imagine the sudden angry growl, the snapping of razor-sharp teeth slicing into his hand and the needles of pain. He didn't relish trying to snatch his hand from the mouth of some wild creature.

But the thing was as still as death.

Moving his fingers upwards, Hitch came to a sudden and horrific realization: he was touching a foot! A human foot!

He reached up with his other hand and felt the hem of a coarsely-woven, grit-encrusted cloth garment hanging from above. Someone was standing silently over him, a great brooding shadow, blacker than the night and less than a foot away.

Hitch was a brave man, a man who routinely faced the possibility of mortal danger in his job, and a man who did not flinch from even the meanest of aggressors. But right now, his primal consciousness, the area whereas that spark, that predominant instinct for survival resides, was flooded by an unreasonable and extreme sense of terror. The amygdale portion of his brain, much quicker than his cognitive awareness, was in high gear driving an animal-instinctual reaction geared to self preservation.

In fact, as his consciousness caught up to his quick & dirty gut reaction, he literally tasted peril! Not that he hadn't before but there was something ominously different in this danger; something alien, dark and threatening. Something insurmountable.

He began to tremble. Goose bumps rose over his entire body. He tried to speak but his throat had constricted as an inner sense warned him that he'd made a fatal mistake in coming into the cellar, one that would cost him dearly.

He closed his eyes and wished to be on the way home to the warmth of an open fire and his cozy log bungalow; to be snuggling up to Martha as she stirred a pot of stew; or to be fly-fishing in a clear mountain stream with the comfort of the summer sunlight on his face. In short, he wanted to continue living.

But, with a certainty reserved for the terminally-ill, or for those miserable prison-bound souls walking the last mile, he knew he was going to die.

Hitch opened his eyes wide, still expecting the blackness to be complete.

Instead he saw a greenish glow suffusing the earthen cellar. Afraid to look up, he felt a momentary shame as tears squeezed from his eyes. He began to tremble violently.

As a final act of free will, he summoned the last ounce of courage in his body and raised his head.

Moments before he died, Bob Hitchcock knew that there must be a God. After all, if you believed in God, you believed in the devil. And conversely, if the devil existed, then God must also exist.

Right now Hitch believed in the devil.

It wasn't hard when a refugee from hell was standing directly over him! Two huge clawed hands cupped his head and squeezed his skull until something popped and shattered; intense, paralytic pain seared his face and neck, radiating into the rest of his body.

Desperately he tried to pull away, to escape, to claim a few more seconds of precious life. But it was not to be as the thousands of nerves in his brain stem were slowly crushed into a pulpy mass.

His dying scream was swallowed up by the dark earth....

And then, he was no more.

~ 5 ~

The child seized Clay by his inner thigh and neck and hoisted him bodily over her head. Without hesitation, she bounded towards the front door, her small hand impossibly encircling most of his neck, thumb and forefinger placing pressure directly on his carotid arteries.

For a split second Clay's mind refused to accept what was happening. This was a *child* for God's sake!

BUT SHE HAD THE STRENGTH OF A GOLIATH...!

"Wait!" Clay tried to yell but his voice was strangled, his throat squeezed closed by the tremendous, vice-like grip tightening about his neck.

He tried again to reach his pistol.

His hand flailed the air....

Clay would later play and replay the events over and over in his thoughts as though the entire event took hours. In fact, it took seconds.

His disbelief rapidly gave way to panic. Her grip had tightened on his throat choking off the blood and life-giving oxygen flowing to his brain. In moments he would be rendered unconscious and totally at her mercy.

Aloft, his body swayed and jerked as they crossed the foyer. He fought desperately to keep from passing out. He couldn't breathe. The flap of his parka was somehow tangled in his holster preventing him from reaching his sidearm. Using his right fist, he pounded frantically at the small wrist and hand gripping his throat. It was like assaulting a cast-iron pipe.

Clay gasped for air, his mind whirling, searching desperately and seeking any means of escape.

HE HAD TO GET AIR...!

Pinwheels of light exploded before his face; a film of red bleared his sight.

His vision was fading from red to black....

HE WAS DYING....

By now, all rational analysis of what was happening had ceased, replaced by a gut-level battle for survival. He was no longer a sane, calm individual, a police officer in full control of the situation; rather he was a gagging, convulsing victim, helplessly caught up in a net of terror and the dreadful conviction that he was being murdered.

They were still a few feet from the front door, when she hurled his body through the air. He exploded through the doorway, double impacts sending shock waves of pain through his body as his legs caught one side of the doorjamb and his skull bounced off the other. His legs folded driving his knees into the pit of his stomach, and his head snapped forward as his body tore the screen door from its hinges, and he hit the porch in a mad roll, tumbling down the stairs.

Blood spewed in a bright red plume from his mouth and nose as he continued rolling insanely shoulder-over-shoulder on the densely packed snow. The mad ride finally ceased and he wound up spread-eagled on his back, gasping fitfully for air, and a good forty feet from the steps.

Dazed and in pain, he gazed blankly up into the sky.

Snowflakes whirled softly down from the heavens, gently settling on his face and eyelashes as the chill of the snow on the back of his neck slowly began to penetrate and awaken his senses. Deep in the recesses of his mind, he suspected that this couldn't be happening, that he was home asleep in his bed in the throes of a terrible nightmare from which he would soon awaken. Jody would be by the bedside, a freshly brewed cup of coffee in hand and a smile on her lips as she gently welcomed him back to the real world.

He indulged in the fantasy for a moment, at peace with his situation. Then, very slowly, hot, mind-numbing pain began to seep into almost every part of his body.

The sound of splintering wood sliced through his reverie like a straight razor drawn carelessly across an unsuspecting cheek; fear welled into his throat.

SHE WAS COMING TO FINISH HIM OFF....

Clay quickly rolled onto his stomach, drew his knees into the snow and painfully levered himself upright.

His left arm was a massive ache; he couldn't move it. His head throbbed and when he moved his jaw, the jagged edge of a shattered molar cut the inside of his cheek. He tried to raise his left arm. Pain brought waves of nausea rolling over him. He started to vomit but nothing came up. Glancing down he saw his left arm hanging uselessly by his side, the hand facing outward at an unnatural angle.

A board cracked again and he looked up towards the house.

The child stood on the front porch in the waning light, a sadistic grin on her face, eyes glowing with a ferocity and maliciousness that both angered and terrified him.

His right hand whipped down and swept the parka aside as he snatched the Glock from its holster with a speed that would have rivaled some of the best gunfighters in the old west. Panting hard, he spit the blood and pieces of teeth from his mouth as he faced her. He jammed the pistol hard against his hip to try to yank the slide back and remembered there was a shell already in the chamber from earlier.

"I don't know WHO the hell you are or WHAT the hell you are, but if you don't stay WHERE the hell you are...I'll blow your little ass to Kingdom Come!" he screamed through battered and swollen lips.

She smiled, a horrible patronizing type of grin, and stepped forward onto the broken screen door lying on the porch. As she moved forward to the top of the steps, she sealed her fate.

Grimacing in pain at the movement, Clay extended the pistol, aimed and rapidly squeezed off three shots. The weapon bucked violently in his hand. The explosions from the .45 sounded like cannons in his ears, the sound both magnified and multiplied as the sharp cracks of the weapon echoed off the trees, building and mountains, and bounced further down into the valley.

The bullets seemed to hit the girl almost simultaneously, the first punching through her chest, the second ripping a hole in her throat, and the third tearing a sizable chunk out of her shoulder. She reeled backwards through the doorway.

Her small body crashed somewhere inside and, for a moment, Clay felt an unholy satisfaction; it was quickly followed by a gut-wrenching sickness. He had shot a child!

He had killed a little girl!

MOTHER OF GOD...WHAT HAVE I DONE?

His head began to spin, his legs gave way and he sank to his knees in the snow. He waited until the mental merry-go-round stopped, then got unsteadily to his feet. Fear drove him into action.

Maybe it wasn't too late. Maybe he could still save her, get her to a hospital in time. Maybe the killing shot hadn't really hit her dead center. He bent over in the snow and threw up.

Praying that he'd actually missed his aim, he began to limp towards the steps to save her.

HE CLUTCHED THE PISTOL WITH A DEATH GRIP....

He stumbled up the wooden stairs, booted the remnants of the splintered screen door to the side and made his way across the porch mouthing a silent prayer he'd find her alive.

HE LOOKED DOWN AT THE PISTOL TO SEE THE SLIDE CLOSED, ANOTHER BULLET WAITING PATIENTLY IN THE FIRING CHAMBER....

Cautiously, Clay moved forward. No blood, a good sign. Still, he prepared himself for the sight of the tiny, wasted body lying on its back in the foyer, her chest a mass of blood, her eyes staring unseeingly at the ceiling. Or would he find her in a twisted, convulsing heap, throat torn open and leaking crimson, head askew and nerves still making her tiny body crawl and twist and jerk as she moaned in agony? Sickened, he shuddered and entered the house.

As his eyes adjusted to the inner darkness of the foyer, he mentally prepared himself for the end of his career. There could be no justification for shooting an unarmed child. Plain and simple, he was wrong. No matter how spooked he was, no matter how frightened, nothing could make it right; no-one could grant him absolution on this one. He'd be lucky if he didn't spend his remaining years doing hard time in prison.

He stared in the doorway.

She was gone!

There was no body!

He'd missed...all three shots!

A wave of joy and gratitude welled up inside him. *Thank you Lord.*

HE SPUN ABOUT...PISTOL AT THE READY...!

Satisfied there was nothing there, he breathed a sigh of relief. His thankfulness was abruptly replaced with a measure of disbelief that he'd missed all three shots. He'd seen them hit her.

OR WAS IT WISHFUL THINKING...?

A new thought sobered him.

Maybe she was wounded. Maybe she had dragged herself away to one of the other rooms where she now lay dying from shock as she bled out.

Clay spotted his flashlight in the foyer over near the wall. Its halogen beam cut a neat swathe through the dark lighting dirt and old pieces of wood on the floor. He'd need the light to check inside for a blood trail. All he had to do was cross the foyer and pick it up.

He tried to step forward.

His legs refused to budge.

It was as though his body was acknowledging what his mind refused to accept; namely that walking through that doorway could, in all probability, be a death sentence.

Face it! Somewhere in that house was an insane SOMETHING that took three direct hits from one of the most powerful handguns in the world and walked away. Whatever it was, it couldn't be from this world.

This is silly, Clay told himself sternly. There is nothing supernatural here. After all, he'd read of dozens of stories about people who had displayed abnormal strength when an emergency or a life-threatening situation occurred; a man lifted a car weighting more than two thousand pounds off his son; a girl held back a streetcar with her bare hands because her sister had fallen in front of it; and the countless hypnotic acts, scientifically verified, which showed people, placed in the right frame of mind, performing incredible physical stunts

"What kind of a cop am I?" he muttered aloud. "There's a mortally wounded child inside and I'm standing out here spooked out of my mind."

He swallowed, vowed to enter the house and immediately felt an unreasonable amount of trepidation returning.

Who was he trying to fool? This wasn't an ordinary child. It was a horror straight out of a Marvel comic book. Its eyes glowed in the dark, it had the strength of ten men and it was hoarding a refrigerator full of blood.

NOT EXACTLY YOUR GARDEN-VARIETY THIRD-GRADER.

Clay took a deep breath and leaned back against one of the porch railing supports. His adrenaline level was falling, his heartbeat returning to a semblance of normality. As it did, the pain of his broken arm became more intense. He groaned and winced with every breath he took. Even a slight movement caused waves of agony to radiate through the arm. Before he did anything else, it had to be restrained in some fashion.

Maintaining a careful eye on the front door, Clay carefully shrugged out of his parka and dropped it by his feet.

There was a small tear in the left sleeve of his uniform and he hooked the barrel of the .45 in the hole and pulled downward to rip it open.

The sleeve parted and he almost fainted from the pain the movement generated. Swallowing bile, he examined the arm awkwardly.

The fracture was about six inches below the elbow, almost midway to the wrist. Massive swelling had enlarged it to almost twice its size and it was already turning purple mixed with angry striations of red.

At least it wasn't a compound fracture, he thought. The bone hadn't broken the surface of the skin. Thank God for small favors.

Holding his weapon under his good arm, he loosened the belt of his pants, gritted his teeth and slipped the broken arm between the belt and his hip. He fastened it as tight as he dared, thereby pinning the arm by his side and minimizing its movement.

Feeling more in control Clay got a fresh grip on his gun. He knew he'd fired three rounds and that meant he had seven more. The clip would be impossible to top up with cartridges from his gun belt with one hand. Even getting the spare clip out of his pouch would cost him great pain. He decided against it.

Before he went inside, he had to get his psyche under control. A clear-thinking pragmatist by nature, Clay was usually a good man in a crisis. He told himself that now was not the time to join the lunatic fringe and assume he was hunting a ghost.

Sure, there were extraordinary circumstances...but certainly nothing that couldn't be explained logically. Frightened by the appearance of a strange man in the house, and fearing God knows what sort of abuse, the child had gone berserk and attacked him.

Case closed.

It was his own, unreasonable over-reaction that now sickened him. Throughout his military experiences, his time with the highway patrol, and as sheriff in Woodstrom County, he'd never been that spooked, never felt fear that intense, nor lost control as he had when he'd drawn his weapon and fired at the little girl.

Whatever. He had to do the right thing and it was time to do it.

Clay stifled a desire to yell for his deputy. If Hitch hadn't appeared with the sound of gunfire, he was probably in trouble himself. Maybe she was with her family right now. He had to find the little girl, assess her condition and get help. He also had to find his deputy.

Steeling his nerves, he brought the weapon level and forced himself to step through the doorway. Crouching in an awkward semblance of a combat stance, he painfully spun to the left and right with the pistol swinging to cover his field of vision. He reminded himself he had to be ready to render first aid if needed.

HIS FINGER TENSED ON THE TRIGGER...!

The foyer proved to be empty.

In his mind, a small voice nagged him, pointing out the seeming cross purpose of his mission of mercy; here he was looking to help the child and yet, if she appeared, he was primed to start shooting again.

He pushed the thought aside. One couldn't be too careful.

ESPECIALLY IF THE LITTLE BITCH WAS STILL BREATHING...!

He carefully scanned the darkened foyer as thoroughly as he could.

Nothing moved.

Slowly, gingerly, he knelt and picked up the flashlight. Unable to hold the .45 and the flashlight in the same hand, he carefully worked it under his left armpit. The pinned arm throbbed fiercely but held the light securely in place.

He checked the floor and walls of the foyer. There was no more blood anywhere; in fact, no sign of the girl at all. He checked all rooms downstairs, noting again that a long hallway led off the dining room towards the east wing and another into the west wing.

If she was hit even once, she would have bled like a stuck pig, he thought. Not to mention shock. She'd never make it down the hall nor up the stairs. So why no blood? Where was the girl?

Clay entered the kitchen and tried to open the French door leading to the backyard. The stubborn lock refused to release.

Finally he stepped back, aimed, fired and blew the lock and part of the door away. Three small window panes cracked from the shock. The door swung open flooding the room with a frigid blast of air. A huge yellow moon was just peaking over the low, shadowy mountains. It threw a pale beige light across the stone patio, its luminescence glinting off the ice-covered swimming pool.

The echo of the shot died away. Clay listened for sounds from the rest of the house.

Nothing but silence! *Where was Hitch?*

The wind blew a thin veil of snow inside the kitchen and he could hear the trees rustling and smell the crisp, clean air tainted slightly by the pungent odor of the pines. It was bizarre; everything smelled so natural and yet the reality of the situation was totally unnatural. If he could just find Hitch, maybe life would return to normal. New waves of pain invaded his back, his side, his head, arm and knees.

He looked to his Glock.

IF HE MET SOMETHING HE DIDN'T LIKE, HE'D GREET IT APPROPRIATELY.

Pushing the pain aside he stepped out onto the patio, slipped and barely caught himself before he fell. Nevertheless, he jarred his arm and more intense stabs of pain pulsed up through his shoulder and across his back. Sweat broke out on his forehead. He was nauseated. He was shivering in the cold night air. His stomach was rolling and churning from the pain. Groaning aloud he called on his years of military and police training to force himself to concentrate on the task at hand.

Moving across the patio, he noted the headless statues near the pool. In the twilight they were becoming grim, indistinct shadows, some with half-broken limbs extended towards him as if in supplication.

He yelled: "Hitch!"

"HITCH.......Hitch...hitch...."

His voice resonated through the mountains with the echo seeming to mock him.

He tried again: "Hitch...if you're hurt...if you can't shout...fire a shot!"

"...FIRE A SHOT...Fire a shot...fire a shot...!"

The echo finally faded. Silence returned.

After listening for a moment, Clay cursed and went carefully down the stone steps into the backyard. He was becoming more afraid for his friend with each passing second. If Hitch had encountered that crazy – he hesitated to use the word "child" – and she chose to go berserk again, she could just as easily have torn his head off.

He debated going for help.

But his deputy might be lying wounded someplace, needing immediate attention. Getting through on the radio was highly unlikely, so going for help might mean an hour or more before he got back.

He ruled that option out. He refused to abandon his friend.

In the yard, he found himself knee-deep in virgin snow. He could barely make out a single set of footprints, their depth already half filled by the thick flakes that were making it more and more difficult to see.

He stared at the prints leading to the angled wooden doors atop a frame set on a pile of earth. Root cellar? One door was covered with deep snow; the other was quickly assuming a new mantle of white. Obviously it had been disturbed. Maybe Hitch was trapped down there. Any sounds he tried to make would surely be muffled by the earth and doors.

"That's where you are, my friend," he said aloud, relief flooding through him despite his pain.

He spit blood and tried to avoid jostling his throbbing arm as he slogged through the snow over to the cellar entrance.

There was a pile of snow adjacent to the bare door. Hitch had probably dislodged this snow as he pulled up the doors.

Clay reluctantly holstered his pistol, then reached down, grabbed the handle and pulled with all his might. The door came up a few inches and then a tremendous weight dragged it back down with a thud. With his bad arm on fire, he sank back panting from the exertion. He tried again, at the same time calling the deputy's name.

There was no response from below and once more he was only able to raise the door a few inches before it slammed back down. And again he was rewarded by needles of agony shooting up the arm, into his neck and face, and radiating across his shoulders and back.

Each time he tried to open the door, it was almost as though someone was dragging it closed trying to prevent him from accessing the cellar. Maybe Hitch was being held prisoner down there.

Clay toyed with the idea of banging on the heavy wooden covering but quickly discarded it. He could illicit a fusillade of shots from the captors. And, if he returned fire, Hitch could be hit.

A momentary vision of the child waiting patiently in the dark below flashed through his mind and he felt a tangible manifestation of fear in his gut. He was also trembling from the pain now and feeling third spaced. Could he be going into shock? After a few deep breaths, he shrugged aside any concerns for himself. If Hitch was down there, Clay was going to get him out!

Using the fuel of his pent-up anger, his desperate need to find his friend, and the fear associated with encountering something which defied logic and reason, Clay desperately grabbed the handle with his good arm. Bracing his feet against the door frame of the root cellar entrance, he summoned every ounce of strength he could muster. He leveraged the pain-induced adrenaline and dragged the door upward with an amplified brute force.

He yelled in triumph as the door came up. Unexpectedly it carried through its arc flopping wide open. The momentum threw Clay backwards into the snow.

He hit the ground with a jolt and screamed in anguish. Tears flooded his eyes and he choked back a sob, then regained control and staggered to his feet. He glanced down at his arm where blood ran freely from an open wound evident through his torn uniform shirt. A shard of grey bone now poked through an ugly purple bruise in the skin.

"Jesus...Jesus..." he cursed, more tears flooding his eyes. He'd compounded the fracture. Rings of pain throbbed mercilessly with each beat of his heart which was now doing a credible imitation of a tom-tom.

Slowly he raised his gaze and dismay flooded every atom of his body; the shock hit him with a series of mental impacts like repeated hammer strikes on his brain.

His own voice sounded from afar: "Oh dear God...no...NO!"

Hitch was there alright. Or, at least, what was left of the man hung in full view. His body lay nailed upside down to the inside of the door, mostly naked and shredded except for a few shards of uniform. Thick, rusted railroad-type spikes had been used to pinion him; one had been hammered through his throat, more through the center of his rib cage, and more through his outstretched arms and feet.

The deputy had been crucified upside down.

But the horror didn't end there.

His head – huge, bloodied eyeballs rolled back, mouth open in a soundless scream – was almost unrecognizable. Clay was looking at a mass of oozing meat, muscle and ligaments strung with glistening yellow fat through which peeked a dull, cream-yellow skull. His head, from the neck up, had been skinned; hardly a square inch of derma remained undamaged.

All the exacerbated might of Clay's hate and anger echoed over the mountains and into the valleys as he screamed again and again. His rage was quickly followed by repeated explosions as he vainly emptied his pistol blindly into the cellar. In the darkness below nothing moved despite the explosions and rounds burrowing into the dirt floor.

The pistol reports and a waning day caused a snow owl to lumber into flight from a tall pine tree nearby and pull itself to a comfortable altitude. It swung over the valley in a wide, sweeping circle. Suddenly its wings paused their motion in flight and it glided in an ever tightening spiral. Far below, a figure stumbled blindly through the woods and down the snow-covered road. Deciding the creature was too large to lift with its razor-sharp talons, the owl peeled off and lazily resumed its nocturnal patrol.

The sound of an automobile engine roaring into life sent it deeper into the mountains in search of other prey.

~ 6 ~

"For God's sake, Sheriff, your damn timeline just doesn't add up," Captain Rodney Stamper of the Vermont State Police, Criminal Investigations Unit, said irritably. He banged his fist down on the interrogation room table in the Waterbury Complex headquarters. An FBI agent, sitting in on the questioning, jumped nervously.

"We've been over this time and again, Captain," Clay replied, feeling his blood boil. "I've told you what happened. Hitch was one of my best friends and I want to catch this bastard more than anyone."

"Then help us."

"How?"

"By telling us everything; there's something missing here."

"I'm telling you what I know!"

"Fine," the Captain fumed. "Then explain how anyone can kill a full-grown, armed 200 pound-man without shooting or knifing him, strip off his clothes, remove the epidermis of his skull with medical precision, and then haul his body up those stairs, nail it to the door and close it again in about ten to fifteen minutes? Not to mention escaping and not leaving any footprints in the snow."

"Perhaps there was more than one," Clay answered.

"There was no evidence of *anyone* being on the estate except for you and Deputy Hitchcock. Not a cigarette butt, not a gum wrapper, not a used match, food container…not even a footprint – nothing!"

"And where the hell is his blood?" FBI Agent Stan Pritchard asked, joining in. "The autopsy showed that the victim was virtually exsanguinated. His vessels had collapsed – nothing left."

The Captain, appointed lead investigator of a special investigative task force set up by the Governor of Vermont, sighed and calmed down slightly: "Let's start again. You went into the foyer, heard some noises and fired three shots."

"That's right," Clay replied.

"And your deputy was nowhere in sight."

"He was outside round back."

"But he could have come through from the back. You said he circled round carrying a Winchester. You're an ex-Army Ranger and a former Florida Highway Patrolman with several commendations; you have a reputation for keeping cool under fire. Why did you discharge your weapon?"

"I already told you. I saw a shadow and it appeared to be carrying a rifle. Last year poachers had taken a shot at a game warden round there. I fired warning shots. I was letting her know I meant business."

"Her?" Stamper asked, looking at him oddly.

"Her…him…whoever," Clay responded.

"You saw a woman?"

"I saw a shadow; it moved like a woman."

"So, you fired *three warning shots* into the outside door frame and the foyer wall!" Pritchard said, in disbelief. "And you have no idea how the front screen door was destroyed."

Clay said nothing. After a few moments Stamper got up and stamped out of the room slamming the office door behind him. Sensing he was gone for good, Pritchard quickly followed.

Abandoned, Clay finally left the complex and drove back home. He felt miserable, angry and guilty as sin. Still, he couldn't tell them *everything*. First, they'd never believe it. Second, they'd wonder what he was trying to cover up.

For Clay, the subsequent investigation into his deputy's death had become his second nightmare. Since it was likely that the perpetrators had crossed state lines, the County and the Vermont State Police had invited the Federal Bureau of Investigation into the case. At first it appeared Hitch's murder was committed by a psychopath who had been hiding in the root cellar of the estate. Next they advanced the theory of a ritualistic killing by some kind of satanic cult. Finally, because of conflicting timelines, lack of supporting evidence pointing to a third person or persons, and an obvious hesitancy on the part of Sherriff Clay Montague to come clean, they began to take a serious look at the Sheriff himself.

A number of factors brought suspicion and confusion. First, his broken arm, contusions and cuts on his head and legs were not all consistent with a fall on the ice – a negative. Next, however, forensic analysis of the three spent slugs from his pistol, recovered from the door jam and wall inside the foyer, confirmed an absence of blood, tissue or hair and fit in with his story of warning shots – a positive.

Finally, his explanation of what he was doing for the time it took the killer or killers to strike seemed vague and remote – another negative. As for the bags of blood allegedly stored in the refrigerator, when police returned to the scene, the appliance stood silent and empty. They knew he was hiding something.

On Clay's part, there was no way he was about to tell them about a 70-pound kid with eyes like a wolf who picked him up and literally kicked his ass; he'd soon be a resident of a state institution where the sleeves of jackets extended well beyond his 33-inch arm measurement.

They were right, of course. There was much more to it. When police and emergency services had screamed back to the Baker place in a melee of sirens and flashing light bars, they found only the body. And, when they began to question Clay in the hospital, even though he was partially sedated from the setting of his arm, he had enough of his wits about him to omit certain details. After all, who would believe that a refrigerator ran without electricity or a little girl with superhuman strength could absorb three .45 slugs and walk away?

Because the victim was one of their own, they pulled out all stops to find Hitch's killer. And, after due course, they stopped pussy-footing around and hinted that more and more it looked like the Sheriff was either guilty or complicit. He had the means and the opportunity; they just couldn't come up with a motive.

Hitch's body was buried two days before Christmas. By then, all the testing, probing and dissection had taken place, the parts were hastily sewn back together and he was delivered to his wife Martha, relatives and friends for a Christian burial – closed casket of course.

The funeral and the week leading up to it was pathetically cruel. Never in his entire life had Clay experienced anything so horrific. He felt totally impotent, powerless to ease Martha's suffering or shield her from the sordid details of the crime. He and Jody had watched her devastation as she fought with the awful knowledge that a man whom she had worshipped, a man whom she had loved so much, had been cruelly and horribly butchered in the most obscene fashion and then continued to suffer indignity after indignity on the pathology table as though he was a side of beef.

Clay and Jody virtually carried Martha through the funeral ceremony, her endless broken sobs promising to never cease.

Many of the town's population of 3,200 people and a huge representation of citizens from Winder County turned out to say good-bye to a well-loved and respected member of the community. This was a man who had been born there, who had gone to school with many of the original citizens, and who had chosen service to his community rather than head for the city, as had so many of his peers.

Townsfolk, tourists and Christmas shoppers silently lined the funeral route formed by Georgian, Federal Style and Greek revival homes and buildings, their heads bowed. The somber parade of automobiles, led by the silent black hearse made its way through the town, down Main Street and over the bridge towards the small cemetery on the hill just outside town. Unfortunately, administrative oversight had resulted in the failure to turn off the town's PA system which continued to croon out Christmas Carols for the shoppers as the funeral procession passed.

In addition to the hearse, three limos and more than 100 private automobiles, there were police cars carrying officers from as far away as Texas and even two Royal Canadian Mounted Police officers in full-dress red tunics; the officers were all silent and brooding as they gathered to pay farewell to a fallen comrade.

As though on cue, dark grey, rain-laden clouds tumbled through the sky on a wild, warm wind, and a single, unseasonable roll of thunder rumbled its presence.

The temperature had risen 20 degrees in the last 24-hours signaling a momentary reprieve from the harshness of the season. Snow had begun to melt and a light drizzle fell speckling the windshields of the cars and bringing wipers to life.

The trees swayed and bent as a monsoon-like wind increased in intensity; store awnings, prematurely unrolled to complement the unseasonably spring-like weather flapped madly; and, the fittings of the town's Christmas decorations clustered on the replicated gas lamps and restored buildings were sorely tested. Christmas wreaths swayed and lifted, silver bells jingled frantically and plastic holly and trim threatened to break loose from their anchors and litter the streets.

The men cursed quietly, the women thought it fitting, and the children were strangely silent as though sensing the end of innocence and the advent of a darker era for their town. After all, this was the first time a Woodstrom police officer had died in the line of duty and it seemed to be an omen, a signal that their tiny, remote and supposedly protected community would no longer be shielded from the ritual horrors of the outside world.

Welcome to the 21st Century, thought Clay bitterly as he wished away the next few hours and tried to comfort Hitch's wife who sobbed quietly between he and Jody in the backseat of the limo.

"Oh Martha...I'm so sorry," Jody murmured soothingly knowing only time and tears would help.

"Nothing will ever be the same again," Martha sobbed. "He's gone...and so is my life." She turned to Clay, her tone pleading, but with a tinge of accusation in it: "Wasn't there anything you could have done to save him? My God, Clay, he was your *friend*!"

Clay swallowed and reached for her, his own eyes threatening to spill over. He hugged her tightly. "Martha, I'd rather be Hitch right now...!" he whispered and she nodded, accepting the sincerity of his words. She buried her face against his uniformed shoulder and shuddered in grief. Clay looked over at Jody and saw the sympathy in her eyes. She reached across Martha and squeezed his hand; she knew it wasn't his fault.

With the numerous eulogies still fresh in their minds, the mourners turned off the highway and bumped over the dirt road that twisted haphazardly up the hill making its way through scattered grey monuments poking through the snow.

Clay glanced idly at the tombstones, knowing that townspeople from more than 150 years ago were buried here, now resident landlords from a time when space wasn't at a premium.

The older section of the graveyard had been left in its original state without the spaces between the older graves being filled in. Unlike many modern citizens, these people had grown up, died and been buried there with room to "breathe." Somehow it would have seemed unfitting to crowd them after their century-old claim to the land.

As they made their way deeper into the graveyard, these older monuments eventually gave way to an orderly, staid rows of tombstones – the more recent departures. Each stone, Clay noticed, now featured a small, melting drift of snow on top, often sitting askew at a jaunty angle, like some morbid top hat signaling the willingness of those below to step out on the town and kick up their heels. Here and there small American flags fluttered, sad monuments to fallen soldiers, while sodden, dead bundles of flowers wilted in the wind. Finally, the long line of automobiles slowed and stopped.

The mourners disembarked accompanied by the muffled thuds of dozens of car doors slamming as the mass of people moved forward. Ahead, the hearse was opened and a contingent of officers – a police honor guard – prepared to remove the casket. Clay's broken arm prevented him acting as pall bearer. He looked over at the black hole of the grave chiseled into the ground and the heap of earth and snow beside it. Trampled, sodden grass around it had deteriorated into mud.

The ultimate reward, he thought, a three-by-six plot and six feet of dirt shoveled in your face. It was just a matter of luck that he wasn't being laid to rest beside his deputy. He also doubted that he would ever be able to reveal to a single soul what had actually happened at the Baker Estate.

In retrospect, the reality defied believability and police investigators were not notorious believers in anything other than cold, hard facts supported by scientific proof and logic. Clay knew there would be more questions – harder, more probing questions as the investigation proceeded.

Scanning the crowd, he noticed two men in long black overcoats and dark pants with black, wide-brimmed slouch hats standing apart from the others. He could just make out clerical collars peeking through the scarves they had wound about their throats. He wasn't surprised because they were strangers; there were more than enough of them in town for the funeral. He was, however, surprised because he'd seen these men about town many times before, but in other modes of dress: as skiers in colorful sweaters, as serious businessmen in suits, and in relaxed clothing acting like tourists and taking pictures. And, all the time they had been priests? Well, even God's servants had a right to a vacation, he thought. And, it was nice of them to show up for Hitch's funeral. He made a mental note to speak to them afterwards.

He left Martha with Jody and moved to the hearse to escort the coffin. His reasons were two-fold: First, out of respect for Hitch and second, to remind himself that he was, at least, partially responsible for the hapless death of a very good man.

~ 7 ~

The child's tattered dress fluttered and snapped in the breeze as she stood under the bare branches of a leafless, gnarled oak tree and watched the crowd of mourners in the snow far below.

She did not feel the cold beneath her feet, nor did she feel the relative warmth of the wind; she merely existed for the moment, content to do her Master's bidding as he waited for the night. Secure in a new location, the basement of an abandoned farmhouse, her Master was still largely nocturnal or a crepuscular being at best. Now, as thunder again rumbled in the darkening sky above her, she focused her attention on the one who had escaped. Later, she would report to her Master.

The group carried the ornate, walnut box with the shiny brass fittings to the hole in the earth and set it carefully down on strapping set above the opening. A man moved forward from the crowd and stood at one end of the grave. He shrugged out of his winter garment and she gave an involuntary gasp.

A low, nasty hiss escaped from her lips as she glimpsed the hated symbol – the golden cross on the chasuble the priest wore.

Soon words of praise directed at the Supreme Being drifted to her on the wind and though she did not understand them, she wilted and cringed in pain; agony wracking her body at the holy supplications and she stumbled back in the snow, her hands covering her ears.

The wind shifted, the words faded and the pain ended. She regained her footing. As she moved back towards the tree again, she felt the attention of one man below. Absentmindedly her finger strayed to the center of her chest, to one of the healed scars from when holes had been ripped through her body. Torn sinew and nerves still dangled from a crater-like open, bloodless wound in her neck. The Master would smooth it when he was ready to do so. Though the pain in her body was constant, she did not mind; it was now a part of her, one of many indignities her small being had suffered. She did not seek relief nor pay the transgressions any heed. They were just there, much as a human would feel a chill in the air or a hunger in the belly. This pain served no distraction and placed no limitations on her.

She looked down the hill again.

Though it was of great distance, she knew that this man who she felt watching her was responsible; that he was the one she had faced before and who wished her Master harm. She found her lips curling back over yellowed teeth as the wind continued to snap her shift about her bare knees.

She smiled because she knew that his time would soon come. The Master had promised.

~ 8 ~

After the honor guard had placed the coffin on the wooden slats, Clay stood at attention in a row with the others. Three Vermont State Trooper in full dress uniforms aimed their rifles skyward and, on cue, fired a gun salute – three volleys, three times. A New York Police Department Sergeant next stepped forward, hoisted his brass trumpet, and played Last Post.

Suddenly Clay found himself staring up the hill at a small, lone figure near an oak tree. He tensed, stared hard for a moment and then abruptly left the honor guard formation and began walking. As he moved past Jody, she looked at him in puzzlement. She spoke softly: "Clay, what is it?"

He didn't answer but continued to stare up the hill as he moved away from her and strode through the encircled group of people.

Jody followed. "Where are you going? The service...?"

"It's her...!" he said, his tone betraying a savage and furious anger lacking even a remote vestige of civility. He reached the outer fringe of the crowd and moved into deep, unblemished snow.

His tone frightened her: "Who...?"

"It's her," he repeated, eyes on the hill and now moving more swiftly.

Jody tried once more walking after him: "Clay!"

He ignored her, running, falling on a patch of bared ground, ripping the knee out of one leg of his trouser uniform, getting up and rushing up the hill. He ran in despair, not knowing what he would do once he reached her, only knowing that he wanted to seize the scrawny little body and shake the truth from it.

He shifted his gaze to the rough terrain and the piles of snow, branches and debris that littered his path as he ran. He covered ground quickly, panting and stumbling drunkenly, catching himself, and rising to run again, boots sending a mixture of snow and frozen sod flying up behind him as he thundered up the ridge.

The sound of his breathing exploded in his ears and he drove his legs to go faster, to move like the wind itself and put an end to his torture. Once he had the little bitch, he would find out what animal had stripped his friend of his life and dignity, turning him into the oozing, mutilated remains they were now burying.

Behind him, Jody was also running, slipping and falling on the hill. She called: "Clay...stop!" She was crying now, confused and hurt at this sudden, bizarre behavior.

The two priests in their black coats had also moved away from the crowd, their hands thrust into their right hand pockets as they moved after the sheriff in a trot. He was running full out. They hurried forward as best they could. He'd put an impressive amount of ground between them.

Below, the service had stopped. The crowd stared upward as Clay followed by Jody and two men raced towards the deserted tree. Reaching it, he screamed in anguish and whirled in dismay, He dashed about left and right, finally dropping to his knees in the wet snow, defeated.

Some mourners put it down to grief, other, less friendly folk, whispered that the sheriff had finally cracked up.

Jody reached him.

"She was here...she was here!" he yelled, as he desperately brushed the snow left and right searching for tracks, for any trace of the child's presence.

Fathers Dermott Murphy and Ronald Langevin reached Jody and Clay. Father Murphy tried to comfort him as Father Langevin seemed to stand guard, his hand still in his right coat pocket, eyes scanning the area.

"Easy lad...easy lass..." Father Dermott Murphy said soothingly, placing one hand on Jody's shoulder and the other on Clay's arm. To Jody, he said: "He'll be all right."

"She was here," Clay screamed. "That *thing* was here, I tell you!"

"Who was here, Clay...who?" Jody whispered, sinking to the ground with him, restraining him, holding him, and comforting him as he collapsed.

Throughout the weeks after his deputy's death, Clay had refused to cry, choosing instead to maintain the stony silence and strength expected of a strong leader.

Until now....

~ 9 ~

A little more than six months after the funeral, Agent Stan Pritchard of the FBI, resplendent in a charcoal grey suit, gleaming white shirt and silver power tie, sat across from Clay in his office, notebook and gold pen in hand. On the desk a small Sony tape recorder whirred softly.

"Quite frankly Sheriff, we're no further ahead in this matter," he said, opening the collar of his immaculate white shirt and loosening his tie to compensate for the stifling summer heat. "One thing would help us all greatly – if you would agree to take a lie detector test." Prichard held up his hand to ward off any protest. "Look, it would help you as well. It would clear you as a..." he hesitated and began again. "Well…clear you as a person of interest. It would also re-establish your credibility and let us all get on with focusing the investigation somewhere else."

Clay sighed and shook his head. He listened to a fly droning around in the office and wished he could find the swatter. He was sure someone had hidden it, just to frustrate him. His *loyal* police force seemed to enjoy frustrating him lately, working around him, and whispering behind his back.

He spotted the fly near the ceiling fan and then ignored it. He wished he could just go home and lose himself in a glass of Scotch, though, admittedly it was a habit that had caused some dissention with Jody lately.

BUT HELL, HE HAD A RIGHT TO TRY AND FORGET....

Granted, he'd not been easy to live with, either at home or at work.

Initially he drove his men pretty hard in the search for clues to the killer. But when he mentioned they keep a sharp lookout for a little girl with unusual eyes, his men looked at him curiously. For six months he agonized over the pros and cons of confessing exactly what had happened that evening but it all boiled down to a simple fact: nobody was going to believe him. There was little to gain and any credibility he had left would be lost.

He thought back to the evening he'd insisted on leaving the hospital after his arm had been temporarily immobilized. Declaring he needed surgery, the doctor refused to let him go without a signed, self-release form. He signed the paper and had Deputy Tom McConkey drive him back to the murder scene; it looked decidedly surrealistic.

The road had been plowed to the house where a portable generator purred loudly furnishing power to the brilliant Klieg lights illuminating the scene. The sound of radio transmissions crackled in the freezing night air as red and blue emergency strobes lit the snow. Troopers traveled back and forth, their boots crunching, their breath frosting in the sub-zero air. Hitch's body remained pinned to the door where it was barely visible through a translucent, polyethylene sheet tacked up to cover the horror. Four uneasy volunteer firemen stood by, crowbars in hand, none looking towards the open cellar door as they awaited word from the coroner. The dead goat had been cut down, dragged to the back and lay stiff in the snow off to one side.

His arm encased in a temporary plastic splint throbbed viciously as Clay watched white-suited forensic experts on loan from the FBI meticulously combing the interior and exterior of the house and root cellar. Down the road, reporters and curious civilians were being impatiently held back behind yellow police tape and several wooden construction roadblocks.

As he watched, Doc Severn, the County Coroner, decided it was time to move the body. The plastic sheet came down and the firemen quickly worked with crowbars to pull out the rusty, rail-road size spikes. They wore purple nitrile examination gloves and carefully handed the gory spikes by their relatively clean tops to a plain-clothed detective who preserved each one in an individual plastic evidence bag.

During the process, one fireman suddenly turned, vomited and was led away by a trooper. The man fell to his knees gulping for air and desperately washed his face with handfuls of snow.

Clay gained entrance to the kitchen, also illuminated with generator-powered bulbs. Of course, there was no sign of the child nor the dozens of bags of blood from the refrigerator. The appliance stood with its door open, strangely free of dust and dirt, and obviously out of place amid its filthy surroundings. Though sorely tempted to ask if any belongings from a child had been found, he kept his silence about the little girl. Using a flashlight in his good hand, he wandered through the entire house with his deputy by his side.

Since that night, Clay weathered an inquest, many visits from the Vermont State Police and, now, again, from the FBI. Because he was a "person of interest," he'd been ordered to relinquish control over the investigation and, further, not to pursue it in any manner.

To the investigators, it was obvious he was hiding something and the FBI judiciously seeded rumors in town in an effort to apply more pressure on him to come clean. He stuck to his story and their frustration and anger grew.

Meanwhile, the gossip and rumors were taking their toll. Morale in the force was poor and his authority had eroded to the point where the men seemed to be operating independent of him – still providing excellent service to the community – but working around him. It was a polite, but cold, conspiracy of silence and benign neglect they served up to him.

With the rumor mill grinding on, the pressure was intensifying. Today, both McConkey and Lefty Drazel, two of his most supportive deputies, had flatly refused to do any further checks at the Baker Estate citing the orders from the FBI. He called their actions insubordination. They called it reality and stamped out of his office.

Pritchard showed up every two weeks to grill him relentlessly, and Winder County presented him a standing offer to take a financial package and resign. Though Jody was sticking through it with him, he hated how tired and haunted she looked. He had repeatedly suggested she spend a few months with her parents now living in Boston but she'd refused.

The FBI agent was speaking again. He'd have to get the fly later.

"Timing, Sheriff...timing," Pritchard was saying. "That's the key."

"I know the timing doesn't hang together," Clay said, for the hundredth time, "but I can't do much more than tell you exactly what I did from the time we got to the Baker place to when I found Hitch. You figured out the timing."

Pritchard's pursed his lips. He was losing patience again as he slowly and deliberately said: "Okay. Let's assume that this satanic cult – or whatever it was – could mutilate and partially remove the epidermis off the head and drain the blood from a full grown man in the time allotted; how could they do it all without you hearing?" Pritchard leaned intently forward, his watery green eyes fastened intently on Clay like a cobra eyeing a mouse. "The pathologist's report said that it was likely done while he was still alive. So he must have been screaming like a stuck pig. And what did they do with the skin? Sell it to the Colonel as a KFC special?"

Clay came out of the chair like a rocket. He was around the desk and had Pritchard by the throat before the agent was even able to rise. The notebook and pen flew across the room and hit the wall.

"Now listen you son-of-a-bitch!" Clay said, through gritted teeth. "Hitch was my friend. To you he's nothing but a name on a report, but he was my *friend*!"

Gurgling for air, Pritchard tried to pry Clay's hand from his throat but Clay stood four inches over the man and outweighed him by twenty pounds. He didn't slacken his grip as he stared at the agent now turning bright pink. "So listen up, Agent Pritchard. I'm going to let go of your throat. As soon as I do, you take your neatly pressed suit and your questions all the way back to Burlington or Washington or wherever you keep that rock you climbed out from under. You hear?"

He let go and the agent dropped, dead weight, back into the chair. He groaned as he sucked in air. It took a full 30 seconds for his color to return to normal.

"Y-You're a madman," Pritchard gasped. "We're gonna-gonna nail you...right to the wall. We don't think there's any satanic worship group involved here, Sheriff. We never did. We think it's some sicko...and that sicko is YOU!"

"Charge me or leave me alone!"

Pritchard swallowed and glared at him. Though Clay's rage seemed spent, taking no chances, the agent got up and hastily backed away. "I-I'm leaving, but I'll be back," he said, heading for the door. Realizing he was missing his briefcase, he retrieved it from the corner and then stood staring at the desk.

"What?" Clay finally demanded, anxious to be rid of the man.

"My recorder..." he said, eyes shifting uneasily from Clay's stare.

Clay swept it from the desk with one hand. It exploded into a melee of plastic and soldered circuit boards on the floor.

"That's okay Sheriff, we don't need that to get you." Pritchard looked at the gold pen near Clay's foot. Clay followed his gaze and then deliberately lifted his heel and ground the pen into the floor. As the casing bent, it popped open and the inner spring sent the ballpoint filler rolling across the floorboards. "That was a graduation present," Pritchard whined.

Clay felt his anger building again. "Well you just GRADUATED asshole! Get out!"

The agent exited his office and stamped across the outer office. Clay expected to hear the door slam but instead, other boots sounded on the floor. Low voices were followed by Pritchard's growl and he heard two men walking towards his office. Clay tensed.

Tom McConkey rounded the corner followed by Pritchard. The middle-aged deputy looked both harried and dissolute as he stood in the doorway. His prematurely grey hair seemed greyer, and the lines in his weathered face seemed deeper today. His hands fiddled nervously with his gun belt. Behind him was Pritchard, looking at Clay with something close to pity.

McConkey said gently: "Clay...?" There was hurt in the man's face.

"What's up now?" Clay asked bitterly.

McConkey shook his head.

"Spit it out, Tom."

The look on the man's face was something Clay had never seen before.

McConkey just stared at Clay, working up the courage to say the words he knew would change his life forever.

Somewhere in Clay's subconscious, suddenly he knew. Before McConkey spoke, that tiny voice inside whispered that, despite his conviction that things couldn't get any worse, they *had* gotten worse. And, there was only one thing that could make matters worse.

"Please God...not Jody," he murmured, feeling his lungs expanding so fast he couldn't exhale to take another breath and get the oxygen he needed. He wanted to run, to escape. If the words were never said, then, she'd be alright, they could move away together from this madness....

"There's been a bad accident, Clay. Jody is-is missing."

~ 10 ~

As they drove to the accident site at Quechee Gorge, Clay fought to focus on the deputy's words. They sped along the two-lane highway, the siren wailing.

"Somehow she missed the bridge...went off to the side and into the gorge," McConkey said. "We found your Explorer upside down in the river at the bottom, the driver's door was open...but no...body...I-I mean...no Jody."

"Maybe it was stolen...," Clay said, desperate to provide any explanation that would see his wife safe. "Maybe it wasn't her. Maybe she's out shopping with someone."

"Sorry...the owner of the Amoco up the highway said she'd just gassed up."

Within minutes Clay was plunging knee deep into the rushing water of the Ottauquechee River and examining the mangled metal that was their SUV with its roof smashed flat and the open driver's door bent in half. Puddles of gasoline still drained from the vehicle' split gas tank into the river sending ribbons of Technicolor water downstream. Professionally, he knew nobody could survive such a violent drop. But inward he kept rationalizing that sometimes the impossible happened. Trying to grab hold of his emotions he took a deep breath and then another and yet he couldn't seem to consume enough oxygen. His head was spinning so he tried to pretend it was someone else's vehicle; the tiny brown teddy bear mashed between the dashboard and the roof refused him his fantasy.

Silently, with quiet dread, he prayed to the God of his childhood. Just one more chance. I'll do anything...but dear God...let us find her alive, he begged. Don't take my Jody from me. Please, please...make Jody alright. It's too cruel to do this again. "I live by the rules...do what's right...you owe me, damn it," he finally screamed aloud. McConkey looked at him with sadness. As though in answer to his demand, he heard a shout from down river and looked up to see three Vermont Highway Patrol Troopers struggling along the rocky, river bank. One held something in his arms.

Clay slipped, stumbled and fell. Spray flew as he charged out of the river towards the men. McConkey was behind him imploring him to wait, to slow down. "Clay, for God's sake, stop; let me see what they've found." But it was useless. Blood was rushing into

Clay's head as he ran and he could vaguely hear someone crying out to God to let her live, let her be alive – a voice that sounded very much like his own.

But her body hung limp in the trooper's arms, a tumble of dark, wet hair cascading towards the grass and rocks of the riverbank, face milk white and beautiful blue eyes closed forever. Desperately Clay wished that whoever was crying and pleading with God would just stop. Wasn't it obvious? God wasn't listening, God didn't care.

But again, the voice sounded all too familiar.

~ 11 ~

After the funeral, Clay went into a prolonged period of situational depression as weeks of mourning gave way to months of incredible longing and loneliness. His beautiful Jody had been cruelly stolen and, with the loss of her life, any desire on Clay's part to continue had vanished. Everything lost value for him. He watched others go about their daily lives feeling like an alien dropped onto a planet with no concept of how to even fake a semblance of normalcy. His depression deepened; it devoured his ability to concentrate, his confidence, and finally his will to live. The silent house, the empty bed, and knowing he would never hold Jody again, nor hear her laughter had become his personal living hell.

Life soon became a downhill slide, a mad toboggan ride into oblivion with his professional and personal self esteem lost in a virtual blur of booze and self-recriminations. He'd stopped answering or replying to phone calls and emails from his sister. And, in the middle of it all, Jody's parents, his sole supporters were, ironically, killed in an automobile accident. Daily he revisited the "What-if?" demons residing in his head. What if he'd been home? What if Jody hadn't felt the need to go shopping? *What if? What if?*

For a short time Clay managed to endure the stares and whispers of the townspeople, the sudden silences in the cafes when he managed to rouse himself from home and go out for a sandwich. Despite his problems, he also noticed the too-quick service by clerks, bartenders and barbers. He was no longer Jody Mather's husband and favored son-in-law of their ex-sheriff. Fair or not, it seemed people were only too eager to believe the worst of an outsider, particularly when the outsider had cost the town the lives of two of its favorite people. Though his grief was sincere and obvious, the town had enough mourners. What they needed was someone to blame.

Six months after Jody died, Clay hired a lawyer, walked into the Burlington FBI office and gave a detailed statement of everything that happened at the Baker Estate. In the following interrogation sessions he spared no detail, no longer caring how far-fetched or ludicrous it all sounded. He told of the little girl and her superhuman strength as well as her invulnerability to three .45 slugs. He stated his belief that somehow she, or an accomplice, had killed and mutilated his deputy.

They took statement after statement, had him interviewed by a forensic psychiatrist and questioned him during three separate polygraph exams. Finally they looked at the results and shook their heads in disbelief. All indications were that he was telling the truth. When Clay asked Agent Pritchard if he was satisfied, the man had just muttered something about polygraphs not being an exact science. It took two passing FBI agents and the examiner to pull Clay off the agent. Quick negotiations by his lawyer citing harassment and provocation eliminated any charges being filed.

With the polygraph results in hand, as well as voice stress analyzer tests showing him innocent of any wrong-doing, Clay's lawyer used threats of legal action to make the FBI and the State authorities publicly declare Clay was not a suspect in the case. But for him and the citizens of Winder County, it was too little, too late.

In November he resigned as Sheriff, sold his house, and moved to Chicago for a time and then to Manhattan trying to lose himself in a large city. Rather than being a salve for his wounds, the anonymity of the city gave him too much latitude. He drank heavily, as much for the anesthetic value as for the quick amnesia it provided. His vague plan to work in private security evaporated.

In rapid sequence he lost his apartment, moved to a boarding hotel and finally wound up living in a perpetual alcohol-induced fog at a Salvation Army Mission; he was as close to the end as any person could be, devoid of ambition or hope. A week after he moved into the mission, he was warned that he could not continue to drink and stay there. One cold winter evening he left with a warning that if he came back with liquor on his breath he would be refused entry. It was Christmas Eve but there was little joy in Clay Montague. He shivered in his suit jacket; he had deliberately left his topcoat in his room.

After a few drinks at a mid-town bar that consumed most of his remaining money, he stepped into the cold and watched Christmas shoppers hurrying about their errands, gaily wrapped packages under their arms. Christmas carols played joyously over public speakers. Eager children, their faces glowing with expectations of Christmas morning hurried obediently along beside their parents. People met, laughed, hugged and shook hands wishing each other a Merry Christmas – it was all part of a world in which he no longer belonged. Tired and beaten, missing Jody even more, he made his way into a deserted alley and lay down by an ice-covered brick wall. He knew the temperature was hovering around -10 below zero. Piles of cardboard, a dumpster and several plastic garbage cans were his only companions. Alone, cold and broke, he found that old habits die hard as he blessed himself and said a final prayer asking God for forgiveness for his inability to cope.

A wino shuffled into the alley, a blanket round the shoulders of a tattered coat reaching to his knees. He dropped to his haunches, propping himself against the opposite wall. He began to drink from a soiled paper bag as he watched Clay, slyly evaluating his potential as a victim.

"You dying?" the old wino asked, yellow rabbit teeth bared through his dirty beard.

"I don't know," Clay whispered. A feeling of numbness was creeping over his body. The busy street at the end of the alley continued to issue sounds of cars passing and the occasional honk of a horn. The strains of *Silent Night*, sung by a parade of carolers passing by, wafted in and then faded quickly as they moved on.

"Got any money?" the wino asked.

"Sorry…," Clay said.

"Can I have your shoes…after you're gone?"

"Knock yourself out." Clay closed his eyes and soon his body began trembling in the cold. After fifteen minutes of violent shaking, he could almost feel his heart-beat slowing as paralysis settled over him. It was better this way, he reasoned. He'd been unable to help his poor mother…unable to save his best friend and deputy…and unable to save his wife. Time to make room on earth for another soul who might contribute more. Strangely he began to feel hot as constricted blood vessels near the skin's surface dilated causing a false sensation of heat. His heart began to labor.

As Clay drifted into unconsciousness, he looked up through half-closed eyes and watched a shooting star moving slowly across the night sky. He didn't question his ability to see the star despite the city lights that usually washed out all starlight. It came to a dead stop. He even believed he saw a bright, arc-white light descending from the heavens and pausing above the city's canyon of buildings where he lay supine. "Strange," he thought closing his eyes. The wino suddenly scrambled to his feet in panic and raced out of the alley in fear of a strange luminescence descending upon them. After a few minutes Clay began to feel tremendous warmth blanketing his entire body. But this was a valid warmth. He tried to open his eyes. He was so tired, he could not. Instead, the Light suffused him with a feeling of peace and acceptance that lulled him into the sleep of the innocent. He sighed, resigned his soul to God and surrendered to the darkness.

The next morning, he was surprised to wake up in the alley still feeling that all-encompassing warmth despite the fact the temperature continued to be well below zero. There was no hangover and, for the first time in months, he felt hungry. He remembered vaguely a light that had come into the alley and its accompanying warmth. Was the memory alcohol induced, he wondered? Or simply his imagination seeking relief from his impending doom? Whatever had happened, he was still alive and so, ironically, were his problems. Inwardly he berated himself for his stupidity. This was hardly the way; he was lucky he hadn't frozen to death. I've had my last drink he vowed as he dragged himself to his feet and walked out of the alley.

Clay hadn't taken two steps before he bumped into a catholic priest on the sidewalk. The man apologized and looked at him with pity. Quite suddenly the look changed from pity to interest.

The priest, a man of about fifty wore a black topcoat and 1950s-styled fedora. A Roman clerical collar was plainly visible at his throat as he stared directly into Clay's eyes.

"Do you need help, my son?"

Clay found himself nodding and Father Terry O'Leary introduced himself, learned his name, smiled and continued: "Somebody has been very worried about you." His brown eyes twinkling, he gently placed a hand on Clay's arm and began to lead him along the sidewalk. Despite the strangeness of the encounter, something inside Clay told him to comply.

"Someone was worried about me?" Clay asked, in disbelief. "Who?"

"Why...the Lord, of course," the priest stammered, with an enigmatic smile. "Remember? Trust in the Lord and thou shall be saved?"

"Hardly likely," Clay responded, somewhat bitterly.

"Tut, tut..." the priest said, moving him along.

Together, they boarded a series of Manhattan buses. The priest kept up a steady stream of conversation designed, it seemed, to enable Clay to maintain his silence and head off any anticipated protests. It centered on the weather, development in New York, the environment and the increased commercialization of Christmas. In fact, few of his points required any return input which suited Clay just fine. He nodded politely every few minutes and spent the rest of his time asking himself why he was so meekly placing his fate in the priest's hands.

As they walked up Lexington Avenue, Clay was startled when they turned into the entrance of an upscale building. Somehow he had believed they were on their way to a church or a public shelter. When asked, Father O'Leary explained that this was the Opus Dei Regional Office of the Prelature where apostolic works were carried out. He began to proudly relay some pertinent statistics and facts about their surroundings. The 133,000 square foot, 17-story Murray Hill Place contained 100 bedrooms as well as chapels, dining rooms, conference halls and offices. It was used by the Opus Dei Personal Prelature to spread the word of Christ's presence in all facets of life, and to encourage people to live their lives for the Lord in a spirit of charity, humility and sanctity.

Clay marveled at the opulence of the building lobby sheathed in various marbles and inlaid with carved woods; busy civilians and priests, carrying briefcases, passed in and out. Father O'Leary had asked him to wait in the lobby and momentarily disappeared. Within a few minutes, he was back. Clay was assigned a bedroom on the 12th floor without any questions or any understanding of why it seemed so natural to meet this priest and to accept his help. He was shown where the dining room was and given a printed handout on meal times. This was followed by a quick tour of a number of chapels – he could choose *any* for his daily devotions, he was told.

All were opulent and many were filled with serious, well dressed and coiffed young male civilians attending mass or simply kneeling at prayer.

As Father O'Leary rattled on, he soon learned that males and females entered through different doors and had separate quarters within the building. Not that the inhabitants would succumb to temptation, the priest said with a lopsided grin, but why give the devil a garden in which to cultivate and perfect his wily ways?

Once he was settled in, Clay was simply asked to meet with O'Leary once a day as part of a "rehabilitation process" which they felt he needed. When Clay inquired why they were doing this for him – there were thousands of homeless on the streets of New York – he was told it was their Christian duty; the Church would help him re-enter society.

Within a day he found his closet wardrobe contained two suits, dress shirts, ties, sweaters, trousers and both dress and casual shoes, all perfectly sized for him. The following day, he entered his room to find his meager belongings from the Salvation Army Mission also stowed neatly in the closet and bureau.

While priests and civilians alike were polite to him in their comings and goings, he was essentially left alone except for his daily meeting with the priest which turned out to be more like psychotherapy sessions rather than the religious indoctrinations he had expected.

As the days passed into weeks, Clay pretty much made his life an open book to Father O'Leary. He also discovered that the kindly, middle-aged man did indeed possess a degree in clinical psychology. And, with O'Leary's help, he worked to repatriate himself into the land of the living and gradually accepted that he was fated to live with his memories. How he would live sober without his beautiful Jody remained to be seen. But, he reasoned, maybe his destiny was to be a life sentence of regrets.

Clay remained at the building for almost two months. He attended a few Christian lectures as recommended by O'Leary and joined a local chapter of Alcoholic's Anonymous. The elderly priest told him he could stay as long as he wished, however, it would be better if he resumed a normal life.

In fact, they had formed a kinship as Clay unburdened himself and O'Leary encouraged him to reconnect with who he was, accept the unfairness of life and find hope in the form of his Savior.

Clay also had the weird feeling that the good priest knew more about him than he let on. When some of his comments or observations seemed too knowledgeable, too uncanny to be mere guesses, the priest shrugged and said he'd advised many men who had lost their way in the past. He should never feel he was unique in his troubles.

Finally, with O'Leary's encouragement, he put on a suit and summoned up the courage to walk into a branch of the First National Financial and fill out an application for a business line of credit with the stated goal of starting a small private detective agency.

The Loans Officer, a nattily dressed little man with an impeccable mustache and bad comb-over as well as imbued with an exaggerated sense of his own importance, had looked over the application, fixated on the absence of collateral, wrinkled his nose and shook his head. He asked Clay to check back in two days if he *still* wanted to proceed. His tone clearly indicated Clay had a better chance of being elected President of the United States than in getting his loan approved.

Two days later, Clay arrived back, ready for the expected refusal. Instead, he found the Loans Officer wearing an entirely different hat. The man had been gracious to a fault and led Clay to a conference room with a long table and chairs. On the table were neat stacks of financial papers and two pens. He even pulled out Clay's chair as he went to sit down and asked him if he'd like some refreshments. He followed this by saying that the bank had reviewed his application and had deposited ten thousand dollars into an account for him. They were also extending him a line of credit of up to one hundred thousand dollars.

At first Clay felt his temper rising. Was this guy being funny? Barely holding his anger in check, he frowned suspiciously at the man and mentioned he'd only applied for ten thousand dollars.

The Loans Officer shrugged and, while looking somewhat perplexed himself, said that the President of the First National Financial had ordered that Mr. Montague be given whatever funds he needed. Within reason, of course. Was one hundred thousand enough?

Clay suddenly realized they were serious. He wasn't about to look a gift horse in the mouth, no matter who had fouled up in the credit approval process. He signed the papers, and was given a leather check book, a balance book, several bank pens and a bank calendar.

As he was being walked to the street entrance, the Loans Officer had moved in close to him and whispered conspiratorially: "C'mon, tell me who you *really* are?"

Clay looked at the little man and decided to take advantage of the puzzling but welcome situation. He tried to mask his distain as he said: "Let's just say there are people in the bank watching how you treat the disenfranchised – the more vulnerable customers – as compared to the well-heeled. Get it?"

"B-But I'm protecting the bank's assets," the Loans Officer protested.

Clay gave him a policeman's look. "It's *how* you do it. You've been warned." The officer's eye grew large, he nodded, gulped and opened the door for Clay, picking lint off his shoulder as he did so. He very nearly bowed as he said good-bye and good luck.

Having cleared the financial hurtles, Clay feared possible complications when applying for his New York State Private Investigator's License. After all, he had been a suspect in a murder investigation. But, everything had run remarkably smooth there also. He wondered if life was just trying to pay him back for some of the garbage it had thrown his way.

Business started slow but progressed to the point where it supported an excellent existence diametrically opposed to where he'd been heading, he reminded himself. Most of his cases involved marital disputes, commercial theft and criminal defense research. Soon he had a steady diet of defense lawyers needing his detecting skills. Things went so well that within six months he'd financed a small loft condo in lower Manhattan and settled into a predictable routine of working and sleeping. He played a little handball to keep in shape, ran five miles daily and attended Alcoholics Anonymous on a quasi-regular basis.

His close friends were few: Fast Eddie down at Belmont, and Paddy Duffy, owner, operator and bartender of the tavern across the street. Fast Eddy never took more than a $10 bet from him and Paddy never served him anything stronger than a Johnnie Ryan Cola as they spent hours debating the talents of the Yankees and the Mets. He also had a few other friends from Duffy's who played poker with him every Friday night in a back room at the bar.

Though there was now stability in Clay's life, something inside him had died, call it a spark, or a zest for living; emotionally he felt…emotionless. Still, though he forced himself not to live in the past, neither did he look to the future. He'd found a spot in his soul in which to hide his memories so they didn't hurt quite as much. Lately, however, he felt strangely restless, as though he had to do something, something he'd forgotten, the calm before the storm. Though it began as a vague and nebulous feeling, it was becoming increasingly real to him. He seemed to be waiting for something. For what, he had no idea. So he continued his work with small investigations of theft, fraud and other crimes. And, he waited.

~ 12 ~

"Comfortable, Sister?" the voice asked from the front seat of the long, black limousine.

"It's wonderful," Maria answered, wishing she could exchange her hard bed back at the Quebec convent for the comfort of the back seat of the automobile. "If I look a little larger when I leave, you'll know I've stuffed these cushions under my habit."

The two men in front laughed.

Sister Maria Michelle Lapierre yawned and sank deeper into the velvet upholstery of the limo transporting her from Rome's Leonardo Da Vinci Airport to the Vatican. A mere novice, she was surprised she was being given the royal treatment again. Pretty heady stuff for a nun-in-training, as she liked to call herself.

Cardinal Malachi had telephoned from Rome to Sister Superior at the convent in Quebec's Eastern Township Village of Rock Island and told her that Sister Maria was urgently needed in Rome again. In the past three years, she had been summoned to Italy twice by the mysterious cardinal, but on each visit, he merely conducted lengthy discussions with her on her faith, on her personal philosophy, her opinion of church teachings and finally on her reported gift of "second sight." And, he always insisted they meet in plain clothes at a restaurant or other facility in the city of Rome, never actually in Vatican City. She must surely be the only aspiring nun to have come to Rome twice before and never made it there, she mused. Oh well, the third time seemed to be the charm. She was told she was being taken directly to Vatican City.

The cardinal had always been evasive as to the reason for his interest in Maria, only saying that future considerations might include her, but refusing to elaborate further. Now she had been summoned *urgently?* Had she somehow done something wrong? Or was this another meeting from which she would emerge as puzzled as she had been from the first two.

Sister Superior had always told Maria that she was an intelligent and sophisticated woman but with the unquestioning innocence and optimism of a child – all wonderful qualities – but qualities which both blessed, and sadly, could betray her. Whatever Rome had in store for her, she had every right to evaluate and weigh its consequences. She mustn't take anything or *anyone* at face value, and that included the cardinal.

In retrospect, Maria knew the elderly nun was probably right as evidenced by the fact she did not fare exceedingly well in a world based on greed, acquisition and, often, deception. Still she held her virtues and her optimism close; she did not want to harden, did not want to change. Indeed, from what little she had been able to learn from the cardinal, it was a strange set of coincidences that had brought her to the Vatican's attention.

Having come from a devout Catholic family and schooled by the nuns at Our Lady of Mercy School in Rock Island, Quebec, and those at Sacred Heart High School in Newport, Vermont, Maria had taken a deep interest in religion after high school and ultimately graduated from university with a degree in theology. From there she attended teachers' college. After graduation, she had become a lay teacher for the Sisters, content to be near them and their world which seemed so peaceful and serene.

As she taught her daily classes of Catechism and English, she felt less and less association with the secular world. It was as though she would find peace only through a closer relationship with God and His workers. She often lay awake at night feeling there was something she was destined to accomplish but not having the foggiest notion of what *it* was.

A year later, she had joined the order as a postulant at 26, spent the required time as a novice and taken her temporary vows just short of her 29th birthday.

Indeed, she had just turned 29, and was attending a religious seminar at Notre Dame Cathedral in Montreal, when something happened that created headlines in the Montreal newspapers and elsewhere.

Maria's fellow sisters were taking her for a birthday lunch at Place Jacques-Cartier in Old Montreal. Suddenly she saw a car careening down the hill, swerving drunkenly from side-to-side on the cobblestones and heading for one of the open-air restaurant patios bordering the square. She had taken flight calling to the people to run and look out for the car that was going to hit them. They gaped blankly at her, forks and wine glasses half raised to their open mouths. Suddenly one of the other sisters pulled her back and asked what she was doing? Surprised, she stopped and looked about. There was no car swerving down the street towards the diners. Nothing was amiss except for the cessation of jovial conversation and the curious looks of the restaurant patrons. Then, content that things were as they should be, they shrugged and went back to their conversations and food. Maria's companions quickly closed ranks and shielded her from some lingering stares as they tried to calm her.

They had barely turned away when it happened. The roar of the automobile, the squeal of tires and a Cadillac Seville, with the driver already dead of a heart attack at the wheel, smashed into the patio she'd just identified. Tables, chairs and people went flying.

All the sisters had immediately waded into the melee of broken bodies and smashed furniture to help. Fire trucks, police and ambulances arrived in minutes and the Urgences Santé paramedics went to work. One of the unhurt patrons, however, said something to a stocky police officer questioning witnesses. He pointed out Maria. She was immediately taken aside and questioned as to how she had been able to forewarn the diners.

A young reporter had snapped a picture of the nun as the officer questioned her. Maria tried to pass it off as a vague premonition but was forced to give her full name, address, where she'd been born and other statistics to the police with the nearby reporter furiously scribbled notes. The man took more photos as she tried to hide her face.

The next morning she was on the front page of the *Montreal Star* under the headline: **PSYCHIC NUN TRIES TO WARN OF DEATH CAR.** And worse yet, the enterprising newsman had back-tracked her to her hometown of Beebe and dug up the story of her childhood friend and how Maria had foretold of her death as well.

The story brought unwelcome publicity to the convent and Maria was roundly censured. Sister Superior had angrily said that no person should know the future; it was a not a gift from God, but a curse from the devil. Maria was to spend the next week at her devotions praying that God would somehow spare her the onus of this curse. Interview requests were resolutely turned down by Sister Superior.

But the story was picked up by *The Canadian Press*, *Reuters* and *The Associated Press*, briefly reaching international mention. Apparently, it was also the reason she had been hastily summoned to her initial audience with the cardinal in Vatican City.

The first request for her presence had been both brief and cryptic; Sister Maria Lapierre was needed in Rome. No reason was given and Maria herself could shed no light on the strange request. Sister Superior was against letting her travel by herself since she believed that each member of the order needed constant companionship and support in their holy vows. Rome, however, insisted Maria come, sans escort and in civilian clothing. Her visit was to be a clandestine affair and under no circumstances were the press to be allowed to know. Sister Superior had finally agreed and Maria was off on her adventure. Surprisingly, both her first and second visits had turned out to be non-adventures with the cardinal seeming to just want to get to know her better.

But tonight, she had been promised, was to be different. When the Air Canada jet landed in Rome near midnight, a rather plump Brother Guy Fagan of the St. Francis of Assisi Order had informed her she was going directly to Vatican City. His companion, a tall, severe-looking Irishman who introduced himself as Father Dermott Murphy, helped pack her bags away with a gruff welcome. They carefully sat in the front seat of a limousine, while she sat in the back as dictated by traditional church etiquette. As she was whisked through the relatively quiet streets of Rome to her appointment with Cardinal Malachi, her excitement grew. What would this visit bring?

Brother Fagan, the more talkative of the two and a Scot from his accent, seemed to feel it was his duty to keep up a running commentary during the journey, particularly when he found out she'd never visited the Holy City. Murphy, concentrating on driving, merely grunted periodically taking issue with Fagan's diatribe but not taking his arguments any further than monosyllabic comments indicating doubt, disbelief and even disenchantment with both history and the brother's observations. Obviously used to this, Fagan took no notice. Maria categorized Murphy as a contrarian.

Though she knew much of its history, she allowed Fagan to continue unabated as he told her that *Il Strato della Città del Vaticano* or, Vatican City, was all of 109 acres, built on the tomb of Saint Peter and was the world's smallest independent state. In 1960, the United Nations had declared the Vatican city-state to be a "war-free zone" an enclave off limits to all military belligerents. It is a state, Brother Fagan said proudly, free of violent crime, welfare, decaying streets and graffiti. "The only thing it's not free of is politics," he added, with a smile.

He rattled on with facts and figures, the occasional one catching Maria's attention as they swerved around corners and accelerated past other cars. What was the hurry, she wondered?

As they approached Vatican City, she gasped at the magnificence of the illuminated dome of St. Peter's Basilica.

"I've always dreamed of visiting St. Peter's Cathedral," Maria said, obviously awestruck.

Brother Fagan turned and smiled. "St. Peter's is not actually, in the strictest sense of the word, a cathedral since it's not the seat of a bishop," he said, not unkindly. "Officially it's really a papal basilica. The Archbasilica of St. John Lateran is really the cathedral church of the Dioceses of Rome. And the official ecclesiastical seat of the Bishop of Rome – His Holiness."

"Score another one for Fagan the Most Exalted," Father Murphy said, dryly.

Maria stifled a chuckle and before she knew it, the dome vanished from sight and they were at what Fagan called the Porta Sant'Anna – the St. Anne Gate. The limo ground to a halt before a huge, ornate, filigreed, iron-barred gate flanked with two ionic columns topped with eagles. Two blue, red and yellow striped-uniformed Swiss Guards examined the Brother's plastic ID cards.

Maria peeked surreptitiously from the backseat at them and couldn't help thinking they looked somewhat ancient and silly in their tin hats, pantaloons and ceremonial amour. The huge gate was slowly swung open with a metallic grinding and creaking.

"Special protocols these days," Murphy muttered, as the automobile accelerated and Maria felt goose bumps rising on her arms with the realization that she had just entered Vatican City.

"Saint Anne of the Palafrenieri, where we attend Mass," Fagan had said tightly, as he gestured to a small, baroque-looking church off to their right. His voice now seemed more perfunctory, less the host and more that of a man with a mission. Old buildings, religious statues commemorating biblical history, and ornate fountains peopled with marble renditions of saints and sinners loomed out of the night and faded away just as quickly; the car occasionally bumped over cobblestoned streets.

Maria glimpsed another stone building to her left and noticed members of the Swiss Guard entering and leaving. White fluorescent light spilled into the street as the door opened and shut. Some only wore parts of their Medici-inspired uniforms as they stood outside in small tight groups and smoked. Perhaps it was their barracks, she guessed. Or those special protocols mentioned.

Though it was one o'clock in the morning, a few robed priests and the occasional pair of nuns glided silently through the narrow streets appearing bent on important and mysterious missions.

The automobile twisted and turned so often she wondered if they were doubling back on their course. Finally they lurched to a halt before a large grey stone building.

While Murphy waited, Fagan quickly led Maria through a magnificent stone archway, into a giant foyer decorated with gold leaf framed religious paintings, colored tiles and cracked but impressive marble floors. They made their way up multiple sets of stairs and along ancient looking corridors of polished marble or granite, all lit by small-wattage, flickering light bulbs.

After a few minutes, they stopped near a single stone column along one of the corridors and Fagan pushed at something near the back of the column.

He watched Maria's expression as a ragged section of a polished stone facade released and slipped smoothly back from the column. Clearly enjoying her reaction, Fagan pushed it sideways until it revealed a stone passageway lit by small light bulbs linked by a heavy black cable. The bulbs were yellowed by time and dust.

"Shortcut," he had said with a grin as they entered and he pushed it closed behind them. They made their way up rickety-thin wooden staircases hugging stone walls, along narrow dusty hallways, and through portal after portal. Fagan told her that many of the buildings in the Vatican had secret chambers and passageways – escape routes for ancient popes who were often assassinated or imprisoned as consequences of failed political maneuvers or because of competitive ambitions or jealousies. This mostly happened from the ninth to the 14th centuries. To be sure, conspiracy theories even surrounded the death of John Paul I in 1978 but, in the end, no concrete evidence of foul play had been provided.

    A few minutes later, they entered an antechamber through a heavy velvet-curtained doorway. His Eminence, Mustavias Cardinal Malachi, clothed in a simple black robe with a cowl at its neck, rose from a thick wooden table around which six other similarly-garbed, somber-looking clerics sat. He moved forward to greet Maria with a friendly grin.

    This room, contrary to the normal splendor of the Vatican she'd viewed in books and via DVDs, was sparsely furnished and lacked any sign of decoration at all. The stone floor was half-covered by a threadbare throw rug under the table, its pattern almost worn to invisibility. The only decoration on the walls was a simple wooden cross sprouting obviously old palm fronds from a Palm Sunday Mass far too many years ago. She also noted that the room was damp and rather cool.

    The other six men sitting around the ancient and much scarred oak table on severe-looking wooden chairs now scrambled to their feet and shuffled forward. She couldn't tell if they were priests, bishops or cardinals since they were all garbed in black cassocks, devoid of any piping, colors or other badges of rank.

    There was a single, large brass pitcher of something and silver-colored wine goblets set before each chair. On the table was a scarlet cloth seemingly hastily arranged over a rectangular shape, possibly a very large book or a box of some sort? Was it to conceal it from her eyes, she wondered?

    Malachi was an impressive man, a shade under six feet with hazel eyes that twinkled with good humor. A thick and unruly thatch of iron grey hair covered his head and he brushed nervously at it the whole time Maria stood before him. He looked very much like British actor James Mason, she thought. The other clerics, an assortment of bald, fat, short, tall, bearded and clean-shaven men, none under sixty she was sure, now flanked the cardinal but remained mute.

    They had stood by silently as Malachi noted her shaking hands and bade her welcome. "My child, so lovely to see you again but you do look utterly exhausted. Are you all right?"

"Yes Your Eminence…I'm just a little nervous," she said, quickly clasping her hands behind her back to stop them shaking. "So nice to see you again as well."

He laughed and lightly touched her shoulder for a second. "Please…again, I ask you to call me Mustavias. Everyone else here does. And, I shall continue to call you Maria."

"Oh…I couldn't your–?"

"Mustavias," he said with a wide smile. "Since Vatican II we've been ordered to become more egalitarian whether we want to or not. Down from our golden thrones to join the proletariat."

"Yes…sir…Mustavias," she said. The name rolled off her tongue like a spoiled oyster.

"My dear, I shall not introduce you to this band of ragamuffins behind me tonight as you would never remember who is who anyhow. You will get to know them all over time. Now we know you are safe, we'll all give you a hearty wave and send you off to your bed."

The group, obviously bone-tired, lifted heavy hands to Maria and gave her a communal wave. She couldn't help but giggle which brought huge smiles to their weary faces. Fortunately they didn't know she was seeing them as human renditions of Disney's *Seven Dwarfs*.

"Now off with you and we shall talk in the morning," Malachi said. He told Brother Fagan to ensure that Maria was fed and properly housed where he had asked. Then, without further explanation, he bid her a warm goodnight, and politely shooed her out to be taken to her quarters.

Maria was a little disappointed that she hadn't learned the mystery of why she had been summoned such a great distance. And what did he mean by saying they were happy to know she was *safe*? Why wouldn't she be safe?

Brother Fagan made no comments as he led her back to the limo and they resumed their wild ride with the grim-lipped Murphy at the wheel.

Expecting to be housed with one of the many religious orders in the city, Maria found herself instead driven out of Vatican City and housed in, of all things, the Holiday Inn Rome West. She was told that if she was hungry, there was a limited room service menu available at that hour and bid good night. All charges would be covered, she'd been told, so order what she liked. Still disappointed over still being kept in the dark as to the purpose of her journey, she soothed her irritation by eating several chocolate bars from the mini fridge and treating herself to a two-hour, bubbling soak in the Jacuzzi tub. These sorts of luxuries were certainly foreign to her experience at the convent.

The next morning, she dressed in her habit, was picked up by Brother Fagan and a different but still silent driver, taken back to the Vatican and dropped off just behind the Basilica. Fagan had pointed towards a small garden to the right. Maria walked over and found herself in a park-like setting surrounded by a hedge and divided by stretches of low stone walls, and walkways. It featured several statues of saints, an ornate fountain and gravel walkways. A hot sun blazed down.

Across from her was a bed of red roses, several park benches standing in the shade of olive trees and Cardinal Malachi resplendent in a heavy black cassock with cloth-covered red buttons, a cape fringed with red piping, and a red watered-silk ribbon cummerbund circling his waist. In his hand he toyed with a small scarlet skullcap, also of red watered-silk that Maria knew replaced the biretta headpiece which was only worn with choral dress. As with most things into which she had delved, Maria had also made it a point to study the various habits and uniforms of the Church.

He turned and looked her way as the sun glinted off a heavy golden Crucifix hanging from a chain about his neck. As she advanced to meet him in the garden, he lifted a hand in greeting. On reaching him she held out the skirt of her habit and knelt to kiss his signet ring. She remembered that though these ecclesiastical rings had once contained a sapphire, they now were simply gold and featured the scene of the crucifixion. She waited for him to tell her to rise.

"We've got to stop meeting like this, Sister," he said, and she looked up in surprise to see him grinning mischievously down at her.

Face flushed, Maria regained her feet, now self-conscious and embarrassed by the solemn importance she had attached to the occasion, juxtaposed against his cavalier and irreverent treatment of her devotion.

Seeing her dismay, Malachi felt like a heel. He immediately apologized explaining that despite the trappings, he wasn't much one for ceremony. He bade her to relax and join him in a stroll through the garden. As her Sister Superior had warned him, she certainly was an innocent with a trusting nature. Was he making a mistake? Did she have the fortitude to do what he asked?

There were a few minutes of polite conversation and he pointed out statues and the history of various saints as they walked. Then he got right to the point and referenced their prior discussions. "What I have to know, Sister, is simple: These *powers* we've discussed, would you be willing to use them to help us?" He paused for a moment and then continued: "In short, we need your precognitive gift to help the Church."

She nodded silently, eyes downcast. "Sister Superior says it is a curse, not a gift."

"Be that as it may, you do see bad things occurring before they happen."

"Yes. But I have no control over these visions."

He nodded. "So tell me again how do they present themselves to you?" He stared at her intently, no trace of a smile now.

"It's like…a movie. Sometimes I think it's happening right away in front of me. I see something happen and then…I sort of … wake up…and everything is as it was a moment before. And then, sometimes, what I have just seen…begins to happen. Sometimes it's within minutes and sometimes much later. Like the automobile accident in Montreal. I-I don't know why but I feel an ominous sense or presence when bad things are going to happen…evil things." She stopped and wondered if he was about to berate her for believing in magic or witchcraft. Instead he pointed towards a tarnished copper box perched on a two-foot high stone wall nearby. Green swathes of oxidation on it surrendered to polished orange gold metal that glinted in the sunlight

"See that box, Maria?" he asked, looking around to ensure their privacy.

She nodded.

"Tell me…do you believe its contents to be good or evil?"

"What's in it?"

"You tell me…!"

"But-but as I said, I have no control over what I see." She shook her head. "Or *when* I might see something. I can't tell what is in an unopened box any more than I can tell what's in your pocket."

"Try…" he said gently, again pointing towards the box. "I just want to know if it's good or evil – positive or negative. Can you tell me that?"

Maria approached the wall where the box rested. It was about 18 inches long, eight inches wide and six inches high featuring two ornate locks. It looked very old.

"Can you feel anything from it? Or, sense anything associated with it? Anything?"

Maria shook her head and shrugged. As she tried again to explain that the visions didn't come because she willed them, she reached out towards the box hoping to feel *something* so as not to disappoint him. Instead, she felt exactly…nothing.

She had just turned around to tell the cardinal she couldn't do it when she felt a warm, deep peace flooding her body; she stopped speaking in mid-sentence and turned back towards the box. Despite the warm sun, goose bumps rose on her arms and neck.

Maria began to concentrate on the box. Suddenly she found herself drawn to it. She had taken only two steps forward when she was hit with an overwhelming feeling of suffering, pain, loss and disappointment. She gasped aloud as needles of agony radiated from her wrists down through her fingers and up her arms. Her ankles screamed in aguish and pain shot to her right side; she bent double, struggling to breathe, her heart racing.

Within seconds the sun, the garden and the cardinal vanished before her eyes, and she was only aware of darkness, of a rough hillside covered by stunted bushes, stones, brambles and small olive trees; lightning flashed amongst roiling black clouds and thunder rolled in angry waves over her head. A violent wind whipped about her, sending dust and small pebbles rattling against her shins as it shrieked in protest at what was to be.

A terrible thirst beset her and a putrid stench of human sweat, blood, dust and burning tallow assaulted her nostrils as a drab blackness, and a sense of hopelessness swiftly grew in intensity. It clouded her brain, drained her strength and suffocated her will. She sensed fear, anger and hopelessness, agony and death, but mostly, she sensed *revulsion* at what was to come. An image of a beautiful, tortured, sensitive man's face high above her filled her line of sight, while somewhere behind her was the soft weeping of women. Startling, unnaturally pale blue eyes were set in a swarthy countenance but they were dulled by anguish and torment. Dried blood streaked His head and face. Rivulets of fresh sweat ran like miniature rivers towards His chin to lose themselves in His beard. A roughly woven Crown of Thorns rested askew on His brow.

Shadows magnified by flickering torchlight in the now darkened day played across His features throwing His expression of sorrow in deep relief. He desperately looked down from a wooden cross for hope or salvation as wounds from rough spikes driven through His wrists and feet pumped fresh blood from behind crusted scabs at every twitch of pain. Yet she sensed that He knew there would be no salvation. There would only be misery. No last-minute reprieve. Somehow she knew He was destined to die as the sound of wildly chanting crowds from afar assaulted her ears. And, of this she was sure; though He gave of Himself willingly to His destiny, He was afraid.

Within minutes the man on the cross desperately lifted Himself upward against the spikes and the ropes binding His forearms to the cross. Taking a final breath, He cried out in Aramaic. "It is finished." Strangely she understood the words. He then slumped and Maria knew His life force had departed. The wailing of women behind her increased in intensity. It wasn't long before the scrabble of sandals on rocks and the metallic clink of a weapon and scabbard heralded a Roman soldier approaching.

A Roman Legionnaire garbed in metal breastplate and leather cingulum suddenly stood before the man and gazed up at Him, half in anger, and half in sympathy. Maria knew the hardened soldier felt sadness at what he was seeing, though he habitually felt nothing at executions. Raising his lance, Legionnaire Longinus thrust its head into His right side and blood and water poured forth. The man on the cross didn't move. Maria cried out in dismay, tears spilling from her eyes in a torrent. The soldier recoiled as a wave of emotion swept through him and she felt his sudden inner torment rebelling against iron-willed discipline and training. She also felt his doubt grow with a swiftness that surprised him.

Why was this one different? Why did he feel such anguish at his deed? The Legionnaire suddenly felt tears sliding down his own face and quickly wiped them away as the tormentor caught the sightless eyes of the tormented. He fell to his knees as lightning split the air again followed by a whipping, crackling sound snaking across the sky and ending in a rumbling explosion of thunder. A burning stench of ozone assaulted his nostrils. The wind grew ever stronger as the soldier became aware of the saltiness of his tears on his lips. He cast his head down, forgetting about the idols and Gods that he now knew were false. Nor did he care what his Centurion or other soldiers in the cohort thought. "My Lord..." he mumbled, in a coarse Latin that she understood perfectly.

Suddenly Maria was flooded by an extraordinary feeling of relief, beauty and incredible, enlightened happiness. The darkness receded like a breaking ocean wave heralding bright sunlight, and with its retreat, she felt her body being purged of all pain, fear, guilt and hate. She was back in the garden.

More tears flowed as she tried to grasp the beauty and magnitude of a feeling of all-encompassing love, of forgiveness and charity, and of a joy and purity which radiated from the box before her and filled every crevice of her mind and her being.

The box suddenly transformed and became a brilliant light. It kept expanding, getting brighter and brighter, its radiance filling her soul with feelings of redemption and rejuvenation until she thought she would burst. Yet she did not shy away from it; instead she wanted more and found herself seeming to float towards the source, wishing only to be near to it, to have it, to touch and hold it, to know the goodness and light as intimately as humanly possible.

She ached in her heart to possess the holy contents and never, never let them go. Gasping for breath, for a brief instant Maria felt as though she was eternal and finally understood the meaning of true love, oneness with the universe and unconditional surrender to a power greater and purer than anything she had ever experienced.

It was too much....

Her head spun and she dropped to the ground, senseless.

Maria was not even aware that she had passed out until she awakened in bright sunlight with birds singing loudly from the olive trees; she was being cradled unashamedly in the arms of Brother Fagan. He must have remained nearby, she thought.

Cardinal Malachi stood above her, now quite pale and looking terribly concerned until she smiled up at him and gasped: "Y-You're right...w-we've got to stop meeting like this, Your Eminence."

His face underwent a marvelous transformation, almost beatific, as concern gave way to relief and he smiled the broadest and most open smile anyone could ever hope to receive from another mortal.

"Thank Heaven," he said. "You're alright?"

She nodded. Her pounding heart gradually slowed to a normal beat. Fagan wiped perspiration from her forehead and upper lip with a starched white handkerchief.

"Child, tell me about the box?" Cardinal Malachi pressed, gently. He knelt down beside her and stared deep into her eyes. "Do you get a positive or a negative feeling from it? What did you feel?"

"Hurt…despair…and then…l-love," Maria stammered, desperately holding back tears, barely able to conceptualize the latent feelings pouring into her, or contain her weeping which, much to her chagrin, suddenly began anew. "It was total and unconditional sacrifice and love. I-I sensed…the presence of-of our Lord and Savior – Jesus Christ." Malachi looked Heavenward and nodded as she continued: "I saw His death…and-and…I knew His triumph!"

Over the next hour she sat with Malachi in the garden and he revealed that the box contained a Holy Relic, a piece of the *True Cross* on which Christ had died, and which had been brought to Rome in the 4th Century from the Holy Land by Emperor Constantine's mother, Empress Helena.

"The *Wood of the Cross* is reputed to have talismanic powers," he said, looking towards the untouched box still sitting on the stone wall. "What you have felt here this morning can only help confirm once again that this is indeed authentic and will fulfill our hopes."

"How would it do that, Your…?" Maria's question trailed off and she tried to remain calm as she began to fully realize the enormity of the vision she had experienced minutes before. Had she really seen Christ die? Had she travelled to another dimension where time was fluid or was it a hallucination of sorts? In her heart, she already knew the answer. Malachi was speaking.

"We hope that, by its sacrifice, it will rid the world of a plague."

Next he bent close and in a voice barely above a whisper, revealed that she would be asked to undertake a mission of grave importance to God and mankind. There would be risk, possible pain and even death. But, he wagered that if she died, she would surely sit with the angels in Heaven. If she lived, whatever path she chose in life thereafter would be blessed by both the Church and Almighty God.

~ 13 ~

It was now more than eleven months since Maria's last visit and her stunning vision in the garden. Shortly thereafter she had been packed off home with orders to pray, meditate on her faith and reflect on her vision. The mission Malachi had mentioned had still not been revealed to her.

After an exhausting two-day trip back to Rome, she was meeting the cardinal in the *Chamber*. This time they were alone and she listened in rapt attention as he laid out the history of Adramelech and his mission on earth to turn the righteous from God.

"A-a demon, Your Eminence," she stammered. "A *real* demon?" They had resolved the stand-off in the young nun's discomfort in calling Malachi by name. She was free to address him as she chose.

"As real as you and I, Maria. We believe he's been here for eons and has been creating unholy and diabolic mischief for as long."

"You've seen him-it?" she asked, incredulously.

Malachi smiled. "Not personally. But I've seen his work. I've seen what it's done to mankind. As a matter of fact, if we look at the long and bloody history of our world – and even our Church – it would be hard to believe that there *isn't* some form of endemic evil running amok down here."

"Oh please, don't misunderstand me," she apologized. "It's not that I don't believe in Satan…."

"I understand," Malachi said. "Just not *here* and not *right now*."

"S-Something like that," she finished, lamely, head bowed in embarrassment.

"Don't be bashful, Sister. You're in good company."

He then laid out the assignment he was asking her to accept – to accompany a group called the *Watchmen* who were guarding a man being stalked by the "Beast" as Malachi occasionally referred to him. Because of certain administration problems, they weren't ready to do battle with Adramelech just yet. So they hoped she would be able to use her precognitive abilities to let them know of any evil presence she sensed – in effect, an early warning system to allow them to move their charge to safety, if necessary.

"But Cardinal Malachi, I must tell you again that I have no control over what I see," she said.

The cardinal smiled and replied: "Sister, if you can sense the sacrifice of the Crucifixion from a piece of wood after more than two thousand years, you will surely sense the malevolence of the Beast. The only question now is: will you do it?"

Maria nodded slowly. "I am ready to serve where I am needed by the Church. That should be understood…." She hesitated.

"I sense a 'but' there," he said.

"It's just that…. Well…are you sure there is a *demon* on earth, Your Eminence?"

He laughed aloud, a deep cathartic laugh that seemed to help relieve him of the stress she observed on his face. "Or, have I been dipping into the sacrificial wine? Is that your true question?"

"Oh…I would never think that," she replied, horrified.

"Oh yes you would," he said, mischief in his eyes. "That's what makes you so valuable. You bring faith tempered with reason. Though they are not necessarily mutually exclusive, all too often people believe they are." He smiled gently at her. "Maria, we would never send you blindly into battle without you being convinced of the Beast's existence. Accordingly, I have arranged for you to spend some time with one of our scholars – someone well versed in the vagaries of the *Hellspawn*."

"But I do believe you, sir," Maria protested.

"Of course you do," he said, a trifle patronizingly. "Belief because of your vow of obedience? I need more than that." Seeing her face reddening, he tried to make up for any offense she'd taken. "Look, in your shoes, I'd also think the old man was a few fries short of a Happy Meal. What you will learn over the next few days will help you appreciate the seriousness of what we're trying to do." He stood up from the old oak table, a sign of dismissal. "Oh, one more thing…you haven't taken your final vows yet, I believe."

Maria nodded. "No, I'm still a novice. I just haven't been ready, despite the length of time; I'm sorry, Your Eminence."

He waved away her concern. "I have spoken to many of your peers and your Sister Superior. You have a good heart and a clean soul, Maria. All too often we have seen Satan and his emissaries turn people's sins and vulnerabilities against them. I personally believe that your good heart will keep you safe. Now, off you go. Brother Fagan is outside."

Maria soon found herself sitting with an elderly translator in the vast Vatican Library for the better part of the next week. She was told that, while there were secret Vatican archives containing state papers, correspondence, papal account books and other documents accumulated over the centuries, these were now open to researchers and scholars. What would be revealed to Maria came from a "Registered Confidential" room. There were barely ten people living who knew of its existence and their knowledge would be passed to no more than ten others when they died.

The translator, an 85-year-old nun named Sister Raphael from the Sisters of the Sistine Order, spent day-after-day painstakingly translating and reading in English to Maria from a selection of ancient Greek, Latin and Hebrew manuscripts out of these secret archives. She said that the collective chosen texts, selected by a secret enclave, and verified for authenticity under a legal and confidential arrangement with some of the world's eminent biblical scholars, was called the *Hellspawn Attestation*.

As they worked, during breaks, Sister Raphael also revealed that the Vatican Library was founded by Nicholas V in the 14th century, and now contained 60,000 priceless codices, 6,000 incunabula and more than 500,000 volumes.

The papyruses and parchments she read from, many more than two millenniums old, were faded, yellowed and cracked, and kept in a walk-in vault whose door was concealed in a small locked room secreted away from the main library hall. Here the documents had been judiciously mounted and immobilized on acid free cardboard and maintained in slices of what proved to be, glass boxes. The boxes, carefully lined up in an oversized bookcase, were each fed a precisely measured mixture of temperature and humidity-controlled air through small yellow hoses fixed to giant water and compressed air cylinders attached to the wall. Sister Raphael explained that the relative humidity was kept precisely at or below 70 percent to deal with, among other things, microorganisms. By housing them in vacuum-sealed glass boxes they were able to prevent attacks by insects, fungi and bacteria, and mitigate the risk of loss which was greater from live organisms than any posed by chemical aging or mechanical damage.

The nun carefully unhooked each thin glass box, and moved it to an old wooden, table-topped lectern. Then, using an ancient ornate, brass-mounted magnifying glass she squinted at each one.

With her voice wavering and cracking, she slowly revealed the secrets of the ancient scribes to Maria as she translated the faded texts word-for-word into English. After finishing each one, she would laboriously return it to the locked room, reconnect it to its individual humidifier, and make a few entries onto a computer screen to re-sequence and circulate the treated air to the replaced glass box. She would then retrieve another, and begin the process all over again.

Over the week, the tale unwound beginning with a time before Genesis. The story included: Lucifer the Beautiful and his sin of vanity and attempt to displace God from His rightful throne; the Heavenly call to arms to battle the usurpers and how Archangels Michael and Gabriel led the nine orders of angels in a Great Battle in the Heavens; and, how Lucifer and his dark disciples suffered defeat and internal damnation to hell.

There were, however, added details including: After Creation, Lucifer was said to have lurked in the shadows and made a cunning challenge to God to test His people, to let earth be the arena to see if goodness would triumph over evil. And that God placed His faith in the order of a people who would be taught right from wrong, and then allowed to freely choose their destiny. She also related how the devious Lucifer had loosed an evil champion, a spawn of hell, in the person of Adramelech onto the earth and how this demon lived, died, and lived again and again. Through the ages, information on it had been gathered and archived and it became know as the *Hellspawn*. But then it faded from the Church's sight for hundreds of years. Though undocumented, there were rumors of it rising and being put into the Deathsleep with blessed stakes in its heart by an assortment of holy men through those years.

Its purpose, the elderly nun recounted, was to confound and confuse God's people. Also to tempt and terrify them. It was to wreak havoc and evil to the extent that humanity at large would finally ask why a loving, merciful and just God would allow these terrible scourges and deeds to flourish on earth; they would then be prepared to explore and possibly embrace an alternate.

Indeed, the *Hellspawn* periodically assumed man's form and sat at the side of many of mankind's monsters, leading to multiple genocides where millions of God's creatures died, including the ovens of Auschwitz, Treblinka and other death-camps where millions of His people were systematically murdered.

But as Maria had spent time with Sister Raphael, her confidence had grown to where she ceased to be a passive listener and began to probe for discrepancies, contradictions or illogical and unsupported conclusions. Not to be satisfied with high-profile and obvious evils, Maria reasoned that a demon with the power he was supposed to possess must have made more of a mark, if he existed. So, she pressed the old nun: "Sister, can you tell me more of his influence? Other than the terrible Holocaust, I mean?"

Sister Raphael nodded and didn't disappoint. From memory she obliged Maria, counting off on her fingers.

"We believe the demon or possibly some of his familiars had a hand in working with dozens of dictators and mass murderers in places such as: Turkey where 1.2 million Armenians died in 1915; East Timor where three-quarters of a million people vanished or were murdered from 1966 to 1998; the genocide in Rwanda in 1994 where another 800,000 died; and, North Korea where 1.6 million died in purges and concentration camps from 1948 to 1994. From 1975 to 1979, 1.7 million people were also systematically eradicated in Cambodia."

Maria stared at Sister Raphael now beginning to understand the significance of the hunt for Adramelech. "He was responsible for *all* that?"

"Indeed, we believe he had a hand in much of it," she said simply. "In each case there was always an 'adviser' or 'confidant' to the perpetrator of these horrors. However, in-depth and painstaking research was never able to find any history on them. They appeared out of nowhere, supported and influenced evil, and then disappeared without a trace." She wasn't finished.

"For instance, we can go back a little further to Stalin's purges from 1934 to 1939 when 13 million of his own people died," Sister Raphael said. "We believe Adramelech took on the persona of a Dimitri Kuznetsov – an adviser to Stalin – who whispered in his ear and caused the deaths of millions." Then she gave a tired and disheartened sigh and said: "But the Chinese win hands down for deaths in their Great Leap Forward of 1958 to 1961, and their Cultural Revolution from 1966 to 1969 which took more than 45 millions lives. Adramelech was also thought to have been instrumental in these cases when he assumed human form and worked with, or advised these mass murderers. Unfortunately we have no way of knowing for sure all of his deeds since we do not have a complete record of when he was in the Deathsleep and when he was active."

Finally, Sister Raphael presented Maria with photographs and copies of paintings and faded drawings depicting mankind's greatest killers including Kahn, Hitler, Stalin, Mao and others. In each rendering or photo, standing or sitting beside some of mankind's most voracious killers, was another individual, seemingly tall, dark haired and handsome. Whether in the 13th Century or the 20th Century, the man was the same. A consistent look of smug satisfaction creased his features as he seemed to stare at the camera or artist with a knowing leer. His face chilled Maria to the bone.

At last Sister Raphael settled back and removed her eyeglasses. "The problem is, Sister Maria, modernity has taken its toll on ancient or traditional beliefs that were once accepted as gospel." The old nun smiled at her own analogy. "Those in the Church today who know of the *Hellspawn's* existence choose to believe that it has been recalled to blackness, or that it never existed at all. Still, as we have trained exorcists in the wings for when they are needed, so too we have always maintained a brigade ready to battle the demon when it surfaces again. Hence, Cardinal Malachi's people."

Sister Raphael then asked Sister Maria if she'd heard of the Dead Sea Scrolls. Maria nodded that she did indeed know about them. In fact, she had written a paper on them during her college days. The nun asked her to detail what she knew about the scrolls.

Maria related how they had first been discovered in 1947 in a cave near the Dead Sea setting off a ten-year search for more ancient records which eventually yielded hundreds more scrolls and artifacts hidden in eleven caves. She moved on to explain the most popular scholastic theory of their origin: that the Essenes had somehow gathered and hidden the scrolls as they abandoned Qumran at the time of the Roman incursion in 68 CE, two years before the collapse of Jewish self government in Judea, and the destruction of the Temple in Jerusalem in 70 CE. Maria covered their history and a brief summation of what information most contained.

Sister Raphael folded her arms and nodded with a slight smile, impressed with Maria's knowledge. Then she spoke in an even more hushed tone. "As you obviously know, within the ancient Library of Qumran, there were three categories represented among the Dead Sea Scrolls: Biblical, Apocryphal (or pseudepigraphical), and finally Sectarian," she said. "The Sectarian scrolls related to pietistic commune and include ordinances, biblical commentaries, apocalyptic visions and liturgical works. But there was one scroll among these, which was secretly spirited away early in the discovery process and hidden from both civilian scholars and the general public by an archeologist who was also a Catholic priest. This scroll dealt exclusively with the *Hellspawn*. It revealed the genesis and a limited history of the Beast. However, buried deep in the text was one critical piece of information which it seems, had been overlooked. I quote: '...until the *Wood* touches this demon, earth will be forever plagued'."

"What wood?" Maria asked, already anticipating her answer.

"We now surmise it is the *Wood of the Cross*," Sister Raphael said. "But this is a recent deduction made purely by accident when a brilliant biblical scholar went looking for ways to help Cardinal Malachi and his people, and studied anew the writings of the secret scroll."

Maria couldn't help asking: "Oh? Who was that?"

"Me," the old nun said, with a gap-toothed grin. She then put away the last of a series of remnants of parchment scrolls. Next she pulled out a leather bound book with its cover intricately embossed and its perimeter pierced and ringed with leather lacing. Maria could make out Spanish writing on its cover but, having only taken one year of high school Spanish, couldn't decipher it.

From this, Sister Raphael read a report of a small South American village and how the village had been plagued by a creature of the night which killed and drained its victims of their blood. After killing a Catholic priest, the creature - betrayed by a frightened familiar - had been tracked down by Catholic monks, burned with holy water, and had a blessed stake driven through its heart. The monks had forwarded a report to Rome and it was duly entered into the secret records.

Next she put aside this manuscript and pulled out a modern file. Inside were newspaper clippings and computer printouts listing crimes of murder and mayhem in various cities and towns beginning in the December of 1989 in and around Panama. They were followed by more murders over the next decade and a half which seemed to spread around the world. These killings were selected because they all seemed bound by a common thread – bloodless corpses for which no perpetrator had ever been caught, tried or convicted.

The elderly nun extracted a faded, typed report from the file and read a brief tale of an American soldier who was thought to have seen the demon in the jungles of Central America, and survived its initial attack. Next, she held up to Maria a horrible tale of a deputy sheriff in Vermont who had been partially skinned alive, drained of his blood and left nailed to a cellar door in a town called Woodstrom. More work of the Beast, she mused. "The soldier from Panama, who lives in New York today, just happened to have been the Sheriff in Woodstrom, Vermont, when his deputy was murdered; we believe Adramelech was tracking him, the Sheriff I mean."

Sister Raphael closed the book and looked at the young novice for a long moment before saying simply: "There is no more that I have to share with you, Sister Maria. But, believe this, child, as you believe anything most holy: It lives again."

Without another word Sister Raphael blessed herself, got up and left the library, her stooped figured weighed down with the burden of uncompromised truth. An old priest instantly appeared and waited patiently until Maria also left. Then he locked the room tight. He watched the small, pretty nun slowly walking away down the corridor. He mused that she looked so tired, vulnerable and alone, almost like a child.

Maria met Brother Fagan for transportation to her hotel. The revelations she'd just heard lent more and more credence to the entire situation now causing her to become even more worried. What if she were unable to use this so-called "power" of hers to sense anything? What if she couldn't perform? Was she about to cause some cataclysmic event simply because she couldn't measure up to their expectations?

The young novice from a small Quebec town sighed and sank back on the limo's cushions. What had she wrought upon herself?

~ 14 ~

The ride back to the Holiday Inn that evening was relatively silent. Brother Fagan knew there was a lot on her mind and said little as he drove, leaving her with her thoughts. When she said good night, he merely smiled and nodded.

The next morning, Maria was summoned to Cardinal Malachi's office. Finally, she thought, she would see how the "other half" of the Church lived. She was prepared for great opulence when she entered the office, but not for what she saw.

As she entered, he stood up from behind an intricately carved and much battered mahogany desk, an African sandalwood letter opener in one hand, a telephone in the other. He continued his phone conversation but motioned her with the letter opener to a cracked, worn but comfortable, tufted leather wing chair in front of his desk. She took a brief moment to look around the office. On the walls hung evidence of Malachi's travels around the world.

There were photos of the cardinal standing beside a spear-carrying Zulu in Africa, shaking hands with a U.S. Navy officer on the deck of what appeared to be a U.S. Navy nuclear submarine, and having coffee with a tired-looking Pope John Paul II. Obviously, the latter was taken after the assassination attempt. She noticed other photos where he stood, a much younger man, beside Presidents Nixon and Carter. She gaped at the Carter picture because, with a huge grin, Cardinal Malachi was holding up a can of *Billy Beer* behind President Carter's head. Another more recent colored photo showed him visiting the Oval Office and sipping coffee with President Obama.

Maria also noticed an assortment of voodoo masks from Haiti, ritual masks from Africa and what she took to be a crossed pair of North American Indian peace pipes.

On the other walls were an eclectic mix of beaded Inuit sealskin moccasins, an assortment of swords, daggers, rifles, pistols and other weapons from various countries, and a worn-looking tiger skin. Nearby, movie posters for classic movies such as *Casablanca, Niagara* and *Citizen Kane* hung next to nautical-looking memorabilia. Cracked and broken pottery, faux Egyptian statuettes, and hundreds of ancient, very dusty leather books completed the décor, effectively lining the other two walls on shelves bowed from the weight of the volumes. His office, thought Maria, looked like a set from an Indiana Jones' movie rather than that of a Prince of the Catholic Church. She jumped as Malachi abruptly dropped the phone on its cradle, and loudly cleared his throat.

He poured coffee from a carafe into a set of heavy mugs, passed one to her without asking if she took cream or sugar, and without even a greeting, essentially picked up where Sister Raphael had left off; he lost no time in cutting to the chase. "Do you believe what Sister Raphael told you? Do you understand the significance?"

"Yes sir," she said, meekly.

The cardinal nodded slowly, weighing her answer, and then dropped a newspaper clipping on the desk in front of Maria. It was from the Gotham Gazette, one of almost a dozen New York newspapers he had scattered about his desk. "Here's one Sister Raphael doesn't have yet," he said.

Maria picked up the clipping. The headline read: **Monster Seen in Bronx**.

"We believe it is Adramelech," Malachi continued. "It's almost as though he's daring…nay, *helping* us to find him."

She watched him turn and approach a window overlooking other Vatican buildings. The cardinal clasped his hands behind his back and spoke as he stared down to the street below.

"Unfortunately Maria, we live in the 21st Century, a time when technology has become the new religion and the ever-faster central processor a substitute for a Supreme Being. And, believe it or not, there are many members of the Church that have signed on to this way of thinking.

"Last week, I mentioned an administration problem that prevented us from going to war with the Beast? Like most things in this world, it all boils down to money…or the lack thereof. For years, our budget used to hunt this thing down has been blindly approved without any need for justification nor financial reporting. However, new technology, some sort of Enterprise Resource Planning system, has highlighted what many see as a miscellaneous item of no value; therefore, the system eliminated our budget for the *Hellspawn* project. Essentially, it grounds us."

"The resources have just been…taken away?" she ventured, hesitantly.

"Exactly. For decades we have, presumably, been operating under the radar. Now, it seems, we have to call attention to our operation and justify our expense." He laughed shortly, without humor. "Can you imagine standing up in front of a budgetary committee of these jokers and saying you need money to hunt down some goblins and ghosts, in particular a demon that would make Buffy's hair curl all by itself? It doesn't wash very well. No…the only way I'm going to get the budget back, is to see the Big Man himself and get him to sign an Executive Order of Reinstatement."

"The Big Man…?" she asked.

"His Holiness." He spun about in frustration. "For more than ten long years, we've been waiting for this demon to show itself again so we could get another crack at it. And now, we're not ready."

"Must it be now?"

"Yes." His tone was uncharacteristically harsh, clipped. "*Now* is when we have an extraordinary opportunity. We have discerned and validated one of the creature's patterns. Apparently whenever a mortal escapes its intentions, it always finds that person and kills him or her. And, it never gives up. We believe we have such a man being hunted by the Beast right now. It tried to kill him in Panama and failed for some reason. Then it showed near a VA hospital where our man was convalescing and took out a priest who had been ministering to him. Finally it went for him in Vermont and failed again. It's as though this man has the most extraordinary luck, or someone or something is protecting him. Anyhow, we are hoping for a fourth try. As I explained before, we've been keeping him under surveillance using the *Watchmen* – Catholic priests providing 24-hour monitoring – while waiting for this demon to show. Also, we have had nearby a group of highly trained and deadly efficient Jesuit priests code-named the *Crusaders*." Normally they would be ready to move in at the first sign of its presence and attempt to kill it.

"Unfortunately when you can't pay your bills, you can't keep everyone in the field. We've scaled back operations and recalled the *Crusaders*. The Church is no longer in a position to act quickly." He gave a rueful shake of his head. "So, to save the intended victim we have a temporary strategy. We'll extract him at the first sign of danger." He gestured towards the newspaper. "And, since the demon's quarry lives in New York and some sort of monstrosity has been sighted in the Bronx, we believe he's nearby, getting ready to strike."

"Then why not just get him away now?" Maria asked.

"We need to keep Adramelech engaged, to dangle the bait, as it were," Malachi said. "We must keep him from going to ground again as he has done so often. We're walking a tightrope, trying to keep him engaged until we're ready for the fight."

"Does this man, your 'bait'," she said it with distaste, "know this thing is after him?"

"No, he doesn't," Malachi admitted, looking her in the eye. "Nor will he."

"This is the soldier I read about?" she asked, "the one whose deputy and wife were killed?"

"Unfortunately...yes."

"How awful," Maria said, feeling sympathy for a man she'd never met.

"Indeed, it is awful. But we've had *Crusaders* murdered by the demon as well. One in Vermont while keeping an eye on Sheriff Montague after the tragedies. Suddenly Mr. Montague packed up and disappeared to Chicago and then New York City where we lost him. We initiated one of the biggest ecclesiastical dragnets in the history of the Church using a cover story about him being a perfect bone marrow match for a sick cardinal as a cover. Luckily one of our priests spotted him in New York. Based on our standing orders, he befriended and sheltered him until we decided what to do. The solution we came up with was to provide some anchors so he didn't bolt into the woodwork again. We helped him re-enter society."

"So you could continue to use him as bait," Maria said, her disquiet not as well hidden as she might have liked.

Malachi shrugged. "Precisely. You must understand, Maria. Mr. Montague is of extreme importance to us. The entire world is the demon's playground. We never know when or where he will strike. He may show up at the elbow of a major world tyrant, or simply murder single victims in some far-away local. This man, however, Clay Montague, gives us an unprecedented opportunity to make the demon come to us!" "

"Please forgive me, Your Eminence ...but isn't that–?"

"Unethical?" the cardinal asked. "Perhaps. But look at it this way, Maria. Clay Montague may be devil's bait, but the rest of the world is the devil's prey."

* * * *

PART THREE

"IN HARM'S WAY"

I love little pussy, her coat is so warm;
And if I don't hurt her, she'll do me no
Harm…

Jane Taylor
I LOVE LITTLE PUSSY

~ 1 ~

NEW YORK CITY
THE PRESENT

Were they still there?

Clay Montague stood back from his second storey office window on a small side street just off West 42nd Street and carefully began edging aside one of the drapes to peer down at the damp pavement below. Both the street and the night seemed unnaturally quiet. Where were the people?

The ingrained dust covering of the heavy curtain material felt gritty under his fingertips. The drapes, a garish red-velvet legacy from the previous tenant now serving time up the river in Ossining, had probably never been cleaned.

Clay had sublet the office from Attorney Abraham Cohen for three years, the exact length of his prison sentence. When he had expressed surprise that Cohen expected to return to law practice afterwards, the lawyer just winked and asserted that you could do anything – if you knew the right people. Perhaps he wouldn't practice officially, but he'd practice just the same.

Directly across from his office window, the Duffy's Bar & Grill street sign winked monotonously on and off, its red neon light periodically sending a warm glow flooding across the night and into the darkened office. Clay had deliberately refrained from turning on the office lights after arriving moments before so his silhouette couldn't be seen from the street.

He peered out. The street reflected the light of a single dull street lamp after the evening's September rain. A low rumble of thunder sounded from afar, penetrating the building. It was followed within seconds by a distant flash of lightning that lit up the narrow, brick-faced urban street.

They were out there again!

As usual, the *Driver* sat in a black Saab parked in the same spot near the street corner just far enough back to be out of the pool of weak, yellow light cast by the street lamp.

The other one, the *Leader* as Clay named him because he was larger and seemed in control, leaned back against the car's fender, arms folded, hat pulled low. Occasionally he stared up towards Clay's window.

These men dressed in black, or *"Watchers"* as he labeled them in his daily journal, had been following him for close to six weeks now, since just after the Lassiter divorce case. At least that was when he first noticed them. Whether the case and the current surveillance were connected, he didn't know. Still, the timing gave him a chronological reference point from which to work as he tried to find out whom they were and what they wanted.

Keeping the curtain open a few inches, he stared at the men below while reaching over and picking up a flask of bourbon from his desk. Absentmindedly he played with the paper seal on the bottle. He didn't dare break it; a single drink could spell disaster.

Having it within reach, within easy access, gave him the comfort of knowing that he had control of the alcoholism; the bottle was tangible proof he had the strength not to take another drink. He refused to think that he kept it nearby...just in case.

Clay peered out again through the office window with large gold letters stenciled on it advertising his service: *Montague Detective Agency – Discreet Private Investigations*. Below, the *Watchers* hadn't stirred from their positions. Whoever they were and whatever they wanted, they were sure taking their own sweet time about bringing him into the picture.

As he eyed them, the man outside the car shifted his weight on the fender, retrieved something from his pocket and settled back once again. A match flared orange in front of his face and then disappeared leaving a small spark at the end of his cigarette.

A flicker of movement inside the automobile diverted Clay's attention towards the dark interior. Certain that he caught a hint of movement on the passenger side, he looked closer. Was that another person in the front seat of the car beside the driver? More movement. Yes, the driver appeared to be talking to someone next to him. This was a new angle – three *Watchers*!

Suddenly the man on the fender turned and looked over the hood of the Saab as the passenger door opened. A black-cloaked figure exited the automobile and came round and stood before him.

Clay watched, fascinated. The cloak looked like something out of *The French Lieutenant's Woman*, he mused. But there was something different about the third figure, something in its motion, something too fluid and easy in the way it walked. Maybe, glided would have been a more appropriate phrase.

Clay was sure it was a woman. Though her features were hidden by the heavy hood, the easy, graceful sway of her movements and her petite size betrayed her gender.

She reached the *Leader* and the two engaged in conversation. After a minute or so, the *Driver* got out and joined them. There was a sense of urgency in the gestures of the trio. They seemed upset over something. Abruptly the woman pushed back her hood to reveal a pixie like countenance.

Clay continued to watch, fascinated by the silent drama being played out below. This was certainly out of the ordinary; they usually seemed so in control, in fact, arrogantly so. He found himself experiencing a vicarious pleasure in this break in routine; the argument was primarily between the *Leader* and the woman. The tall man shook his head vigorously. She nodded back, equally firm. She appeared to be standing her ground as the *Leader* threw up his hands, turned away for a few moments and stared down the street. The *Driver* shrugged.

Tired of the silent charade, Clay let the curtain fall back into place. He had tried to confront the *Watchers* more than a dozen times since they began following him. He'd been unsuccessful on every occasion; they were just too good at their craft.

For instance, if he headed for the elevator right now, he was sure they'd be in the car and pulling away by the time he reached them. If he leaned out the window and called to them, they'd ignore him as though he didn't exist. But, if he jumped in his car and drove away, the black Saab would settle in behind him, a few car lengths back. And though he was pretty good at shaking tails, he had been unable to shake them. At last count he had more than 35 photographs of them now but not a single, identifiable facial image.

Gently he shook the warm flask, listening to the wash of the liquor slide back and forth, while idly wondering how they'd react if he just leaned out the window and took a shot at them. Perhaps a single slug in a front tire would have them question the wisdom of continuing to annoy him? But then the NYPD would get all upset.

He allowed himself the fantasy for a few more seconds but finally sighed and put the bottle back on the desk. His mouth was getting too dry.

The worst case he could come up with was that he was again a suspect in Hitch's murder – that, after all these years, the FBI was tailing him and hoping he's inadvertently provide some further clue to Hitch's death.

Eventually he also discarded that notion; even the FBI was never quite as polished in their pursuits as these people seemed to be. Besides, when you tailed someone, the general idea was to do it surreptitiously, to covertly gather the evidence to hang them with later. These people obviously didn't care whether he saw them or not, as long as there was no contact to determine who they were.

He also wondered if they were following the wrong guy. If so, the joke was on them. He went over everything he knew about the *Watchers* in his mind.

They always worked as a team of two – at least until tonight – and drove a Saab. But not necessarily the same Saab. At least, the autos had different license plates.

Though they could, at times be short, tall, fat or skinny, their dress never varied either: black suits, black broad-brimmed felt slouch hats that covered their faces, and long topcoats. And, there was another, somewhat ominous fact he'd been able to ferret out; the *Watchers* had some powerful government connections. He'd asked a friend at the Department of Motor Vehicle Registration to run their plates to determine ownership; she'd called back, highly excited. There was nothing in the registry on these plates. But they weren't fake, just listed as un-issued! Who had access to un-issued plates?

Obviously someone very influential had taken an interest in him. *But why him?*

Curiously though, after all these weeks he never felt threatened in any way. So far they had proved benign. Not that he could bank on their behavior remaining benign, but for now they weren't threatening anything other than his privacy.

Clay looked back out at the three figures in the street. They were still engaged in deep conversation. He'd thought about calling the police several times, but was relatively certain they'd be gone by the time the cops arrived. Also, with his PI license up for its renewal, he didn't need some over-worked, pissed-off member of New York's finest turning in a report to the Department of State, Licensing Division, saying that he was seeing bogeymen.

Clay stepped back from the window, lit a Pall Mall and blew the smoke into the middle of the room. Though he rarely smoked any more, the tenaciousness of his shadows was making him increasingly edgy. The red neon light sliced through the crack in the curtains, and captured the smoke for a brief instant. He allowed his thoughts to whirl and spin with the crimson smoke curls as they expanded and swept into the center of the room, formed brief alliances, broke apart into separate clouds and eventually dissipated. Though the years had passed, he missed his Jody just as much as ever. The result in the romance department was he'd been on a few blind dates set up by friends but they all soured. He couldn't seem to maintain a relationship. The loss of Jody and Hitch and the suspicions and accusations had changed him forever. He likened himself to a living tree hollowed out by rot. Outside the tree looked perfectly normal while inside it was essentially a vacuum. Of course he could still be amused and annoyed but it seemed life had taken a rasp to all the sharp edges of his feelings and filed them away leaving him without passion. Or perhaps his emotions had been dulled as a form of protection. Whatever, it wasn't fair to the ladies he dated so he stopped. And he stayed alone. A self-imposed exile insulated himself and others from being hurt.

He drew on the cigarette again, absentmindedly watching the end flare bright red and then fade to a dull glow as he took it from his lips and inhaled deeply. The calming effect of the nicotine soothed his frayed nerves, providing solace for his imagination.

He peeked out the curtain again. What in the hell were they up to? Maybe he could see more if he used his binoculars. He butted out. That's your last cigarette, he promised himself…again.

~ 2 ~

The feeling of dread became too strong for Sister Maria Michelle Lapierre and she jumped out of the Saab and came round to the figure leaning against the fender.

"We must act now," Maria said to Father Dermott Murphy. "Cardinal Malachi said we can't allow anything to happen to this man." She dropped her hood.

Murphy, a stocky man of about 45-years of age, had the build of a weight-lifter. A bullet-shaped head with close-cropped, black hair liberally salted with grey topped powerful shoulders and a barrel-like chest was visible even through his coat; there was no doubt that, physically, he was a man to be reckoned with. His twinkling blue eyes, however, offset his intimidating appearance, and when he smiled and spoke in his soft Irish lilt, he quickly charmed those he met. Tonight, however, he wasn't being charming. Father Ronald Langevin watched Murphy and Maria argue.

Murphy dropped his cigarette and it sizzled on the wet pavement as he coolly appraised the young Quebec woman. Mother Mary, he thought, she's too pretty to be a nun. He ground the butt under his heel as he took in her flawless, slightly tanned complexion, her petite heart-shaped face, generous dark eyebrows and bobbed nose over full red lips that didn't need any lipstick to make them attractive; she was blessed with a perfect countenance.

Murphy grimaced and reached under the collar of his black topcoat. He squeezed a finger between his perspiring neck and the Roman collar that seemed to have a choke-hold on his Adam's apple. He made a mental note to stop trying to squeeze into an adjustment that fit him when he was twenty. "Everything is fine," he declared. "He's in the office, quite safe."

Maria wasn't listening. Again she was feeling the chill of something black and ominous approaching. They didn't have much time. She stared at him. "Father, something is going to happen."

"We can't jump the gun every time you have a bad feeling, Sister," the tall priest said.

Maria looked up towards the darkened window where Clay Montague kept his office. Though the streetlight was dim, she was certain she saw the curtain moving. She turned back and stared desperately up at Murphy.

A boiling cloud of oppression and evil was growing exponentially in her mind; no images so far but still a frighteningly real dimension of the imminent arrival of some form of terror. She had never felt anything like this in her life before.

The driver of the Saab, Father Langevin, got out of the automobile and came round to join them. He was shorter, stockier and friendlier than Murphy. He had been the one who settled her in St. Pat's rectory in New York and done the briefing.

The blackness was growing near.

"It's coming...I feel it!" Maria said to Langevin.

Father Langevin reacted: "We must get him out of there!"

"Father Murphy is SUPPOSED to be in charge?" Maria answered, throwing up her hands and daring him to act; perhaps she could shame him into action.

Father Murphy looked at her. "How can you be sure this creature is near?" It was a direct challenge.

"Father, I know you don't believe that I have this *ability*, but you must realize that Cardinal Malachi would not have sent me here on a whim. Listen to me! Please!"

Murphy shivered and wished for a hot toddy to warm the chill invading his bones. It had begun to drizzle again. If this kept up, he was bound to catch another cold and wind up hawking into a handkerchief for weeks on end. Couldn't the Vatican come up with a healthier way to use the Jesuits than sending them after demons that might exist only in the minds of some senile old cardinals breathing the rarefied air of the Vatican? After all, they might be chasing some homicidal maniac as opposed to something supernatural, despite the horrific murders. "As you noted, Sister, I am in charge here," he said, finally.

Sister Maria sighed and said a quick Hail Mary to avoid making a retort. She looked over at Langevin who shrugged and turned the palms of his hands face up in a gesture of futility.

"Dermott," Langevin ventured, timidly. "Maybe we should listen."

"My God, man, not you too," he replied.

Maria's eyes flashed and she stamped her foot in anger, realizing at the same time how little girlish was her gesture. "Listen to me, both of you! I'm not here because I asked to come. Now Father Murphy, if you'd just stop worrying about catching cold and realize that we have a job to do, maybe we could get on with it!?"

Murphy stared at her. "What did you say, lass?"

"I said we could get on with our job before it's too late!"

"No, the bit about me catching cold...why did you say that?"

Maria shrugged angrily. "I don't know...that's what you're worried about, isn't it...and we're all about to catch a lot more than a cold unless we do something *now*!"

With her comment, Murphy began to wonder if there was more to this nun than he had supposed. However, he was under orders not to move prematurely. They must keep the Beast engaged.

He looked up at the detective's window. What must the man think, he wondered? Did he know he was the worm on a hook? That the Church was spying on him? Or that the Church's benevolence towards him wasn't merely Christian charity? Murphy remembered the deputy's funeral in Vermont. That particular debacle had cost two good men and Montague's wife their lives.

At the behest of Rome, Montague had been under a reduced form of surveillance by the local parish priest of Woodstrom as he had been for years. But when the deputy had been murdered in such a hideous fashion, Murphy felt the priest must have banged some holy gong since the Vatican sprung into action and ordered the *Crusaders* and him and Langevin on site immediately.

The *Crusaders*, posing as skiers and antique hunters, all tough as nails and skilled in the most deadly martial arts, the ritual of exorcism and deadly weaponry, had descended on Woodstrom determined to put an end to Adramelech and his work. Shadowing Montague, they awaited the creature's return with orders to find and kill it at any cost. Father's Murphy and Langevin were there in Vermont for additional support.

But then, other than a brief appearance by Adramelech's familiar at the deputy's funeral, nothing happened for almost six months. When Montague's wife had been killed, they were sure Adramelech had caused her death in a fit of vengeance against the sheriff. The same evening, Father Lesage – one of the *Crusaders* – had also been found dead in his room.

It hadn't been an easy death; they spent four hours cleaning up the blood before they could secretly transport the priest's remains back to their aircraft in Burlington. After that, the Beast vanished again.

Scratch one priest, one deputy and an innocent woman.

After the Woodstrom affair, Montague eventually resigned and virtually disappeared, setting off an unprecedented hunt by the Vatican. The orders had been: find the ex-sheriff. His description and photo were secretly sent to every parish and church organization in the Eastern United States, with a cover story and a request to keep the matter confidential.

The search had culminated when a priest, working out of the Opus Dei headquarters in New York, had accidentally found Montague. With the Church's help, he put some sort of life back together.

Unknown to him, of course, the awesome influence, and political, and monetary forces of the Roman Catholic Church had been there under the surface, quietly opening doors and smoothing his path to re-enter society. Murphy had enjoyed his assignment of being Montague's secret guardian angel; in particular putting that officious little bastard of a Loan's Officer at the First National

Financial in his place with a threat to the bank's president to withdraw many tens of millions of Church money if the bank didn't comply with their wishes. That and a secret guarantor signature secured Montague his credit.

Scanning world news and discovering multiple murders in New York two months ago, Rome had decided to step up the surveillance of the detective on the suspicion that Adramelech was at work again. But with the *Crusaders* recalled due to monetary concerns, the current plan was to remove Montague if he proved to be in harm's way.

Now, they'd been sent this nun with some hocus pocus ability to sense evil and tell them when this creature was nearby. Inwardly, Murphy wondered how *that* idea had been sold.

He looked again at Maria who was standing rigid on the sidewalk a few feet away. Oh no, he thought, don't tell me she's going into a trance, or having some kind of fit.

Maria was staring at something down the street in front of their automobile.

Murphy followed her gaze and groaned aloud: "For God's sake, it's just a child, Sister." He began to move forward towards the small, barefooted waif. The child was purposely walking up the damp sidewalk towards them.

"Don't move!" Something in Maria's tone conveyed both a sense of fear and menace raising the hairs on the back of Father Murphy's neck.

"What's the matter," he asked, disturbed by the intensity of Maria's look as she stared towards the child. He turned towards her in annoyance.

Slowly the young novice reached beneath her cloak, drew out an eight-inch, silver Crucifix and extended it towards the small figure.

"Sister Maria, cut it out –!" Murphy's sentence was interrupted by a thin scream and a vicious hiss reverberating off the brownstone and brick walls of the surrounding buildings. He spun around and looked back in shock at the little girl.

She stood about twenty feet away, legs wide apart, eye sockets glowing with a fire-red incandescent as though someone had just lit a torch in the middle of her skull. The problem was that *now* she was standing three feet up in the air…on nothing. Her mouth was open and drooling, exposing long, needle-sharp teeth. As he watched in disbelief, the little girl suddenly descended back to the street, clamped her upper teeth over her bottom lip and shredded it by scissoring the fangs back and forth. The flesh parted and blood spurted from her mouth a good three feet out onto the sidewalk and then poured down her chin.

The child grinned at them, a bloody-toothed, mirthless smile.

"Holy shit!" Father Murphy exclaimed in a momentary lapse of priestly decorum as he stared, sickened by the sight.

If Maria had not been so terrified she would have laughed at his abrupt turnaround.

The child had stopped walking now and just stood on the sidewalk, transfixed by the sight of the Crucifix, savagely whining and snarling like a whipped cur.

"Get Mr. Montague," Maria whispered quietly without moving, holding the cross as far forward as possible as the sound of the snarling increased in savagery.

"But Sister –!" Langevin protested, glancing fearfully at the child.

She cut him short. "Do as I say!"

The two priests' didn't hesitate. They raced to the opposite side of the street and along it towards Montague's building, keeping a wary eye on the child as they drew parallel with her. She didn't seem to notice as she stared in fascination at Maria's Crucifix. The clatter of their footsteps died away as they entered the building leaving Maria on the sidewalk, alone and frightened.

Still smiling her bloody smile, the child backed up a few feet and danced sideways into an alley. The moment she was out of sight, Maria's fears intensified. She didn't know this child-thing's capabilities. She continued holding the cross up pointing towards the alley. She waited a few minutes, and then a sixth sense made her turn around and look behind the Saab.

The small bloody-mouthed figure was coming at her from behind. It sported a wicked grin, was less than fifty feet away and was skipping closer by the second.

~ 3 ~

Clay found the Tasco binoculars in the third drawer of his filing cabinet jammed between papers in a file folder under V for Vision. He extracted the heavy glasses, breathed on each eyepiece and then used his tie to scrub off a thick layer of dust covering the outer lens.

Wandering back to the window, he shook out the plastic strap, put it around his neck and pulled open the curtains a crack and then thought: What the hell! He yanked them wide.

The tavern sign blinked on and off filling the window and office with its scarlet brilliance. Clay shielded his eyes against the glare and stared down at the black Saab.

Now the lone figure of the woman stood beside it staring down the street and holding something before her like a shield. Clay noted it was raining again as he tried to find the object of her attention. There was no sign of any person or automobile; the street was virtually deserted.

He looked back at the woman and was surprised to suddenly see a small figure appear and begin approaching her from behind. The woman spun about to face the figure. Still grasping something in her hand, she suddenly thrust it out in front of her, like a warning.

Puzzled, Clay shaded his eyes from the neon light. He'd just begun to raise the binoculars when he felt a jolt race through his entire system. The figure on the street facing the woman was a small child, a girl! And there was something disturbingly familiar about her.

Clay pressed closer to the window and stared at the tiny waif-like figure below. His mind raced: could this be the one who attacked him years ago, just minutes before he found his murdered deputy?

Judging from her height, she seemed to be about eight years old. And, like the girl back at the Baker house in Vermont, and on the hill at Hitch's funeral, her hair was a sodden, tangled mess and she was clothed in a dirty, tattered dress.

He narrowed his eyes, squinting to make out her features.
WAS IT POSSIBLE?

He dismissed the idea. It was impossible. The child he'd encountered would have been a teenager by now. The little girl below was nowhere near that age. He told himself that his imagination was working overtime. After all, what were the chances he'd encounter her hundreds of miles away, in a city of 18 million people?

Still he couldn't shake a nagging and urgent suspicion that she was the one. He continued to stare down at the child who stood unmoving in the rain, rooted to the street. She faced the cloaked woman who was also frozen in a curious posture of confrontation, her hand held high in the air.

What the hell was going on? He raised the field glasses to his eyes. The woman was holding a Crucifix aloft. His heart racing, his breath quickening, he focused them on the child. "Damnit to hell!" His oath was loud and bitter as her pale, milk-white face leaped into view. It was her! There was no doubt! She was standing calmly in the street a mere stone's throw away!

Her mouth yawned open, bloody froth dribbled from her teeth and her eyes gleamed wickedly, as they had so many times in his nightmares. She still wore that same expression of quiet, cunning detachment as she stared at the woman in the cloak.

Then, as he watched her through the binoculars, the child slowly shifted her gaze from the woman up towards where Clay stood in his window. Somehow she knew he was watching her. She stared straight up into his lenses.

Ever so slowly, a grin of recognition spread across her face. Her glowing eyes met his. As he watched, they lost their pupils and became milk-white orbs that bulged outward and expanded, becoming larger and larger until they completely filled the lenses of the binoculars; great luminous discs awakening his hidden fears and his darkest thoughts as they probed the faraway corners of his mind. He could feel her trying to seize control.

A wave of nausea washed over him as a malevolent force poked and pried at his mind. He shuddered and tore the binoculars from his eyes. Outwardly trembling, sweat running freely down under his collar, he knew without doubt: it was her!

A sudden wave of anger cowed the fear he was feeling and he silently vowed that she wouldn't get away this time.

Clay dropped the binoculars onto his chest and spun around to get his revolver from his desk drawer. A new thought brought him up short and he whirled back to the window.

The street was still empty except for the woman and the child. Where were the others – the other two men!? He leaned his face flat against the window pane and looked up and down the street. No-one in sight.

Where the hell were they?

Below he saw the child shift from foot to foot as though her feet were cold. The woman still stood silently before her, a cowled guardian keeping her at bay with the Crucifix. Did this woman, now tied into this bizarre nightmare, not realize she was in mortal danger! He watched as the child moved a few inches forward; the woman retreated a step, thrusting her hand out farther. The child moved forward again.

Again the woman retreated.

Somehow he had to warn her. To get her away from this hellion.

"Damn it to hell," he groaned aloud, grabbing the window frame and trying to force the window up. Locked.

He reached up and tried to twist the lock open; multiple coats of paint over the years had invaded the window tracks and completed an effective seal holding the window solidly in place. It was no use. He would have to break it!

He spun back towards his desk to get something heavy to drive through the glass and stopped dead.

Shadows flitted across the window in his office door. There was someone or *something*…outside!

~ 4 ~

Father Murphy and Father Langevin slammed through the front door of the detective's building, their wet shoes skidding on the polished granite floor; they barely remained standing as they clambered inside. Their hard sole shoes beat double staccatos as they ran forward.

"I never would have believed it," Murphy said.

"What…kind…of creature can stand…in midair?" Langevin panted as they crossed the foyer, still slipping and sliding. They headed for the elevator.

"Did you ever see the old *Exorcist* movie?"

"No."

"Well skip it…I think we just got a taste of the real thing." Murphy stabbed the elevator button repeatedly. It refused to light up. "They must turn the damn thing off in the evening."

They ran for the stairwell, pushed open the door and began running up concrete flights of stairs. The frantic pounding of their dress shoes echoed up and down the stairwell chimney like a nail gun on full auto.

"What do we do when we get up there?" Langevin yelled to Murphy who, by now, was a full flight of stairs ahead of him. He found himself gasping desperately for breath.

"Use the pistols...if necessary," Murphy shouted back, also out of breath from the exertion.

Langevin looked up to see him banishing his heavy .50 caliber smooth bore pistol. The breach-loading triple barrel weapon had been custom made for the job. As he took the stairs two at a time, he dug his own pistol out of his topcoat pocket.

They continued upward for another few seconds until Murphy let out a yell of triumph. Langevin grabbed the pipe style railing and pulled himself up the final flight to the landing where the older priest was preparing to open a door with a large orange number 3 painted on it.

"Mon Dieu...!" Langevin gasped, the air rasping painfully down his windpipe. "One minute...let me catch my breath!"

"Get ready," Murphy said, his adrenaline level at an all-time high.

He readied his pistol, yanked open the door, stuck his head through and then disappeared. Langevin swallowed an acid-like bile rising into the back of his throat. He followed him.

They were in an office corridor lit only by a single fluorescent light at each end; an energy-conscious building management was obviously doing its best to help save power. The corridor itself was silent except for the faint buzz of the fluorescents.

Holding their pistols at the ready, the two priests moved quickly and quietly down the carpeted corridor towards Montague's office. They arrived at the mahogany door half-filled with a frosted, ripple glass window on which the detective agency's name was stenciled in Times New Roman-style gold letters.

"Try knocking on the door," Langevin whispered.

"And say what? We're here to save you from the devil?" Murphy shook his head. "Dollars to doughnuts he's armed and pissed off after all he's been through. He'd welcome a chance to take a shot at us."

"What if he's not in there any longer?"

"The elevator is out of commission, and we didn't pass him on the stairs. He's got to be in there. When I pull open the door, you cover him...then we talk…fast!"

"Right."

"Ready?"

Langevin licked suddenly dry lips. "Go ahead!"

Murphy reached for the door, grasped the brass knob and tried to turn it. It was locked.

~ 5 ~

Clay barely had time to glimpse the shadow of a figure in a broad-brimmed hat outlined in the office door window before he heard the door knob creak.

"Cripes!" he muttered, dropping the binoculars and diving for his desk to get at his Ruger. He yanked open the drawer and grabbed the butt of the snub-nosed .45 revolver.

Everything happened extraordinarily fast.

Outside, Murphy cursed, and he and Langevin immediately drew back their heavy pistols and slashed at the frosted pane in the door.

It shattered inwards and great shards and plates of glass collapsed onto the office floor exploding into hundreds of pieces as the two priests leaned through the window frame with their weapons leveled.

"Hold it!" Murphy shouted, even as Clay, bent half-way over and pulled his revolver out of a desk drawer. "Stop!"

Clay glimpsed the two *Watchers* with weapons pointed at him but he'd gone too far to give up now. He dropped to a half-crouching position, snapped up the weapon and squeezed off two quick shots towards his assailants.

"He's got a gun--!" Langevin yelled needlessly as the Ruger's muzzle flash illuminated the room and the deafening roars and tongues of fire spit towards them.

The crash of the shots filled the room with slugs tearing into a corner of the mahogany door frame an inch from Murphy's head. They blew shards of wood splinters into his temple near his left eye before slamming on through the wall on the opposite side of the corridor to lose themselves in another office.

"Shoot!" Murphy cried desperately, already squeezing the trigger of his weapon.

Langevin began firing, the soft muffled plops of his shots an impotent-sounding response to Clay's third and fourth cannon-like reports.

By the time the detective began to squeeze off another shot, he had been hit twice in the chest and his firing reflected it with a bullet crashing into the far wall. The blows stunned him and though he was vaguely aware of pains in his chest, it was only for an instant.

He squeezed the trigger again even as he felt further stabs of pain in his stomach, and shoulder. His final shot went wild, hitting the chain holding a large lamp suspended over his desk. It immediately dropped and exploded onto the desk's surface in a burst of metal and glass pieces.

Slowly, ever so slowly, Clay's sight began fading. He tried to fight the weakness, to make himself stand and fire again, but his head whirled. He groaned and pitched forward onto the top of his desk. The Ruger clattered to the floor as he became totally limp, rolled off the desk and landed with a crash face-up. His chest, stomach and shoulder were bleeding through his shirt.

At the door, the two priests looked at one another.

"Are you okay, Dermott?" Langevin asked.

"Yes, quick, get inside!" Murphy said, as he wiped away the blood and tears flooding his left eye. He kept his gun trained on the man on the floor.

Langevin reached through the broken window for the door lock. "Your eye...?"

"Just a few splinters...."

Langevin reached inside, twisted the lock and they entered the room. Pieces of glass crunched underfoot as they advanced cautiously. The stench of gunpowder hung heavy in the air.

"Do you think we killed him?" Langevin asked fearfully. They approached Clay cautiously. The detective lay unmoving on his back, his eyes half-open, staring at the ceiling.

"Keep him covered," Murphy warned, kicking the Ruger away from Clay's hand. He bent down and quickly felt for a pulse in the neck.

Clay groaned softly.

Dear Lord let him be alright, Murphy prayed as he looked at six bleeding wounds in the man's chest and torso. They had hit him six out of six shots despite the confusion and danger. He was relieved to find a pulse but it was alarmingly weak. Murphy spotted one of the six silver cylinders with plastic feathers on the floor. "We have to get the others out of him right now! Too many hits. This stuff can kill him."

Murphy searched Montague's desk until he found a letter opener in the form of a medieval dagger. Langevin flipped up the detective's tie, ripped open his shirt and Murphy began probing the wounds with his make-shift instrument.

The dim light made it almost impossible to find the small, narcotic-laced darts in his chest.

"Hurry!" Langevin urged.

"Can't see," Murphy said, yanking a small penlight from his pocket. He flicked it on, grasped it in his teeth, bent closer and squinted at the small bleeding holes. "Got one!" He happily extracted a vial-like dart with a plastic feather, dropped it in his coat pocket and went after another. He grunted in satisfaction again and pocketed his prize as Langevin used his fingers to grab some protruding feathers and yanked out two more vial darts in rapid succession. "One more left…where is it?"

Langevin scooped up the errant dart lying on the floor, and pocketed Clay's pistol as well. "Dear God…what about Sister Maria!" he asked, suddenly remembering the young woman they had left at the mercy of the child thing.

"Forget her!" came the harsh reply. "Either she's okay or we're too late; in either case this man is our priority."

"Is this all?" Langevin said.

"There's one more deep in his chest," Murphy answered. "The doc will have to get it." He reached down to lift Clay. "Damn, they said to shoot him only two or three times at most. The narcotic is fast acting but dangerous in quantity."

"What have we done?" Langevin asked regretfully, shaking his head.

"What needed to be done," Murphy said feeling for a pulse in Clay's neck again. "It's getting weaker!" The detective's body was also beginning to trembling violently.

"His breathing is barely there," Langevin said. "They said the drug was relatively safe but too many hits could send him into anaphylactic shock."

Without a word, the worried looking Murphy reached into his pocket, extracted a covered syringe containing Narcan, a narcotic antagonist, and removed the plastic cover. He nodded to Langevin who pushed Clay's sleeve up and encircled his wrist with his fingers and squeezed; a vein bulged in the back of Clay's hand. "C'mon, c'mon," Murphy said through clenched teeth. Finally the priest felt confident enough to slowly introduce the needle into the pumped up vein in the detective's hand. As he'd been taught, he pulled back the plunger until blood entered the syringe's cylinder, and then quickly depressed it sending the contents into Clay's bloodstream.

"When we get him to the car, get on the cellular and alert the plane," Murphy said, slapping the cover back on the needle and pocketing it. "Tell them what happened; make sure Sick Bay is ready." He paused for a few seconds and then added: "And then pray like hell we're not too late!"

~ 6 ~

Sister Maria leaped backwards, stepping on the hem of her cloak and almost falling. Barely catching herself, she regained her balance.

The child drew menacingly closer.

Though the tiny figure radiated malignity, Maria's sense still warned her of a greater evil forthcoming, the inevitable arrival of an iniquitous being of greater power and destruction. What she faced now was merely the appetizer before the arrival of a darker main course fixated on torment and slaughter. Images of the approaching creature tried to enter her mind, but her consciousness refused to accept them, fleeing aimlessly ahead of the specter of the great carrion as a leaf flees before a cold autumn gust.

The child was crying now and making soothing, baby-like sounds as it advanced with arms outstretched as though seeking comfort. Maria retreated but the pitiful wails tugged at her natural kindness and maternal instincts.

For a moment she felt her resolve weakening; suppose this little girl was just a child, a lost homeless soul captured and held prisoner by the creature? Suppose she was trying to escape, looking to Maria for help? Could she turn her down, coldly deny her human compassion and fail to give aid? Had she lost all empathy in a world seemingly gone mad, a world no longer bound within the parameters of any accepted reality? After all, there was nothing really supernatural about the child...except that her eyes were strange.

...AND SHE WAS ABLE TO STAND THREE FEET IN THE AIR ON NOTHING!

Maria looked at the child again, and all doubt left her. An ink-black cloud of malevolence smothered the young nun. She gasped for breath and shivered miserably in the cool, night air as she fought her natural feelings of concern and pity for the child. Deep in her soul she knew her survival depended on keeping a cool head and using the power of her faith to ward off this evil.

Slowly, she now felt a great fatigue coming over her; she was so sleepy. As her arm grew tired and her hand began to droop, the child seemed to gather strength from her weariness and began to advance. Maria remembered the Crucifix and thrust it high once again.

The child stopped dead less than thirty feet away and smiled craftily at Maria, sighing with the exhausted patience of an angry parent when a stubborn youngster refuses to give up its will.

Suddenly the little girl reached a finger up to her face, there was an audible pop, and her left eyeball leaped out of its socket and plopped grotesquely down onto her cheek. Attached nerves and muscles kept it dangling there as a tiny river of blood and yellow mucus flowed from the empty gaping socket above the eyeball and ran off her chin. The child smiled, a horrible yellow-toothed mocking grin.

Maria's stomach turned over again; nausea threatened to send her retching into the gutter. Heart pounding, she felt her head growing tight as pinwheels of light danced before her eyes. Dear God, she thought, don't let me pass out! She closed her eyes and began to pray aloud. "Hail Mary, full of grace, the Lord is with thee, blessed art thou amongst women...."

The tightness in her head began to subside and she held the silver cross tighter and higher, willing it to banish the evil, praying for the power of God to help send this thing back from wherever it came. Her voice grew louder as she neared the end of her prayer.

"...now and at the hour of our death...Amen!"

Maria opened her eyes.

The waif was still standing there, her head cocked to the side as though puzzled over the fuss. Her eye was back in its socket; Maria wondered if it had ever truly been plucked out, or if it had been part of some macabre mind game. Was any of this real, she wondered numbly? But there was little time for introspection. The child grinned and reached a hand up under her gown. She probed her lower belly, struggling with something between her legs. A live entity suddenly bucked and thrashed, pushing out her gown, twisting into it and then retreating back, only to plunge forward a moment later like a berserk garden hose, bending, curving and shaking itself to get loose of the folds of the dress.

A geyser erupted from beneath the shift, soaking through the material in a huge yellow stain that dripped and puddled onto the street as something under her dress angrily hissed and spat.

For a brief moment Maria thought the child was giving birth, then, with horror, saw her small hands reach down and grip a black, beaded head poking from under the hem of her garment.

The child yanked at the head, and long, writhing black coils spilled from between her legs.

Dripping phlegm-like venom, the snake's head whipped frantically about, forked tongue repeatedly licking out to sniff and test the air. Suddenly it paused its aimless search, its small, black eyes fixed on Maria.

Maria cried: "No...! In the name of God – stop!"

Grinning insanely, the child dropped the head and continued pulling the slippery snake from under her dress, foot-after-foot, hand-over-hand she worked until finally its tail emerged and it dropped onto the sidewalk.

Like a flash, the serpent slithered its ten-foot length across the wet pavement towards the transfixed nun.

READY OR NOT....!

The child grinned widely as, before Maria could move, the serpent was at her feet, rearing upward, pushing and probing against her clothing, trying to get under her cloak, to climb her legs.

In her mind, Maria knew with horrified certainty that it was trying to enter her; a vision forced itself into her mind – the snake worming its way up her leg, into her body and thrusting itself upwards until it burst through her internal organs and snapped its fangs directly into her heart...!

A LOVELY DEATH IS ON ITS WAY....!

Maria screamed!

Terror overwhelmed her. She dropped her Crucifix and leaped backwards! Panic washed away any vestige of control as she found herself coughing, gulping and filling her lungs with of air, vainly trying to satisfy an oxygen need that refused to be satisfied. The street whirled madly. She heard a hiss of exultation from the child as she staggered back. Barely able to stand, Maria retreated backwards around the front of the Saab.

The snake shot off the sidewalk and under the car heading straight for her feet again.

Maria looked desperately about, spotted the front door of the automobile, tore it open and leaped into the driver's seat. She slammed the door closed.

Safe!

A wave of relief was quickly followed by hollow thuds as the angry snake leaped against the driver's side of the automobile. Its flat head slammed repeatedly against the window; fangs released splashes of thick, yellow gore which pooled and ran down the surface of the glass.

With a small cry, Maria drew back, pushing herself as deep as possible into the upholstery. As she did so, however, she glimpsed the child in the rear view mirror. She was running for the back door of the Saab.

Maria hit the automatic lock button. The four door locks snapped shut just as the child seized a handle. Locked outside, she rattled it frantically up and down.

Maria screamed; she had to get out of there!

The keys...

...were in the ignition and she fumbled frantically to get the automobile started. The ignition caught. She pulled it into drive and jammed her foot down on the accelerator. The tires spun madly evaporating wetness on the street. With tire smoke rising to mix with the night mist, the automobile screamed away.

Maria was half-way down the street when she realized she had left Father Murphy and Father Langevin at the mercy of the child-thing. Slamming on the brakes, she twisted the wheel, trying to make a U-turn in the middle of the street. The automobile spun half-way round, sliding sideways down the wet pavement, then bumped over the curb, mounted the sidewalk and finally dropped back onto the street facing in the direction she had just come.

She accelerated back down the street, switching on the headlights as the automobile picked up speed. The beams picked up the waif in the middle of the road looking small and helpless.

Maria continued to accelerate towards her. She hit the horn. "Get out of the way!"

The child dropped to her knees in the roadway, head tilted upward, hands clasped in mock prayer.

"Jesus, Mary and Joseph…move…get out of the way!" Maria screamed at the child, knowing she couldn't be heard.

The child remained kneeling, seemingly lost in a trance-like devotion.

"Get out of the way!!"

Though knowing in her heart that the figure was merely something monstrous in the guise of a little girl, Maria couldn't bring herself to run her down.

At the last moment, she pushed down hard on the brakes and twisted the wheel to the left in an attempt to avoid her. The car skidded wildly again, the back end slewing to the left and right.

As the careening automobile slid towards her, the waif suddenly picked something off the roadway and stood up.

Holding up the wriggling serpent like a prize, she grinned directly at Maria through the windshield just as the car slammed into her at a 45-degree angle. There was a metallic clunk and the child vanished under the automobile. It jumped slightly as one back tire rode over her small body. The slide continued for another 150 feet before coming to a stop in front of Montague's building just as the doors burst open and the two priests staggered out. Murphy had the unconscious detective slung over his shoulder in a fireman's hold.

"Sister!" Murphy yelled, spotting Maria in the automobile. "Over here."

"I hit her!" Maria cried, throwing open the door and jumping out.

"Get back in and drive!" Murphy shouted. The child was already rising from the street.

Maria looked back. She gaped at the miraculous recovery. The child, unscathed, stood immobile on the pavement. The young nun needed no further urging. She yanked open the rear door of the Saab on the driver's side. Murphy came round and slung Montague inside across the back seat as Langevin lost no time in getting in the front passenger seat.

"Never mind, I'll drive," Murphy said, throwing his pistol onto the back seat after Clay's inert form. He motioned Maria inside.

Obediently she climbed in back with the detective, glad that the priest was now taking command. She looked out the back window.

The child was now walking towards the car. She held the snake midway in one hand. Slowly she began to whirl it by its tail.

"Please go now, Father," Maria called. "She's – it's not human."

Murphy stood at the open driver's door of the Saab and stared at the little girl whipping the snake round and round in a heated frenzy. Faster and faster the snake whirled, forming a shimmering, black, hypnotic spinning wheel, drawing the eyes of all towards its center where her small, pale hand pumped frantically.

The reptile was just a blur now, its passage through the air creating a whine growing louder with each passing second. The child continued walking towards the automobile, eyes blazing with a mixture of hate and anticipated triumph.

Father Murphy stared in morbid fascination, hypnotized by the sight of the whirling reptile and the child's glowing, alien-looking eyes.

"Father! Get us out of here," Maria yelled again, from the back seat. Somehow she knew that if this thing reached them, they would all die a quick and horrible death.

The priest failed to move; he was frozen.

Sensing the danger, Langevin reached over through the open driver's door and grabbed the back of Murphy's coat. "Dermott! Get in!"

Jolted by Langevin's shout, Murphy felt sweat running down his face. Paralyzed he fought the child's seductive eyes and an icy power that gripped his mind as he struggled inwardly to regain possession of his will. His resolve swung wildly between revulsion and love for the girl advancing towards him.

He tried to resist but found himself sliding back into her snare. He was captivated by the warmth of her eyes. They were so tender, so forgiving, and so full of promise. They offered him the pleasures of nights immersed in the warm folds of female flesh, the power of riches beyond his imagination, the heady raptures of fame and adoration…and a multitude of other delights never experienced before on earth.

IT WILL ALL BE YOURS, FATHER.

"She's a devil! Murphy, you stupid ass, get in the car!" Langevin screamed, again.

Murphy heard the distant insult yelled at him and was surprised that Father Langevin would dare speak to him in that tone. But he also didn't care a great deal. After all, he felt so fatigued, so numbed by life and all its trials that he wanted nothing more than to surrender his will to comfortable and secular pleasures.

COME WITH *ME*, HOLY MAN. SUCK THE FORBIDDEN FRUIT…!

Maria was out the back door of the car in an instant and facing the priest. Stepping between him and the child, she brought her hand up high in a wide, open-handed swing and the vicious crack of the slap echoed up and down the street like a pistol shot.

Father Murphy's head snapped back, his face stinging. Summoning the last bit of strength he possessed, and calling on the decades of regimented prayer, discipline and sacrifice that fed his inner spirit, he tore his eyes away from the child and stared in confusion at Maria standing before him. Her eyes were both terrified and angry at the same time.

"Suck it up, Father!" she shouted, simultaneously amazed and appalled at her use of such an expression. "Get in the damn car!"

He looked beyond her.

Less than 40 feet away the little hellion was approaching rapidly. She tried to entrap his mind again. Loathsome tentacles of evil clawed at his psyche. Quickly Murphy looked away. He realized how close they were to destruction and took his own silver Crucifix from a pocket. "Chew on this you little heathen," he yelled, and flung it full force at the child. It whipped end-over-end straight over her head. Like a cat unable to stop itself from responding, the child slammed the snake into the ground, leaped up instinctively, stretched, and amazingly snatched the Crucifix from the air with a single hand.

A long, bowel-wrenching scream ripped through the night as her hands closed on the blessed object. For several seconds she stayed aloft. There was an electric snap and a brilliant arc of light. Pain shot through her body with the swiftness of a lightning bolt and she gave a spasmodic jerk and shrilled once more. As though blown out of the air by a shotgun blast, she abruptly plunged to the ground howling in agony.

Hitting the pavement, she rolled, twisted and turned. She continued to grip the Crucifix like a live electric wire, unable to let it go, unable to free herself from the agony and the seizures shaking her small being. .

Alternately snarling and shrieking, she clutched it to her belly, bent double until she had rolled herself into a ball and brought up her bare feet to try and pry it free from her hands. Her toes dug and flailed at it like an angry feline, toenails splintering and ripping as she gouged her hands and arms in an insane rage to be free of the cursed object.

Feeling a strange and unholy satisfaction at someone else's pain, Murphy pushed Maria into the back seat and slammed the car door.

The Saab squealed away.

~ 7 ~

Smoke and the stench of burning hair and flesh rose from the small figure wailing and rolling on the wet pavement as a huge, ant-like creature suddenly swept down like a giant locust onto the street. Adramelech, now part-creature, part-man, landed gracefully on powerful legs near the child.

Lifting a huge, triangular, horned head, hooded yellow eyes took in the scene. Nothing stirred except the child. She quivered and moaned weakly at his feet. The creature reached down and grabbed the child in one hand. Carefully avoiding touching the metal cross, he picked her up and shook her like a dead rat.

The Crucifix dropped from her grasp and clattered to the pavement. The creature gave it a vicious kick, sending it hurtling across the roadway with a metallic rattle to slam into the curb and spin towards an overflow drain. It hung for a moment in the grate, twisted with the current of rainwater washing from the road, and dropped from sight into the bowels of the sewer.

The creature flung the child to the pavement where she landed with a snarl and turned to confront her new adversary. On sighting her Master, she slunk down as low as possible, whining and pleading for mercy.

But the Beast ignored her; he was intent on something else.

Adramelech leaped upwards to the building ledge just outside the detective's window. There he paused, but only for a second, and then, spreading his arms wide, he sailed forward.

The window and frame exploded inwards and the Beast disappeared from sight.

The sound of the last tinkle of breaking glass faded.

For a moment all was silent, then...

...the quiet of the street was shattered by a primitive, visceral roar of rage surging into the night. The cry grew louder, building into a furious crescendo of angry abandon and disappointment. Parked car alarms began to wail up and down adjacent streets, windows suddenly glowed with light, and soon sirens sounded in the distance; the din continued to increase in intensity.

Below, the terrified child began to weep in fear and despair. Trembling violently, desperate to escape retribution, she began to beat her head against the pavement. Harder and harder she smashed it until the skin of her forehead split, and great clots of blood and splinters of bone flew through the air. As the front of her skull caved in, the sounds changed from the sharp cracks of bone, to the meaty thuds of wet tissue slapping the concrete. The membrane surrounding her brain ruptured and bits of white jelly and brain matter spattered the street as she frantically pounded it, faster, harder, faster, harder....until finally, exhausted, she collapsed in defeat. She was already spontaneously healing even as, above her on the ledge, the creature stood poised once more.

There was no escape; even through trying to attain the unattainable – death. After all, death was her Master...and right now, it was not pleased.

~ 8 ~

As they raced through the back streets, Father Langevin spoke urgently into a cellular telephone. Though Maria couldn't hear what he said, there was no mistaking his tone.

"What's the matter with him?" Maria asked, as she tried to pull Clay to a sitting position. "Why is he unconscious?"

"The Narcan is not working," Murphy said. "Sister, try and get him awake! Slap him! Yell at him! Wake him up!"

As Maria struggled with Clay's six-foot frame, trying to sit him up, she couldn't help noticing that he was a handsome man, well-muscled and fit.

Clay's suit jacket draped open exposing the front of his torn white shirt now soaked crimson with blood.

The car rounded a corner almost tilting onto two wheels, tires squealing in protest.

Maria fell sideways onto the unconscious detective. "What did you do to him?" she screamed at Murphy, pulling herself upright.

The priest said nothing but concentrated on his driving. Something made her look down and she saw the high-tech looking pistol on the floor where Murphy had thrown it.

"You SHOT him!?" Her voice was high, her tone one of disbelief.

"We're taking him to a doctor."

"You shot him!" she repeated, too shocked to make sense of what was going on. "We were supposed to save him! Why did you shoot him?"

"We had no choice," Langevin said, tensely.

"Choice?" Maria pulled open his shirt and surveyed the wounds that were bleeding freely. "My God, you shot him…he's dying!"

"Those aren't bullet wounds," Murphy said. "He was hit with tranquilizing darts."

"Darts? He's bleeding so much!"

"We shot him too many times…too close," Langevin admitted, realizing Maria wasn't privy to details of their weapons.

"We have to get him to a hospital!"

"We're getting him to a doctor," Murphy insisted, spinning the wheel again and turning north on 2nd Avenue. He planned to cross the East River on the Queensboro Bridge and head north again on Vernon Boulevard. From there they'd be able to make their way to Grand Central and hit La Guardia. He muttered a quick prayer of thanks for traffic being fairly mild.

Maria grabbed Clay's wrist and felt for a pulse. If it was there, it was indiscernible. She stared at his chest; he wasn't breathing! "You've killed him…" she cried. "He isn't breathing!"

"What?" Murphy demanded. "What are you saying!?"

"He isn't breathing; I can't find a pulse!"

"Oh my Lord," Langevin said, twisting in the front seat.

Maria dragged Clay sideways until he was lying prone on the backseat and tried to jam herself sideways to kneel on the floor. "Move your seats up," she yelled at the two priests. They complied and she managed to wedge herself upright in the cramped space.

Langevin was also kneeling and extended backwards over his seat now, trying to reach back to give Clay CPR. Once the detective was on his back, Langevin lifted his fist and pounded once on his chest and then leaned over, cupped his hands just under the breastbone and began to push rhythmically downward as he counted aloud: "One...two...three..." After 30 seconds of compressions, he stopped.

Maria, remembering her life-guard training from high school, pinched Clay's nose, pulled his head back to open his air passage and waited. As soon as Langevin ceased pushing on Clay's chest, Maria leaned forward and blew into his mouth until she saw his chest rise.

Langevin went back to his rhythm for another thirty seconds and Maria blew into his mouth a few more times.

They jointly worked on the detective for two minutes. It seemed more like hours before he choked, gasped and began breathing on his own. We must be on a freeway now, thought Maria as the ride changed from violent turns to straight and smooth. She felt the detective's wrist again. The pulse was feeble but seemed to be growing stronger.

"Are we near the hospital?" she called, her heart pounding. There was no reply from the front seat. This time she screamed: "Answer me! Are we near the hospital?"

"We're less than five minutes from La Guardia," Murphy said. He sped up to race through an already red light to a chorus of horns.

"La Guardia? We don't need an airport...we need a hospital, you –!" She didn't finish and was immediately sorry for what she'd been about to say. Murphy didn't seem to notice.

"There'll be everything we need at the airport, lass," he said patiently.

"Drive to a hospital...please!" Her voice was panicky, shrill. "He may need surgery, he may be dying."

"There'll be everything we need at the airport," Murphy repeated, stubbornly.

Still kneeling on the front seat Father Langevin looked at her with genuine concern. "We couldn't help it, Sister. Together, let us pray for his recovery. In the name of the Father..."

The priest blessed himself and Maria followed suit.

"He'd better recover," Murphy snapped, to no-one in particular. "If he dies, we may wind up envying him."

~ 9 ~

The Vicar of Christ and Successor of Peter, was becoming increasingly mired in a jungle of red tape and bureaucracy that could strangle the best of intentions before they even reached him, thought the Most Reverend Mustavias Cardinal Malachi.

Malachi inwardly fumed at the bureaucracy that was overwhelming the Romana Curia as he strode swiftly across the Piazza di San Pietro directly in front of the Papal Palace. Decades ago, the prestigious American Institute of Management had judged the Catholic Church's administrative body one of the three most efficiently administered organizations in the world; he wondered how it would fare today. Right now, despite his personal decades-long participation in the Curia he found its processes inherently destructive to his own agenda. What was most astonishing, however, was that despite incorporating new technology to improve its processes, they seemed to become more complex and maddeningly slower.

As he walked, he nodded and smiled politely at groups of sightseeing tourists thronging the piazza under the boiling sun. He also marveled again at the sheer power exuded by the architecture of the Vatican: the statues of the Saints gleaming in the sun, the pillared arms of Bernini's double colonnade and the omnipresent dome of St. Peter's Basilica, a white beacon of Christian hope against the blue sky. It made most people feel small and insignificant. Mission accomplished.

Lately, he thought, the Curia seemed to be occupied by administrators more in love with their rules and business processes than anything else. For instance, gaining an audience with the pope, something relatively simple for people at his level in the past, was proving to be almost impossible thanks to a new Curia-developed process that demanded he fill out forms, most which featured questions which he couldn't and wouldn't answer. And, the man who controlled the pope's calendar was certainly enjoying his new power compliments of the revamped processes. Malachi felt his face redden with anger at the stupidity of the entire affair. He remembered a mediaeval saying: *'Timeo mon Petrum, sex secretarium eius'* which, roughly translated, meant: 'I don't mind Peter; it's his secretary who scares me.'

He knew that while most Holy Fathers had understood full well the power and influence of the Curia, few popes had ever been able to bring it to heel. Most merely worked within its ever-shifting framework. Like any government with its league of mandarins, leaders would come and go but the bureaucracy would live forever. And, even most popes had quietly accepted the occasional abuse of power it wielded. Through the ages, the most perceptive popes had manipulated the power and abuses to their own advantage.

One thing was sure; though the function of the Curia was primarily to put itself at the pastoral service of the pope for the good of the Church, and help him bring the message that "Christ has Risen" to the billion Catholics around the world (and any others who would listen), there was also multiple hidden agendas quietly in progress through the old-boy networks to fulfill personal goals, strike alliances, perform or repay favors, and carry out personal vendettas.

As far as Malachi was concerned, the Curia, far from being a collegiate sanctuary for the faithful, was in fact a coldly efficient, politically-oriented congress where empires were built and destroyed, and alliances welded tight or viciously savaged. The vindictive relish of those who had been betrayed would lie still and wait, sometimes for years, for the opportunity to repay the debt. And, having been in Rome for thirty years and in the Vatican for twenty nine of those thirty, he knew that debts were always repaid.

But what had wrought this angry evaluation of the Curia by Cardinal Malachi? A mere two minute telephone conversation with one of the pope's secretaries had been enough.

Monsignor Giuseppe Lopez, Prefecture of the Pontifical Household, and the one who handled all access to His Holiness these days, had flatly refused him a private audience with the Holy Father. Pleading overwork and a full calendar, Lopez had suggested Malachi try for early December, months away. No longer consigned merely to handling official visits, Lopez's new powers appeared to have swelled his head.

Malachi had argued the critical nature of his mission, its need for secrecy and the most serious ramifications if he were not allowed an audience. Still Lopez had held fast while gently pressing for information on the subject of his *urgent* visit. After all, Malachi's application papers had not been fully filled out.

Fortunately Malachi knew from experience that the Monsignor was a bit of a gossip – no, no, that was unfair. The Monsignor merely shared most of his information with Bishop Pastoni who was the biggest gossip in the Curia. It would be disastrous for any mention of the *Hellspawn* to surface before he could prove its existence to the Holy Father and make him aware of the dangers. He'd be damned if he'd spill the beans first to the *Joan Rivers* of the Holy City. *Can we talk?*

If word got out prematurely, there would be legions of naysayers who would leap to the fore. They would laugh at the very idea of a spiritual entity having taken bodily form to invade earth, even though they based their lives, careers and daily existence on the belief of same.

And, once they stated their positions, they would not be allowed to drift back into the woodwork, or quietly sit on the fence. Since they argued against such an occurrence, they would be expected to back up their position, to fight him and to prove the folly of such a belief.

The resulting battle would not be pleasant. Malachi's motives and his mental capacities would be questioned. And they would conduct an aggressive campaign to discredit him. Before long they'd have Malachi firmly in bed with the UFO nuts and New Age cuckoos.

No, he had to inform the pope directly and have the active support of the Holy Father before he could reacquire his budget and quietly recommit his forces to track and destroy Adramelech. He knew the Holy Father was a no-nonsense man with an analytical mind who, once informed, made quick and irrevocable decisions. So he would have only one chance to make his case.

He sighed tiredly as he walked. Here he had the biggest spiritual bombshell in hundreds of years and he couldn't inform his commander-in-chief because of the whim of a clerk. Of course Malachi understood the need for process and security. Unfortunately, he was also sure the refusal was mere petulance over his own reluctance to furnish a reason for his access request. Well, he thought, so much for the official route. Now he'd have to try the back staircase. Malachi was thinking of the unofficial channels which were occasionally able to by-pass the front-office screening of the Prefecture of the Pontifical Household.

Of course, he knew full well that access to the back staircase depended directly on one's span of influence among the papal secretaries within the Curia. And, it didn't hurt any if those in strategic positions, or those who had the ear of the Holy Father, owed you a few favors. Still he felt reasonably sure that if he brought Archbishop Bortnowaska, the pope's personal secretary, into his confidence and convinced him of the threat, despite the new "process improvement" he could be assured of a papal audience. Bortnowaska was a fair and reasonable man.

He pondered the best approach: through an official appointment with the secretary, or should he just ensure he made contact at the Papal Mass the next morning?

He decided to wait until they sat down after Mass for the usual repast where he would ensure that he gained a seat next to Bortnowaska.

Invariably, when Monsignor Lopez saw them together, he would guess immediately what Malachi was up to, so he would have to move fast. Lopez might get in a snit and find some ingenious way to head him off at the pass.

It would probably be better to tempt Bortnowaska, drop a hint of something big and ask him to attend a meeting of *The Seven*. Once the Archbishop was faced with a united front of Cardinal Malachi, two Bishops, a Monsignor and the three official Anti-Christ Watchers from the older orders of the Benedictines, the Franciscans and the Jesuits, and they shared their knowledge of the *Hellspawn* with him, he would doubtlessly act. The question was, would they get to see the old boy, or be judged mad as the proverbial hatter?

Malachi stopped for a moment and pulled a small solid-state recorder from his pocket. He made a brief note to get copies made of the ancient testaments and news clippings before he met with Bortnowaska. He hoped access to such information would convince him of the urgent need for the meeting.

He resumed his trek across the square from the 1,100 room Papal Palace towards the Curia Generalizia dei Gesuite, the Jesuit headquarters where he kept his office. As he walked, he lifted his face towards the warming sun and idly wondered how Saint Peter would react to the surrounding extravagance if he were alive today.

Likely he'd be impressed...not!

~ 10 ~

"Charter 104, taxi runway 31. Wind is three ten degrees at five...altimeter thirty-one inches." The controller's voice was mechanical sounding and raspy with a brief bout of static. First Officer Danny Gostini keyed back an affirmative and looked over at Captain Wayne Bowden.

"Let's go Danny old boy," Bowden said, bringing the nose wheel around a bit as he advanced the throttles of the Airbus A320.

The 162,000 pound airplane began to roll along the taxiway. Gostini checked off the taxiways they passed on the way to runway three one. They both watched the ND groundspeed readout to monitor taxi speed.

"What about the lights?" asked Gostini.

"The special set? Not tonight if you don't mind. Sooner or later the FAA is gonna have our ass if we turn them on before we're airborne and in international air space."

The co-pilot chuckled and began the routine of the pre-takeoff checklist.

"Flaps two, Wayne," Gostini said.

"Roger....flaps two," Bowden answered.

"Trim four degrees, nose up, rudder zero."

Gostini confirmed the flaps were deployed properly. "Two indicated on the screen," he said.

"Wing and engine anti-ice off," Bowden continued, touching a switch over his head. "Takeoff data...." he paused and his expert eyes scanned dozens of instruments including the artificial horizon, the initial altitude the flight was cleared to, and the RDMIs to make sure they were functioning properly.

"Takeoff data reviewed and set," Bowden continued. He moved the side joystick full up and down, then full left and full right to ensure the flight controls were working correctly.

"Flight controls...check," he said.

They droned on through the checklist as they approached runway 31 and were told by the tower they were cleared for takeoff, given departure instructions and told to intercept their enroute at thirty-five thousand feet.

Bowden called out the indicated take-off speeds from his computer display: "One four five…one five zero…one six zero."

The pilot lost no time as they swung into position. He lined up the nose wheel on the white centerline stripe as they completed the final pre-flight check.

"The cabin is advised…weather radar and anti-ice are off."

They finished their checks and Bowden grasped the two thrust levers.

"Charter 104 rolling…" Gostini reported into the microphone as Bowden slowly advanced the thrust levers forward into the take-off detent.

The aircraft engines increased in pitch and the A320 began lumbering down the runway. The speed built and the runway stripes, illuminated by the powerful landing lights, disappeared under the nose with increasing speed.

Bowden and Gostini both kept their eyes on the airspeed indicator as they rapidly ate up the runway length. The needle crept towards V-1 the go, no-go decision speed. They knew that before V-1 they could reject the take-off, put the engines in reverse and slam on the brakes to avoid plummeting off the end of the runway. Once they hit V-1, they were committed to flight.

"One hundred" Gostini called out, cross checking airspeeds for accuracy.

The airspeed indicator speed was passing one hundred and thirty knots…one hundred and thirty five knots…one hundred and forty five….

"V1…rotate," Gostini said, a moment later.

Bowden eased back on the joystick and the nose of the aircraft rose into the air. His eyes probed the vertical speed indicator watching for evidence they were beginning to climb. The needle started moving upwards.

No matter how many times he flew, Bowden always felt that tiny bit of relief at this moment. Though many pilots would maintain that they commanded their airplanes with the nonchalance of a drive to the corner milk store, medical tests monitoring their blood pressures at the moment of takeoff told a different story. Once the thrust levers were advanced to the TOGA position, their blood pressures surged right up there with the engine thrusts.

"Gear up," Bowden said, as he felt the craft kick free of earth's gravity and slowly pull itself skyward.

The jet climbed at a 20-degree pitch angle as Gostini reached forward to the instrument panel and pulled a black lever up.

The soft whine of the wheels retracting was followed by a muffled thump as the nose wheel settled into the wheel well. They could hear it still spinning in its well as the doors closed. The vertical speed indicator reacted sharply to the decreased drag and the aircraft leaped upward as though suddenly lighter.

"Gear up," Gostini confirmed, seeing three amber indicators.

Bowden eased the joystick to the left in a climbing left turn as the jet soared upwards. "Flaps one…." Then: "Flaps zero."

Gostini complied and grinned at him for no particular reason other than to pass an unspoken message that he was happy to be in the air again. Bowden understood and returned his grin.

"Next stop London," Gostini said.

"Yeah...and then Rome. Where, if I weren't married, I'd be looking for Roman maidens."

They had the luxury of a straight climb to their assigned altitude to intercept their High Altitude Jet Airway already dialed into their navigational system.

"Wayne...what's going on back there?" Gostini inclined his head towards the passenger compartment.

Bowden shook his own head. "No idea...but whoever they brought aboard looked in pretty rocky shape. I got a quick look in the sick bay before they closed the curtain. Dr. Butler and the new nurse were working on him."

"I bet their patient didn't go through channels neither. Sooner or later…big trouble."

Bowden grinned at the co-pilot. "Hell, he can't get in any trouble...he's got the power of the Roman Catholic Church back there. They can grant him absolution for just about anything."

"Even ducking immigration?"

Bowden grinned at him. "Even ducking immigration."

Gostini shook his head and did a reasonable impersonation of Sergeant Schultz from *Hogan's Heroes*: "I see nuutttinnn...!"

Bowden chuckled as he watched the altimeter. With their route already programmed in the computer, once they left the Terminal Radar Service Area (TRSA) zone and passed into Class A airspace above flight level one eight zero, and attained altitude, it would be time to let the automatic pilot take over and fly them to London's Gatwick Airport.

After some sleep, the second leg would take them from London to Rome. Though the A320 had been fitted with auxiliary tanks that gave it direct flight capability, the pilots still needed to rest. The Vatican hadn't sprung for a relief crew; Bowden and Gostini were it.

As Gostini confirmed an altitude change with the control tower, Bowden settled back in his seat and thought about the mysterious passenger and their own curious arrangements with the Vatican.

Some time ago, both he and Gostini had been approached by Father Claude Lamontagne, a Jesuit priest with the Romana Curia. The Church had leased an A320 from United Airlines and needed two high-time, airline pilots to fly it on an on-call basis. The caveat was they were on call 24-hours a day at half pay. Full pay when they flew.

Since him and his friend Dan Gostini had been laid off by Eastern Airlines in an expense cut, they jumped at the contracts. Bowden had a small mortgage on a house in Atlanta. He and his wife Susan also had a new baby on the way. With Susan on pregnancy leave from her nursing job, they needed the money. So what if the position was somewhat strange? He and his bachelor co-pilot saluted and gratefully signed their new and generous contracts. They were also made to sign legal, non-disclosure letters stating that anything they saw or learned, while in the employ of the Church, would remain confidential. Disclosure of information deemed confidential by the church would mean repayment of all monies delivered to them by the church from the beginning of their contract. What it all meant was anyone's guess, but they both signed it. They could keep their mouths shut.

Since then, they had largely been on stand-by. They had to carefully monitor their flying hours to meet the Federal Aviation Agency's 6-month minimum guidelines for carrying passengers. In short, to act as pilot in command and co-pilot, they had to make five take-offs and landings within each six month period to stay current. Generally, it wasn't a problem as they'd fly a cardinal overseas or transport what they called the Quad-Squad, four silent, unsmiling priests – who looked more like commandos than men of God – somewhere in the world. In the previous year, however, they were short one take-off and landing in their six-month requirement, and so were instructed to take the A320 on a flight to Paris, via Milan, Stuttgart, and Brussels, where they landed and took off from each city before returning to Rome.

Then last year things picked up. Suddenly they were advised the plane would be undergoing modifications and the aircraft had been taken in for a retrofit.

When they signed for delivery two weeks later, both he and Gostini were surprised to find a quarter of the rear passenger cabin had been converted into a fully outfitted Medical Sick Bay, complete with an operating theatre featuring what surely must be the latest compact medical diagnostic and treatment equipment.

The rest of the aircraft was taken up with an office (complete with computers shielded so as not to interfere with their instruments) a FAX machine and multiple telephones as well as six sleeping compartments – three with double beds and three with a pair of bunk beds – and a general room with TV, a couch and two chairs, lamps and tables. A small galley with microwave, eating table and chairs bolted down completed the retrofit.

The aircraft was also outfitted with auxiliary fuel tanks in a section of the lower cargo hold extending their range to more than 2,600 nautical miles thus giving them transatlantic flight capabilities. Their two General Electric CFM56-5 engines had thrust ratings between 25,500 and 27,000 pounds giving them power to spare. In addition, however, they also had a curious set of auxiliary "LED visibility" lights inset along the fuselage and down each wing, carefully crafted so as not to interfere in any way with lift. At least, Father Lamontagne said they were for visibility.

The drill, during night flights, had been to switch them on illuminating the edges of wings and body of the aircraft once they were aloft and at their assigned altitude. Bowden, citing his captaincy of the aircraft, demanded to know the reason for the lights and had muttered about possibly contravening international regulations. However, the Jesuit priest, Father Lamontagne merely smiled and said all navigational lighting requirements continued to be met and now they were just illuminating God's work.

The same year, Lamontagne had been replaced by Bishop Flavius Aquila. Their new boss, an elderly man, spoke little other than to give them their flight orders. During transit he worked at his desk in one stateroom and rarely visited the flight deck.

Bowden sighed and wondered if he should flip on the "visibility" lights. He decided against it. What the priests didn't miss, wouldn't hurt them.

He turned control of the aircraft over to his co-pilot and took out a World Aeronautic Chart. If he had any idea about what would happen over the next seven-odd hours, he would have immediately requested a new vector and altitude to take them directly back to La Guardia where he would have happily resigned. After all, Captain Wayne Bowden wasn't in any hurry to make Mrs. Bowden a widow.

~ 11 ~

Doctor Rennie M. Butler steadied himself on his feet as he felt the A320 lift off. As usual, the angle of climb was sharp. He and his nurse, Susan Swaga, hung onto the operating table on which Clay Montague lay strapped and naked with IVs in both arms. He'd been catheterized and she was taking his blood pressure as they climbed.

The nurse nodded in satisfaction. "BP is 100 over 60...."

Butler smiled for the first time in almost half an hour and glanced around the cabin for his penlight to check Clay's pupil response. He still couldn't get over the completeness of the facilities and the amazing array of medical equipment on board; the Church had spared nothing.

The Sick Bay of the A320 cabin had been paneled in stark white and contained down-sized pieces of most of the medical devices found in any modern hospital's emergency department.

Along one wall were drug cabinets, oxygen cylinders, a portable x-ray machine, a trauma wagon complete with defibrillator, and various other and sundry pieces of medical equipment including a heart-lung machine and a resuscitator. He had been told that there were X-Ray technicians, perfusionists and anesthetists on call in various cities. If needed, they would be waiting at the nearest airport and would be at his disposal. And they had hired a nurse who told him she was also sworn to secrecy.

An operating table capped by powerful lights was bolted to the center of the cabin floor. Next to it rested a secured instrument tray now cluttered with stainless steel scalpels, retractors, scissors, empty disposable hypodermic needles and a number of bloodied cotton sponges – remnants of their efforts to stabilize Clay and repair the wounds compromised by the priests' attempts to dig the darts out of his chest with a metal letter opener.

As a general surgeon and trauma specialist at St. Elizabeth's Medical Center of Boston, the prior four years had seen Dr. Butler spending more time in operating rooms than out. In truth, he was burned out, and becoming less and less effective. Seeing that he needed some rest, the hospital had approached him on behalf of the Catholic Church who needed a full time surgeon who would only perform emergency work a few times a year. The Hospital Administrator had introduced him to Father Lamontagne and given his blessing to a two-year leave of absence provided Butler returned to St. Elizabeth's two years hence.

Doctor Butler had been placed by the Church on permanent call with a generous weekly stipend and merely had to fly with the aircraft when it went to certain locals. Since he was single, this was no great hardship. He had comfortable quarters on board, plenty of reading material and an extensive DVD collection to choose from. The only condition of employment was that he never disclosed anything he witnessed during his tenure. Also, when he was away from the aircraft, he had to respond to his pager or a cell call immediately. Failure to comply, said Father Lamontagne, would result in instant dismissal and a very forceful complaint registered with the American Medical Association that would cause him no end of grief. He was amused at how the Church seemed to work: extend the carrot and then show him one freaking big stick with a nail in the end of it. Butler mulled it over for a day and asked himself if it was worth it. When he expressed doubts, they simply doubled his salary.

Since then he'd been to Rome, London, and Paris more times than he could count, Berlin twice, various South and Central American cities including Bogotá, Panama City and Santiago. He'd also flown to LA, Boston, Las Vegas and New York more times than he could remember. And they'd flown to Burlington, Vermont, and stayed there for a week the previous year. It was there he had his first and only patient – till now. One of the four priests they typically flew with had been brought to the aircraft in Burlington VSA – Vital Signs Absent. There was nothing he could do – the man had been almost torn to shreds as though he'd been attacked by a berserk animal. He had told Bishop Aquila that they required the county coroner in to attend but he'd been ignored. They simply shut the aircraft doors and took off for Rome. It was then the Bishop had unlocked a locker along the fuselage near the bathroom that turned out to be a small refrigerated "morgue" with two drawer compartments. Whatever the dead man's function had been, he wasn't replaced. No grieving, no regrets and no explanations.

When his second patient, Clay Montague, had been brought across the La Guardia tarmac in a black Saab, and transferred on board, his pulse had been rapid and weak, his respiration shallow, blood pressure bottoming out and pupils beginning to dilate. According to Father Murphy he had been injected by six darts containing 20 mg. of Ketamine each. They'd tried to counteract the drugs by injecting him with Narcan but it hadn't worked. His heart had temporarily stopped on the way in but now he did have a pulse. Butler saw right away the man was in hypovolemic shock.

The doctor and his nurse went to work. They immediately applied the MAST trousers, gave him oxygen and started two large bore IV lines to deliver a crystalloid solution for volume replacement.

Now he listened with satisfaction as the patient's heartbeat grew stronger. Though, on entry to the aircraft, the patient's chest and belly showed six wounds, all except one were now closed with antimicrobial surgical dressings. The last required stitches. The young woman, who hurriedly introduced herself as Sister Maria, had initially told Butler that she thought there was still one dart in the man's chest and she had been right. He retrieved a stainless steel affair measuring an inch and a half long that was composed of a plastic feather over a metal ampoule with a sharpened hollow tip to administer the narcotic intramuscularly on impact. Although Butler recognized Ketamine as a general anesthetic that was considered relatively safe in the medical community, the patient had been injected by too many darts, too many times and gone into shock. With Clay's heart resuming a normal rhythm and his BP satisfactory, he'd repaired the wounds.

Clay groaned and Butler leaned close and shouted. "Clay...wake up! Can you hear me? Wake up! Clay...can you hear me?" He continued the litany for a few more seconds as his patient fought the narcotic and struggled to regain consciousness.

Fifteen feet towards the rear of the aircraft's Sick Bay, a chastened Father Murphy, Father Langevin and Sister Maria were visible through the half-open privacy curtain. They sat on a small, white, leather couch as Bishop Aquila paced angrily back and forth.

The priests were dressed in black suits, their Roman collars gleaming under their dark shirts. Father Murphy now sported a small dressing centered at the corner of his left eye that the doctor had insisted on applying once his primary patient had been stabilized.

It was hard for Butler to believe that the pretty girl in the dark grey wool skirt and red sweater seated beside them was a nun. Unlike many clerics or nuns he'd met, and in particular those dour personalities for whom he now worked, she seemed to have a sense of life, optimism and a mischievous happiness about her.

Butler looked back and had a fleeting thought; if a man's life hadn't been hanging in the balance for the last thirty minutes, the whole scene he was viewing might have been funny.

The bishop, squinting through thick glasses, thundered his rage at the two priests. Occasionally he'd lose his balance as the plane hit a mild downdraft or updraft, but then, on regaining his equilibrium he would vent his fury anew. The wounded priest would alternately argue and retreat into passive submissiveness, argue and retreat again. He tried tuning them out as he worked. It didn't work.

"He had a revolver...he was shooting at us," Murphy retorted once, not willing to fully accept blame.

"Were your lives more important than this mission, Father?" Bishop Aquila asked, tartly.

"No, Your Excellency."

"Are you aware of the consequences if he dies?"

Langevin and Maria remained quiet.

Murphy looked up and slowly nodded his head. "We're in deep dung?"

"Father!"

"Sorry, sir."

"Were you not aware of the power of the tranquilizers?"

"Your Excellency, when someone is trying to blast your head off...!" Murphy left the sentence hanging.

"So your well-being was taking precedence over his...?"

"Of course not...but extracting him meant we had to stay alive."

"We were all told the drug took 10 – 15 seconds to work...." Aquila said.

"That's an eternity when you're taking fire...."

"Taking fire? You sound like a pro, Father."

Murphy's face reddened. "You wanted him out of there. We got him out!"

"He's no good to us if he's dead!"

Maria could contain herself no longer. "Your Excellency, we did the best we could under the circumstances. The child we told you about was not…well, it wasn't *human*. We were under virtual siege."

"Enough!" The bishop glared at her and motioned towards the doctor and nurse. Maria's cheeks flushed with embarrassment.

Butler heard the latter exchange and decided to spare the two priests and the pretty young nun further harassment. "Pardon me, Your Excellency," he called from the Sick Bay. "The prognosis for Mr. Montague is a full recovery. Whoever chose Ketamine as the agent knew what they were doing. It's a relatively safe anesthetic…in reasonable doses."

"But his heart stopped," Maria protested.

"Perhaps…but I doubt it," Butler responded. "Likely you just failed to find a pulse."

"Sure, he wasn't breathing neither," Murphy said, in his heavy Irish accent. He immediately wished he'd kept his mouth shut when he received another glare from the bishop.

Aquila looked back at Butler, nodded and then made his way up to the detective's side. His relief was evident. "He'll be okay?"

"A little groggy over the next few hours but after that he'll come round." Butler decided to stretch the truth a bit and give Murphy and Langevin a hand. "Mind you, the man's chest will be a little sore, but if Father Murphy and Father Langevin hadn't acted so quickly in extracting the darts, he might have received too much narcotic to recover; it might have been much more serious." In fact, the complete dosage had been delivered on impact. Prompt or slow removal of the darts didn't affect the volume of the drug delivered one bit.

Somewhat mollified Aquila grunted and nodded. "Very well. What now?"

"I'm going to try and get him up very soon and walk him about."

"Doctor, this will be a long trip to Rome and I'd rather avoid this gentleman's questions till we reach there," Bishop Aquila said. "Could we keep him lightly sedated for the remainder of the trip?"

Doctor Butler looked at him strangely.

"Without endangering him, I mean," the bishop added, hastily.

Butler shrugged and nodded. "After he responds initially we can let him sleep it off."

"That's excellent news, Doctor. We're in your debt."

Butler and the nurse remained with Clay while the rest retired to a small office where a careful debriefing of every single thing that had happened that evening took place.

The aircraft had leveled off and had now settled on its transatlantic course. Exhausted from their ordeal Murphy and Langevin finally flaked out in a small double cabin, Maria curled up on the sofa and Bishop Aquila retired to a slightly larger sleeping cabin over the wing. Doctor Butler offered to stand the first watch over their patient. The nurse accepted his offer and gratefully retreated to her small aft cabin near the tail.

~ 12 ~

They had been cruising for three hours with the morning horizon still far away when the tedium of the overseas flight suddenly gave way to terror.

Gostini was gazing out the windscreen at the beauty of a bloated moon hanging like a self-illuminated ball. It sent shimmering silver moonbeams through the black velvet sky to sparkle like distant diamonds on the ocean far below. He checked their position with Gatwick Control. Suddenly the A320 staggered in flight. There was a huge bang and a thud as though something hit the aircraft.

Bowden, immersed in a novel snapped the book shut and shot upright in his seat, eyes scanning the instruments.

"What the hell was that!?"

Gostini, his eyes concerned, stared back in surprise then looked out the window off to his right.

"I don't know. Something hit us! "He didn't believe it himself.

"At three five zero? I doubt it. Unless it was a damn meteor."

Bowden satisfied himself that their instrument readings were okay as Gostini bent sideways and stared out his window, looking back towards the wings of the aircraft not quite visible to him. Oh my God," he exclaimed, suddenly recoiling from the glass in an instant.

"What is it…what's wrong?" Bowden's voice was tense.

"N-Nothing."

"Dan, what did you see?"

"N-Nothing…I'm a little tired, Wayne…m-my imagination is running away with me." He was almost hyperventilating from shock. What he had just witnessed spawned the physiological "fight or flight" reflex. Adrenaline surged into his system and increased his breathing to infuse his muscles with much-needed oxygen to accommodate whatever action was needed. Cautiously he peered out again. He breathed a sigh of relief, his heart rate slowed. There was nothing there.

Bowden was about to press him further when he spotted the needle on the airspeed indicator unwinding. For a moment, he couldn't believe his eyes. The ASI was now reading three hundred and seventy-five knots and quickly unwinding to three hundred and sixty…three hundred and fifty…three hundred and forty!

"We're losing airspeed!" Bowden switched off the auto pilot and eased the nose down fully expecting to see their airspeed increase. Instead, the erosion continued.

At the rate they were losing speed they could expect to stall out in less than a minute or two. The pilot felt his mouth go dry as he grabbed the throttle levers and eased them from their cruise position towards the second to last detent near the front of the pedestal.

The engines whined, eating up the Jet A-1 fuel on increased thrust as the readouts showed them advancing their engine power. The EPR gauges showed healthy engine thrust but the ASI showed continued erosion in airspeed.

Another 25 knots bled off.

"What the hell is going on?" Bowden muttered, over the roar of the engines. He scanned his instruments. Engine thrust was near maximum and all systems appeared to be functioning normally except for their airspeed that continued to unwind at an alarming speed. "We need another flight level." He pushed the stick forward.

Suddenly the urgency of the stall warning indicator assaulted their ears.

He stared at the altimeters. They showed them at flight level three five zero, thirty-five thousand feet. And yet he had the stick shoved as far forward as possible. At this moment they should have been in a screaming dive. Instead they seemed to be hanging in the sky, as though a hook was attached to their tail.

The stall indicator continued to sound, their air speed dropped to 110 knots and yet their altitude remained constant at three five zero; they shouldn't have been flying at that speed. There was only one possible conclusion....

"Instruments are haywire," Bowden said, through gritted teeth as he peered out the window at the ocean still far below.

Suddenly they heard another tremendous bang, followed quickly by another. The EPR numbers plummeted just before the cockpit went black. The aircraft lurched and the nose dropped. As both pilots watched in shock, their glass cockpit went dark. The giant aircraft staggered, yawed to starboard and began plummeting towards the moonlit sea.

"Flameout!" Gostini said, tightly. "Sweet Jesus…we've lost both engines…!"

~ 13 ~

For many of those invited to the Sunday morning Papal Breakfast in the Vatican, it was an opportunity to make up for any fasting done through the week, for others, merely a tempting feast and an opportunity to spend some time with friends and co-workers from other functions within the Vatican. It was a time to share stories and concerns, and relax in the solidarity of ecclesiastical camaraderie. The invitations were carefully rotated so that most major players in the Romana Curia had the opportunity to attend a few times a year.

But sadly, like at any major gatherings of like-minded individuals, it was also used for internal politicking, gossip, innuendo, character assassination and the forming and breaking of alliances. Careful observation of who sat with who, who avoided who, and in what direction surreptitious glances were cast while discourse took place in hushed tones among the noisy babble, quickly allowed even the most casual observer to realize a certain reality: beneath the surface of joviality, the busy rattle of plates and cups and the pious serenity permeating the gathering, a living, breathing and very real web of intrigue lurked.

As silverware clinked and more dishes rattled, Cardinal Malachi helped himself to another piece of whole wheat toast and sopped up the remains of his broken egg yoke. He had barely managed to resist the overflowing plate of crisp Canadian bacon to his left and the croissants, eggs Benedict and platters of pancakes and waffles waiting to be smothered in highly prized, imported Taylor's Matchedash Gold Maple Syrup to his right. If he gave in, he knew that his blood sugar would go through the roof initially and then drop him like a broken freight elevator.

He glanced around the room.

The Roman trattoria in which they ate was composed of a single, stucco-covered, grotto-like room. Measuring 140 by 80 feet and therefore much longer than it was wide, the side walls gradually curved inward to form a rounded, dome-like ceiling.

At a height ten feet above a man's head, arches had been cut into the walls; each arch featuring an intricately carved, decorative plaster molding or archivolt framing it with the work of an artist dead for at least the last nine hundred years. Gladiators wielding swords, mothers carrying well water in urns on their heads, and warriors whipping crazed chariot horses lay etched into the mortar. The colors, though faded with time, were still vivid enough to render a certain life-like quality to the artist's work.

Along the far end of the room, opposite the entrance, was some intricate scaffolding on which folded polyethylene and closed paint cans revealed that the initial steps towards the preservation and restoration of the fading artwork had begun.

Eight and 16-foot tables had been carefully arranged in rows facing the west side of the room where the head table, draped and elevated on a small platform faced all the others. From here, His Holiness smiled benignly down on the regular tables occupied by legions of clergy engaged in a feeding frenzy of food and gossip. The Pontiff seemed to take great satisfaction in his breakfast initiative that gathered his senior people more closely about him and gave them a forum and an excuse to rid themselves of the silo mentality so prevalent in large organizations. The message to his flock was simple: Despite your often solitary disciplines, we are a family.

Malachi, seated near the end of a table, felt the comforting bulge of the envelope in his breast pocket; it was stuffed with down-sized copies of sections of ancient scrolls, newspaper clippings and a transcript of his recent air-telephone conversation with Bishop Aquila. The Bishop, now en route to Rome with the ex-soldier who Father Gallo had initially discovered, as well as Sister Maria and the two Jesuits, had called immediately after take-off. His words, though seemingly innocent, had been grim. There was little doubt that their "friend" was back. Some friend.

Malachi sighed and thought of the immediate future. At best it seemed bleak, at worst laden with dire nuances of doom. Fussing and worrying wouldn't help, he told himself sternly. Instead, he congratulated himself on a brilliant series of strategic table maneuvering that secured him a spot beside Archbishop Dominique Bortnowaska, the pope's personal secretary. Of course it was also fortunate that, rather than staying at the head table near His Holiness, which was his perfect right, Bortnowaska seemed to view each Sunday morning as an opportunity to spend time with his brethren occupying positions not quite as exalted as he.

Bortnowaska was a heavy set man with a round, beaming face framed by two cauliflower-like ears. A pugnacious, red nose featuring a prominent bend to the left, the only remaining evidence of his early career as a prizefighter, was set in the middle of his good-humored countenance. A confirmed pragmatist to all who knew him, he was not a man to take advantage of his station nor throw his weight around as had been the case with some previous papal secretaries. He was well liked and respected by most.

Across, and much farther down the table, Malachi saw the thin, reedy face of Monsignor Lopez eyeing him suspiciously. Doing his best to ignore the look, Malachi reached over and poured Bortnowaska more coffee. Bortnowaska, seated to the cardinal's left, thanked him and spooned two heaps of sugar into his cup.

Leaning forward, Malachi happened to catch Lopez's eye again and smiled innocently back at the man while raising his coffee cup in a silent toast.

The Prefecture of the Pontifical Household flushed beet red, rapidly averted his eyes and attacked a double plateful of sausages and pancakes with religious zeal. He was obviously worried that Malachi was now trying to circumvent his authority and obtain a private audience with the Holy Father through means outside his personal discretion. Of course, he was dead right, but Malachi wasn't eager to telegraph his intentions.

The cardinal motioned towards Lopez and mused to Bortnowaska that being such a staunch guardian of the Holy Father's calendar certainly seemed to give Lopez a huge appetite.

Bortnowaska eyed the Monsignor, chuckled and added cream to his coffee. "When you work as hard as he does at being a major prick, it's inevitable that you burn up calories," he said.

Malachi stared at him in surprise but then couldn't hold in a laugh. He'd never heard Bortnowaska speak ill of any man, much less in such crude street language. He tried to recoup and said innocently: "Yes...I understand he can be difficult."

"Difficult...crap! He's an ass!"

Malachi laughed again.

"Anyhow, Your Eminence, you said you wanted to ask me something?" Despite his momentary candor, Bortnowaska's tone had now become polite and respectful in deference to Malachi's station. He smiled quizzically at the cardinal.

Malachi dropped the pleasantries and gave the Archbishop a serious look. "I have a matter of grave importance which I must present to His Holiness."

"And when will you do this?" Bortnowaska inquired, politely.

"Never...if Monsignor Lopez has anything to say about it," Malachi returned.

"Ah...so that's it."

"Regrettably he says that he can't fit me in until December."

"And even as we speak, we are being watched," Bortnowaska confided, his tone amused. He'd obviously locked horns with the Prefecture before.

Malachi picked up a silver sugar bowl, and using its reflection, managed to steal a clandestine glance at Lopez. He was watching them alright, a fork full of dripping pancake pieces halfway to his mouth.

"The syrup is at our end of the table now," Bortnowaska continued. "Maybe you could trade with Lopez; the syrup for an audience with the Holy Father."

Malachi shook his head: "Were it so easy...."

Bortnowaska fixed him with a stare. "Anyhow, since when can a Prince of the Holy Roman Catholic Church *not* squeeze in a few moments with his revered leader?"

"Since the Curia has initiated dozens of new rules and even more new forms demanding reasons for access and a bunch of other useless minutia. Alas, I alone need a good hour at least to present my case, plus I have six other committee members who must bring certain facts to light to substantiate our needs in this matter. Ideally we could use two, maybe three hours. And, as you know, I am not privileged to stroll into the inner sanctum at will. His Holiness and I are not particularly close."

Bortnowaska studied Malachi closely. "You're a free man, Mustavias," he said, using Malachi's Christian name in a friendly gesture. "After he has his third coffee – you'll find him semi-civilized then – march over and ask him for the time." He pointed to the head table covered with flowers where the white-robed, rotund bulk of the Pope could be seen sipping coffee.

As Malachi watched, the Pope seemed to be smiling wearily and nodding in reply to the animated conversations of a group of visiting North American Bishops seated on either side of him. Each appeared to be vying with equal determination for his attention. The Holy Father's head movements resembled someone watching a tennis match.

"You know how he is about protocol. He'd send me back to Lopez."

Bortnowaska sighed. "Yes...I suppose you're right. And by trying to bypass Lopez, you'd turn him into an enemy for life."

"Exactly."

"But if I get you in through the back staircase, Lopez will still not be pleased."

"But I'll be in..." Malachi said, with a slight smile. "After that, I'll gladly take his arrows in my back; this matter is critical." He extracted the envelope from his pocket. "This must be held in the utmost confidence but I can show you –".

The Archbishop held up his hand. "Not necessary. I'll do what I can for you. Of course, Lopez still controls his calendar so my only chance will be during some of his personal time or when I hear of a cancellation before Lopez does. My reward will be to stick it to the Prefecture for a change."

Malachi grinned, smiled his thanks and added: "You haven't asked me what it's all about."

Bortnowaska returned the smile. "Well, it must be none of my business or you would have told me."

"I do find it hard to understand what satisfaction Lopez gets out delaying me."

"Power...exercising his power," the Archbishop said, with a chuckle. "Much the same as goes on in some of our smaller parishes. You know why local church politics can be particularly vicious?"

Malachi shook his head.

"Because the stakes are so small," he responded, with something akin to a giggle.

Malachi smiled and put a hand on Bortnowaska's shoulder. "You're a rare bird, my friend."

"So I'm told," the Archbishop answered, rising as he unsuccessfully tried to stifle a loud burp. "Your leave, Eminence?"

Malachi smiled at the formal respect for his rank and gave a good-natured shrug. If Bortnowaska managed to get him in, he would be in this man's debt forever. The Archbishop gave him a wink and a wave, stifled another burp and made his way out of the room. It seemed he wouldn't have to give the man the envelope after all. He was being taken on faith.

Malachi caught sight of Lopez watching Bortnowaska leave. He hadn't been fooled; as the man disappeared he immediately shifted his gaze to Malachi. They found themselves staring at each other and Lopez quickly looked away. The anger in his beady little eyes fairly crackled.

The cardinal sighed and wondered why men felt so compelled to establish personal fiefdoms on earth and guard them with the jealousy of mad lovers? Life would be so simple if everyone practiced what Jesus preached and stored up spiritual treasures in Heaven rather than seeking petty victories on earth. But, in all fairness, Malachi also couldn't help enjoying a certain amount of inner pleasure over having taken the first step towards thwarting the Curia's bureaucracy, so who was he to give lessons in humility?

He glanced round the room which was now alive with people excusing themselves as they headed for their morning constitutions. Coffee, like beer, was never bought, merely rented, he thought with a chuckle and decided he'd better make a pit stop in the washroom before heading back to his office. But first, decorum dictated that he await the departure of the Holy Father who was rising even as the bishops followed suit.

Across the room, the Pope caught Malachi's eye, looked briefly at the heavens and gave him a wan smile indicating his weariness with his admirers. As he walked, he tried to rub the stiffness out of the back of his neck.

Malachi returned the smile thinking: so near and yet so far. He understood that the Holy Father didn't dislike him; it was merely that he didn't know him all that well. After a pope was inaugurated and established, as with the routine of his predecessors, he would customarily move people, with whom he had worked and was familiar into positions of power. Lopez had been one of his crew; Malachi had not.

The Pope now hastened his departure, moving through the shifting throng of clergy who clustered in his path. His stature was slightly bent and he walked with difficulty.

His rheumatism must be acting up, thought Malachi. As he waited, he couldn't help reviewing portions of the last 24 hours. His thoughts filled him with a mixture of concern, excitement and a healthy dose of trepidation.

At midnight he'd received word that the Vatican's leased A320 aircraft was en route from New York to Rome. It was quickly followed by the carefully worded air-telephone call from Bishop Aquila. "It begins Mustavias. As you know, we did not have the tools on hand so we removed the package. There was an obvious dark envoy present but our people moved quickly and successfully. According to reports, there can be no doubt we are dealing with *it*!"

Obviously, Adramelech had taken the bait and since the *Watchmen* couldn't bring in the *Crusaders,* they carried out Plan B and moved in to save Montague. Further details would have to wait until the man either reached a secure telephone or arrived in Vatican City.

With a six-hour time difference between the two cities and a brief sleep-over at Gatwick, he figured they had an ETA of three hours from now. On board were the witnesses he needed to show that their "prophecies" were unfolding. In fact they were taking place much quicker than any of them would have imagined, or preferred! He prayed inwardly that by removing Montague from harm's way, they hadn't tipped their hand. The creature was cunning; it must already know that the hunt for it was on again, but hopefully not that the Church had an ace up its sleeve.

The Pope was now near the door, bowing slightly and shaking hands with the many clerics lining his escape route. Lopez was already at his side, his own perceived self-importance manifested in the way he mimicked the Pope's gestures and occasionally shook hands with someone whom His Holiness had missed. The look of intense disappointment on the passed-over prelate's face as he caught Lopez's hand instead of the Pope's, made Malachi chuckle. Lopez didn't seem to notice.

His good humor quickly faded as he made ready to follow the Pontiff outside. He might have a better idea of how good a hand he actually held when the aircraft landed. Idly he wished that right now he was with Aquila sailing gaily somewhere above the clouds, listening to piped in music and sipping champagne. Oh, for the life of a jet-setter.

~ 14 ~

"Mayday...Mayday...Mayday!" Gostini shouted, over the scream of the stall warning indicator as the stick shaker vibrated and the A320 stalled out and then plummeted earthward through the night sky like a mortally wounded bird. He'd tried radioing their position moments before but had no reply from Gatwick or any other control center; an infernal static crackled madly through the headset. Now they were broadcasting to anyone on the 121.5 emergency band.

When the engines died, they had lost their last generator and all power. A Ram Air Turbine, a small propeller-driven emergency auxiliary propeller that powered an emergency generator, had immediately dropped out of the fuselage and was now providing enough power for a few basic standby instruments, flight controls and some linked hydraulics. Despite this, their hi-tech jet plane now featured the instrumentation and control of a World War I Sopwith Camel.

The roar of their dive was building, audible to the pilots as the big jet plunged towards the waves.

Outside, in the frigid night air at thirty thousand feet, a small man-like shadow let go the freezing aluminum of the huge tail and peeled away from the sinking aircraft; its eyes glowed with a fiery brilliance as its skin wings filled once more with wind and it soared aloft.

The Beast circled in the pale light of the full moon and watched the jet drop towards the black ocean waves far below.

Inside the cockpit, both pilots, oxygen masks now clamped over their faces, fought the hollowness in their stomachs and their own escalating fear as they frantically sought to control the aircraft and regain power in the eerie luminescence of the emergency lights.

Both engines had rolled back and flamed out. Thankfully he still had some hydraulic assist due to their emergency generator but it was at a minimum and Bowden was largely relying on skill to maintain control. Keeping the airplane flying and under control depended solely on having enough air slipping past the surfaces of wings, the rudder and ailerons for him to manipulate them and influence the attitude of the craft. That meant keeping up the airspeed through a dive. In turn, once they ran out of altitude, they also ran out of flying time.

Corded muscles standing out in his neck, Bowden held the aircraft in a steady descent as Gostini flipped switches to attempt a restart of their engines. He set the APU bleed to on, the engine selector from normal to IGN/START, the ENG MASTER switch to ON and tried again

"We're at two four zero..." Gostini yelled to the pilot, the underlying fear in his voice kept strictly in check by his professionalism. "They won't spool up!

Bowden stole a glance at their working standby altimeter. Its needle steadily unwound bringing them ever closer to their fate. Twenty-four thousand feet didn't give the pilots much time, barely minutes before the plane hit the water. He decreased the angle of their dive to gain a few more precious seconds in the air.

One wing dipped and Gostini, watching the captain struggle for control of the aircraft, grabbed his stick and helped as he called out their altitudes and they plummeted towards the earth.

"Come over sweetheart," Bowden said, through gritted teeth as their combined strength managed to straighten the jet.

They were still in a controlled descent but the seconds were ticking away. Their only hope lay in regaining power.

"Let's go…try again," Bowden said, knowing that the manual called for an attempted restart; in the event of continued failure, they were facing what was clinically termed: a water landing. In reality, a crash into brick-solid water that would see their life expectancy reduced to nil. Gostini tried to relight number one engine.

Bowden mentally said a quick Our Father and wondered what it would be like to die. If he had to take the jet in, it would certainly break up and explode in the giant sea swells. The end would come quickly. But even if they somehow managed to ditch and hold the aircraft together, and through another miracle were able to evacuate the jet before it settled and slid beneath the waves, freezing to death in the icy Atlantic waters wasn't exactly a win.

On impact, an Emergency Locator Transmitter in the tail of the jet would be automatically jettisoned and electronically signal a satellite pinpointing their position. Small comfort that some bodies might be recovered.

"She won't respond –!" Gostini said.

"Restart again...RESTART...!" Bowden yelled desperately, angry with whatever powers had chosen to make this his last day on earth. He longed to see his wife and know their baby, and to make amends for any of his failings. More than anything in the world he wanted to simply tell her he loved her and their unborn child. Now he wouldn't have the opportunity.

"I'm trying..." Gostini cried, even as he checked his own remaining instruments. The ASI gauge showed their airspeed at two hundred and eighty knots.

The plane dropped lower.

Suddenly the heavy plane began to vibrate as it descended through a temperature inversion. It pitched, swayed and bumped much as an automobile would driving from pavement onto a gravel road filled with potholes.

The pilot rammed his feet tighter on the rudder pedals and fought to hold it steady. If it heeled over he might not be able to regain straight and level flight; it would begin a death roll that would seal their fate.

"Oh Jesus...we're not gonna make it!" Gostini said.

The resignation in his copilot's voice sent a tremor through Bowden.

The aircraft abruptly pitched to starboard and the pilot felt a jarring blow as his head slammed against the cockpit window ledge. He cursed as blood ran down the side of his face. With a groan he managed to straighten the wings once again.

"Eighteen thousand...try again!" he yelled, his voice quaking as the aircraft's stick-shaker vibrations began again. Quickly he lowered the nose further.

Gostini leaned over and again threw the switch for engine number one. This time there was a whine, a pop and one red light on the control panel over his head switched to green and the engine spooled up.

"One's up!" he yelled, in jubilation.

The aircraft was suddenly alive with instruments returning to life. The cabin lights came on. Instrument needles jerked to position, digital readouts magically reappeared in their previously dark instrument windows, the weather radar glowed, and the radio crackled in both their ears.

"Advance the power... slow and easy!" Bowden said, through gritted teeth, unwilling to take his hand from the stick; he needed to keep the wings level. Beads of sweat ran unheeded down his cheeks and under the collar of his shirt.

Gostini advanced the throttle on number one.

As the hydraulics took hold, the stick responded and Bowden found himself easing back into his seat. The nose of the aircraft was rising but suddenly the plane heeled to the right as the starboard wing dipped. He quickly eased the stick forward and to the left until they were again on an even keel. If it stalled now, there might not be time to recover. He had to keep it slowly dropping until they had enough power to fully level out and then regain altitude. The Flight Management System was now working and Bowden immediately off-loaded work to it.

They were at forty-five hundred feet as Gostini punched up number two and the turbine whined and roared as though nothing had been amiss. The copilot gently eased the throttle to the second detent as Bowden now pulled his control stick back; the nose of the jet slowly lifted level.

"C'mon sweetheart!" Bowden said, the joy in his voice evident as their rate of descent finally showed zero.

The welcome G forces of acceleration started to push them both back in their seats and Gostini's eyes flickered to his altimeter. They had been at less than thirty-five hundred feet ASL when the artificial horizon finally showed them in level flight. At their previous rate of descent, they had been seconds away from doom.

The altimeter was now gaining feet, breaking four thousand and then five; they were in a full climb. Only now did Bowden identify the strange pounding in his ears he'd assumed had been the buffeting of the aircraft; it was the blood pumping from his heart. Well, he thought, if it took the last few minutes and didn't give out, I won't have to worry about my next medical.

The reprieve filled the pilot with an exultation, unabashed, uncompromised happiness that permeated his every sense; they weren't going to die. He found his mind clear of all worries and regrets; the accumulated mental baggage that typically weighs down every human being had magically been cast off at the doorway to death. His senses were unbelievably alive and sharp: he was certain he could now hear every screw straining and the composites flexing as the jet blasted upward towards the stars. In fact, he could smell the ripeness of the leather in his week-old shoes, feel the rough cotton of his starched shirt collar rubbing against some beard he'd missed shaving, and even detect a certain metallic taste in the air furnished from the compressed air cylinders feeding his mask. He was alive! There was veracity after all in the saying: to truly live, one must almost die.

Gostini, smiling wanly in relief, was also scanning the instruments. All showed normal functioning. "What the hell happened!?"

"I don't know...but it could happen again," Bowden said, now discarding the euphoria for the reality of their situation. His eyes were still on the vertical speed indicator. "Get out the manuals."

The pilot's pronouncement was as sobering as it was accurate and Gostini pulled out the operational manuals even as his thoughts drifted back to a few minutes before. Had he seen what he thought he'd seen outside the window? Impossible. It must have been a trick of the moonlight because nothing could live outside at 35,000 feet; the temperature was easily 50 below zero and there wasn't enough oxygen to keep a bird alive, much less anything else.

And yet...it seemed so real. When the dull thud of something hitting the aircraft had come, Gostini had been sure it was on his side and he'd instinctively glanced out the window and back towards the starboard wing position.

At first he thought he was staring at an old coat near his window, that it had somehow gotten snagged in a service bay door or some such thing and managed to miraculously remain throughout their flight. But then, just as quickly, he'd realized that there was no service door where the 'coat' was alternately spinning wildly in the air and being flattened against the skin of the aircraft by the tremendous slip stream. Then, to the copilot's horror, the supposed coat had taken shape!

It had ballooned out as though inflated by some mysterious force, and he found himself looking at a naked, leather-skinned, winged and horned creature clinging to the side of the aircraft. As he gaped, his numbed brain tried to deny the sight of the monster staring squarely at him through his window less than three feet away. Yellow, slanted eyes, shining like glowing embers, imprinted on his brain as the creature hung by fingers somehow sticking to the aluminum of the aircraft. Huge folds of wings flapped wildly on its back and a hole in the face yawned open where a mouth should be. Razor teeth gleamed in the moonlight. And then it was gone!!

It had vanished in the blink of an eye; it had to be an illusion...

...and yet it had seemed so real!

"Captain...?" It was Bishop Aquila, his face deathly white. He stood in the doorway. "What happened?"

"We don't know but it could happen again, Your Excellency! Please go back and belt yourself in."

"A malfunction...?"

The jet was in a steady climb now, breaking fifteen thousand feet, behaving as though they had just rotated out of La Guardia.

Trying to understand what had gone wrong, Bowden scanned the instruments again. They all read normal. Then why had they suddenly lost their airspeed? Why had they experienced almost simultaneous flameouts in both engines? There had to be a freak lightning strike that hit the plane. Or perhaps they had flown into some atmospheric anomaly that somehow formed a vacuum bubble starving the engines of the oxygen they needed to run. For a minute or two before they dropped, they had seemed to hang motionless in midair, almost as though suspended by their stabilizer from a giant skyhook. Nothing made sense which made him increasingly uneasy; whatever happened could repeat.

If it had been a headwind that somehow snuffed them out, it had to be the mother of all headwinds! And anyhow, while their groundspeed might have eroded, their airspeed wouldn't. Of course, Bowden didn't believe it had anything to do with a headwind. But, at the same time he didn't know what to believe. He looked over at Gostini. "Get Gatwick on the horn and inform them we had a double engine failure, descended to four thousand, reason unknown and we are now reassuming our original flight level and vector."

"Captain...?"

Bowden looked back at the bishop. If he wanted to keep his job, he'd better be a little more circumspect in his treatment of the old gentleman. The man was clearly frightened. "Everything's operating normally now, Your Excellency." The pilot realized he was speaking into his oxygen mask, pulled it off and continued: "We lost our engines...we're not sure why...but they seem to be fine now."

"Will we turn back?"

"No, we're past the point of no return...it's shorter to continue."

Suddenly a thought seemed to hit the old man. He stared at Bowden: "The running lights! Are they on?" There was urgency as well as a hint of concern in the old man's voice, almost as though he knew what the answer would be.

Bowden reluctantly shook his head. "Nor will they be." The bishop vanished from the cockpit.

~ 15 ~

High above the Atlantic Ocean, Adramelech flew purposely on demon wings back towards the city from which he had first risen to seek vengeance on his prey. His speed outpaced any form of aircraft. Barely minutes into his return flight, miles ahead and tens of thousands of feet below, the first glow of the millions of lights of the distant New York shoreline lit the night sky.

Now he paused in flight.

Within seconds he had abandoned his arrow-straight singular route, and circled and soared on the high winds going neither forward nor back. Buffeted roughly by the unforgiving jet stream, he scarcely noticed it as he tried to decipher his feelings.

A sixth sense, an evil omnipotence, had begun to overcome him, needling at his confidence, crying dire warnings until finally persistence paid off; the creature took heed of his instincts.

SOMETHING WAS WRONG.

The former feeling of triumph, the satisfaction of killing, had now been replaced by a nagging failure, an uneasy sense of an incomplete victory.

After a moment he knew! He knew with a dreadful, supernatural clarity, with a terrible conviction reserved for those with second sight; his prey continued to live.

Fury and rage choked the Beast. He turned his flight and began to retrace his path back through the purple sky. Powerful wings of skin reinforced with boney ribs drove him forward and up, filling and lifting him higher.

He continued upward until he sensed a powerful wind at his back. Relaxing only slightly, he sped back towards the point where he'd had left the jet plunging towards the sea.

As the seconds turned to minutes, the creature streaked through the dark air under wisps of cirrus clouds which had now begun to join and thicken. A hundred miles on, they became cirrostratus and, in turn, some distance further, changed to balls of cotton-like cumulus. Finally, as hundreds of miles fled by, the cumulus changed to great towering mounds of cumulonimbus rain clouds. Inside them lightning flickered and snapped, and ear splitting crashes rolled into peals of thunder.

The Beast took advantage of warm air currents and rose in a graceful circle high above the thickening cover until he found himself flying over a dull white carpet punctuated by columns of skyscraper-like mounds jarring upwards through the misty floor. These pyramids of nature continued to vent their fury. Bolts of electricity, with temperatures hotter than the surface of the sun, betrayed a savage internal wrath.

Illuminated by a pure white light bouncing off the clouds, he glanced upward and saw a crystal ring of ice pellets forming a circle around a full moon. In the eastern sky the first signs of gold appeared as the dawn made ready.

Suddenly, he swept to a stop and stood upright in mid-air, his ribbed wings beating a relentless tattoo that kept him stable. Now he was but a tiny silhouette in the night, his monstrous head turning left and right as he listened to the distant roar of aircraft engines. His foe drew nigh.

He strained again for the sounds of the engines vowing that this time he would not toy with these insignificant mortals. He would pierce the skin of their vessel like a needle through a balloon and let it explode.

The shrill whistle of the straining jet engines grew in intensity, piercing the night ahead of the Beast.

The craft was somewhere below, somewhere underneath the rolling white clusters.

This time there would be no error.

Like a falcon hunting its prey, he folded his arms close, pulled in the wings that jutted from his back and dove like an arrow forward and down towards the sound.

Barely five miles ahead, the huge A320 jet suddenly burst through the silvery clouds into the moonlight and rocketed upwards at speed as it headed towards its former cruising altitude. Adramelech stopped his descent and then surged upwards, preparing to get above and ahead of the aircraft.

~ 16 ~

"Dear God!" Maria said, her racing heart slowly returning to a normal beat. She had been sure they were all about to die when the aircraft dropped and continued to drop for so long. Everyone was wide awake now except their charge; she looked over at the private detective who had blissfully slept through it all. He continued to breathe normally, strapped securely into one of two hospital beds sharing the sitting room.

Dr. Butler had poked his head out from his stateroom looking very pale. Seated on the couch, the two priests looked relieved as both had been saying the Act of Contrition as salvation for their souls during the aircraft's dive. Bishop Aquila was making his way forward to the cockpit again which he entered without knocking. Maria could barely hear him.

"Turn the visibility lights on!" Bishop Aquila ordered in a no-nonsense tone holding himself steady in the cockpit door as the jet climbed.

Bowden could feel a resentment building inside him. The lights might be a further drain on their electrics. In fact, he wondered if the auxiliary light system had not been installed properly and somehow compromised their electrical system and the on-board computers. Perhaps it had been responsible for the engine failure.

"Your Excellency, something went very wrong and we almost crashed," Bowden said busily checking his instrument readouts while scanning the horizon for weather abnormalities. "Please go back and sit down."

"The lights!"

Gostini stared from Bowden to the Bishop.

The old man's face was red with fury.

"I can't put them on right now!" Bowden said, his voice clipped. "I'm not doing anything that might endanger this aircraft; for all I know those auxiliary lights might have shorted something out."

"That wasn't what happened," Aquila said, his tone certain. "There are events unfolding that you do not understand, Captain."

"I'm sorry; I'm in command here, Your Excellency, and you *will* leave the cockpit... please!"

Again Aquila vanished from the doorway, slamming the door.

Gostini sighed with a sinking feeling in the pit of his stomach. Though he agreed with the Captain's reasoning, he wondered if this would mean their dismissal at the end of the flight. If they landed safely, of course.

"Jesus...we almost pranged this SOB a few minutes ago and that man is worried about how we look...!" Bowden's voice died as he twisted to look back at cockpit door opening again. Aquila entered.

Gostini followed his gaze and could scarcely believe his eyes.

Bishop Aquila, silhouetted against the cabin lights was difficult to see but there was no mistaking the black revolver he held trained on Bowden. "Captain Bowden, you will either put on the visibility lights or I will...I will remove you and let First Officer Gostini complete the flight."

The Bishop followed up his threat by cocking the revolver. Despite the dull whistle of the engines, the hiss of the cabin airflow and a custom installed soft chime warning the cockpit door was open, the metallic click was still distinctly audible in the cockpit.

~ 17 ~

Adramelech adjusted his trajectory from above and headed for the jet as it arced upwards seeming to make for the moon. His speed accelerated as he adjusted his aim towards the widest part of the aircraft, just behind the wing.

There would be no time to delicately open veins, no time to languish and suck the sweet, life-giving nourishment of his victims. It would merely be a neat, efficient fulfillment of an ancient reality: all who saw the Beast must die. Then he would continue his insidious work confounding the mortals of the planet and seducing them to choose Satan's lair.

Though finding the soldier had been long and difficult, he would finish what he had began so long ago in the jungle; he would ensure the man's death.

As he sped towards the jet, the Beast toyed with the idea of puncturing the jet, grabbing the soldier and hurtling down to an altitude where there was enough air to keep him alive.

Once they were in comfortable flight, he could open the soldier's throat.

His arrow-like figure ripped towards the aircraft at blinding speed...3000 yards...2000 yards...!

An explosion of light suddenly blinded him. He instinctively peeled over to the side missing the jet completely.

The Beast filled his wings again, pumped powerful muscles and climbed above the jet which had leveled off at 35,000 feet. He stared down in hate, a low rattle building in his throat.

A thousand feet below the creature, the jet sailed on, now a brilliant symbol of power and hope riding the night currents of a jet stream in the troposphere.

With the reluctant flick of a switch by Captain Bowden, the visible outline of the aircraft had changed completely; the jet's visibility lights had illuminated the main wing and fuselage to form the shape of a brilliant, shining Crucifix.

Abruptly, his rage now dissipated by the familiar weakness associated with the symbol, he turned back towards the city. In fact, he was growing stronger every day and there would be another time for the soldier. Right now he would return to preying on the malcontents and underworld figures of the earth, the gutter people, the disenfranchised, and society's castoffs; he could easily win the most vulnerable, those wretches without jobs, security or hope.

Again he would assume human form and preach to them of a god that cared, that shared their pain and one who, so long ago, had been banished from the Light because of his affinity for the underdogs and his thirst for knowledge and understanding. After all, with Adramelech's help those on the road to hell would surely meet their black lord and master a little sooner.

* * * *

PART FOUR

"THE MISSION"

On a starred night Prince Lucifer
Uprose
Tired of his dark dominion swung the
Fiend...

George Meredith
LUCIFER IN STARLIGHT (1883)

~ 1 ~

Bowden stretched in the cockpit and looked forward to landing in Rome, having a hot shower and a good sleep. For both he and Gostini, the last couple of days had been particularly grueling. Though he wondered if there would be more fallout from his refusal to turn on the visibility lights, after the confrontation the bishop had treated him as though nothing untoward had happened.

They had flown the remainder of the New York-Gatwick leg without incident but he had insisted on having the aircraft thoroughly checked at Heathrow Airport in London. Because their mayday calls had not been received by Gatwick or any other control center, Bishop Aquila asked Bowden not to file any sort of incident report; they didn't want any publicity. The captain agreed, but in exchange, had extracted the agreement for engine inspections. The result: they spent two days longer than originally planned for the flight.

Their unconscious patient, and his nurse and doctor remained on the aircraft with the aft section containing the sick bay and sleeping and eating quarters locked up tight. Power for lights and air conditioning was furnished by an auxiliary generating unit they ordered hooked up to the aircraft. The rest of their passengers had retired to a nearby hotel while Bowden and Gostini saw to the check-up. They also bunked at an airport hotel but different from the bishop and his crew.

British Airways had been gracious enough to furnish maintenance assistance and the aircraft had been meticulously examined by an army of engineers, mechanics and avionics' technicians. They were merely told the engines had been running rough, quit and then restarted. Countless diagnostics were run, the engines were probed, prodded and the aircraft even test-flown in the Gatwick circuit. It performed flawlessly. Neither the mechanics nor any other member of the maintenance team could find any reason for the aircraft's strange behavior.

Since both engines cut out within moments of each other, and there was ample fuel on board at the time, the only possible explanation they could come up with was a computer malfunction which failed to show up on the diagnostic records. The fact they couldn't trace it, nor had other Airbus 320 experienced it, was not very comforting. No-one was particularly satisfied with that explanation, but it was all they had.

Finally the aircraft had been pronounced fit and the British Airways Chief of Maintenance, as well as the team of mechanics, signed off on the airworthiness of the A320.

Bowden telephoned his report to Bishop Aquila staying at a hotel near the airport. The elderly clergyman had been straightforward and friendly on the telephone. This confirmed the bishop's suspicions: their troubles on the flight had *not* been mechanical but more of a "church" matter. He patiently explained that if Bowden had turned on the visibility lights when they left La Guardia, there would have been no trouble; God would have guarded them.

Bowden was more inclined to place his trust in an aircraft engineer at the moment, but he stayed mute. During their preflight planning for their next leg, he and Gostini spent extra time noting alternate airports along their route and ensuring their altitude would give them a sufficient glide ratio to reach them where possible. They began referring to those legs where there weren't any "glide" alternates as "dead legs", the implication being that if the bug returned and they lost power, they'd likely wind up dead.

The priests, the nun, and the bishop had arrived and been boarded.

Once again Bowden had marveled at the ease with which the entourage had slipped through Customs & Immigration at Gatwick. The church was a power unto itself.

They would set down in Rome after dark Bowden thought as he eased the throttles forward and the big jet thundered down the runway and lifted into the sky.

The flight to Rome turned out to be uneventful, yet both pilots were still cautious as they entered the traffic pattern for the Italian capital.

Bowden moved the stick to the right bringing the heavy jet around from his holding pattern to intercept a long, slow final approach to Leonardo Da Vinci International airport. In front of him was an American Airlines DC-10 and an Alitalia Airlines 737 that would touch down and clear the runway first.

"So far...so good," he said to Gostini.

The copilot grinned uneasily and shook his head as though saying to hold the congratulations until they were safely on the ground.

They were now passing through five thousand feet in their descent towards Rome. Bowden turned the plane slightly and successfully intercepted the Rome VOR radial for the beginning of their VOR approach.

Gostini's altimeter unwound counterclockwise, barely one revolution per minute. His altimeter was set to height above the airport. He carefully watched it and periodically called out altitude readings to Bowden. They passed the outer marker, entered a low cloud bank and outside the windscreen everything went black. Gostini craned forward to catch sight of the runway.

"Wayne?" Gostini called to Bowden.

"Yeah...?"

"I dunno how to say this...but I saw something funny just before the flameouts."

"What?" Bowden asked, incredulously. "Why the hell didn't you speak up before?" He was both surprised and annoyed that his first officer had withheld information.

Though curious, Bowden's eyes flicked back to their airspeed: this wasn't exactly the time to be sidetracked. Their airspeed held at 165 knots. He checked the DME window. They were still about ten miles from the airport. He felt the aircraft settling and eased the throttles forward slightly, alternately watching the EPR gauges and the vertical speed indicator. He needed to hold the thousand foot-per-minute descent, remain exactly on the glide path and get the runway in sight. "So...what did you see?"

Gostini hesitated, swallowed and then bravely continued on: "I thought I saw some sort of figure hanging onto the fuselage...right after that thump."

"A bird carcass?"

"No...."

Bowden looked over at the copilot, puzzled by his tone. He nodded towards the radio. "Tell them we're inbound."

Gostini keyed his microphone: "Charter 104 inbound on final, over."

The cockpit radio crackled: "Roger, Charter 104, we have you, you're looking good, over."

"Thank you, sir," Gostini said, and released the transmit button.

With the affirmation from the tower, both pilots returned to the business of landing their aircraft. They would not make contact with the tower again until they touched down. Then Ground Control would direct them to their bay.

They broke out of the overcast with wisps of cloud illuminated by their powerful landing lights whipping by the nose of the aircraft. Ahead and below, the lights of Rome stretched for miles, a carpet of unbroken, sparkling, colored jewels that, as they settled lower, resolved themselves to be the lights of houses, apartments, and domed buildings interspersed with rows of intersecting street lamps. On the roads and highways thousands of headlights from ant-like traffic moved resolutely towards individual destinations.

Gostini liked and respected Wayne Bowden. He certainly didn't want to be seen by him as being some sort of wacko, still, he felt he owed the pilot the truth – or at least, what he perceived to be the truth.

As the A320 sank lower and lower, he lost himself momentarily in the beauty of the city. He never tired of night landings; the city lights took on the appearance of friendly beacons welcoming him back to the sanctuary of civilization after another prowl through the night skies. They entered another cloud and everything vanished.

"Gear down," Bowden said, interrupting Gostini's thoughts. As they broke through the mist the runway lights of the airstrip appeared. "There we are...dead ahead."

The pilot had purposely refrained from deploying the gear earlier just in case they ran into more engine trouble. Bowden preferred they have as little drag as possible in case they lost power suddenly and needed to glide.

Gostini obliged, reached forward and pulled the landing gear lever. The rumble of the nose wheel extending shook the floor panels beneath his feet and he felt the jet momentarily stagger as their drag increased. Though he had felt the same sensation thousands of times before, this time, for a split second Gostini felt concern as the aircraft slowed. If, as happened during the New York-Gatwick leg of their flight, they did lose their engines, they would undershoot the runway and wind up a smoldering melee of metal and body parts somewhere on the streets below. He stared up at the green lights indicating the wheels were down. "Gear down and locked," he said.

Sensing the strain in his co-pilot's voice, Bowden gave him a look and asked: "What did you see out there, Dan?"

Gostini hesitated: "A...some sort of man...or something."

"A man!? C'mon!"

"Well...more like some kind of manlike creature." He immediately regretted his candor.

Gostini stared straight ahead hardly daring to look at the pilot though he could feel his friend's eyes boring into him. He shouldn't have spoken. They needed a sterile cockpit for landing anyhow.

Bowden stared at his first officer for a full three seconds, a relative eternity during a landing, and then turned away and concentrated on the DME on his instrument panel. As he mentally tried to rationalize what his copilot had just said, he watched the tenths of miles ticking off: 5.7, 5.6, 5.5....

The aircraft continued its descent, now at a mere 200 feet per minute. He checked their approach airspeed: 165 knots.

The VOR needle centered.

Everything A-Okay.

Beside him, as though nothing out of the ordinary had been said, Gostini began running through the final pre-landing checklist. Every moment or so he glanced at a list clipped to his knee.

"Ignition," he said, reaching up and pushing the switches to the continuous position. "No smoke...radar's up and off...gear down...! He glanced at the annunciator panel - small squares which would light up while giving an audible warning if anything was wrong. Every square was A-Okay - good news.

"One thousand, instruments cross-checked, landing memo green," he continued, reaching to the center control pedestal to grasp the spoiler lever and pull it into the armed position.

"Dan?"

Gostini looked at the pilot: "Yeah?"

"Maybe you should take a rest after this flight...eh?"

"Wayne, I saw what I saw! It was a-a...humanoid...a-a creature of some kind."

There was no reply from Bowden.

Gostini pressed his point. "I know you're eyeing the fire extinguisher in case I flip out but I swear to God there was this-this THING...hanging onto the fuselage just behind my window!"

Bowden cleared his throat: "We'll deal with it after landing."

"Damn!" Gostini said, angry with himself for speaking up.

"Let's just forget it," the pilot said. "When I'm tired, I've seen some pretty strange things out the windows too..." He grinned and added amiably: "Once I thought I saw Rocky the Flying Squirrel out there but my first officer said I was nuts. It was definitely Bullwinkle J. Moose."

Gostini didn't laugh and Bowden took the rejection with a shrug. Instead the co-pilot retreated into a moody silence, watching the twin rows of runway lights reaching up for them. Blue taxiway lights led off to the right and left down in front, and he could make out the lights of another airliner shooting towards the sky from an alternate runway off their starboard side.

"Here we go," Bowden said, pushing the nose down a fraction and further reducing power. "Hello Rome, are we glad to see you!" The runway rushed towards them as the computer's metallic voice counted out: "200 feet...100 feet...50 feet." At 50 feet he cut power entirely and brought the nose up three degrees to flare for landing. A welcome jolt announced they were down.

~ 2 ~

Clay felt himself being lifted to his feet. Still groggy, he barely managed to grab hold of the edge of a white metal table before he teetered and almost fell. His legs felt rubbery and weak; the inside of his mouth was most certainly coated with fuzz. He had thrown up a few minutes ago which made his stomach feel better. They'd allowed him a quick rinse with mouthwash, to use the bathroom and then escorted him back to a couch.

The doctor, who had introduced himself a few seconds earlier as Dr. Butler, helped him maintain his balance with a hand under his arm.

"You're just a little rocky, Mr. Montague. It'll pass."

"Yeah...thanks Doc."

Clay's mind was whirling. He had awakened less than five minutes ago to find himself in some sort of medical dispensary along with Butler and a nurse who deliberately ignored his questions as they repeatedly encouraged him to get to his feet.

He had been helped up, led along a short corridor and into what looked like an operating theatre and seated on a white, leather couch. Despite his best efforts, he had promptly fallen asleep again.

Now he raised his head and looked over at three men dressed in black suits and clerical collars busily gathering up papers, coats and hats. The elderly priest was obviously in charge as he murmured orders to the other two. The doctor and nurse had disappeared.

Where the hell am I, he wondered looking carefully about the interior of the room for the first time. The operating table and various other pieces of medical equipment around the walls confirmed he was in a medical center of some kind. But where? Was he still in Manhattan? Or somewhere else in the city? And, how long had he been unconscious?

As Clay's senses became more acute, memories flooded back: the office, the *Watchers* breaking through the door, and the impacts of the slugs hitting him in the chest.

He'd been shot several times.

Cautiously he raised his hand to his chest expecting to find it swathed in bandages. Though his chest was awfully sore he couldn't feel any bandages through his clothes, merely what seemed to be a number of small pieces of taped gauze on his chest.

Now he realized with a start that he was dressed in garb similar to the priests. He felt the constriction of a clerical collar about his neck and fingered it curiously as he gazed down at his own black suit. He knew he should feel anger but he only felt confusion.

The tallest priest had stopped his business to catch the detective's eye. Clay was sure he was one of the *Watchers* – possibly the Leader.

"Fancy that," Clay said with a wry, if weak, attempt at humor. "I must have slept through my ordination."

Father Murphy grinned: "Just a precaution, Mr. Montague."

"Who are you? What's g-going on?"

"You're safe." The new voice was soft and feminine and came from his right.

Clay turned and almost fell sideways on the couch. A small hand grasped him firmly by the arm as he shifted his gaze to a young woman in a red sweater and a grey skirt who held him steady and stared up with genuine concern in her eyes.

"Will you be able to walk?" she asked, her voice light, almost musical and having the slightest French accent.

"I-I don't know," he said, doubtfully. "Where am I?" Neither the girl nor any of the three priests made any comment; the men merely went back to gathering up their wares. The girl smiled.

Clay looked down at her again and took in a pair of huge, dark eyes and a classic bob haircut; her dark brown hair framed her small, heart-shaped face. Her naturally red lips, moist and parted, revealed a slight overbite, but just enough to give her a hint of mischievous impertinence to an otherwise open, honest face. She was only slightly over five and a half feet, he guessed and incredibly attractive. For the first time in years, he felt a strange thrill permeate his body and his heartbeat quicken.

Clay then became distracted by a throbbing through the floor. The low rumble of some sort of furnace he decided. Suddenly the thunderous roar of what could only be a jet aircraft taking off also filled the room. He looked towards what appeared to be an open doorway twenty feet forward of where he stood. At the same time he noted the cylindrical shaped ceiling and walls of the operating theatre. It told him enough.

"We're on an aircraft," he said in surprise.

Father Murphy nodded, stuck out his hand and grasped Clay's in a firm handshake: "We may as well get acquainted. I'm Father Dermott Murphy....this is Father Ronald Langevin and Bishop Aquila." The other two followed suit and shook hands.

The young woman merely nodded. "I'm Sister Maria," she said simply.

Despite the grogginess and overall confusion, Clay still had the presence of mind to feel a certain disappointment; she was a nun. He quickly chastised himself. What did it matter? Right now he obviously had major problems since he'd been drugged and kidnapped by...clergy?

"We'll explain everything very shortly, Mr. Montague," Bishop Aquila promised, all business now. "I'm sure you have many questions."

Clay nodded and looked at the other two men. "You're the *Watchers*," he said to Murphy and Langevin as they donned their black coats and wide-brimmed hats.

"Our group is called the *Watchmen* but we can go with your title." Langevin said.

"You've been following me for weeks."

"More like years," the priest ventured, with a slight chuckle as he buttoned his coat.

"Years? And you shot me," Clay continued, feeling his temper rising as he remembered them firing at him; he rose unsteadily.

"These men saved your life, Mr. Montague," Aquila said, stepping between them and gently placing his hand against Clay's chest.

"Saved my life? Like hell! They shot me..."

"...with tranquilizing darts," Aquila finished.

"Darts?"

"Yes," Murphy chimed in. "We used darts on you..." He touched a small white bandage near his eye and added wryly: "...while you tried to use a small howitzer on us!"

The dry witticism softened Clay's anger and he relaxed. Darts? That explained the absence of bandages and why he was so groggy. "I've been asleep for…how many hours?"

The priests looked at each other.

"Actually…days," Murphy corrected.

"Days…" Clay repeated, still dazed. He looked closer at Murphy and Langevin. There was something familiar about them. He strained to remember. Finally…"You guys were at Hitch's funeral. You followed me onto the hill!"

Murphy nodded. "We were there. We've been doing our best to look after you for years," he admitted, with a tired sigh.

"I thought Catholic priests were into bingo, not kidnapping," Clay said.

"This isn't a kidnapping," Maria said. "More of a rescue mission."

Clay turned to her. "And I suppose you're mystery woman from the Saab?"

"I was there," she said gently. "We had to get you out."

Suddenly the image of the cloaked woman facing the child on the rainy street came back to the detective.

"The kid..?" Clay asked, hoarsely. "Where is she?"

Maria gave a faint shudder. "I don't know and I don't want to know."

Clay shook his head trying to clear it. After years of self-recrimination and guilt, his one hope, a single link with the past, had been within his grasp. Something told him the child was the same one he encountered so long ago. If he could bring her to the FBI, he could find out who butchered his deputy and remove any lingering shadow of doubt that might still hang over him. "Listen to me," he said to Maria and then swept his hand towards the priests to include them all. "I want to know where that child is, or so help me, each and every one of you will be standing trial for kidnapping!"

"If that happens, Mr. Montague," Langevin answered, gently, "then you will already be dead...or at best killed shortly thereafter."

"Don't threaten me," Clay said, shaking off Maria's hand.

Murphy looked at him and said quietly: "It's not a threat, my son, it's a fact. And you wouldn't be harmed by us. You'd face something a lot worse. Something you faced before. We're here to protect you. Please believe me; please believe in *us*!"

For some unfathomable reason, Clay did believe him; whatever their purpose, in his bones he knew these people were not out to harm him.

"Enough!" Aquila said, thrusting a passport into Clay's hand. "You're Father André Maisonrouge from Niece, France, in case we are stopped. If we bump into the wrong crowd, we may have to go through customs and immigration. At least until we can summon our man here."

Clay looked at the passport. It was French. He thumbed it open to find a photo of himself in clerical garb. As he took in his half-open eyes, the memory of a flash of light came to him. They must have photographed him while he was only partially conscious.

Without further ado, Clay was led to a set of stairs at the door of the plane. Cool night air wafted through and helped him clear his head, even though it was mixed with the kerosene-like odor of jet fuel.

Father Murphy turned to the doctor who had reappeared. "When we're out, close the door and have Captain Bowden move the plane to our assigned post as usual. We'll contact you tomorrow."

The doctor nodded.

Clay, Maria and the three clergymen all stepped out of the plane onto a metal ramp with a stairway extending down to the ground. Murphy stopped Clay from descending the steps and told him to hang on. Everyone grasped the railings as the steps, attached to a small vehicle underneath, moved away from the aircraft and stopped when it was well clear of the wingtip.

It was a cool, moist night. An absence of stars signaled it was slightly overcast. Their hard soled shoes rang hollow on corrugated aluminum as they walked down the metal staircase mounted on the truck. More roars of jets taking off could be heard in the distance and Clay noted that they were disembarking about a mile from what seemed to be a main terminal building. He could make out a hub of activity surrounding the building topped by a control tower on which a beacon slowly rotated intermittently sending a brilliant swathe of cloudy light cutting across the night sky.

"Move quickly," Aquila said into Clay's ear as they descended.

"Where are we? Where are we going?"

"To a comfortable bed. That should make you happy."

The bishop was right. Clay couldn't wait to rest his unsteady legs. As they descended, he saw other out-lying buildings around the field. Amid the taxi-ways and main strips there were scores of large jets clustered around terminal ramps. It was raining as they came off the steps; their heels clattered onto the cool tarmac and they marched hurriedly towards a long, black limousine about three hundred feet from the plane. The automobile's emergency lights were rhythmically flashing a silent red tattoo into the pools of water lying on the wet pavement; Clay noted a wisp of smoke curling from the automobile's exhaust pipe.

The truck with the steps welded to its frame pulled away. Its orange light flashed as it sped off across the field.

Clay glanced back and noted that the white A320 had no markings other than registration numbers on the tail. It seemed to be waiting for something on the apron. Its strobe light flashed. He could just make out the pilot above them in the warm, amber glow of the cockpit lights.

Glancing towards the terminal building again, he saw that amid the rumble and whistle of departing and taxiing aircraft, comparatively small airport luggage carriers scurried from aircraft to building. Fuel and catering trucks, as well as fork-lifts piled high with crates, moved purposely about their business. Hosts of men in coveralls and yellow safety vests swarmed like worker bees beside and around the planes gleaming in the floodlights. Figures worked at open baggage compartment doors, or clamped refueling hoses to the undersides of wings. Other workers walked about with orange cone lights in hand to receive incoming airliners at their gates.

"Why didn't the driver park closer," Aquila grumbled, glancing nervously around as they continued walking towards the limousine parked near the grassy border of the tarmac.

"Where's the driver?" Father Murphy asked, expecting him to jump out and open the back door. "He couldn't miss us landing." His tone conveyed a modicum of uneasiness.

Idly, Clay wondered if he should make a break for it. The priests and Sister Maria were doing their best to surround him, but short of Father Murphy, Clay figured he could easily break away.

Whether he could evade being recaptured was another matter. He was still pretty weak.

Maria seemed to read his mind for she crowded closer ushering him quickly towards the automobile. They moved in an awkward form of a huddle, the two priests casting quick, nervous glances to the left and right, and even upward into the sky.

"Don't think about running, Mr. Montague, you could be killed!" Maria warned, her tone worried.

"By you?" Clay asked, beginning to breathe heavily from the exertion, his strength ebbing quickly.

"Don't be ridiculous," she said, tightly. She looked over at Murphy. "Father, there's something here…I feel it. I *really* feel it!"

Clay felt apprehension wash over him like an ice cold shower. Murphy looked at her and raised his eyebrows. He held up his hand and they all stopped.

Behind them, the port engine on the A320 suddenly increased in intensity to a loud whine and the aircraft began to turn away. Its jet wash momentarily whipped a wind at them but it quickly swept past as the aircraft made ready to roll to its overnight parking location.

Clay felt Maria stiffen and draw a deep breath. He was surprised to see both Langevin and Murphy now clutched heavy, silver Crucifixes in their hands. The two priests started to move forward from the group, Murphy on the perimeter and Langevin towards the back door of the vehicle.

"Wait!" Maria called, her voice low but nevertheless conveying an urgency few could ignore.

At the automobile, Langevin froze and then gingerly removed his hand from the back door handle; the priest cautiously backed away from the door.

Maria had been holding Clay's arm tightly, crowding him in her hurry to get him into the limo. Now, with her body still pressed close to his, he felt her beginning to tremble. Silently she began to draw him backwards, away from the vehicle. "Mother of God!" she whispered, her eyes wide. "There's something here!" She was looking towards the darkened driver's window while backing up and pulling Clay.

Aquila stood his ground and called out loudly: "Driver!"

Though Clay could make out the form of a man sitting at the steering wheel, the figure failed to respond to the bishop's voice.

"Cripes!" Murphy exclaimed tersely as he and Langevin rejoined the group. He nodded to Langevin.

Both reached inside their jackets and pulled out heavy, black revolvers with their free hands.

"More darts?" Clay asked sarcastically, wondering if he was dealing with the church or the Mafia.

"Not this time," Murphy mumbled. "Ruger .44 Magnums with +P-loads and hollow-points…dipped in holy water and blessed by a cardinal; some good they'll do if we've been compromised."

Despite the tension, Clay was impressed. He knew weapons and the .44 Magnum was one of the most powerful handguns on the planet. The +P-loads indicated higher-quality gun powder in larger quantities, and hollow points or dum-dums delivered maximum stopping power. These boys were sporting handguns that could literally bring down a rhino.

"Sister, open the driver's door and stand back," Murphy ordered, holding his revolver steady. Clay saw that he had exchanged his Crucifix for a small but powerful halogen flashlight. He and Langevin moved forward and covered the front door with their weapons.

Maria relaxed her grip on Clay and he felt Aquila immediately grab him by the arm. He was pulled back further from the limo.

"Now wait a minute," Clay began, as Maria advanced to pull open the driver's door. "Don't let her–!"

His protest was cut short as Maria pulled door open and jumped back. The body of the driver pitched out of his seat and hit the tarmac on his side. From the way he landed and rolled limply onto his back, arms flopping out, Clay sensed immediately the man was dead.

Maria gave a small cry, and turned away.

Murphy's light centered on the body. The driver had been a priest, his white collar now splashed with blood. The middle of his chest was an explosion of vacant redness gleaming wetly in the automobile's flashing emergency lights. His eyes were moist, luminous, black disks, fixed and dilated and still conveying a final sense of impending horror and doom.

"It's been here," Maria whispered, as Clay and the Bishop moved forward and stared at the driver.

"No kidding," Murphy said, his tone bitter.

"Mother of God...!" Bishop Aquila said softly, making the sign of the cross even as he watched Langevin kneel beside the chauffeur and feel for a pulse.

"I doubt you'll find one," Murphy said tightly, looking down at the body. "His heart appears to have been ripped out."

Langevin stared at the man's chest, nodded silently, blessed the body quickly and backed away from the corpse. Together, they all retreated a good fifty feet from the automobile for a council.

The limo's front door now yawned open; a dull interior light emitted a warm invitation to enter the shelter and escape the chill of the misting rain. Clay noted that the Bishop now held a small revolver in his hand.

"I'll drive," Langevin volunteered.

The limo was parked at such an angle that any illumination from the retreating aircraft's flashing beacon was hitting the rear of the vehicle but being effectively screened by the darkened privacy windows. Even with the added glow of the dashboard lights, it was difficult to make out the interior of the rear seat.

"Sister, is it still here?" Murphy asked without taking his eyes off the open door.

"I-I can't tell...there's still a-a sense of-of oppression...of blackness," Maria answered, her voice quivering. "I-I don't know if it's residual…or-or….maybe it's still here."

"Yes or no!?"

"I-I don't know...." She shuddered, looking sick.

"Dandy," Murphy said.

"We can't stay out here all night," Bishop Aquila griped, impatiently.

"Alright, let's see what we've got!" Murphy said, taking charge. He strode forward shining the long, black halogen flashlight at the automobile. He circled the vehicle once, spotlighting it and trying to see into the back through the privacy windows.

Approaching the open front driver's door once again, he coughed as he inadvertently inhaled a mouthful of drifting exhaust fumes.

Langevin moved in a half-circle around Murphy towards the front of the vehicle. He stopped at the hood, his revolver aimed directly at the windshield for a clear shot into the interior. He was making sure that Murphy's body did not block his line of fire.

The taxiing A320 now sent out a piercing whistle as the pilot advanced the throttles slightly; it was almost a thousand feet away. Bishop Aquila glanced desperately back at the moving plane as their one line of retreat was withdrawn.

Like a soldier chucking a grenade into an enemy bunker, Murphy suddenly leaned forward, exchanged the flashlight for his Crucifix and chucked it onto the front seat of the automobile. He beat a hasty retreat from the open door and spun to point his weapon.

They all waited, staring at the limo in silence.

The engine continued to purr quietly, the tailpipe emitting its exhaust which was beginning to pool around the car in the still night air.

Nothing happened.

After about thirty seconds, Murphy nodded to Langevin who straightened, pointed his weapon in the air and carried his own Crucifix towards the back of the vehicle. Murphy joined him and grasped the back door handle of the passenger compartment. Licking dry lips, the priest felt his heart accelerating as Langevin readied his Crucifix. Murphy quietly began to recite the Our Father. He pulled the door open....

Langevin forcefully threw the silver cross inside. It smacked against the opposite window in back. Murphy slammed the door and recoiled.

Barely breathing, revolvers fixed on the back door, they waited....

Nothing happened....

Up till now, Clay had been mesmerized by the ominous warning from Maria, the discovery of the body and the subsequent actions of the priests. But heaving Crucifixes into the automobile like grenades, and expecting something to happen strained credulity. Why the hell didn't they just call the police? After all, a murder had been committed and they were tampering with a crime scene.

"This has to be reported...," Clay began, but a quick look from Murphy silenced him.

They continued to wait, the priests and nun staring towards the back door as if expecting someone or something to emerge from the limo. Did they really think the killer would calmly await their arrival?

A few more seconds passed.

Clay sighed and looked over towards the main terminal, easily a half mile or more away. Airport workers continued about their business. If he yelled for help, they'd never hear him because of distance and aircraft sounds. He glanced at his companions who continued to wait for something to happen. His mind was finally beginning to clear and the incongruity of the situation was becoming more evident with every passing second.

When nothing happened, Murphy advanced and pulled open the vehicle's back door and carefully looked inside. Satisfied, he turned towards the others as though to invite them forward. Suddenly, sensing something, he spun desperately and fired his weapon into the limo.

At almost that exact instant, a huge, black form exploded out of the back seat. A mushroom of fire and wind hit Murphy and drove him backwards down onto the concrete. He hit hard, his head bounced off the ground.

Maria screamed and grabbed Clay by the arm.

Though the events of the next few seconds took place with blinding speed, they also seemed to happen in a maddening, slow-motion sequence that sucked away split-second reactions and mired them all in a fluid-like world where words and movements were lengthened and stretched into bizarre contortions of time lapsing into itself.

Though there was no time to actually see anything, Clay knew instinctively that a massive, deadly force of some kind was rushing towards them.

For a fraction of a second he was sure the limo had exploded and they were about to be engulfed in a fire cloud. A pressure ball of air fleeing before a specter of fire roared directly towards Clay, Aquila and Maria. It was only Clay's lightning reflexes, gained through his military and police training that saved them.

His left arm smashed into Bishop Aquila's chest knocking him flat as he grabbed Maria with his right hand and dragged her to the ground. He rolled in mid-air and flung himself face down on top of the girl as Aquila landed nearby on his back.

An obscene stench of ozone and sulfur washed over them as Clay heard a wild flapping, felt a rough leather-like object scraping his back, and momentarily swung his head to glimpse two red-filmed eyes burning in a sea of shadows blacker then the night sky.

The crack of gunfire sounded as though from a great distance and a savage shriek split the air directly over them followed by a blinding, crimson flash turning night into day.

Clay instinctively turned his head and buried it in Maria's shoulder to escape the light as he covered Maria's eyes with his hands.

The crimson light incandesced into a pure white fire as heat singed the back of Clay's head and he pressed his hands harder over Maria's face.

Beside them, Bishop Aquila moaned as he stared directly upward into the fire-pink light...

...and in an instant...

...it was gone!

Whatever had uttered the blood-curdling scream, and forced them to the ground, had vanished in a split second leaving behind only a shrill of wind as a cold bequest.

SILENCE...

...then the sound of the jet engines of the retreating A320 grew from a faint whisper to an increasing roar as their hearing gradually returned.

Clay rolled off Maria. The three of them sat up, sickened, dazed and confused. At first Clay could see nothing. After a few seconds, his sight returned.

Bishop Aquila and Sister Maria were sitting nearby holding their heads as they recovered.

"Heathen bastard...!" It was Murphy scrambling to his feet near the limo, crimson flowing freely from a scalp laceration over the back of his white collar.

Clay managed to get up as Maria also scrambled to her feet. Beside her, Aquila sat quietly, drawn and pale. The lens of his glasses had fused into cracked, opaque circles, the wire frames askew on his nose. He didn't remove them.

Langevin, colorless and shaking badly, stood near the side of the limo with his smoking revolver in hand. He stared into the night sky directly over the tail of their aircraft moving on the taxiway. "Holy Mother of God! It-it...went straight up...over there," he stammered, motioning with the barrel of his revolver upward at clumps of low grayish clouds illuminated by airport lights.

Clay looked upward but saw nothing except the pale light of the moon now peeking from behind the darkening clouds. He looked across the field towards the air terminal somehow expecting a reaction. Instead, oblivious to everything except their personal responsibilities, the workers continued to swarm around their giant aircraft and octopus-like boarding tunnels.

The sounds of the machinery and aircraft engines must have drowned out the shots, Clay reasoned staring at the others. "What in the hell is going on?" he asked anyone who would listen.

The priests ignored him, Maria cast him a look that seemed to be half pity and half fear, and Aquila continued to sit in stunned silence on the ground.

Clay tried again. "What just happened?"

Suddenly Aquila began to weep, whether from relief, sorrow or anger, Clay wasn't sure. Langevin quickly moved to where he sat on the tarmac. "It was here – it was truly here!" the bishop said repeatedly between sobs. "This is no longer an abstraction, no longer an idea…and not something we have to take on faith any longer. Oh my…oh my…!"

"It's gone, Your Excellency!" Langevin said, soothingly using the more formal address for the bishop. He put a comforting hand on the old man's shoulder. "Here, let me help you up."

Aquila allowed himself to be hoisted to his feet. He pulled his ruined glasses from his face and wiped his hand across his eyes, took a deep breath and gave vent to a new emotion. "It knew!" he said tensely, anger and frustration evident in his tone. "It knew we were coming. It knows everything! How in the name of God are we supposed to defeat something like *that*?"

The two priests and Maria glanced at each other in embarrassed silence.

After a moment Father Murphy squared his shoulders and said: "We must get to the Holy City."

No-one moved.

"Now!" he added, forcefully.

They sprung into action. Murphy moved to the back of the limo, hesitated and then looked through the open door. Steeling himself, he ducked inside and, a moment later, emerged with a tight smile and Langevin's Crucifix in hand. He moved to the front, pulled a lever inside the automobile and the trunk popped open.

"Father?" he said, politely to Langevin. He reached down and grabbed the dead man under the arms.

Langevin nodded, tucked away his pistol, took the corpse's feet and together they deposited the dead man in the trunk and slammed it shut.

"I'll drive," Murphy said, spreading his coat across the front seat to soak up the mess of blood. He wiped the steering wheel with a white handkerchief which rapidly turned red. "Father Langevin will ride shotgun up beside me and the rest of you in the back." He hesitated and added, "If that's okay with you, Your Excellency."

"That's fine," the Bishop answered, slowly holding out his hand, "but you'll have to help me please. I'm afraid...I'm blind."

~ 3 ~

"Where are they!?" Cardinal Malachi demanded, as he anxiously paced the length of the *Chamber*. He looked towards some thick woolen, wine-colored drapes along one wall covering a hidden passageway through which he expected Bishop Flavious Aquila and his group to enter at any moment. The curtains failed to move.

Five other clerics sat at the heavy oak table in the center of the room, exchanging worried looks but saying little. Other than the table and seven chairs, a threadbare area carpet that had once portrayed a colorful scene from Paul's first missionary journey to Rome, four corner standup lamps bouncing indirect light off the ceiling and a scarred wooden cross on one wall, the room was bare of furniture. A thick, iron chandelier hung by a long and rusted chain directly over the middle of the room. Receptacles on it were filled with half-melted lumps of hardened, black candles which had not been lit for hundreds of years. Coffee cups, a brass ashtray in the shape of a splayed monkey stuffed with butts, a few wine bottles and partially filled glasses littered the surface of the wooden table.

The walls themselves were of rough-hewn stone, into which the remains of rusted, iron ringbolts were set, evidence of its historical function as an interrogation chamber. During the Roman Inquisition in 1252, the room had been well used when Pope Innocent IV authorized judicious torture as a means to secure evidence of a heretic's wrongdoing. The thick walls would have effectively muffled the screams of the victims as they were forced to fabricate transgressions to stay the molten iron from their quivering flesh, or avoid having their feet slowly roasted over open fires. The reward for admitting heresy was a quick and merciful death, versus one that could drag on for many days.

Set deep in the bowels of the earth of Vatican Hill, beneath the Borgia Tower area, scarcely a few hundred yards away from the venerated basilica, the *Chamber* and the passage to the room was known only to a handful of Vatican personnel. Here, *The Seven* carried out their mandate under a strict oath of secrecy. As a covert organization they were thus able to support each other in daily political maneuverings within their defined responsibilities without any open acknowledgement of their hidden connection.

When Malachi was confirmed as leader of *The Seven*, he learned he was chancellor of a group that had been in existence for eight centuries. Before taking the oath of secrecy, however, Malachi made one thing clear to all: if he was going to be held accountable for the success or failure of the hunt, things would be done his way.

In addition to Malachi, *The Seven* were composed of: Father **Benito Gallo** who had first discovered evidence of a new *Awakening* and who was also a replacement recruit; Bishop **Flavius Aquila**, head of the *Watchmen* group, now en route to the Vatican with the detective; Monsignor **Heinz Rautenberg** who oversaw the *Crusaders*; Father **Fredrick Gant** who was the *Keeper of the Relic* and doubled as their finance officer; Bishop **Jean Castilloux**, who was in charge of *Public Relations*, or, as he'd like to say, assuring the absence of any press or public relation; and, Father **Peter Austin**, a no-nonsense former Canadian arctic missionary who came late in life to the priesthood and became their *Provost Marshal* of sorts.

With the exception of Father Gallo, to all others, the *Hellspawn* was still an unseen bogeyman; none had personally witnessed the reality of the Beast. Still, faith was their business and like good soldiers in the army of God's service, the group accepted the premise as proven.

Malachi watched Father Gallo, his old friend from his seminary days, and he worried. During the last few months the old man had been drinking heavily and become increasingly distant. Of course, though he consumed inordinate amounts of spirits, Malachi had never seen the priest exhibit signs of drunkenness; he seemed to be immune to the effects of the alcohol. And, though he insisted on attending meetings, he was generally silent; he seldom volunteered opinions on any actions.

When Malachi had assumed leadership, he'd been given a number of documents. One was an ancient diary which chronicled the known church-sponsored hunts for the creature beginning in the 12th century.

From 1140, the Catholic Church had taken a greater role in defining Satan and his ability to influence human behavior. And, with reports of sightings and then the discovery of a supernatural beast that defied logic and had powers beyond those of mortals, a spawn of Satan had been recognized. Entitled the *Hellspawn*, it was tracked down in 1145 and put to death with a blessed stake driven through its heart. But, according to the diary, it eventually arose again after some years.

Each time, the Church – acknowledging the demon's resilience – had formed new organizations to hunt it down and kill it.

Through the ages it continued to be cornered and killed; sometimes by local parishes. The manner of execution varied: most involved blessed stakes or pikes driven through its heart; or the occasional beheading with a sword christened with holy water. Neither kept it down sufficiently long. As time progressed, Bishops were asked not to scorn too much if informed of any unnatural or even supernatural phenomena within their jurisdictions and to act with blessed weapons against any manifestations of evil. They were also to report the events to Rome. That way they collected and centralized files on the demon.

But specific directions as to how to best it, were still wisely left to the individuals responsible. After all, the clerics of old knew that the tools of death available to a 12th Century monk or priest would be far different from those common to a 21st-Century hunter. The only advice that Malachi's late predecessor had left, was a note for his successor that simply read: Pray to Almighty God it remains still during your reign.

"They should have been here an hour ago," Malachi said, the tension obvious in his voice. His words were quickly absorbed by the walls and rounded ceiling of the *Chamber*.

"Perhaps there was a delay in landing," Gallo ventured, running a hand through his thick white hair. Gallo found he needed to talk, to say something. Lately his mind wandered so much, it was often hard to determine where he was and why he was there. Convinced he was beginning to suffer from dementia, he concentrated extra hard on the tasks at hand. If only they knew of the suffering he had endured, they would have been only too glad to excuse him his lapses.

In reality, he was lucky to be alive. When he had surfaced in England six months after he vanished from the veteran's hospital in upstate New York, his inability to remember who he was or where he'd come from landed him in a hospital. A nurse discovered his Bible with his name in it and his cassock packed away in a sack in a corner. The hospital administration called Catholic Church officials and asked if they knew a Father Benito Gallo.

Malachi had been advised that his old friend was not dead and immediately had him brought to Rome where he underwent extensive therapy and counseling. He eventually replaced a newly deceased member of *The Seven*.

But even after Gallo had returned to Rome, he was unable to talk about what had happened to him for months. It was only later, after many therapy sessions and fortified with a number of glasses of wine, that he had revealed his story in confidence to Malachi. He covered it all from the initial kidnapping until, after six months captivity and mental torture, he awoke one evening to find his cell door standing open; at the foot of his mattress was his cassock wrapped around his Bible – both stuffed in a soft cloth sack. Was he to be freed?

Suspecting some cruel joke, he made his way down some stairs, along some passages and through a great room decorated in an old English style with clan banners, suits of armor, broadswords and pikes on the walls. He noted a huge stain-glass window at the end of the room boasting some hellish scene. He skirted isles of couches and chairs in the great room, and finally found a foyer and two heavy 12-foot high front doors made of thick walnut planks reinforced with decorative iron stays. They were locked. When he heard a noise, he retreated to a stairway which descended to another lower level. There he found a corridor which eventually turned into a rough stone tunnel; he followed it to an opening in a cliff overlooking an ocean. It was dark, but he found ledges and paths leading him across the cliff face to a dry creek bed that led upward from the cliff face. He surfaced about a mile from a towering castle looming out of the mist – his place of torment.

After wandering for two days, exhaustion drove him to sleep fitfully beside large rocks for shelter from the moor winds at night. Finally he came across a road. Later that day, he was picked up by a

Scottish motorist with a brogue so thick he could barely understand him. When asked where he was headed, Gallo, confused, simply answered: "Home."

"Then you'll be going to the ferry, I suppose," the Scot said, noting the remnants of his Italian accent. He drove him to a seaside town where a ferry was in port. Gallo had walked on board behind a family; no-one challenged him for a ticket.

He hitch-hiked his way to London on a lorry but by the time they reached the city, the driver, seeing him sweating and trembling uncontrollably, brought him directly to a hospital. There he was admitted and treated for exposure and extreme dehydration. Identification in his pocket resulted in a call to Rome. When the call came, Malachi sent Father Murphy and a plane to bring him to Rome.

For the next few months, the *Crusaders* had been charged with finding the castle where Gallo had been held. The search had gone nowhere. It was as though it had vanished off the face of the earth. They couldn't even find the lorry driver who had given him a lift.

As Father Gallo went through therapy, he remembered more and more details of his captivity. What he didn't understand was why he had been freed? Again, though there were many hypotheses put forward, nothing seemed to make sense. In the end, they went back to simply trying to find the demon. Amen, thought Gallo. Good luck to us all if we find it.

The cardinal surveyed the others in the room. Despite the disparity of their ecclesiastical rank, they were all dressed in simple black robes for these occasions. It was a sign that as members of *The Seven* they were equal in hierarchy and voice. Only Malachi had the final word on decisions.

The rules, set many years ago, were wise and complete: no attempts at brinkmanship, no petty vendettas and no attempts at self-glorification. Instead, they searched for commonality to prove that they shared more together than they owned individually. And, they recognized that, collectively, the sum of their group was stronger than its parts.

The only truly democratic choice they made was in regards to language. Since four of the seven men spoke perfect Italian, but the other three had only a passing knowledge of the language, (and yet all spoke reasonable English), they decided to use English as their common tongue.

Finally, they resolved to dedicate their lives to the fulfillment of their singular purpose. Under the Supreme Pontiff, and within the doctrine of theological or canon law, and in the name of the Holy Roman Catholic Church, these learned men and servants of God were united in their desire to kill or, at least, banish Adramelech back to whence he came.

Under the Supreme Pontiff indeed, Malachi mused to himself. The flaw in that rationale was that the Supreme Pontiff changed. And, with each new pope the degree of commitment from the Holy See changed.

It was fine that years ago, Pope John Paul II had, on his appointment, again endorsed their mission, and even increased their funding through the miscellaneous item in the Vatican's annual Financial Operating Plan. And that he encouraged them to continue their important work. In fact, everything worked even after Paul's death with newly appointed prelates benignly sanctioning their mission without fully understanding it. Malachi's budget had been faithfully renewed each year. But when the Curia accountants implemented their new software programs, his budget disappeared. And, because their mandate was so secret, Malachi needed papal approval for reinstatement of the monies. One-by-one they had to shut down various operations around the world. While some line items such as the lease on the aircraft, the pilot's salaries and the *Watchmen* had been covered in advance, they had had to recall their official "hit" squad from New York. And, with His Holiness an innocent prisoner of his bureaucratic Prefecture, getting the budget renewed was taking longer than he had expected.

Well, Malachi hoped he'd taken care of that problem and that Bortnowaska would get him the time needed to convince His Holiness of the urgency of their mission. He relit his cigar and looked at his companions who were now getting as restless as he. A heavy pall of smoke hung in the air despite the fact that Malachi was the only one smoking. He puffed furiously on his thick Havana as he faced Gallo. "They landed on time," he said shortly, deliberately eyeing the man's wine glass. "But I can't raise Aquila on his cell. Nor any of the others."

"Perhaps they're caught in traffic," Monsignor Rautenberg interrupted, his deep voice, and thick German accent seeming to lend an air of wisdom and finality to whatever he said. "Captain Bowden told us he dropped them at the limo and they were preparing to depart when he last saw them."

The man could order a ham sandwich and make it sound like a reading from the gospel, Malachi thought. He shrugged at the latest excuse and resumed his pacing. Rautenberg was being unusually optimistic since he usually saw doom and gloom around every corner. Now, well past eighty, the Monsignor had come to the priesthood as a much-decorated German Luftwaffe pilot from WW II. He was known in the group for his resourcefulness, his kindness and his courage. The man had been shot out of the skies three times, had two Iron Crosses packed away in his room, and limped from having taken a British Spitfire's .303 caliber machine gun bullet through his right thigh. How, even with rehabilitative therapy, he managed to get up and walk after doctors had pieced his splintered bones together in a ten-hour operation, astounded his medical team. Still, when it came to hard decisions regarding his *Crusaders*, he never hesitated to call the shots. Nor would he ask them to do anything that he wasn't prepared to do himself.

When Malachi thought about another member of his team, Father Gant, he also had faith in his ability to do whatever needed to be done. A brilliant man, he seemed almost comical when he walked since he was bent forward at a 35-degree angle. It was as though the top half of his body was anxious to arrive at his destination before the lower half caught up. In reality Malachi knew scoliosis had set in and was taking its toll.

A wiry, tough 65-year-old, still sporting a crop of red hair and without an ounce of fat on his body, Gant brought endurance, strength of purpose and pragmatism to their little group. As *Keeper of the Relic*, Gant was a critical component of Malachi's team since it was he who would determine if circumstances warranted risking the Church's treasurers which he guarded like a jealous uncle. It had been tough enough to persuade him to lend the Relic for the test with Maria. So it was critical that he be fully informed, and fully cognizant of why they had to risk damaging, and possibly losing the Relic in this venture.

The others were also all good men, Malachi thought.

"Aquila would call if there was trouble," Father Austin ventured, seated at the end of the table.

The cardinal looked over at him and smiled. "If he could..." he said, thinking the man looked exactly like what he had been – an arctic missionary. His heavy beard, thick eyebrows and lumberjack hands seemed to suit him more for the far north rather than duties in the Vatican. Yet Malachi knew that the man had strength of character and an iron faith that was enviable. And he had given up much to minister to Inuit within Canada's Arctic Circle.

During his time in the north, he survived a violent polar bear attack, as evidenced by horrible scarring on his face, and twice been trapped on Arctic ice flows with his young Inuit charges and almost froze to death.

Most people felt uneasy in Austin's presence because of his size and somewhat grizzled appearance; he used his beard to hide a now deformed chin and lips. His muscular frame, and wild hair promised a ferocity of personality, totally at odds with the man's eyes that betrayed his true nature; he was the personification of a gentle giant, a loving, sensitive man who felt genuine pain at the hurt or sorrow of others.

Finally, Bishop Jean Castilloux, their Public Relations man had a seemingly simple responsibility – deal with any potential press coverage of any of their groups. In fact, his job was quite complex. If word got out that the Catholic Church was actively hunting a true demon, they would experience a major credibility problem, or even panic in the Christian world. To avoid discovery, Castilloux had developed a host of linked cover stories and proactive strategic actions to mitigate any PR disasters.

Malachi thought of the other members of their team: members of the *Watchmen* group tracking and guarding Lieutenant Clay Montague, as well as the *Crusaders,* a grim squad of trained killers. These men had all been put through the British Army's Special Air Services (SAS) assault and counter-terrorism training, reputed to be the toughest and most demanding combat training in the world. Varying in strength (depending on circumstances) from three to four men, they were ready for anything as they were armed with Smith & Wesson Model 500 .50 caliber revolvers, Brugger & Thomet MP9 submachine guns, grenades, holy water, incense, blessed hosts, silver bullets, blessed stakes and heavy mallets. Indeed, formidable weaponry. Practical as well as spiritually focused men, this current "squad" was merely a modern representation of dozens of other church hunter/killer groups that had once existed.

From the *Chamber*, Malachi's group would periodically send out designates to gather facts on suspicious murder sprees and report. There was little doubt when the *Hellspawn* had been involved – exsanguinations, mutilations, motiveless and random killings were his mark. Twice during the past few years, they had been close behind him.

In fact, they had actually dispatched the *Crusaders* to locations in France and Spain. Sadly, they were unsuccessful in their apprehension attempts. In France he had escaped minutes before they arrived with their tools of death. And in Toledo, Spain, another *Crusader* had been successfully separated from his team, lured to a back alley, and paid for his mistake with his life.

They regrouped and realized that one fact now seemed indisputable. According to their analysis, each time *it* managed to attack, rest and reappear, it had become stronger and less vulnerable to holy objects; each time, the power of Christ affected it less and the traditional weapons favored by the hunters from the church also had less effect.

One other bit of information also surfaced. As it grew stronger, it was able to shape-shift into human form at will. According to the last victim who died moments after being discovered, the only things that didn't change were the demon's eyes – lifeless, reflective and mesmerizing. Hit them with a flashlight and they glowed with a wolf-like fire that seemed able to laser a smoking hole in one's soul.

Now it was on the move again. This time they had to find it and kill it. If they didn't, the world would soon know the dark dominion of satanic rule.

Malachi's cell phone suddenly let forth a chime of the *William Tell Overture* and he snatched it up. It was Father Murphy telling him they were on their way and needed medical help. Bishop Aquila needed an eye doctor. He would call back when they were closer.

~ 4 ~

Whatever happened to them back at the airport was beyond his understanding Clay decided as the limo bounced and swayed. In fact, the entire situation was like something out of a Cohen Brothers' movie. After being shot in his New York office with tranquilizing darts by a couple of men who turned out to be catholic priests, and flown God knows where in an aircraft outfitted like a medical center, he now found himself on the equivalent of Disney's *"Mr. Toad's Wild Ride."* They were roaring through the back streets of an unknown city with a body in the trunk, a bishop desperately needing medical attention, and a nun who, so far, seemed like the least crazed of the bunch.

After the explosion, Bishop Aquila had decreed they skip Customs, and the limo had bumped over grass with its lights off as huge jets took off and landed around them. At one point they waited until a lumbering 747 the size of a small building landed a mere 30 feet ahead of them on the strip making their vehicle lift and shudder. Then, without hesitation, and with lights off, Murphy floored it and crossed behind the jet where they were buffeted and almost overturned by vortices twirling off its wingtips. They could hear the sudden roar of its jets reversing as they made the grass on the other side. The priest then steered around some bushes, braked, and unlocked a padlocked gate in the security fence. Within a minute they were bouncing over a small hill and onto a highway.

Since they talked about Customs, they must have left the United States, Clay reasoned. They'd been on the road for almost 20 minutes now and he'd given up trying to spot landmarks through the darkened back window and the drawn window curtains. Instead he was trying to elicit any bit of information he could from his companions. As of yet, he hadn't decided if they were truly his saviors or were his jailors; he only knew that he was still with them and no-one was poking a gun in his ribs to keep him there.

Clay tried once again. "Where are we?"

"You are safe," Aquila said.

"Thanks, but that's not what I asked?" He was feeling more awake now.

"But that's what I answered, my son," the bishop returned dryly, but not unkindly. Aquila sat on an upholstered bench with his back to the driver while Clay and Maria faced him from the back seat of the limo. His glasses were gone, the skin around his eyes was extremely red, and a milky, cloud-like substance covered his eyes. Though he couldn't see at all, he claimed not to be in pain. Finally he sighed once more and whispered, "You are in Rome."

Clay took this in without a word. He was in Rome? He watched the others in the car.

The old man held a tumbler of brandy in hand given to him by Maria from a small bar in the limo. He awkwardly slopped the liquid into his mouth every few seconds, scarcely paying heed to the amounts dribbling down his chin and onto his dark suit.

"Father Murphy said we'll get you a doctor when we arrive, Your Excellency," Maria said, reaching out to clasp his free hand which lay curled in his lap. It felt cold and clammy to the nun.

The bishop didn't reply but just stared unseeingly ahead with the same flat, facial expression he'd maintained since his momentary lapse of control on the tarmac.

"We're on our way to a hospital, I hope?" Clay ventured. No one answered him. Deducing that Maria was his best hope of an answer, he pressed again. "Sister, what happened back there?"

Before Maria could speak, Aquila whispered again: "Adramelech."

Clay looked at the man. "Adramelech?"

The bishop sighed and took another slug of brandy. "In Panama you were touched by evil...by the supernatural, Lieutenant, so please learn to accept it. Denial only leaves you vulnerable. If you can suspend your worldly beliefs for a time, and realize that there is a spiritual world that occasionally crosses over into ours, you might survive this. Now, please...let us all rest. We have no idea what trials await us."

Clay felt goose bumps rise as the vague image of a giant shadow turning towards him in the stifling heat of a jungle night flashed into his mind. He shivered and shook his head at the memory. Get a grip, he told himself harshly. That memory was false, the remnant of a nightmare.

Aloud he said, "I don't exactly believe in the supernatural, sir. The only thing I met in Panama that was evil...was the enemy and they carried Chinese T65 Assault rifles...among other armaments."

"Not true, Lieutenant," the old man said. "Or your wife and your deputy would still be alive. Now if you don't mind...?" He settled back against the cushions to rest but didn't close his eyes.

Clay stared at him. Jody and Hitch would still be alive? They weren't kidding. Obviously they *had* been following him for years.

The rest of the journey was conducted in awkward silence over the next 25 odd minutes. The limo accelerated, slowed and sped up again until it finally slowed and stopped. There was a hurried conversation with some form of guards and Clay heard the groaning and squealing of a huge iron gate being opened in front of them. Beside him, he felt the warmth of Maria's thigh pressed against his. She didn't seem to notice and the vehicle smoothly accelerated through the gates. It pulled to the curb a few minutes later.

They all disembarked by a five-story, stone building with yellow lights glowing from rows of windows above. It looked somewhat like an older, traditional New York apartment building except for the fine stone work surrounding its balustrade and doorway. It was a relatively bright night and in the light of the moon, he could make out eerie gargoyle-like carvings staring down at them as they gathered on the sidewalk.

A hurried conference was conducted in the warm night air by his companions as pairs of nuns in billowing black habits periodically swept by on the sidewalk. The occasional priest or brother also strode by, their demeanors conveying an urgent errand as they suddenly materialized out of the darkness and were quickly swallowed up by the shadows again.

Clay could barely make out what Murphy and the bishop were saying other than they were arguing over something. He strained to catch what he could.

"...see the doctor now," Murphy argued.

"I'll see him when I'm ready," returned Aquila. "Take me to the *Chamber*."

They argued for a few more moments in low, guarded tones and finally Murphy threw up his hands. "We'll ask the doctor to attend him there." He and Maria helped Aquila back into the automobile.

"Good bye," Maria said to Clay, slipping back into the limo after the bishop and leaving Clay and Father Langevin on the sidewalk.

Clay felt his stomach sink. Why he felt that way, he wasn't exactly sure. After all, the huge losses in his life had paid one dividend; there wasn't a lot more in this world that could hurt him any longer. And, with his emotional and caring side numbed by his tragedies, he had been content to accept the penalty of loneliness, a fact born out by few friendships and zero love affairs since Jody's death. Self-preservation had rigidly kept his emotions in balance, a simple equation that said that the less he had – the less he had to lose. Clay just couldn't risk losing any more.

So why the sudden concern, he wondered. Why did he feel a knee-weakening sense of loss at her departure?

He stared at Maria arranging herself in the back of the limo beside the bishop. She looked up at him out the open back door and caught his eye. They stared at each other for a moment, her eyes plainly mirroring a sudden confusion. He felt a stirring within himself that he couldn't understand. She said nothing. He kept mute. The only sign she gave him was a barely perceptible raising of her eyebrows and an enigmatic smile.

As Clay looked at her a moment longer, his heart beat faster and his palms began to sweat. He swallowed and realized with a certainty reserved for sinners and saints that he was deathly afraid that he might never see this girl again. But, at the same time, he acknowledged to himself that he was being ridiculous. She was, after all, a nun.

Spotting worry in his eyes, Maria raised a hand in good-bye. "Father Langevin will see to your needs," she called softly through the open door. "Don't worry, Mr. Montague. God has watched over you so far. All will be well."

Before Clay could answer, Father Murphy slammed the back door, resumed his driver's seat and the automobile pulled smoothly away into the night leaving him and Langevin alone on the sidewalk under the night sky.

Inside the building, Clay was led up a winding set of creaking wooden stairs, along musty corridors featuring yellowed drawings and painting of the Sacred Heart of Jesus. They moved past graphic renditions of recognizable biblical parables and through stone archways into which the likeness of various saints had been carved; they scowled down at him. As he and Langevin moved they encountered no-one in the hallways and finally reached a door in the corridor that was carefully unlocked by the priest.

"It's rather sparse but at least you can get some sleep here," Langevin explained, opening the door. Hinges that could have used a good oiling, squeaked loudly.

Clay entered and saw at once that the priest had not exaggerated. The room contained a simple wooden bunk, a desk with a small lamp, a wooden chair, a foot locker and a large armoire. Other than a wooden cross on one wall, and a naked bulb hanging from an electric wire from the 20-odd-foot high ceiling, the only other feature was a twisted stream of fly-paper with several dead guests clinging to it. And, over the bed, on a plaster wall yellowed by time, another ancient-looking painting of the Sacred Heart of Jesus was displayed.

The naked bulb cast a weak, yellow light on the plastered walls which he guessed had been painted white at one time. Another door led to a washroom, and a single small window set high in the wall, completed his new surroundings.

"I really didn't deserve the Royal Suite," Clay said. A tired sigh escaped him.

Langevin chuckled. "The opulence of the Vatican – of which you hear so much – is hardly extended to those at the level of monk."

The Vatican, thought Clay. So that's where we are. Why wasn't he surprised? Outwardly he merely shrugged at Langevin and went over and sat on the bunk, grateful to be off his feet again. The springs came through the thin mattress and dug into his hips and posterior. He was feeling less groggy now and inpatient to be back in charge of his own destiny. "I'd like some answers," he said finally, sitting up straight.

Langevin shook his head. "I'm not authorized to tell you anything." The priest crossed to the walnut-stained door in the far wall, opened it and entered. "Bathroom with shower here, razor, toothbrush…all the comforts of home." His voice echoed hollowly in the tiled room.

"Then what's to prevent me from leaving here and going to the police?" Clay called.

"Curiosity?" Langevin ventured, smiling as he came back into the room.

"Not good enough."

"How about self-preservation?" Langevin had stopped smiling. "After all, if you weren't here with us in body tonight, Mr. Montague, I can assure you that you would most certainly be *a* body in New York. Or worse."

Clay felt his temper rising. "Enough of this nonsense," he said. "I can take care of myself. You can't just walk up, drug a man and take him out of the country. There are laws, even in Italy!"

Langevin nodded toward the footlocker by the bed and continued: "You'll find pajamas, and an assortment of clothes in there and in the armoire. Size forty, 15 inch neck, 33 inch sleeve…32 inch inseam if I'm not mistaken."

Clay tried again: "Can you tell me just one thing?"

Langevin sighed, obviously felt sorry for him and shrugged. "Depends."

"I saw that driver tonight. Why was he killed? And what kind of murderer rips the heart out of his victim?"

The answer hit Clay like a bucket of ice water.

"The same kind of killer who skins his victim from the neck up and crucifies them upside down," the priest said with a look that sent shivers up Clay's spine. "Now I'll bid you good night and see you…sometime."

His tone said he was through answering questions and without another word, he turned on his heel and left the room. The door closed softly.

Clay waited two minutes and then tip-toed to the door and tried the knob. It wouldn't budge. It was locked from the outside.

At least now he had a clearer idea of who they really were. They were his jailors.

~ 5 ~

The next day morning came earlier than usual for Sister Maria Lapierre.

A gentle tap on her door at 5:00 a.m. cut through her nightmare like a careless scalpel slicing into a doctor's fingertip. Instantly awake, she bolted up, heart racing and realized there was no faceless entity from hell chasing her on a lonely, rain-swept street. Maria gazed at her surroundings in confusion; within seconds, however, the memories flooded back and she re-oriented herself.

She looked down to see she was clothed only in her bikini brief panties as she sat up on the narrow brass bed. Vaguely she remembered having taken a moment to remove her sweater, bra and skirt the night before, and then, surrendering to a mind-numbing weariness, she had collapsed back on the coarse wool of the bed's hand-woven quilt. Judging from her position on the bed, she's scarcely moved all night. Her cloak had been hastily thrown over a chair. She squinted at her Seiko still strapped to her wrist.

"Five A.M.…!" she groaned and was interrupted by another, more urgent rap on the door. Instinctively she covered her bare breasts with her hands and then dropped them as she realized she was alone; no one could see her nakedness. And for sure no-one would be allowed to see her bikini briefs. Though a novice, Maria embraced a single weakness – a love of provocative underwear and sleepwear. Perhaps she would give them up as a sacrifice when she took her final vows, she thought. But not just yet.

"Just a minute!" Maria called out.

Taking in the Spartan decor of the room, Maria swung her legs over the edge of the bed. A heavy wooden bureau, unframed wall mirror, table and a single ladder-backed chair completed the furniture of her assigned domicile at Our Lady of Mount Carmel convent. Even the cracked, plaster walls, a rosy pink muted by time and moisture, failed to offer any form of creature comfort such as a painting or wall hanging. Predictably, a tarnished brass cross hung over her bed with withered Easter palm fronds tucked securely between the splayed figure of Christ and the cross. Her packed suitcase sat near the bureau. Actually she thought, she would have preferred the Holiday Inn again; it had a Jacuzzi in the bathroom.

Rubbing the sleep from her eyes, Maria stood, yawned and stretched, hoping to banish the aching weariness that seemed to have penetrated every muscle of her small frame. As she did so, she caught sight of herself in the mirror.

The golden rays of the morning sun, streaming through an open window across the room, painted the ripe firmness of her half-naked body a golden yellow. She felt a momentary pride in the fullness of her small but firm breasts, dark nipples standing proud and erect. For a brief second she found herself thinking of Clay Montague and wondering what it would be like to be with him.

She pushed the thought away even as she felt the vague, deliciously warm sensation of her libido stirring in her loins, and the familiar flush reddening her neck and cheeks. Embarrassed at her shamelessness, she pushed the thoughts aside. Would she never be free of her sexuality she wondered with annoyance? After all, she would soon take her final vows and become a Bride of Christ. And, He knew her every thought.

Quickly she pulled the blanket off the bed to wrap around her body and went to answer the door. Passing the open window, Maria looked out and spotted a lineup of birds singing with wild abandon outside. Two ancient olive trees, set on a carefully manicured lawn just beyond the window opening, provided ready-made bleachers for the feathered chorus; no doubt successive generations of these birds had used them down through the ages, she thought. She was thrilled to be in Rome again. For a young Quebecois who had never been farther than Montreal prior to her Rome visits, she was certainly making up for lost time.

It was a beautiful fall day, warm and full of promise. Though she felt tired, she also felt an underlying current of happiness throughout her whole being. Her thoughts returned to the detective again, and she angrily forced them away and recited a quick Hail Mary; it was madness to have any feelings other than Christian charity for this poor man. Besides, if everything went according to Cardinal Malachi's plan, she would be spending more time with him than even he realized. She had better get her feelings under control as they certainly didn't need any post-adolescence nonsense to compromise or complicate their work. Also, the cardinal had made it clear that what they would ask of her and the detective was highly dangerous.

The rap sounded again, even more impatient this time. As she crossed to the door, Maria could hear traffic outside the bedroom window as early commuters made their way to work.

"Yes?" she said softly, without opening the door.

"Morning devotions in-a-forty minutes, Sister," a gentle voice said, the lyrical Italian accent giving the English words a sing-song quality.

"I'll wash and be down directly," she replied.

"Please no late, Sister Maria," the voice pleaded, the tone, apologetic yet insistent. "Mother Superior doesn't like anyone to be late for morning devotions...even guests."

"I'll be quick like a bunny."

"There was a puzzled silence from outside and finally: "You have a rabbit in there, Sister?"

Maria laughed aloud. "No, no...I'll be very fast."

"Thank you, Sister."

Maria heard nothing further so she crossed to the washroom to perform a scaled down version of her usual morning routine. She put toothpaste on her brush and took it into the small shower with her. The pipes creaked and groaned as she cranked up the hot tap. Despite selecting the maximum setting on the tap, the water never got above tepid. She shivered as she brushed her teeth and thought about the previous evening.

The detective had looked so distressed when she'd said goodnight. For a moment she thought he was going to protest her leaving. In turn, as she'd met his worried gaze, she'd been shocked to feel her heart do a strange flip-flop, the kind she'd felt as a schoolgirl when she was getting a crush on a boy.

This was silly, she told herself again. She certainly wasn't any school girl and, as a nun, affairs of the heart no longer existed for her. She had promised undying devotion to the Father.

Still, there was something about the detective that attracted her. Perhaps it was the quiet strength mirrored in his sensitive, grey eyes. Or, the set of his jaw and the underlying determination and confidence in the way he moved as the drugs had worn off. Despite only a passing knowledge of his history, she could sense that Clay was a man of integrity, someone bruised and battered by life, but who still clung to a fierce pride in himself and his actions.

Then she also remembered the feel of his muscular body covering hers as he pushed her to the tarmac the night before. Though his position in the overall scheme of things had rendered him somewhat vulnerable, he still came across as a take-charge individual, a man who would carefully weigh his options and make his move when the time was right.

Cardinal Malachi had told her he was also man who had been terribly hurt, his life thrown into a shambles by accusations of conspiracy in the death of a friend and fellow police officer. This had been quickly followed by the loss of his much-loved wife.

For another brief instant she again allowed herself to be catapulted back to the evening before at the airport as Clay reacted instinctively to the nightmare exploding out of the back of the limo. Again, she felt his strong arms dragging her down out of harm's way. And, as they hit the tarmac, she remembered the feel of his body on top of her putting himself in danger to protect her from whatever was happening; it was a bittersweet memory considering the loss of sight for the bishop.

The smile that had played over her lips moments before, vanished as reality set in. A man was dead and she was facing an unknown future, one that the cardinal indicated might be both frightening and perilous. She sighed; the day seemed to hold less promise.

Maria ran fingers through her wet, tousled hair and opened the plastic shower curtain to reach for the shampoo on a ledge nearby. She caught sight of herself in the bathroom mirror through the steam from the shower and winched at the raccoon-like circles under her eyes. The hours these people kept were not exactly routine.

Last night, after they had dropped off Clay and Father Langevin, they'd driven to a lengthy meeting in the *Chamber* where she had first met *The Seven*. Cardinal Malachi and five other grim-faced clerics had insisted on grilling her and Fathers Murphy and Langevin while Bishop Aquila received medical attention from Doctor Carlo Casaroli, the Pope's personal physician. He examined Bishop Aquila's eyes in a corner of the *Chamber* as Father Murphy delivered his report.

Father Murphy's narration held everyone spellbound. The Beast's familiar had heralded his coming after Montague again. Their plane trouble also seemed too coincidental. And, finally, it had been waiting for them at the airport where it had killed their driver. On occasion, Murphy required prompting by Malachi when he stumbled over the more unbelievable portions of his tale, yet, with encouragement he gamely pressed on. At his conclusion, he had stood silent.

The clerics had nodded, almost as one, seeming lost in thought. All except Cardinal Malachi. "So these were supernatural happenings...you saw evidence of the extraordinary with your own eyes, Father Murphy?"

"I suppose so, Your Eminence. Something blasted out of the limo...and that child should have been killed outright when she was hit by the car. There may be perfectly rational explanations...?" His voice had trailed off.

"A die hard skeptic still, Father? Despite what the Relic did for you?"

Murphy's face had reddened and he looked down, almost in shame. "You didn't let me finish. While there may be other explanations, I couldn't come up with any."

"Thank you, Dermottt," Malachi said, kindly. "Hang on to that pragmatism, I'm sure we'll need it." He turned to the others. "It's working; it's trying desperately to find our man." All nodded.

In the corner, the doctor was peering through an instrument and shining light into the bishop's eyes. He murmured questions and the Bishop Aquila nodded or shook his head. Malachi switched off a small tape recorder he held in his hand. Maria noticed it for the first time when he clicked it off. It was an older model. He attempted to change tapes, put one in backwards, grumbled and finally slid it in properly, snapped it closed and hit the record button.

Next, she was asked to relate what had happened to her from the time she went on watch with Murphy and Langevin up until they arrived at the Vatican that evening. She was cautioned to include every detail of what she saw, heard or felt, no matter how trivial.

Nice method of cross-checking, thought Maria. Of course if they really wanted independent verification, they would have kept her out of the room while Murphy spoke. Obviously there wasn't an over-abundance of Perry Mason fans in this group or they would have been aware of the protocol for calling a witness.

"Before I begin...how is Bishop Aquila?" Maria asked, her voice nervous.

From the corner Bishop Aquila had sighed and called out: "Never mind my child. Tell them what happened."

But Malachi kindly saw fit to intervene. "Doctor? How is our friend?"

The physician had snapped his penlight off and looked up." My initial diagnosis is the optic nerves have been burned. In effect they have been destroyed, Your Eminence. We must get His Excellency to a hospital immediately. I will call ahead for a specialist, but I do not hold much hope. I'm sorry, Flavius."

Horrified, Marie wanted to go to the man but the cardinal had stopped her with a glance. "We are almost through. Your story, Maria...please."

Hardly a breath was drawn as Maria described the foggy street where their Saab had been parked and the events that transpired. When she finished, there was more silence for a moment and then a deep sigh from Cardinal Malachi.

"The child...that's the familiar again," he commented to the others.

"She was mentioned in the 1880 case," Monsignor Rautenberg agreed.

"...And the 1905 case in Katmandu...and in 1973 in Vietnam," Bishop Castilloux echoed. "Not to mention Vermont. The child of hell...The Little Witch."

Malachi nodded. "And something else worked; Sister Maria gave enough warning in New York for us to save our man. Pity our *Crusaders* weren't on site. Another lost opportunity."

There was murmured assent from the others.

"One thing does give me pause," Malachi continued. "Those very expensive auxiliary lighting we had installed on the aircraft to represent a Crucifix…?"

"They weren't on, Mustavias," Bishop Aquila called from the corner. "The pilot did not follow our procedures for flight."

"You set Captain Bowden right, did you?"

"Damned straight," the bishop answered.

Despite everything, they had all laughed.

For Maria, however, she was now convinced that something wicked was indeed loosed upon the earth and she was suddenly frightened of the future.

The water started to go cold in her shower. Darn! She thought angrily and began to scrub doubly hard at the shampoo covering her hair as her thoughts returned to the detective. To take her mind off him she began humming a refrain from the Broadway musical *South Pacific*. It turned out to be the melody from the song: *I'm gonna wash that man right outta my hair!* She shook her head in disbelief and annoyance with herself. What's this, she wondered – irony or omen?

~ 6 ~

Cardinal Malachi sipped his morning coffee in his cluttered office and pondered his strategy for that afternoon. His imminent meeting with Sister Maria and Clay Montague would determine if the detective was willing to team up with Maria to help attract this ancient horror.

Though reports said Montague did not fully remember his jungle experience, Malachi still felt that recent events, as well as exposing Adramelech's role in the murder of his deputy and his wife, would encourage him to cooperate. If he agreed, he and Sister Maria would stay in close touch with the *Crusaders* and sound the alarm if they were lucky. Or "unlucky" depending on how you viewed it, he thought wryly.

Malachi took a deep breath and tried to assuage his guilt. Making Montague the figurative Judas Goat was not something he relished, however, this was an unprecedented opportunity to entice the demon to present itself – and then kill it. Maria had already proven her abilities to sense evil. That would give them some protection.

He sighed and went to take another sip of coffee. His thoughts shifted to Sister Maria. It was Monsignor Rautenberg who questioned the wisdom of their novice staying at the Holiday Inn. What if someone recognized her from newspaper photos and asked why the "psychic nun" was in Rome? Malachi agreed that he had a point. Despite discovery being unlikely, why take a chance? He had cancelled the Inn reservation and decided he'd have to rouse a friend.

A quick call to Sister Angelina of the Secular Order of Discalced Carmelites and she provided sleeping quarters for Maria. He had chosen the Carmelites because their lives were largely contemplative, consisting of prayer, penance, and hard work. A low profile was exactly what was needed in Maria's case and, at two o'clock in the morning Sister Angelina had welcomed her young sister to their humble surroundings a mere six blocks from the Vatican.

So, after being up for many hours and flying one third the way round the world, Maria would have found herself ushered into a cloistered convent housed in a small (and rather drafty) early European maison. However, by that time, he reasoned, she would have been happy to have any place where she could lay her weary body down.

She was a very special young woman as far as Malachi was concerned, one of those genuine people who seemed born to a life of kindness, service and selflessness. There was also a certain innocence about her that made him feel like a heel. After all, Montague was an ex-soldier and police officer; he was used to risk. But how, in good conscience, could he ask this relative *innocent* to tie herself to their "bait?"

He grimaced at his empty coffee cup and wondered for the umpteenth time why he had chosen this time to give up smoking. Though he allowed himself the occasional cigar, he desperately needed a good dose of nicotine. To distract himself, he decided to check his iPhone for messages. It failed to initiate and he shook it, grumbling aloud to himself. Had he forgotten to charge it *again*?

~ 7 ~

Clay awoke but lay unmoving, staring at the water-stained plaster ceiling through half-opened eyes. He was in another strange place and he'd be damned if he'd move until he figured out exactly where he was.

Slowly the memories returned: the aircraft flight, the limo with the dead driver, the macabre events surrounding whatever it was that exploded out of the back of the limo and, finally, his utter exhaustion leading to one of the deepest sleeps he'd ever had. No doubt that had been augmented by whatever drugs were still in his system.

Abruptly he threw off his covers and stood up. The room was in semi-darkness except for a brilliant shaft of sunlight streaming through the small window high overhead. He stared at the dust particles illuminated in the relatively brilliant ray for a moment, and then took in the sparse room. He was feeling more like a prisoner with every passing moment.

Clothed only in his shorts, he padded silently to the door and tried the knob to confirm that it was indeed locked. It opened easily. Surprised, he cautiously stuck his head out and found himself staring at a plain carpeted corridor vanishing at either end down sets of stairs. He could make out further alcoves along the corridor where other doors were inset making him suppose he was in a dormitory of some sort.

When Clay looked for the clothes he'd shucked the night before, the black shirt, pants and clerical collar had vanished. He opened the doors to an armoire in the corner. Inside, he found two pairs of gabardine slacks, two pairs of medium weight cotton khaki pants, a choice of cotton shirts in various colors, socks, underwear, light sweaters, a heavy canvas Lands End jacket, two pairs of loafers, a pair of sturdy boots, two sports jackets that matched the slacks, and two suits. A brown leather suitcase rested in the corner of the wooden wardrobe. On checking, he noted they were all his approximate size so he selected a combination of Gap Khaki trousers, a blue Hugo Boss shirt, a navy sweater and a pair of striped boxers. He picked navy socks and wine-colored loafers and took them into the bathroom where there was an assortment of toiletries.

He shaved, showered, dressed and was brushing his teeth when there was a sharp rap at his door. It was followed by the creak of door hinges and the sound of a familiar voice.

"Mr. Montague?" Father Murphy called. "Are you up yet, lad?"

"Hang on," Clay said, his voice sounding hollow as it reverberated in the tiled bathroom. He finished his toiletry and came out to greet Father Murphy who was looking as fresh and rested as if he'd just come off a two-week vacation.

"Good morning," the priest said, with unbridled enthusiasm as Clay appeared. "It's almost noon. Care for a mug of coffee and a bit of breakfast before we start our day?"

"You can have whatever you'd like," Clay said. "I'm getting out of here."

"I hardly think so, Mr. Montague. At least until you've heard what we have to say."

"Who is *we?*" Clay asked. "And, I repeat to you what I told Father Langevin. Kidnapping is against the law; or has that little detail slipped your mind?"

"Mr. Montague, since we left New York, your office has been cleaned up and restored, a message tells prospective clients you are on assignment and we have provided for rent, utility and other payments. Your car has been returned to your condo parking and the super has been notified you'll be away for some weeks."

"And, what if I go to the police," Clay asked.

The priest looked at the detective and gave him an easy grin. "The power of the Vatican is more than most people know in this city my friend; even if you go to the *Polizia Municipali*, they will merely send you wherever we ask them to, including back here. You have no money, no credit cards, no identity papers or passport…not even your own clothes…virtually nothing other than what we provide. Do you think a good Catholic police constable will take your word that the most Holy Roman Catholic Church drugged and kidnapped you from New York and spirited you away on a Roman holiday? You'll wind up in a white coat at one of our less distinguished hospitals, drugged to the gills, playing crazy eights and drooling in your shoe. Or, you can have breakfast with me. And then a meeting with Cardinal Malachi who will explain everything."

Clay stared at the smiling priest feeling his temper beginning to rise.

Father Murphy clapped his hands together as he gave Clay an appraising look. "So…what do you say?" His smile was somewhat infectious, a complete turnaround from the grim priest of the night before. "I can answer *some* questions," he continued, by way of incentive.

As they sped along in a small Fiat, Father Murphy glanced approvingly at his watch. "Good! This restaurant only opens at noon but I know the owner, Giulio, and he'll be pleased to rustle us up some Eggs Florentine," he said. "It's in the Camp de'Fiori area and is a favorite of the Vatican Monsignors and the prelates." Clay barely heard him. He found himself constantly jamming his foot down on an imaginary brake pedal as they raced through the streets of Rome paying little heed to others.

The priest deftly dodged hundreds of fearless, jay-walking pedestrians, and crisscrossing swarms of motor scooters and small automobiles piloted by equally insane drivers competing for space and distance on the broad avenue.

"Look out...watch it...!" Clay said, as an enterprising motorist in a mini car pulled a u-turn in front of them and, amid a crescendo of protesting horns, headed across the traffic as he darted for a side street he'd missed. "These people are nuts...how do you drive here?"

"You get used to it," Murphy answered with a chuckle as he squared off against an aggressive scooter in a roundabout and won. The rider in the helmet gave him a one-fingered salute and then, seeing Murphy's white collar, blessed himself and shouted an apology. Murphy chuckled and granted absolution with a wave.

They parked on a small side street named Via Monserrato. After locking the auto, they walked for about 75 yards past ancient looking buildings bathed in the noonday sun, reached the Church of Monserrato, turned left onto Via Barchetta and found their destination – Da Giulio. The warm autumn sun felt good on Clay's face. He noticed that Murphy carried a large envelope by his side as they walked.

"Too bad it isn't dinner time," the priest said as they entered. "They do mainly home made dishes here and their gnocchi with truffle is the best in Rome." He continued to rattle on about the quality of the food as a waiter seated them in the bright yellow room with white vaults curving from the walls to the ceiling. "You are eating in a 16th Century palazzo, my good man."

With Clay's agreement he ordered them both Eggs Florentine and coffee. He added an order of sweet rolls and settled back to watch Clay as the waiter departed. Neither man said anything for a full two minutes until finally Murphy sighed and broke the silence. "So...what's new?"

In spite of himself, Clay laughed. "You mean other than being shot, shanghaied and smuggled halfway round the world?"

Murphy grinned. "Aye. Other than that?"

"Incidentally, am I free to leave, Father?"

"You're not a prisoner, Mr. Montague."

"Clay is fine. You've gone to a lot of trouble to get me out of New York. Why?"

"Without our intervention your life expectancy was measured in minutes."

"Really? From who? That little girl on the street?"

"You've made it plain enough that you don't really want to know. And for now I'm not allowed to tell you very much. You will meet Cardinal Malachi in about two hours and everything will be made clear. I'd just like to show you some photographs – to wet your whistle, as it were. For now…patience is a virtue."

"So is honesty."

"Idealists would think so, wouldn't they?" Murphy grinned. He was enjoying himself.

The coffee arrived. They both drank it black and in silence. As they waited for the eggs, Father Murphy carefully laid the brown manila envelope on the table and removed four large photographs from it. He slid them across the table to Clay.

Clay picked up the first photo and stared at an 8 X 10 of a magnificent golden Crucifix inset into a metal-looking gold box with a religious image of Christ's Crucifixion embossed in relief on the box; it was guarded by two small, sculpted, angel figures with lances crossed.

Father Murphy watched Clay's face and finally reached across and pointed at an indistinct, slender, twisted blackened piece seeming to rest inside a crystal portion of the vertical bar of the Crucifix just under a golden circle which connected the vertical post with the horizontal crossbeam. "Very nice," Clay said, not exactly sure of what he was looking at.

"Three fragments of the True Cross of Christ brought back from the Holy Land by Empress Helena," Murphy explained patiently. "That's what the tourists see."

"From the actual cross?"

"Without doubt."

He examined the second photograph that showed what looked like a decaying piece of wood mounted under glass in an oval gold frame supported by an intricately carved stand. There appeared to be a few letters of some sort of text carved into the wood. "And this is...?" asked Clay.

"The Titulus Crucis," Father Murphy said, reverence in his tone.

"Sorry, that puts me no further ahead, Father."

"The Titulus is one part of the proclamation that was nailed onto Christ's cross when he was crucified. It identified him as Jesus of Nazareth, King of the Jews. It was also found by Empress Helena, mother of Emperor Constantine in the mid-AD 320s when, as a 70-year-old woman, she made a pilgrimage to the Holy Land and reputedly excavated it, the true cross and a series of nails from the site of His Crucifixion. The walnut proclamation was cut up into three pieces. One given to Constantine, one stayed in Jerusalem and one was sent to Rome. This piece came into the possession of Gerardus Cardinalis S. Crucis, that is, Gerardo Caccianemici, Archbishop of Bologna and titular cardinal of Santa Croce, who ruled as Pope Lucius II from 1144 to 1145. It seems that his choice of a special box for the Titulus and the markings from his cardinal's seal indicate it must have taken place before 1144 and his proclamation as pope."

"How can you be sure it's real after 2,000 plus years?"

"Many reasons. One, for example, is that we know that the Roman Prefect, Pontius Pilate, signed and sealed Christ's death warrant in Latin," said Murphy. "If we look at the Latin that is on the Titulus, we see that it says Jesus the Nazarinus rather than Jesus the Nazarenus...it spells the translation of Nazareth with an *I* rather than an *E*. In paintings of the crucifixion, or anywhere the INRI is spelled out, the spelling is always *Jesus the Nazarenus*. Follow me so far?"

Clay nodded.

"Now *Nazarenus* is later Latin, Vulgate Latin, which is correct for the 4th and 5th centuries. Of course, a Roman bureaucrat like Pilate would have known that the correct Latin spelling is Nazarinus with an *I* as shown on the Titulus. It predates any Latin version of John's Gospel and therefore can't be a later forgery. It must belong to the period of Pilate who would only write and accept classic Latin."

Clay looked up, impressed in spite of himself. "So the church believes it's real?"

"Gospel," Murphy said with a smile. "Cardinal Crucis decided to secret it away and it remained a hidden treasure for the next three hundred years. It was found during restoration work on the mosaic of Santa Croce in 1492 when part of the ceiling was taken away. You see, the reason for it being hidden in that particular spot might very well have been the artwork in the mosaic itself in St. Helena's chapel. This artistry was sponsored by Emperor Valentinian III who ruled from 425 to 455. It showed scenes from Helena's voyage to the Holy Land and, in particular, her discovery of the *True Cross*. Since the Cardinal and his authorities had decided not to display their portion, the worthiest, symbolically most meaningful – and also the safest – place to hide it from attacking Visigoths was behind the mosaic which showed the moment of its discovery. When a layer of damaged stucco was taken off on February 1st in 1492, they saw a brick with an inscription reading **TITVLVS CRVCIS.** When they removed the brick, they discover a niche and a lead box with a description of its contents. Inside was the Titulus. It's been displayed to the public on and off since it's discovery back then. Right now anyone can see it in the Chapel of the Passion Relics at Santa Croce church in Gerusalemme. I'd take you there if we had time. Unfortunately time is something we have precious little of at the moment."

"So, again, it's authentic?"

"Experts claim it is, though others maintain that these and all other relics are a lingering cultural manifestation of an illiterate world."

"All right…what about this?" He held up the third photo.

Murphy merely gestured towards it. "What do you think?" The third photo, creased and spoiled by time, showed what appeared to be a close-up of a blackened four-sided, squared nail about 12 centimeters long; there seemed to be a new head attached. It rested in red velvet lined open box. "Very nice," he said. "Don't tell me this is what I think it is?"

Murphy nodded. "A nail from the cross on which Christ died. Also retrieved by Empress Helena."

"An original nail?"

"Yes, though they added a new head that had been broken off."

"If you say so." He picked up the last photo, a petrified-looking blackened object about eighteen inches long, three inches wide and tapered to a point. A pen in the photo gave it scale.

"And this is…?"

"The largest known piece of the *Wood of the Cross* in existence today. This has never been made public. It was found in a second box behind the Titulus, but never announced. How can we be sure this is real? It's common knowledge, through the ages, that there has been a thriving traffic in fake relics. Some maintain that if all the reputed pieces of the *True Cross* were assembled in one spot, we'd have enough wood to build a national forest."

"You're not making much of a case for its authenticity."

Murphy smiled. "Carbon dating and historical records showed it was from the right time period and we have a mostly unbroken evidence chain that tells us it was one of many pieces brought back by Helena. It's walnut, the type of wood used by the Romans. But that proved nothing. It could have been from a number of crucifixions. Something else convinced us of its authenticity."

"And that was…?"

"By merely laying this Relic on a medically-documented, end-stage cancer patient, the tumors vanished in 24 hours. And stayed away. For eight years…so far. Medically impossible."

"Really?" Clay said, giving him a hard look. "You see, that's one of my problems with the Church, falsely raising hope for a miracle through prayer and faith."

"I couldn't agree more."

"Then how do you know the cure resulted from exposure to this piece of petrified wood? Was the diagnosis accurate? Did someone follow this person home? Watch them for eight years?"

Father Murphy took a deep breath and, for the first time, Clay glimpsed a range of emotions momentarily swirl across the man's face. He even felt embarrassed for the priest as the man briefly turned away to wipe his eyes with a Kleenex. This was hardly the Murphy he'd seen last night, the weapon-carrying, hard-bitten, dogmatic soldier cleric on some nebulous mission for the all-powerful Roman Catholic Church. He waited as the man regained his composure and cleared his throat. Finally, he looked Clay straight in the eye and said: "I'm here, aren't I?"

"You? You were the dying cancer patient?" Clay thought for a moment and slid the photo back. Gently he said: "You've heard of psychosomatic healing? Maybe through your belief in the power of this-this…?"

"…miracle," Father Murphy finished for him. "Afraid that doesn't work. You see I have what we call *conditional* faith. Can't help it. Despite what I do…I'm a 'show me' type of guy. My guts were being eaten out by cancer, I was 90 pounds, MRIs showed tumors with tumors on the tumors, and I was all set to meet my Maker. When one of the world's leading oncologists tells you that you're dead meat, it's prudent to book a plot somewhere. I had given up. I'd made my peace with God and was even looking forward to learning the truth of life's greatest mystery – are we but a flicker of light in a moment in time, or do we go on in some other form? Get my drift, lad?"

Their breakfast arrived and they talked as they ate. Murphy told him of his battle with the invasive lymphoma, his radiation and chemo treatments, weight loss, terminal prognosis and, finally…at deaths door…his miraculous healing. He had been chosen as a guinea pig to see if the relic might have any positive effect on him. The results were far more than dramatic. They were miraculous. He went on to voluntarily deliver a brief synopsis of his life.

Murphy was an Irish schoolboy who had grown up in civil-war torn Belfast and abhorred the violence that he witnessed on a daily basis. He was an only child, born late in life to his parents who doted over him. But by the time he was in university, they had both passed away leaving him enough of an inheritance to fund his college education. He had chosen theology as an elective subject and was fascinated by the origin, growth and hypotheses of organized religions around the world. It was during his first year that he began to suspect that he might have a calling to the priesthood. After several months of discussions with his parish priest and the local bishop, he had changed his subjects to more closely reflect those of a theological major. By the second year he was sure. Now, Murphy confided, 25 years later he found himself chasing something that belonged in a Stephen King novel.

"And what, exactly, are you chasing?" Clay asked.

Murphy shook his head, slowly. "Something that we all wish would go away. But it won't. So I and some other dedicated souls have a job to do."

By the end of breakfast, Clay felt a new respect, a closeness and even a liking for the priest. He pushed his plate away and finished off his coffee. "So who is this guy…Adramelech? The Bishop mentioned him last night?"

"I'll leave that to the cardinal."

"What's the point of all this?" Clay gestured at the photographs.

Murphy studied him closely as though trying to assess how he was doing so far in his unofficial presentation.

"Perhaps to soften you up? Perhaps to convince you that there may be more credence to what we're about to tell you than you'd care to admit. Perhaps to convince you that there is a God in Heaven and a devil in hell. Finally, to ask you to suspend disbelief long enough to give us a better chance at saving your life." He looked at Clay. "And maybe the souls of billions from eternal damnation."

Clay raised his eyebrows, bemused. "Souls of billions? Pretty high stakes, partner."

Murphy eyed him and regretfully shook his head. "All I know is that the game is not over. I'm sorry. I've said too much. And, His Excellency, Bishop Aquila, also spoke prematurely last night. Cardinal Malachi is supposed to fill you in."

Clay sighed. "Was that child on the street the same one from Vermont? And if so, how come she didn't age?"

"Later, lad. Later."

"Then tell me this," Clay said. "Last night I smelled propane. Is that limo powered by propane?"

"Yes, I believe it is," Murphy answered, slowly.

"Then that's what happened. A small leak and when the gun was fired into the back, it set off an explosion." Clay settled back in his chair, a satisfied smile creeping across his features at having solved the puzzle.

"Works for me," Murphy responded perfunctorily and drained his cup. "Now I have to get you back to the Vatican my boy before they set the hounds after us and I have to do a round of penance. That might entail an absence of grog for a week or two and that would not be a laughing matter."

As they left the restaurant, Murphy tried to press a wad of Euros into the owner's hand but he was dismissively waved away. "I'll rack you up for a new set of indulgences at the ecclesiastical bank," he called to the man as they exited. The old friends both laughed.

~ 8 ~

Malachi's secretary was out to lunch so Murphy used the brass shrunken head door knocker to softly tap on the heavy oak door of his office. Clay looked at it and raised his eyebrows at Sister Maria standing beside them. She tried to look serious but the ghost of a smile played across her lips. An impatient acknowledgement came from inside and Murphy opened the door, ushered them in and eased it closed silently behind them. He didn't enter.

"Good afternoon, Your Eminence," Maria said, a slight nervousness in her voice.

"Sister Maria…Mr. Montague…welcome to my humble abode," Cardinal Malachi said, jovially. He'd given up trying to get Maria to call him by his Christian name. "Just move those papers and books to the floor and drag the chairs up here." He seemed to be searching for something on his desk piled high with dossiers, unopened mail and file folders of every description. They did as he asked and sat down. Malachi finally selected a bubble-pack envelope from a pile of papers, extracted a brown manila folder and glanced briefly at the contents. "Undoubtedly, after everything you've been through, you must have a few questions, Mr. Montague."

"A few," Clay admitted, careful to keep sarcasm from his tone. He stared at the cardinal in his black suit and white collar desperately trying to remember where he had seen him before. After a moment it came to him. This was the man who had briefly appeared at the VA hospital in upstate New York just as he was being discharged. So he was a colleague of the old priest who vanished?

Clay glanced around the office at the various weapons on the walls. He knew weaponry and recognized ancient blunderbusses, a Lee Enfield .303, a 7.65 "sportized" Mauser, two crossed, silver .45 caliber frontier-style Peacemaker Colts, a Mossberg .22 and an assortment of rapiers, cutlasses, scimitars, and foils. The remaining walls featured glass display cases showing various archeological artifacts as well as heavy bookcases containing cracked, leather-jacketed books whose spines featured faded, gold lettering.

On the cardinal's desk sat, for all extents and purposes, a real human skull with a half-melted candle sticking out through a hole bored in the top. Obviously an original from the Edgar Allan Poe School of Interior Design, Clay thought.

The Cardinal finally sat forward. "Do you believe in evil?"

"Evil as in evil deeds?" Clay asked, surprised by the question.

"Call it an intrinsic evil. A force without any desire or chance for redemption."

Clay shrugged. "In my police work I've run across suspects who appeared to be motivated purely by evil. I guess, as a man of God, you are constantly surprised by the evil man perpetrates?"

Malachi laughed and sat back, his chair creaking. "Quite the contrary, Mr. Montague. I am never surprised by the evil men do. I am, however, often surprised by man's inherent generosity and goodness of spirit."

"Was that the spirit in which I was kidnapped?" Clay couldn't help himself.

"Actually it was," Malachi said with a genuine smile. "Essentially you're here because of what you saw on your last night patrol as a soldier in Panama." The cardinal rocked absentmindedly in his chair and fixed Clay with an unwavering stare. "Do you remember?"

Clay sighed. "So many years ago? The night I was wounded?"

Maria watched him intently.

"Correct," Malachi said.

"Alright, I thought I saw something odd. But it might well have been just a dream I had in the VA hospital."

"Do you remember what happened at the Baker estate in Vermont the night your deputy died?"

Clay felt the goose bumps hairs rise on his arms and neck. "Of course." His tone was now more cautious.

"Anything extraordinary happen there that evening? Anything of consequence?"

"A good man died."

Malachi sighed, got up from his desk, turned and looked out his window. He clasped two strong-looking hands behind his back as he gazed at dozens of ancient Vatican rooftops, some emitting smoke through centuries-old chimneys. These rooftops had covered up so many secrets, he thought. Some good; some best forgotten. But some of the bad had to be brutally kept alive so that those in the present could learn from the past. And, his job today was to stir up some of the less desirable realities of the past.

Clay glanced at Maria again. She seemed to be deliberately avoiding his eyes as she stared at the cardinal's back.

Finally, Malachi spoke without turning: "I have a copy of your final report to the American FBI regarding the murder of your deputy. The whole thing: the girl, her superhuman strength, you firing and hitting her multiple times, and her apparent resurrection…the works. Have I left anything out?" He turned and sat back down.

"They thought I was delusional," Clay said, slowly.

"But we both know they were wrong, don't we? It all happened, just as you described and what killed your partner was something unholy, something from beyond the boundaries of what the FBI or any other police force was willing to investigate or acknowledge as reality."

"You believe the report?"

"Yes," Malachi said, simply.

"Do you know who killed Hitch? That little girl?"

Malachi shook his head. "I doubt it. We believe it was something much worse. Her master…an arch demon known as Adramelech."

"An arch *demon*?" Clay rolled his eyes slightly. "You're not serious?"

"Deadly serious. The Catholic Church has been hunting it in one form or another since we first formally confirmed its earthly existence…about nine centuries ago. We believe, however, that it's been around for eons. Records show we have occasionally 'put it down' but it always returns."

"And who's the kid…another…*demon*?" Clay could barely get the word out.

"Her name was Rosalita Hickox, a Mexican child run over in 1840 by a wagon transporting gold from a mine in Sonora, Mexico. From our research we've discovered she was from a fairly rich family that, as was the custom, had seen her laid out in their living room before burial. But the same night she vanished. She was later seen *alive* a number of times in the company of a large stranger who was reputed to only appear at night. The family, believing she had somehow made a miraculous recovery and been kidnapped, pulled out all stops to find her. They succeeded up in Monterey, California.

The story goes that she was, in fact, a zombie of sorts. They found her alone one evening and her mother and father seized and transported her to their Monterey domicile. Then they called in the local parish priest. The next morning, the Marshall was called to their residence where he found the parents and the priest murdered. The child was gone."

"And how did she get from the year 1840 to now?" Clay asked, disbelief riddling his tone.

"From what we can tell, he sometimes 'stashes' familiars after they have fulfilled his needs. Later, he returns to where he has interred them and they reawaken, ready to serve again. In effect, he makes them immortal until he is finished with them."

"Sir, with all due respect…," Clay said, shaking his head; he wasn't about to buy into a story that he'd been attacked by a 170-year-plus child corpse that had been brought back from the dead by a demon. No matter what had happened to him in Vermont.

"The Marshall's report noted one strange thing," Malachi continued as though Clay hadn't spoken. "Despite the horrific mutilations, there wasn't a drop of blood where they lay. And, the local doctor said they had little left in their bodies. Clean as bled-out pork." He grimaced.

Maria added her voice to the discussion. "I know this sounds absurd, but I saw her on the street outside your office in New York. What she did defied logic. She had unbelievable powers."

"I know…. " Clay's voice, almost a whisper, broke slightly. He took a deep breath. "I know…because I've seen it. Who is she? How can she take three .45 caliber slugs and survive?"

"You're not listening," Malachi said, with annoyance. "She's *immortal*! Just like her master, Adramelech. The only thing that can put her, or her demon boss down is a stake, blessed by a man of God, driven through her heart."

"Like in some vampire movie?"

"According to Sister Raphael that's where most of the bogeyman and vampire stories come from," Maria interrupted. "The only things that affect him are what have come out of the legends: Crucifixes or crosses representing Christ's sacrifice, holy water and other blessed objects. On the other hand, consecrated ground and religious statues have little effect. A Crucifix seems to work against him but reports over time have noted that even holy objects are losing some of their effectiveness each time he returns to life. It seems the longer he lives, the stronger he becomes. And, as near as Sister Raphael can tell, Adramelech has been awake again since the invasion of Panama."

"You're asking me to believe that there's some immortal demon thing running around in the 21st Century?"

"Sort of what you asked the FBI to believe," Malachi responded, his eyebrows arching in challenge.

Touché, thought Clay. Still, he shook his head in disbelief even as he asked: "So what's this *thing* been doing for twenty-plus years?"

Malachi raised his hands: "Guatemalan civil war, Darfur, Rwanda, Iraq, Bosnia…we see his handiwork everywhere. And we always find a shadowy figure whispering in the ears of despots, dictators or warlords – someone without any retrievable history who invariably vanishes after the disasters. His purpose? Destroy faith and hope. As Roman poet Ovid said: 'Take hope from the heart of man and you make him a beast of prey.' Adramelech's specialty!"

"So why am I here?"

"Do you believe in God, Mr. Montague?"

"I believe there's a difference between right and wrong."

"Nothing more?" Malachi sat back. "Do you know that more and more scientists and scholars are looking at Big Bang cosmology that brought matter, time, and space into existence, and other amazing discoveries such as an expanding universe, and are concluding that the idea of a transcendent power is entirely possible…and reasonable? That someone or something – take your pick – is responsible for our creation. That it wasn't an accident or mere happenstance."

"I'm sorry but I haven't kept up with theories on our origin. I've been a little busy trying to figure out why the Catholic Church has kidnapped me." Clay was getting tired of the dance.

"Of course. Let's approach this from another angle. You were raised a Catholic. Do you believe in the Catholic Church? In its holy mission to bring the world to Christ?"

Clay pondered this for a moment. "I was raised a Catholic. And, as a boy I believed everything I was supposed to believe. But as a thinking adult, I see the church as just another powerful organization with a goal. I'm just not entirely sure what the goal is these days."

Malachi sighed. "It's true. We have become heavily bureaucratic, out of touch with modern reality and, sometimes we lose sight of our God-given charitable mandate. Sometimes we pursue earthly power and wealth rather than focus on the spiritual side of mankind. These are self-acknowledged failings which we strive each day to overcome. And we pay the price as people turn away from God and the church."

Clay nodded, both surprised at this admission and grateful for the candor. It was hard not to like this man.

"However," Malachi continued, "when the lure of prestige subsides, when the bright lights flicker and die, and we find ourselves adrift in this increasingly dark world, every true priest worth his salt will come down on the side of God and His teachings."

"Really? *Every* priest?" Clay regretted his barb even as he said it but Malachi did not blink.

The cardinal caught his meaning and sighed. "You'll notice I said 'true' priests. These men who invaded our ranks have done a very effective job of shaming our Mother the Church. They did not come to the priesthood as innocents and then were corrupted. They came as they were and brought their dirty little secrets with them. How could we know? Unfortunately, when we did know, too many decision-makers became terrified of the consequences of a few evil men and didn't handle it properly. We have more than 400,000 priests around the globe serving the spiritual needs of 1 billion Catholics – 17 percent of the world's population. Show me any organization this size and I'll show you much more corruption than what we have. But don't get me wrong, I am not defending a *single* one of them. Slowly we are working to rectify the wrongs where we can. Undoubtedly, Satan is laughing long and hard at our naivety."

Malachi rose, crossed to a sideboard and poured himself a drink of water. He held up the jug to Clay and Maria but both shook their heads. He resumed his seat behind the desk, took a healthy drink, set it down and made a small steeple with his fingers. He sighed and settled back.

"Let us get back to the problem at hand. First I'll tell you *who* Adramelech is according to ancient text. We first find him as an arch demon of hell. In fact, at one time he was the president of the Senate of the demons. In Judeo-Christianity he is also known as the Chancellor of Hell. In Poet Robert Silverberg's short story *Basileus*, he is described as: 'The enemy of God, greater in ambition, guile and mischief than Satan.' That's an apt description. Let us just say that we believe Satan saw Adramelech's power and his ambition, and so decided that he didn't need anyone around to compete for leadership after all the usurpers were banished from Paradise. He summoned Adramelech and gave him an earthly mission: to triumph over God's creatures and turn them from the Trinity. It is only with God's goodness that we have survived so far."

"Meaning no disrespect, sir," Clay said, "but I really find it hard to believe there is any defined power for good when I watched my poor mother pray to die because of her suffering. I saw my beautiful young wife, who never hurt anyone, smashed to pieces in a senseless accident. And, I saw a salt of the earth guy like my deputy, tortured and murdered for nothing. So when you ask me if I believe in God…quite frankly, I don't. I'd be much more inclined to believe in the devil. *If*…I believed in anything these days."

"Quite understandable since you've seen his representative up close and personal," Malachi shot back.

The image of the large cloaked figure looming over the young soldier came back to Clay again and he shuddered. "I don't know what I saw that night…if anything. A doctor told me what I thought I *saw* was merely a personification of evil that I created in my mind."

"We all take comfort in rationalizations, Mr. Montague. Perhaps it was a personal nightmare. You just have to ask yourself that, if it was a personal nightmare, how come it fits so well as a catalyst for what followed?" Malachi leaned forward over the desk. "Let's put aside our theories and get down to brass tacks. You're a detective. I'd like to hire you to do some detective work for me."

"This keeps getting more bizarre."

"Hear him out," Maria said, quickly.

"Mr. Montague…listen carefully. I run an organization of *Daemon Elit* – Demon Trackers. We have met with varying degrees of success but we need help – professional detecting help. The Vatican will pay you a thousand dollars a day plus expenses to find Adramelech and tell us where he is." Malachi sat back and waited.

"And how am I supposed to do that?"

"He has a nasty habit of calling attention to himself by murdering people. In quantity. For their blood. For instance, there have been a string of murders in London, England, recently.

Streetwalkers have been dying at the rate of one or two a week. And Scotland Yard reports they are drained of blood – Adramelech's MO. The police are looking for a modern day Jack the Ripper."

"The Millennium Ripper," Clay said, recalling a news report.

"We should be so lucky," Malachi said. "This Ripper is not human."

"Assuming there is any credence to this story of some sort of blood-sucking monster, I have to ask why?"

"Why what?"

"Why does it need blood?"

"We can only suppose that Satan has some perverted sense of humor. As the blood of Christ was to be shed for all mankind, he ensured that his creature needed the blood of mankind to help him continue his battle against Christ and all He stands for. If you saw Adramelech in his 'natural' embodiment, you'd know immediately that he's a very different breed of cat – too monstrous to move within our society. But after he awakens each time, and ingests human blood, he attains the ability to become, at will, more human. In other words, he is a shape shifter."

"And, if I believed any of this," Clay asked, "what stage is he in now?"

"We've no idea. We do know this: He is knowing, but *not all knowing*. Powerful but *not all powerful*. He can be killed but only by a holy instrument blessed in the name of God. And after a time, he returns from the dead. Or a temporary incapacitation – whatever you care to term it. That much we know for certain.

"We also had a priest kidnapped by him and the little girl you met. That was in 1990. This priest claims to have seen the horrors of hell but remembers little else. Then for some unknown reason, he was allowed to escape his imprisonment."

"*Allowed* to escape?"

"Yes."

Clay thought back to the VA hospital and probed his memory for the name of the priest who disappeared. "Father Gallo?"

Malachi stared at him for a moment and then a slight smile crossed his face. "Very good. You not only remember, you are able to put together diverse happenings and to look for patterns or clues – the sign of a good detective."

"How did he get away?"

"Essentially he walked out. But he knew well the legend: that Adramelech tracks down and kills –" Malachi stopped abruptly. "Anyhow, we brought him back to the Vatican and this has become his safe-house of sorts. As it has been for you." The cardinal smiled. "A thousand dollars a day, Mr. Montague?"

"If I took on this...assignment," Clay said, "where would I begin?"

"London. You'll work with Sister Maria."

Clay thought again for a moment. Something was missing. "Surely an organization like the Vatican already has detectives it can recruit? Vatican Police...whatever? Why me?"

Maria looked at Clay but again quickly looked away. The detective sensed an uneasiness as Malachi answered in a deliberate, matter-of-fact tone. "Let's just say you are somewhat aware of what you're dealing with. And, you have the added incentive of knowing that it savagely tore up your good friend Hitchcock...and then sent your poor wife plummeting to her death over a cliff."

Despite knowing the cardinal was deliberately playing to his desire for revenge, Clay couldn't help rising to the bait. For the first time in his life, he actually felt his blood run cold.

~ 9 ~

The child pulled her knees close in a useless attempt to keep warm. Once again, though she felt nothing physical, habit made her try to warm herself as she crouched in the corner of the dank London sewer. She was so tired and yet she could never sleep. For hours, a thousand tiny silken threads of cobwebs had flowed around her as hundreds of spiders worked their magic to create their intricate traps and capture and crunch the ever-present insects crawling busily along the stone floors and walls. From her feet to her head, she was virtually half hidden by a gauze of webs. No insects avoided the child as there was no movement nor any tell-tale temperature elevation to alert them to the presence of a living body. But other sewer predators were not so easily fooled. They knew a potential meal when they saw it.

Two large rats, with nostrils twitching and red eyes blazing raced towards the girl. The child's own eyes lit up like twin fires and a deep, very low growl grew in her throat as she bared scissor sharp teeth. Some primitive survival instinct, honed by millions of years of existence, warned the rodents this campaign was a particularly bad idea and they abruptly stopped, peeled off, and ran squeaking in terror back the way they came.

More sounds. At first Rosalita thought they were returning. But then she heard heavy footfalls approaching. Her Master strode out of the shadows sheathed in a dark suit and a long black cloak that dragged unheeded through the puddles of water and animal urine forming tiny lakes in depressions left in the ancient cracked stone floor. She looked up at the strong, pale face, and the greenish yellow eyes. She felt such a surge of love and devotion that she could barely contain herself. Eager to please, she prostrated herself on her stomach, raised her buttocks and waited. But he was there for another purpose. A large hand picked her up by her shift and she was suddenly on her feet. Gently he brushed off the webs that fell like angel gauze to the stone floor.

"We have work to do tonight, Rosalito," he said to her, his voice deep and guttural. "Those who have seen must be destroyed. You, my dearest, will bring me more sustenance – two to give me the strength I shall need. So go. Bring back what I ask. I eat first and then we shall commence the hunt."

The child felt the hand release her and she quickly scurried towards an iron door that concealed stone steps leading to the London street grill above. Though its rusted condition and formidable weight would have prevented most strong men from opening it, she grasped the handle and easily pulled it wide with its metal hinges screeching and popping in protest. She must not displease her Master…for he could make even the dead feel pain and terror. She moved ahead purposely.

Slipping through the opening, she made her way up the steps towards the surface. Above her she could now see that it was dark and raining. And, as she climbed, she could hear the swish of the occasional car blasting through rain puddles pooling on the pavement. All she had to do was find two women plying the oldest trade in the world and lead them back down the stone steps to her Master. If they didn't come willingly, then she would take them anyhow.

Once a younger call girl had refused to accompany her and tried to scream when she was seized. The child had simply reached up, grabbed her throat and squeezed until her larynx ruptured and blood boiled out of her mouth. The screaming had ceased immediately, as soon did her struggles. Fortunately her heart had continued to beat so that when Adramelech pierced her veins, it was an easy meal.

Either way, she could not return empty handed. Tonight, two more women would yield up their life-sustaining nourishment begging and thrashing about as they so desperately fought for life.

Rosalita looked up at the squared grill leading to the street above and easily pushed the 125-pound weight to the side. As she pulled herself up, she noted two ladies of the evening walking towards their favorite corner, barely 25 yards away. She turned away knowing they had seen her.

The taller one caught sight of Rosalita and both came to a halt.

"Hey child, you'll catch your death. What in the name of Heaven are you doing out dressed like that? What are you up to, luv?"

With her back to them, Rosalita's eyes began to glow as a wicked grin crossed her features. She played the game, turned and held out her arms for help. Cooing softly in sympathy they came to her willingly.

~ 10 ~

Captain Wayne Bowden adjusted his large frame on the hotel bed, shook the London Times open to the city section, and sighed loudly at the headlines: **SCOTLAND YARD INVESTIGATES PROSTITUTES' DISAPPEARANCES.** A kicker ran under it reading: **Millennium Ripper prowls Soho.** The story probed the disappearance of up to nine working girls in Soho and the finding of two more bodies which were under prolonged examination by Scotland Yard's forensic pathology department. Though little news had been officially released, the press had managed to retrieve one bit of information; the bodies had been mutilated and virtually exsanguinated. From this came the speculation that some form of modern day Jack the Ripper was on the loose. Bowden shook his head. A sidebar story was headlined **Highgate Murders – Has Ripper moved to The City of Shadows?**

It told the story of two teenage girls being found killed in Highgate Cemetery with battered skulls and gaping holes in their throats. With no signs of robbery or rape, the reporter speculated as to whether the "ripper" had moved north of the city to Highgate Cemetery – a centuries old burying ground with an extensive system of architecturally significant tombs, mausoleums, statues and catacombs.

"Ready to grab a bite?" Copilot Danny Gostini called exiting Bowden's washroom while drying his hands with a small white towel. He threw the cloth on Bowden's extra bed.

"Hey, mess up your own room," Bowden said with a chuckle as Gostini quickly retrieved it and returned it to the washroom. "Yeah, let's go. Café Latino on Frith Street okay?" He neatly folded the paper and placed it on the side table.

"Sounds good. I'm tired of Café Nero," the First Officer answered affably. "We can walk." He glanced at the newspaper's headlines. "God, I thought crime in America was bad. Seems London is catching up."

"No franchise on nutcases," Bowden said. "When I was a kid and read stories about Jack the Ripper, I used to think we'd evolved since the last century. But then the Boston Strangler, Son of Sam, the Yorkshire Ripper and all those others made me realize the human race is pretty much stuck with its mixture of good, bad and indifferent. Unfortunately, their punishments hardly ever fit their crimes. They plead unhappy childhoods or insanity and the judges say: 'Poor boy, we didn't understand you'."

"For justice, my friend, you need politicians with the guts to pass the right legislation. Most live on a financial strata that isn't touched by crime and so don't give a rat's ass."

"You got that right."

Five minutes later the two pilots, clothed in slacks, wool sweaters and waterproof windbreakers were making their way through the very streets of Soho named in the article, pausing occasionally to look in shop windows and then moving on. A light but chilling mist seemed to have thinned out the usual crowds so they hadn't bothered with dinner reservations. Neither man was super hungry and they'd decided that if there was a prolonged wait, they'd find a coffee shop and settle for a couple of sandwiches.

"Did we get any marching orders from Rome now that the majors on the power plants are done," asked Gostini, referring to their return to London for scheduled major overhauls on both A320 engines.

Out of habit, Bowden checked the pager on his belt for updates. No further messages. "Just what I received previously: Return to Rome tomorrow. The doc and his nurse will be at the airport by 0800 hours and fly back with us. Then, as usual, we wait. But, again, we have to be ready to move at a moments notice. For what…or why…who knows! The only thing I've figured out so far is that they are looking for someone."

"Blimey!" Gostini said in an exaggerated British accent. "Did I ever tell you I did a stint with FedEx ferrying everything from ant farms to a killer whale, as well as private work with the Saudi government transporting a prince's six wives to wherever he needed them. And yet, this is the weirdest assignment I've ever had! A couple of times I even heard references to a demon. *Demons!* Boy!"

"No kidding," Bowden said, dryly. Their footsteps echoed hollowly on the deserted side street they'd taken. "I heard the new Bishop and two of his priests talking last week about the 'Relic.' Anyhow, when one priest saw I was half listening, he came up and slammed the cockpit door. Not a very friendly fellow."

"No…they'd never make it as stand-up comics."

Bowden laughed. "Yeah, welcome to my world of denial, servitude and self-flagellation."

"They don't beat themselves anymore," Gostini said, his tone defensive.

"Aw…the eternal Catholic," Bowden returned with a grin.

Gostini laughed, somewhat self-consciously. "When you've been raised in the Church, it never quite leaves you."

"Maybe we wouldn't have this gig if we weren't Catholics. When I was interviewed, that was the first question they asked me."

"Me too. But they seemed to be more interested in the fact that I was a bachelor and could be available 24-hours a day." He stopped and looked at a Swiss Rolex Submariner watch in a jewelry store's window. "Always wanted one of those. Ever since I read that James Bond wore one."

Bowden laughed again. "My Tag is good enough for me. Anyhow with the extra overtime premium we're earning for stand-by, you should be able to afford one soon."

"I don't know," Gostini said as they resumed walking. "No guarantees on the length of this assignment. They could pull the plug anytime."

"So far…so good. Besides they have tons of cash."

"Every organization has controls," the co-pilot answered. "Just because they have cash doesn't mean they want to spend it on an aircraft and two pilots sitting around waiting for God knows what orders. Or orders from God." He laughed at his own joke, already feeling bad for saying it.

"Hello!" Bowden came to a stop as a young, barefoot child stepped out of an alley about thirty feet in front of them. They stopped in surprise. "What the hell is a kid her age doing out on a night like this? And dressed like that?" He felt an immediate anger towards her parents as he looked about to see if there was any sign of them. Strangely, the street seemed to have grown quieter than it had been; the usual underlying throb had abated. Other than for themselves, it was deserted.

The child looked at Gostini, raised her tiny forefinger and brazenly beckoned him to approach her.

"Hey little girl…stay there please!" The voice rang out from behind them and Bowden and Gostini turned expecting to see some very worried parents. Instead two helmeted London Bobbies had appeared and were hurrying towards them, their night sticks swinging.

Bowden swung back round towards the child and started as she moved and the muted glow of a street lamp fell on her face. Her eyes lit up like a Halloween pumpkin and for a brief instant he could only think of the eyes of an animal caught in the headlights of a car.

"Missy…stop!" the second officer said, as the constables drew abreast and passed Bowden and Gostini. The child had turned abruptly and darted back into the alley from where she'd come.

All four men hurried forward but when they came to the alley the child was nowhere in sight. The Bobbies quickly gave the pilots the once-over. The taller constable spoke. "She isn't one of your lot is she, sir?"

"No, we saw her about the same time you did," Gostini said. Bowden nodded in agreement.

"Right, off you go then," the second copper responded. "We'll have a look-see down there." They hurried into the alley which appeared to be very long and very dark.

"Did you see her eyes?" Bowden asked.

"Her eyes? What about them?" Gostini probed.

"Nothing. Must have been a trick of the light." The pilot shrugged off a vague feeling of uneasiness and they began to move forward. Suddenly there was shouting from the alley behind them followed by a man's shrill scream splitting the air; both men knew immediately that it wasn't the scream of a child; it came from one of the constables. As one, he and Gostini barged into a convenience store to summon help.

~ 11 ~

Cardinal Malachi fidgeted impatiently in the ante-chamber as he cooled his heels in preparation for his long-awaited audience with the Holy Father. Archbishop Dominique Bortnowaska, the big man's personal secretary, had happily come through for him and scheduled thirty minutes for "ecclesiastical discussion" as a cover for his true purpose. Malachi was disappointed that *The Seven* had not been allowed to accompany him, but together, they had labored for more than ten hours putting together an abbreviated *PowerPoint* presentation with newspaper articles and other cryptic documents necessary to highlight their case. His laptop would run the presentation while he backed it up with pieces of parchments and original documents signed out of the Vatican Library under pain of death, if damaged or lost.

Malachi's singular purpose, of course, was to elicit a papal waiver restoring his budget; their entire mission was rendered impotent without it. With their Vatican Bank credit card accounts in danger of being declined for everything from jet fuel to lodgings, it was becoming an enormous nuisance limiting the movement of the *Crusaders*, the *Watchers* and even *The Seven*. And finally, they were getting close to Adramelech; he knew it with every fiber of his being. And with some luck, they now had a weapon whose power he hoped would snuff out this scourge once and for all.

There was a muffled crash of what sounded like breaking glass inside from the Pope's office and Malachi stared at the heavy carved mahogany doors. The sound served as a tension breaker as he smiled to himself wondering if the Holy Father was breaking up the furniture. He'd heard that at times he could give in to temper. Not that he was prone to throwing things, more like he didn't suffer fools gladly and had made this fact well known.

Malachi wondered for the umpteenth time if he'd ever been briefed on the existence of *The Seven*, much less their mandate. The Holy Father was reputed to be pragmatic to a fault. Though the church was intensely spiritual as well as, admittedly, selling a certain amount of mysticism, talk of arch demons and the like might not sit too well with the Vicar of Christ in a 21st Century setting.

Still there was no alternative. He'd pulled in every favour, exercised a few threats and even arranged for Monsignor Giuseppe Lopez, the Prefecture of the Pontifical Household, to "win" a three-day sabbatical (via a non-existent contest) to Nice on the French Riviera where he would also attend a hastily-arranged seminar on *Exploring Celibacy Vows in the Modern Priesthood*. The Bishop of Nice, a very old friend, had been only too happy to help out and hurriedly lined up speakers, a set of rooms and fake attendees for the "seminar." With weasel nose out of the picture, Malachi knew he was reasonably certain he wouldn't be preempted.

Suddenly the tall doors opened and Bortnowaska stuck his head out. "Mustavias, old friend, His Holiness will see you now."

Malachi abruptly stood up, felt his Notebook sliding and grabbed at it while dumping all the papers from his half-opened briefcase onto the terrazzo-tiled floor. Heels clicking on the marble floor, Bortnowaska quickly came out to help him gather them up. Not far behind him shuffled a familiar figure dressed in immaculate white, sporting a small silk skullcap; a heavy gold Crucifix dangling from his neck. The Holy Father was smiling kindly at Malachi's predicament through the doorway. He motioned by throwing his hands in the air with a "best laid plans of mice and men…" gesture and then re-entered his office and headed to his desk to await their entry.

As Malachi stuffed newspaper clippings, budget sheets and photocopies of ancient scrolls back into the leather satchel, he noticed with surprise that his hands were shaking. It didn't take much to realize why. So much was riding on his personal persuasiveness during the next thirty minutes. In fact, everything was riding on it.

He heard the distant ringing of the phone as he rose with his reclaimed papers. He could now see Bortnowaska already picking up the receiver, speaking briefly with someone and then handing the phone to the Pontiff as he shook his head. Quickly he came out of the office towards Malachi, an apologetic look on his face. "My friend, I'm sorry. We've a bit of a legal emergency and I can tell you it will take some time to resolve. I will reschedule you as soon as humanly possible."

"Can I wait?" Malachi pleaded

"I'm sorry, it will serve no purpose. I will call you later, I promise. Mustavias, we have *no* choice but to deal with this now. I am so sorry." Looking sympathetically at Malachi, Bortnowaska backed through the heavy doors, pulling them shut as he went.

Feeling beaten, Malachi nodded resolutely at the closed doors and turned slowly away with his computer and leather satchel. If only they knew his true purpose, all other emergencies would pale in significance. The first part of the conundrum he found himself in was that he was representing a spiritual problem in an increasingly secular world. A corollary, unfortunately, was that their spiritual problem was rapidly becoming more secular by the moment. And, only God knew how fast it would grow. Already the newspapers were reporting on mysterious multiple murders that seemed to have no motives and no discernible perpetrators.

Malachi decided to stop into the Basilica on his way back to his office. It was time to once again test the power of prayer.

* * * *

PART FIVE

"THE HUNT"

"...Fancy thinking the Beast was something you could hunt and kill!" said the head...

William Golding
THE LORD OF THE FLIES

~ 1 ~

British Airways Flight BA2542 sailed westward through the blue morning sky over an unbroken bed of white clouds below. With nary a bump to betray the fact they were flying at more than 500 miles per hour, for all Clay knew, he might have been having breakfast at his own table in Manhattan rather than trying to scoop up the remnants of two over-easy eggs on a piece of toast from a meal tray at 35,000 feet.

According to Malachi, it was cheaper to send them via commercial carrier than bring their own aircraft back from London where it was undergoing a scheduled and paid for major engine overhaul. Though the engines had undergone an intensive inspection less than two weeks ago, the "major" was required by law.

Beside Clay, in another oversized and comfortable 767 seat, looking quite fetching and professional in a plain grey suit and ruffled white blouse, Maria sat quietly reading a London newspaper while intermittently sipping black coffee from a china cup. The Vatican had sprung for *Club Europe,* a form of business class and Clay settled himself more comfortably in the leather-like seats. They were at least three inches wider than normal and he had oodles of room for his long legs. Infinitely better than "sardine class" – his customary habitat when he flew.

"There were two policeman murdered in Soho last week, same area where the prostitutes have been vanishing," Maria said, quartering the paper and handing it to Clay. He quickly dropped the toast back onto the plate and read of the killings. Reporters, who managed to get on scene before it was well-secured and taped off claimed that the victims looked like they'd been attacked by a wild animal. There was even reports of dismemberment. According to the press, Scotland Yard had refused to comment on the homicides.

"Sister, I—"

"Call me Maria," she admonished, with a slight curve of her red lips accentuating her natural dimples. "Remember, we're supposed to be your average married couple."

Clay nodded but couldn't help noticing the healthy shine of her hair nor a form of merriment that forever seemed to lurk in her eyes as though she was privy to a private joke. She was a bit like a dolphin, he thought, with a natural smile in the curve of her lips. No wonder people seemed to like her immediately. In fact, in the brief time they were together he'd already seen ample evidence of an inherent attractiveness that seemed to magically open doors as she'd requested pre-boarding, and then a more private seat location near the bulkhead. Fortunately the flight wasn't crowded and the young male flight attendant, smitten by her easy manner and charm, had accommodated them. And, he'd been around several times since with newspapers, pillows, and even an open bottle of champagne – any excuse to spend a few moments making small talk with her. Small wonder.

"And here's a story of two teenage girls being killed in Highgate Cemetery in northern London two nights ago," she said. "There's even speculation that it may have been the work of the Millennium Ripper."

"Maria, just to clear up any misunderstanding, I still believe we're searching for a madman," Clay said. "A very intelligent and cunning killer but one with his feet planted firmly in our world."

"How can you say that after what you've seen," she asked, more puzzled than upset.

"All I've seen have been a bunch of people shadowing me for months with some rather obsessive and excessive notions."

"And what about Vermont? You saw what was done to your deputy. You shot that little girl and yet she's still alive."

"I know…I know…but who's to say she was the same girl as the one in New York?" He shook his head. "As for Hitch…I don't know. It could have been some crazed sect or something got to him and then cut out before I got there."

"And Panama?" She issued the words like a challenge.

"Panama…was-was nothing more than a nightmare. It all happened so fast I barely saw anything."

"I think it's a case of you don't *want* to believe. Perhaps it frightens you?"

"Perhaps it does," he admitted with a shrug and then sighed. He sat back and closed his eyes.

Maria, however, wasn't content to let it all lie. "Do you think these senior members of the Church have nothing better to do with their time than chase goblins? These are learned men, Clay."

"Men who believe in the supernatural, miracles and the tangible power of prayer?"

"I believe in all those things," she said, simply. Then, with her jaw jutting forward at an angle that betrayed a natural stubborn streak, she said: "What do you think came out of the limo that night? What blinded Bishop Aquila?"

"Propane explosion set off by Murphy firing his weapon. You felt the heat."

"A gas explosion ripped the heart out of the limo driver?"

"That happened before we got there. I'm not denying that the Church is in conflict with a violent and deadly adversary, Maria, but asking me to believe a demon is roaming the earth...."

"Shush, Clay," she warned, bringing her finger to her lips.

He realized his voice level had been rising and he resumed an undertone. "I don't know what happened that night. If you recall, I had a fair amount of drugs pumped into me."

Maria shook her head looking somewhat disappointed. "I wish you were right. But what I saw outside your office in New York that night sealed it for me. She levitated in front of me. And when I accidentally ran over her, I felt the wheels of the automobile bump over her body, and yet she stood up immediately afterwards and acted as though nothing had happened. You were unconscious at the time."

"Yes, I seem to miss all the good parts, don't I?" he said, with a wry smile. "And why *me*? Not to appear narcissistic, but why am I in the middle of this mess?"

Maria pondered his question for a moment and then softly said: "God has plans for all of us, Clay."

"Plans? You believe God has an individual plan for me, for you...for every human being on this earth?"

"Yes I do. I believe that some of us fit into His plans. I believe He helps us find our way when we are lost in life. I believe that if we ask Him for help, and believe in Him, He will provide the help we need."

"If it fits in with His plan?"

"Perhaps. Look at what has happened to you. You met Adramelech in Panama...."

"Allegedly."

"You survived. And then you survived again in Vermont. And you survived in your office in New York. And then at the airport in Rome. Maybe it was all for a reason, Clay."

Clay didn't say anything. Maria's prompts reminded him of a cold alley in New York City. Was that all part of a plan? But why him? As devil's advocate he could also ask: why not him? He smiled at the irony and Maria saw this and immediately took issue.

"It's not necessarily preposterous, you know. Throughout history there have been many, many instances of God intervening purposely and directly in people's lives. Indeed, the Bible tells us of dozens of instances."

Clay held up a hand. "Forgive me but I wasn't laughing at the idea, Maria. I was just thinking of something else. Maybe there is a plan for us all. It would be more comforting to believe so. And if that helps anyone sleep better at night, I would even encourage that thinking."

"But you must not only think of it only for others, Clay. *You* must have faith. *You* must believe that God loves you."

There was silence between them for a few minutes and finally Clay closed his eyes and thought about the past few days. After he agreed to do some sleuthing for the Church, he'd been sent to Sister Raphael in the Vatican Library who, through a legion of documentation tried to convince him that this *Hellspawn* – or Beast as she sometimes called it – actually existed. She presented him with historical portraits from Church reports, as well as with newspaper and microfiche records of his supposed crimes against humanity. Its reason for being, she theorized, was to prepare the earth for demonic rule.

After his sessions with Sister Raphael, he was certainly convinced that she believed it was real; still, when he emerged into the light of day, he could not bring himself round to their apocalyptic vision. Instead, he'd decided to pursue the killer and reserve judgment on his/her or *its* origin.

His educational phrase was followed by a photographic session and the issuance of a new American passport in his own name. His New York Driver's license, Private Investigator ID and several credit cards in his name, were also returned to him from his wallet which had obviously been confiscated when they took him in New York. He'd been told there would be other necessary tools waiting for him in London. One "tool" he had specifically requested and he had been surprised that they didn't give him an argument about it.

Finally, he and Maria had spent time with Father Murphy going over the exact process to be followed should they locate the hiding place of this Adramelech fellow. If they found anything, they were to avoid contact at all costs, phone a cell number immediately, and give the exact location and time of their find. They were not to try to engage it; merely report its location and get the hell out of there. Apparently, a team of Jesuit priests would then be quickly sent to their location to settle the matter.

Malachi said that if they were lucky this time, it would be annihilated for all eternity. Also they would be operating with the security of the *Crusaders* nearby but neither he nor Maria would know their exact whereabouts. If the detective and the nun were taken and compromised, the cardinal didn't want the attack team taken out through inadvertent betrayal. It was much safer to have the information on the team's whereabouts compartmentalized.

Malachi had also hit Clay with another bombshell. Sister Maria had a well-documented history of a psychic ability to sense impending evil or danger. So he was to listen to her in every instance and act accordingly. Malachi had held his hand up when Clay protested, and stood firm. The cardinal admitted that at one time he thought her abilities might have been a bunch of malarkey. Then he'd seen proof himself. Not to mention Father Murphy, a notorious skeptic, who now confirmed her abilities. In fact, if she hadn't been present that night in New York, and given Murphy and Langevin advance warning of Adramelech's impending arrival, Clay would likely not be alive at the moment.

And all this happened in three days. Three days in which he found himself more and more attracted to Maria. He'd tried to dismiss it, fight it, or recognize it as a hopeless cause. It didn't work.

"Are you asleep?" Maria asked, gently.

Clay opened his eyes. "No, just going over a few things in my mind."

"I just wanted to say that I understand why you're skeptical and I hope I didn't offend you."

"I've a rather thick, albeit secular, skin," Clay said, with a slight smile. For a moment he considered telling her he was glad to be working with her, no matter what the circumstances, but then thought better of it. "Why don't you get some rest yourself?" He turned slightly and lowered the back of his seat but not before he saw a slight disappointment in her eyes. She wanted to talk. He didn't. What he needed now was some time to adjust to what was happening in his life. He had gone from being a run-of-the-mill private eye with no solid direction in life, to being on an international assignment hunting down some sort of serial killer for the Catholic Church. Hard to top that for weirdness. He was also bothered by the fact that his feelings for Maria were growing by the hour. No percentage there either, he thought.

"Good idea," she finally responded as he heard her settle back. "Next stop London."

~ 2 ~

After landing in Heathrow, Clay and Maria picked up a silver Toyota Previa from Hertz. True to his word, Malachi, with the Church's seemingly limitless influence, had arranged for a metal case housing a .44 caliber Ruger Blacktop Magnum with 100 rounds of ammunition, four Maxfire Speedloaders and a shoulder holster to be in the trunk. Though it looked more like a frontier Colt with its long barrel, Clay knew he'd never have a problem with it jamming. It was more accurate than many shorter-barreled handguns and would virtually stop any living thing in its tracks. Whether his quarry was living or not was a matter still up for debate.

He loaded the weapon, donned the holster and felt a whole lot better. Their mad quarry better hope he wasn't looking at the business end of this weapon.

Also in another case were two press employee cards identifying them as reporters for the Associated Press News Service, as well as a *British Concealed Carry Weapons Permit* for a restricted weapon. A laptop computer, various and sundry hookups and a small compact printer completed the equipment.

Clay and Maria checked into a suite at the Halkin Hotel later that afternoon. They were posing as man and wife. Malachi had booked them a room with two beds to keep Maria close to Clay should Adramelech come after him. The cardinal was banking on Maria sensing any form of potential "attack" as she had in New York, and then being able to alert the *Crusaders*.

The room was uniquely comfortable with a pair of antique-looking beds, a roll-top desk and a genuine grandfather clock ticking loudly in one corner. The best concession the room offered, however, was double bathrooms. Clay insisted on taking the smaller one with just a shower stall. The larger one offered a bathtub and he caught Maria looking longingly at it. "I'm not exactly a bubble bath type of guy," he said, transferring his shaving gear to the smaller one and then unpacking his Vatican purchased wardrobe.

They ate dinner at a small fish & chips restaurant within walking distance of the hotel and then returned to watch some television. Clay found himself laughing at a Fawlty Towers marathon while Maria grimaced at his choice. He offered to switch channel but she shook her head and immersed herself in a copy of the *Montreal Gazette* they'd picked up at a W H Smith store while out for supper. Still, whenever he started to laugh, he caught her looking over the edge of the newspaper. If he caught her eye she simply shook her head again and dived behind it for cover once more. Finally he switched the TV off in favor of conversation.

As they talked, he was surprised to find that she had attended high school in Vermont not that far from where he had lived. In fact, they had both attended Sacred Heart at different times, shopped in Newport, and swam in Lake Memphremagog. Finally, Maria began to yawn.

"I'll take the left bed, if that's okay," Maria declared.

"Me too," Clay said, and then laughed at how wide her eyes opened.

She finally got the joke and returned his grin. "Got me."

"I certainly did," he said kindly, now feeling embarrassed at taking advantage of her obvious innocence.

"You're a nice man, Clay." She said it openly and honestly. "I'm not worried."

He felt himself flushing with pleasure at her remark. But then she brought him back to reality with her next sentence. "But this isn't a lark, you know. We have to take what we are doing very seriously if we want to get out of this alive." Feeling his face flush he nodded and turned away.

They retired to their individual bathrooms to perform their nightly rituals. Clay emerged from his bathroom first, got into bed and clicked on his reading light. He shook out a copy of the *London Times* they'd found in their room and began to explore details of the Millennium Ripper attacks in a feature article. After a few minutes, Maria came out of her bathroom clothed in a heavy, red terry-cloth robe, smiled self consciously and sat with her back to him on her own bed. A whiff of soap or shower gel drifted over.

"Shall I set it for five-thirty?" she asked, fidgeting with the alarm clock.

"Sure," Clay responded, amusement in his voice. "Wake me at eight."

"I'm sorry. I'm so used to rising for morning devotions."

"That's okay…whatever time you'd like is fine with me."

She sat there and Clay realized that when he was in the army and so many decisions were made for him by an established routine, it was sometimes difficult to make small personal choices on your own when given the opportunity. Likely Maria experienced a similar conundrum because of her vocation. "Why don't we compromise," he said. "Say…seven thirty?"

"Okay." She stabbed a button on the clock repeatedly, stood up, dropped her robe and quickly climbed under her covers. Just as quickly, she rolled back out, knelt by her bed and spent ten minutes in prayer.

Clay couldn't help noticing she was wearing 60s-style baby doll pajamas. A nun in baby dolls? Despite his best efforts, he sighed. She was cute as a button and he felt like a letch. She soon dove back into her bed and pulled the covers up to her chin.

"Clay?" Her voice now sounded tiny and a little worried.

"Yes?"

"Do you–do you think everything will…work out?"

"Well, let's see. According to your boss, we're chasing an immortal emissary of Satan and his evil familiar who have murdered millions of people over thousands of years. We carry useless weapons, are in an unfamiliar city with no idea where our backup is hiding, and are in the dark on this thing's location or what it's up to. Heck, what could go wrong?"

Despite herself, Maria laughed. "You know we're only supposed to find him. That's all."

"So I've been told."

"I know you want to avenge your wife and your friend but that's not our job." She waited for a reaction. When none was forthcoming, she began again: "We can't kill him; you know that? We can slow him down but nothing short of special and very holy remedies will finish him."

"Did you see the movie, *Dirty Harry*?"

"Dirty who?"

In spite of himself, he laughed. "Never mind, Maria, I think I may be carrying a solution that will make this fellow's day a little more difficult."

"When we find him or even get close to where we think he might be, we have orders to call the special cell phone number and leave the area."

He looked over at her. "I promise I won't put you in any danger, Maria."

"It's not me I'm worried about Clay; I – I don't want you hurt neither."

"Thanks…." He went back to reading his newspaper but not really absorbing any of what he was reading. She'd voiced a concern for him. Was it possible…? Stop it, he told himself.

After a few minutes of tossing in her bed, Maria punched her pillow a few times and then softly asked: "What was she like?"

He put down the paper. "Who?"

"Your wife…Jody?"

Clay sighed. "She was someone who deserved better than what she got. If I'd never met her, she'd likely be alive now."

"It wasn't your fault."

"Wasn't it?" His tone was bitter. "According to the cardinal, she died because of this thing I supposedly met in Panama. Even if that isn't true, what she went through in Woodstrom wasn't pleasant; maybe it contributed to a moment of inattention on the highway. And it killed her."

"I'm sorry. I shouldn't have brought it up."

"That's okay; it was a long time ago." *And yet the hurt and regret were both fresh as a daisy.*

"You must never blame yourself, Clay. These happenings began long before you or I were even born. There is nothing any of us could have done to prevent what is unfolding."

"You mean like innocent people being killed by a madman."

"That and more. We happen to have become part of a battle between good and evil that, according to Sister Raphael, began at Creation. We have to trust in God to see us through it."

"God and the Ruger Firearms Company."

She ignored his sarcasm. "As I said before, I know you're a decent and wise man, Clay. But please, also put your trust in the divine power of God and He will give us the strength we need."

Clay was sorry for trying to be smart. "Mind if I ask you something, Maria?" he asked, snapping off his reading light, ditching the paper and settling back.

"Of course. Ask away."

He felt braver in the dark. "Why did you become a nun?"

"I'm a novice still…I haven't taken my final religious vows." She paused and then added: "But I hope to when this is all over."

"And that means…?"

"Well you just don't join an order…like Girl Guides or the Boy Scouts. First you go through a period of time as a postulant. You take certain religious training and then are received as a novice, which is what I am. Novices are not admitted to final vows until they have completed more prescribed training and proving called the novitiate –."

A trifle impatient, he interrupted her. "Right. So you could still…back out?"

She laughed, though it sounded more like a giggle in the darkness. "You mean like backing out of a deal to buy a used car?"

"Something like that."

"I suppose a person can back out of anything."

"You haven't answered my original question. Why?"

"I'm sorry. It was a calling…from God. When I was a little girl, and I would get visions of the future, I used to think that I was cursed because all I saw were bad things – things I couldn't prevent. But I also felt there was something I was meant to do. Some sort of 'calling,' I guess. And when I went to school with the nuns, I began to admire their strength, their resolve, and their kindness. As I grew older, I realized that they were unique in a cruel world. And I wanted the peace that they seemed to possess. I finally came to the conclusion this could only come from a closer relationship with God who inspired this peace."

"Have you ever thought of a…normal life?"

She laughed again. "This is a normal life for me, Clay."

"Sorry…of course," he answered, lamely. What he did see, however, was that this nun was beginning to occupy his thoughts more and more despite their bizarre quest. These were the first feelings he'd had for a girl since Jody died more than a decade ago. In fact, he was feeling like a school boy with his first crush. Though he tried to fight it, and though he realized he barely knew her, the feelings refused to leave. During their training together, they enjoyed some laughs and some serious discussions. His admiration for her, her faith and her kindness grew as did his personal feelings for her. Now he chastised himself again; it was ridiculous to fall in love with a Catholic nun.

"Are you okay?" Her voice out of the blackness startled him and he tried to cover his thoughts wondering if she sensed anything.

"Yes…yes…I'm fine. We better get to sleep. We'll need to be in top form tomorrow."

"I know you're concerned for me, Clay. And, I think I may also be picking up some other feelings from you…but we have a job to do. And its success must come first… no matter how you may feel about me."

He figuratively slapped himself on the forehead. Was he nuts? Worse, was he that transparent, or was she really psychic? She must think I'm an idiot, he moaned inwardly regretting his unwarranted feelings for her. "Understood," he finally managed to croak aloud, feeling his face flush with embarrassment. He silently thanked God that the lights were out. He rolled over, but it was hours before he slept.

~ 3 ~

The next morning, following Malachi's orders on how to get started, they drove to the Metropolitan Police Headquarters building with Clay finding the left hand driving to be a challenge. The building was fronted by a metallic triangular sign that slowly revolved announcing that it was the Metropolitan Police Headquarters on one side – Working for a safer London – and the New Scotland Yard on the other side. It wasn't hard to find and when they drove up to it on Broadway, S.W.1., they encountered a modern steel and glass building with ample parking for staff and visitors alike. Clay took off his shoulder holster and stored the .44 caliber rig under the front seat before they exited the automobile.

As they walked alongside the building looking for an entrance, Clay again marveled at the city. London was a study in contrasts. For example across Broadway from the ultra-modern Scotland Yard building, was a typical, leafy English park, while across Victoria Street, the Strutton Arms featuring traditional English pubs such as The Old Monk and something called The Pub offering good food and real ales. Farther along the Ichi Riki Sushi House added its diverse fare.

A yellow coated Bobby gave them directions to the public entrance. Inside, Clay and Maria were kindly asked to state their business by a professional but pretty police woman sporting three sergeant stripes on her jersey. They asked for Chief Superintendent Ian Cruickshank and the sergeant nodded and asked them to both sign the register. She then made a quick telephone call to Homicide West. After hanging up, she asked them to have a seat in a comfortable waiting area just off the lobby. Police constables, dark suited men with laden briefcases, and a parade of other civilians moved constantly in and out of the doors. Clay looked up and caught the eye of the attractive desk sergeant who was on the telephone and looking their way.

Clay and Maria had been told that Malachi had set it up with Scotland Yard for them to gain access to briefing papers and reports on the Millennium Ripper. They were hoping that the police had found some sort of pattern that might telegraph where he might strike next. They had not been authorized to tell Scotland Yard *why* they were interested – just that the Vatican had an interest in the killer.

It wasn't long before a tired looking, grey-haired, stocky man resembling actor Nigel Bruce who played Watson in older Sherlock Holmes movies, approached with his hand out. He was wearing a badly rumpled tweed suit and white shirt; a dark paisley tie was loosely wound around his open collar, the Winsor knot tugged loose.

"Mr. Montague I presume," he said, with a twinkle in his eye. He grasped Clay's hand firmly and gave it a friendly shake. Despite being obviously exhausted, he cavalierly kissed Maria's hand as he introduced himself. "Detective Chief Superintendent Ian Cruickshank…at your service."

"Oh!" Maria said as his lips brushed her hand. "I'm Maria Lapierre."

Clay smiled at Maria's grin and obvious pleasure at the courtly manners, even as he judged the inspector to be a bit of a rogue.

They stopped at reception once more where Cruickshank retrieved two visitor badges which they were asked to snap on.

He led them to an elevator and several floors later they exited into a busy office setting, the clacking of computer keys punctuated only by ringing phones and the constant buzz of conversations. After traversing three corridors they settled in the Chief Superintendent's office with the door closed.

"So, how is our esteemed cardinal?" Cruickshank asked

"Very well, sir." Maria said. "He sends his regards."

"And do return mine," Cruickshank said, with a slight smile. "Now Mr. Montague…Miss Lapierre…I'm happy to help my friend any way I can, so what can I do for you?" As he waited, he tapped a few keys on his computer, examined something, raised his eyebrows and turned back to Clay and Maria.

"Essentially, we're investigating the Millennium Ripper story and wondered if we could access some of your files," Clay said.

"He told me that much," Cruickshank replied. "What do you hope to find?"

"Information on where, when and how he struck," Clay said, slipping into his investigative role with surprising ease. "Also, we wondered if you had any ideas or theories on where he could strike next. If it's confidential, we're happy to sign any non-disclosure forms you might have, of course."

"Very thoughtful of you," Cruickshank said. "No, we don't know where he might strike next or when. Wish we did. But why would the Vatican send two investigators to inquire? Bit out of its realm once the last rites have been administered, what?"

"We were just asked to get information on the murders–," Clay began, but the Chief Superintendent held up his hand.

"Now old boy, let's keep this friendly shall we? I need you to level with me." Cruickshank's gaze had hardened just a shade. "Why is my friend interested in this fiend? He just sent me a short email asking me to cooperate with you two and little else. I haven't been able to raise him on the horn since."

Clay looked at Maria who shrugged. "I'm afraid we signed a confidentiality agreement with our employer…" Clay began.

Cruickshank held up his hand again. "I would hope you wouldn't be trying to delve into my case and perhaps use the information to get in my way and muck it up, would you?" He stared unblinking at Clay. "Bad form, old boy."

Clay decided the best route was to be truthful, to a point. He handed over his New York Private Investigator's license. "I'm a private detective hired by Cardinal Malachi to find out as much as I can about these murders. Why, I have no idea. Naturally I intend to cooperate fully with Scotland Yard if I discover any leads."

"Naturally," Cruickshank replied, dryly. "And the lovely Miss Lapierre?"

"My assistant."

He sighed. "I daresay I shall have to get hold of Mustavias again to find out what's up."

Cruickshank, seemingly more relaxed now, passed back the license and agreed to allow them to review some "Ripper" files in a briefing room.

They spent the next four hours going over a series of gruesome murders in and around London. They reviewed the recent murders of the two London Bobbies in Soho, the murders of multiple known prostitutes and of two teenage girls in Highgate Cemetery, two days prior. They even found a map of the cemetery with the positions of the murders clearly marked. The report said that though forensics had finished with the area, the crime scene was still taped and guarded by a constable. Maria noted the location of the last murders.

Finally, gathering up their notes, they tried to see Cruickshank to thank him for his help but were told he was out. Wearily they left Scotland Yard. On the drive back to the hotel, they decided to get washed up, grab a bite to eat and head up to Highgate Cemetery to see where the teenagers had been found.

Back in their room, Maria pulled a map of Highgate Cemetery off the Internet and printed it via their small compact printer. It came with a set of driving instructions. Clay studied the London map on how to get to Highgate.

Later, as Clay was brushing his teeth, he noticed a five o'clock shadow. Ordinarily he would let it go, but for some reason he pulled out his razor and shaving cream. As he shaved, he heard Maria on the telephone reporting to Cardinal Malachi on their first day's progress and their plan to go to Highgate Cemetery that evening. "Don't worry," she was saying. "We'll be careful."

~ 4 ~

After dining at the Aberdeen Angus Steak House in Soho, Maria and Clay climbed into the Previa and headed north on Highway A-1 in the twilight towards Highgate, also billed: *The City of Shadows*. They hoped to find the taped off crime scene and talk to the constable guarding it.

Darkness quickly overshadowed them as they drove up the one-way, brick-walled Swains Lane which bisected the cemetery; they began looking for the entrance. They passed various townhouse-looking complexes on their left. According to their notes, the cemetery was divided into east and west sections with the murders having taken place in the western section. What the victims had been doing there after dark was still unknown. Because of its relatively wild state, the western section was closed off to visitors with only guided tours allowed. Newspaper reports had speculated that the two teenagers were just looking for thrills amongst the gravestones; testing societal taboos, as it were. Their attempt to tease fate resulted in their murder by some wayward fiend.

It was dark now and a cool mist was settling quickly over the area making the pavement greasy and bringing a fog-like consistency to the air. Street lights assumed halos and visibility became more and more limited. They drove slowly on the narrow, one-way road, passing the yellow lighting emanating from small houses and cottages, and eventually found themselves rounding well marked bends as they ran parallel to a spike-topped, rusted ornamental steel fence with a three-foot-high brick base and spaced brick columns. Clay slowed the car at a sign on the fence reading **Danger – Keep Out**. They continued on under a canopy of hundred-year-old trees hanging formidable leaf-laden branches over the road, Highgate Cemetery now on both sides of them.

"It's a little spooky," Maria said. "I think...." Abruptly she stopped and looked over at Clay, her eyes widening in fright.

"What's the matter?" Clay asked.

Maria stared at him in horror, slowly shaking her head. "Dear God...no!" she managed to get out a fraction of a second before it happened.

Something heavy smashed onto their automobile roof driving the entire vehicle down on its springs as the roof caved in a good two inches. Maria screamed. A branch crashed through the windshield in front of her; a deadly tentacle reached out to pinion her at chest level.

At the same time, Clay's foot involuntarily hit the gas. With spinning, smoking, screaming tires they shot forward. Slammed back in his seat, he lost his grip on the wheel as he began to realize that it wasn't a branch poking through the windshield but something alive. A blackened arm with a claw-like shape at its end was scrabbling wildly about looking for a purchase. Meanwhile, Maria cowered desperately in her seat, arms pulled back in horror.

Clay was clawing at his gun when the automobile slewed sideways, hit the brick fence base and careened through it scattering bricks and hunks of mortar. Freed of its anchor, the attached wrought iron, spike-topped fence hit the hood and was deflected upwards where it rotated twenty feet in the air. The automobile surged through into the graveyard. Behind it the piece of fence smashed to earth upside down and embedded its steel spikes in the ground. The car bumped forward mowing and pulverizing smaller, brittle gravestones that exploded on contact until, with a metallic crash of tearing metal and bursting glass, it smashed into a large, upright stone monument.

Silence....

~ 5 ~

Father Gallo made his way down the corridor towards Cardinal Malachi's office walking very slowly, his arthritis causing him to bend over like some Frankenstein Igor creature. His shoulders ached constantly these days and yet he couldn't straighten them out for relief. He had a herniated disc in his back and was spending more and more time in the company of ice packs and heating pads. But that wasn't what disturbed him most. Rather it was his *blackouts*. Sometimes they lasted for minutes, sometimes hours. Once he went to bed on a Tuesday and awoke on a Thursday.

He even found himself in different clothes so he knew he'd been up and about; but, doing what? Going where? He refused to tell anyone since it would doubtlessly mean a battery of tests and hospitalization. Perhaps they were mini-strokes, he reasoned. Whatever they were, he seemed none the worse for wear so he continued to keep mum.

Oh to be young again, he thought. To experience the sheer delights of a body unfettered by age and to be free of his calling. To be able to partake of the delights of youth. For a few delicious seconds, his mind drifted back to his one and only sexual experience.

He was 18-years old, a seminary student in Rome on his first week-end pass to visit his father and mother in the village of Siena up north. He remembered his excitement at the railroad station as he'd run through the bursts of steam billowing from under the panting steam engine. Clutching his hemp-woven sack containing a change of clothes, an apple and his toothbrush, he climbed aboard the train. There he secured a seat in a compartment inhabited by two bored-looking young men in heavy turtle-neck sweaters and wool jackets.

Before long, a squeal of releasing brakes, the clanging of the bell on the steam engine and a sudden jerk announced their departure. The great locomotive slowly chugged its way through the back streets of Rome rapidly gaining momentum as it headed for the open countryside with a happy Benito humming as he looked out the window.

The two young men turned out to be architectural students originally from a small northern Italian village near Florence. They were ebullient fellows, good-humored as well as bright conversationalists. Later he also found out they all shared an extraordinary fondness for the grape.

He struck up a conversation with the young men who were soon trying to talk Benito out of wasting his life in the priesthood. There had been a spirited exchange of ideas, lively and yet friendly, an experience he found both refreshing and exhilarating after having spent the summer in deep devotion and prayer. The quickness of debate and the scoring of rhetorical points through calling on the powers of his own knowledge and deductive reasoning excited Benito in a manner in which he had not been excited for many months; obviously he thrived on discourse as opposed to dogma.

The journey north was long and arduous. Soon however, out came two large bottles of wine. Young Benito had been talked into imbibing..."just a sip."

Within an hour, with much good-natured laughter and back-slapping encouragement, he was roaring drunk and eager to experience life. They got off the train in the dark in the moderately sized village of Grosseto and stumbled down the cobblestone streets at one o'clock in the morning searching for a bordello. The students had been keen to show Benito all he would be missing by becoming a man of the cloth.

The local village constable had finally been roused by the citizenry to quiet the drunken louts staggering through town. He threatened to lock them up, but then realized he would be able to use this late night visit by the students to explain his absence from his home and icy cold wife; through dumb luck, within his grasp was the means of paying a nocturnal visit to his mistress. All he had to do was quickly deal with the young men.

The constable followed the most expedient course of action possible: he gave them wonderfully simple directions to the local whorehouse and accompanied them part of the way.

As they thanked him profusely for his hospitality and waved good-bye, the constable hitched up his trousers and wandered off humming "O Solo Mio"...in a direction opposite to his own home.

Within five minutes, the boys had found the modest whitewashed house covered with lush bougainvillea and trumpet flower vines. They noted the red lamp in the window and soon gained entrance through flashing a thick wad of lira.

Benito, his inherent shyness repealed by the drink, had brazenly chosen a short brunette named Carmelita. She had flashing dark eyes, wide hips and an ample bosom. After his companions whispered in her ear, the girl laughed, took Benito upstairs and over the next few hours became both a lover and a teacher to the young seminary student.

He awoke a few hours later, aching, confused and sick. He looked at Carmelita's naked body sprawled beside him and slowly realized with horror what he had done. He had compromised his celibacy; he had betrayed his God and the vows he was destined to take.

His face reddened with shame, and between bouts of throwing up into a commode she pulled from under her bed, he cried softly. She was both perplexed and then confused at her weeping customer. At first she thought he cried with joy at the wonder of his experience with her and she seized him in her hand to let him know that it didn't have to be over. As a simple soul in all but the art of love-making, she failed to make any connection between their act of nature and his utter disgust with himself. Was he a man or was he not? He drew away from her as though she were a leper and tried between sobs to explain the magnificence of his sin.

When Benito confessed he was a seminary student and soon to be ordained as a priest, her eyes grew wide with fright. She'd blessed herself and fell to her knees to seek forgiveness from God.

He'd dressed quickly and stumbled downstairs abandoning her and his friends before they even knew that he'd awakened. When he last saw Carmelita, she was silhouetted in the doorway with her devotions forgotten. The yellow light from the oil lamps spilled out around her as she screamed at him to come back and pay for her services.

He'd quickly found and boarded an early morning southbound train and returned immediately to the seminary where, with great shame and humbleness, he tearfully confessed his sins to his father confessor, ran out of the confessional and back to the dormitory where he made ready to leave and go back home.

He'd just finished stuffing his few simple belongings in a canvas duffle bag when there was a knock on the door of his cell-like room.

Father Bullo, a visiting professor and a Jesuit known for his harsh disciplinary beliefs, asked to enter. He sat quietly on the thin mattress covering Benito's wooden bunk as the chastened student packed.

The priest, with the crinkled grey hair and severe brown eyes, allowed himself a gentle smile as he saw Benito's wet cheeks. He proceeded to speak in a low, modulated and almost hypnotic tone. For the next twenty minutes, Benito listened in rapt attention as Father Bullo delivered a gentle admonishment for his actions and then a lecture on the powerful temptations of the flesh and how to avoid them in future.

He led the boy through a theological lecture on the evils and the goal of sin as well as the purpose of the sacrament of confession – a gift from God to wipe away the sin and the guilt of all those who were weaker than He.

He patiently showed Benito, through examples in the scriptures, of the many followers of Christ who had fallen prey to the devil's tricks and yet who had risen up afterwards to become iron Christians – some even went to their deaths as martyrs for the Church.

Finally the Jesuit had asked Benito: "Why do you still cry my son...and why do you still ready your clothing?"

Benito said, "Because I have sacrificed my purity!"

"There are many before you who were not pure."

"But they were not like me! I-I...." He swallowed and gathered his courage. "I enjoyed it, Father...I wantonly fornicated like an animal and I enjoyed it!!"

The priest looked at him with amusement: "So did I, my son...when I tried it. In fact, the beauty of womanhood was the singular most powerful reason for me to reject the call of God. But deep inside I knew God was testing me to see if I would sacrifice even this great gift which He had bestowed upon humanity. My love of The Trinity triumphed...and here I am."

Benito had stared at the Jesuit. "You...?"

Father Bullo nodded. "We did not all come to our callings from saintly backgrounds, my young idealist. Often we came, not because of purity...but because of sin, and because we recognized the severity of our sin and sought to make atonement for our failings. Obviously, you are a young man of conviction, humility and true remorse, excellent qualifications for someone who has chosen to serve Christ. And your adventure was *not* a mortal sin; no final vows have been taken."

More than a half century later, Gallo wondered what the good Father would say now about his charge if he were alive and able to evaluate his career as a rabble rouser and constant thorn in the side of the Vatican. Gallo certainly wasn't a candidate for sainthood.

He shuffled up to the cardinal's door and used the brass knocker; Malachi bellowed to enter. He did so just as the cardinal put down the telephone.

Within five minutes Gallo had been briefed on Sister Maria and Clay's progress, and their plans for the evening to see if Maria could sense anything at Highgate Cemetery where two teen-age girls had been murdered. Gallo noted that Malachi was looking more tired than usual.

"My friend, I have to admit that I'm beginning to be concerned over our course of action," Malachi confessed to Gallo. "I'm also concerned about Sister Maria and our detective friend. Do we have the right to put them in mortal danger?"

"Mustavias, you must facilitate the apprehension of the Beast," Father Gallo responded without hesitation. "You know that. Their lives, my life or even yours should all be sacrificed to stop this abomination. I've often wondered why you didn't use *me* as bait long ago."

"You've never been strong enough, Benito," he answered, wearily. "Now I need your help."

"Are the *Crusaders* in position," Gallo asked.

"Yes. We used every remaining cent in our budget to get them into the field. They have a room on the floor directly above our friends. Of course Maria is unaware of this; safer for everyone in case Adramelech is looking for our team to strike first."

"So if Maria and Montague get close to Adramelech, they dial the cell number and our men will be there in short order."

"Exactly," Malachi said.

"And the *Crusaders* carry the relic??"

"Not right now. It's a concern because Father Gant won't have it popping all over the world. When we think we've found Adramelech, we have to fly it to them right away. And then pray it works."

"Let's hope so," said Gallo. "But what if it doesn't?"

"More corpses," Malachi muttered. "And among them will be our dear sister and our detective. Which brings me to another point?"

"And that is…?"

"I'd like for you to join them in London."

"Why thank you," Gallo said, in amusement. "I've yearned to be on the bleeding edge."

Malachi ignored him. "You've been within its grasp and are one of the few to escape from it. You may be able to give them the edge they need in terms of experience and judgment."

"While my imprisonment is a fact, I've mentioned I wasn't exactly a model of strength and defiance," Gallo said bitterly.

"Maybe not Benito but our army friend is not yet fully convinced he is dealing with anything supernatural and may act accordingly. Maria can only do so much. I wouldn't ask you to risk this if I didn't think it was critical."

Gallo swept his concerns away with a wave of his hand. "What does it matter? I am an old man who has had a long and interesting life. I can leave tomorrow."

"Thank you," Malachi answered, simply. "I'll have arrangements made."

"I understand from our mutual friend Bortnowaska that your audience with the Holy Father was not successful?"

"It never happened. Some other emergency came up. Our aircraft is back in Rome but we're trying not to incur more expenses until we settle this budget issue."

"Am I to hitchhike to London," Gallo asked, with a smile.

"No, old friend, I'm sure we can do better than that," Malachi answered. "There's a commercial flight booked for you already:

First Class." He was interrupted by the telephone ringing. "Malachi," he answered.

Gallo watched closely.

"What? Now? Thank you...no-no...I've been trying to gain access for so long...I'll be there in fifteen minutes." He hung up.

"What is it?"

"Speak of the devil," Malachi exclaimed, and then laughed shortly at what he'd said. "That was the Prefect...Giuseppe Lopez. He says I'm *in*! The Holy Father wants to see me right now."

~ 6 ~

Nothing stirred in the night as billows of steam hissed from the automobile's fractured radiator. Clay shook his head to clear the cobwebs and found himself looking through a glassless window frame with most of the shattered windscreen lying on the dramatically shortened and buckled front hood. He was amazed that both headlights were still cutting swaths through the mist and fog, though now at cock-eyed angles. They highlighted the large monument they had hit; it was topped by a formidable stone rendition of a Crucifix.

"Maria...are you okay?"

"I-I think so," she said. They stared at each other for a moment in shock.

"Jesus Christ," Clay muttered in sudden realization as the Ruger magically appeared in his hand. He pointed it towards the roof and there was a brilliant flash and a deafening bang as a foot-long muzzle flame burned a hole in the overhead roof fabric, and the bullet tore a hole in the car's ceiling. Maria screamed again. With ears ringing, he apologized. "Sorry...sorry. Gotta get him. Are you sure you're okay?"

"I...yes...I'm not hurt –!"

He pushed his door open. "Good. Stay here...stay down!" His seatbelt clicked open and he threw himself out of the car onto the leaf covered grass, rolled once, scrambled to his feet and extended the revolver towards the automobile's roof.

Nothing....

He spun around, weapon at the ready and then started as he saw movement a hundred yards away near a mausoleum. Cocking his weapon he ran towards the spot where a vague form had silently melted back into the shadows. In a few seconds he stood where the form had been but he saw only shadows.

"Clay...Clay!" Maria shouted, but there was no response; the sound of his running footsteps faded into the night. She spit out a piece of something. Tasting the saltiness of blood, she realized it was a nugget of safety glass. The distant hoot of an owl made her realize she was alone; the Beast could be stalking her right now as she sat trapped and helplessly in the car. Despite the shock, Maria had no doubt about what had attacked them; they were both in mortal danger. She tried once more: "Clay! For God's sake, answer me. Come back!"

There was no sound except a growing patter of raindrops against the metal of the automobile. She had to call the *Crusaders*. She looked for the cell phone in her hand bag lying open on the seat. The phone was now lying on the floor mat, its face smashed in and its back lying beside it.

The acrid smell of antifreeze sizzling on the heated engine block and the sweet smell of spilled gasoline made her realize that at any moment the automobile could burst into flames. She undid her seatbelt and was relieved to find the door opened easily.

Maria tumbled out of the car and got to her feet, her legs rubbery. Cautiously she inspected herself once again. Her only injury seemed to be soreness from where the seatbelt had dug into her chest wall between her breasts. She stared around, caught sight of the stone cross topping the monument they struck and realized why the Beast had vanished.

In the light from the car's headlight beams Maria surveyed the rest of her surroundings and found herself looking at a scene from a gothic horror movie.

All around her were mausoleums, monuments, gravestones and tombs heavily overgrown with vines, ivy and weeds. In various corners, stone angels and gargoyle-like creatures stared mutely at her as though angry at the invasion of their sanctuary. From a tree off to her right the owl hooted again and Maria looked back towards where they had come through the fence. Carefully she began picking her way among the broken tombstones towards the road. Two huge booms followed by a single distinctive whine as a bullet ricocheted off rock sounded from somewhere behind the concrete wall of a tomb. With this, she cast caution to the winds and ran towards the safety of the pavement and out of the cemetery.

Nothing stirred as she stood on the pavement of the deserted roadway....

A few crickets took to chirping....

She tried again: "Clay...where are you?"

A cold silence was her only answer.

~ 7 ~

Meanwhile, a quarter mile away, slowly making his way down a stone corridor with burial vaults on both sides, Clay lowered his .44 after firing twice at movements off to his left. The stench of cordite stung his nostrils. He tried to rein in his beating heart as he realized he was being unconscionably reckless; those shots could travel a mile. At the moment, however, he was spooked enough that he'd thrown caution and training to the wind. Whoever had landed on the roof of the car wasn't only big, he was also amazingly strong to have smashed his hand through the safety glass.

Clay pulled the spent shells from the cylinder, manually thumbed three fresh rounds into it and flipped it closed. He moved softly through the cemetery, carefully placing one foot in front of the other, trying his best not to step on branches that would snap and betray his position. He worked his way patiently around gravestones and explored every shadow as he moved in a half-crouch, silent as an Indian hunter. His Army Ranger training was coming in useful as he carefully picked his way around small twigs on the ground that could snap and betray his presence. He held the revolver in the classic two-handed grip, ready to fire.

He cautioned himself that there was supposed to be an English cop standing guard somewhere in the cemetery, so he's better be more careful. In fact, if the constable had heard the gunshots, he may have already summoned more police.

Still, whoever or *whatever* they had encountered that tried to grab Maria wasn't going to get a second chance if he had a say in it. If this was something supernatural he was hunting, as Malachi and Maria claimed, why had it run?

Maria! "Damn it," he muttered aloud, realizing he'd left her alone in his pursuit. What if his quarry had doubled back?

Abruptly he turned and began quickly making his way towards where he thought the wrecked automobile was located. After a minute he stopped dead and surveyed a number of different stone monuments, entrances to catacombs and stone archways. He had come through an archway, and around a catacomb…but which one? There were two in his field of vision. He tried to remember exactly where he'd come from. A forest of huge oak trees loomed over everything; it was truly a city of shadows.

He had to find Maria.

Throwing caution to the winds, he called out her name.

No answer…

…just the sound of raindrops splashing into shallow puddles.

Slowly Clay turned in a complete circle, his weapon ready. Nothing immediately recognizable.

He was lost!

~ 8 ~

Maria walked cautiously down Swains Lane, her heels echoing hollow on the damp pavement. Ahead of her, set into the walls of the laneway was a tan, neo-Tudor house or lodge of some type. She vaguely remembered reading about Swain's Lane Lodge in information she'd gleamed about Highgate Cemetery on the net. It was supposed to be vacant if she remembered correctly with Camden Town Council arguing over its use and the cost of refurbishment.

As she approached the two-storey building, she noted that a door fronted on the lane, and it was flanked by two windows below and two above; the door stood ajar. Suddenly she became aware of a darkness gradually invading her psyche.

It was near…

…and she was alone.

Inside the lodge, Adramelech waited. His current incarnation, while less horrid, was no less imposing. In fact, he could pass for a human now despite the milk white flesh and the eyes that glowed red in the faint light from the street lamps filtering through the dirt-streaked windows on either side of the open door. He raised a muscular arm; nails that were more like talons gleamed at the ends of his claw-like fingers.

He waited patiently.

She was getting closer….

He could hear Maria's quickened breathing, smell her sweet perfume and even the fact she was at her time of the month. He would kill her quickly, forego any pleasures and wait for her partner to come looking; he knew his true quarry wouldn't be far behind the girl. After so many years, he would fulfill the satanic requisition and kill the one who dared escape him.

"Clay...!" Maria called, in case he had come this way and was in the house. "Clay...are you in there?" She trembled as the sense of foreboding grew ever-so-slowly larger and more suffocating. Where was Clay? Was he hurt? Dead?

The Beast drew near the door being sure to remain in the shadows. She approached death without any inkling that the end was near. Once she stepped through the doorway, he would decapitate her quickly so no further sound would be uttered. "Come, my little sanctimonious bitch...come to your better," Adramelech whispered into the emptiness of the room.

"Clay...I need you...I'm frightened," Maria called again from outside. A sense of dread and revulsion was clouding all other thoughts from her mind. She began to tremble, felt nauseated and desperately reached under the neck of her sweater to pull up a four-inch silver Crucifix attached to a pewter chain. She held it before her, reached for the lodge door and pushed it inward. It creaked and groaned but swung three-quarters open. The inside was pitch black.

Maria stepped towards the doorway.

"Maria!" The voice was strong and commanding. Clay strode hurriedly down the lane, revolver by his side, his footsteps echoing off the walls. "Get away from there. God knows, that madman could be inside."

Maria backed out and Adramelech moved swiftly opposite the open door where he could remain in the blackness while he watched Clay and Maria embrace. As he coiled muscles and readied his strike, Maria's Crucifix flashed reflecting the headlights of an automobile speeding down the laneway. He froze as its sound alerted the pair and they looked up in sudden concern.

The black Saab began braking the moment the driver spotted Maria and Clay who had virtually nowhere to run. Clay dragged Maria to the side of the lane, against the wall. The automobile slithered sideways and then fishtailed but somehow maintained control until finally it came to rest a few feet from them. They approached the driver's open window.

"Are you alright, sir," asked a 40-something male with black hair and sporting a square crew-cut. He was dressed in a navy-blue turtleneck and dark navy pea jacket. His piercing grey eyes and lantern-like jaw gave him a rugged, handsome quality. Beside him, and in the back seat were seated two other very fit looking men of about the same age. There was something strange about their sudden appearance; too coincidental. And they looked to be very capable fellows.

Cops, thought Clay. How was he going to explain this one? He kept the weapon low and behind his back. "Yes, we're fine thanks. Just got a bit of a scare when we saw you coming."

The driver nodded with a slight smile. "My fault, I shouldn't have been driving so fast." He hesitated for a moment and glanced briefly at his companions. "I'm Kit Nathaniel. Can we give you a lift anywhere?"

"No thanks, we're fine," Clay said, realizing that the driver had an American accent. At the back of his mind there was a nagging feeling he'd seen this man before. He now surmised it was unlikely they were cops with that accent; perhaps American military personnel.

"You're sure you don't need a ride?" It was a swarthy Mediterranean type with an Italian accent in the back seat leaning forward.

"No, we're fine," Clay assured them.

"Do you have a cell phone?" the driver inquired politely, observing the darkness.

"Yes, we have a cell," Clay answered. There was no way he and Maria were getting in a car with a trio of strangers.

"We'll get back on the road then. Sorry to have bothered you." He nodded, carefully straightened the car and accelerated smoothly away up the lane. The brake lights flashed momentarily near the gaping hole in the security fence but then, surprisingly, the car accelerated and vanished.

As the sound of the motor faded, at the same moment, Clay and Maria realized that they were holding hands. They quickly separated. Flustered he started to apologize for the embrace a few moments before and felt himself reddening. "Sorry about grabbing you...." he said.

She smiled at him and he felt his heart quicken.

"Relax Clay...I'm not made of stone either. I was so frightened by what I was feeling, I needed your arms around me for a moment. So don't apologize. Thank our merciful Lord, the feeling is gone now. We're safe. At least for the moment."

They walked back up the lane towards the gap in the iron fence with Clay lamenting the condition of the Previa. It was likely a write-off. "You think that was your 'demon'?" he asked.

"You don't seem impressed."

"Oh I was impressed alright but if he's so damned powerful, why did he to run?"

"From all reports, he cannot stand the sign of our redemption – a Crucifix. More than any other holy symbol, the instrument of our Lord's sacrificial death repels and weakens him. We just happened to crash into one that was fifteen feet high."

Clay looked up at the monument looming over the ruined car and nodded. His hand instinctively checked the oversized shoulder holster and weapon now under his jacket. "Did you sense anything back there?

"I did…but it's gone now."

No sooner had she uttered her words than they heard the shrill sound of a police whistle. It was cut off in mid-note followed by a distant but unmistakably terrified scream.

~ 9 ~

The blue lights of a dozen marked and unmarked police cars flashed off Highgate Cemetery's vine-covered trees and ancient-looking tombstones as uniformed Bobbies, plain-clothed detectives and others milled about. The squad cars' retro-reflective livery markings of yellow and blue contrasted with the staid surroundings of the cemetery.

The inevitable crowd of curious onlookers had gathered with a contingent of press off to the side. Police cross-talk punctuated by bouts of static poured out of police radios as Clay and Maria watched Chief Superintendent Cruickshank approach them from the other side of a line of police tape. An ambulance, its doors open stood off to one side. It would not be making an emergency run tonight; the coroner was already on-site.

"I say, it just beggars belief that this fiend could do that to the young constable," Cruickshank said to another detective as they ducked under the tape. Cruickshank was wearing the same suit he'd had on earlier in the day but he was missing a tie, his shirt collar open. He looked tired and sad. His companion just shook his head and moved off to confer with another individual in a suit while

Cruickshank approached Clay and Maria. They watched him studying them intently as he drew near.

Clay had learned from a constable assigned to stay with them that concerned citizens had telephoned police because of the noise of their car crash, some shots and the voices in the cemetery. Clay and Maria had been running towards where the scream had originated when police arrived, their Claxton-like horns blaring. Clay had the presence of mind to shrug off his holster and revolver and throw the rig under a bush near the laneway before they got close. When the squad cars pulled up, Clay and Maria were immediately held by police. It wasn't long before Detective Chief Superintendent Cruickshank arrived on the scene, recognized them, got a scaled down version of their story, and then left to examine the body of a young constable found near the yellow, taped-off crime scene where the girls had been murdered. Clay had doctored his story only slightly saying someone landed on their roof, smashed through their windshield with a revolver in hand and tried to shoot them. Clay had wrestled it away and fired through the roof losing control of the car in the process. When they crashed, he lost the revolver but gave chase.

Maria learned from a paramedic that the policeman who had been guarding the crime scene had been brutally attacked and killed. It had been an hour since Cruickshank had made his way to where the body lay and he was now grim-faced on his return.

"So you were on your way here when you were 'ambushed' by someone?" he asked.

"That's correct," Clay said.

"Why? Why would anyone want to ambush you or Miss Lapierre?"

"Maybe the Ripper was waiting for his next victim?"

"So he jumps from a tree onto the roof of a moving vehicle without even knowing who was inside? You can do better than that, Mr. Montague."

"I can't explain it," Clay answered. "I can only tell you what happened."

"What did he look like? Can you give us a description?"

"I never laid eyes on him. I was chasing after a shadow in the cemetery. All I can tell you is that he was abnormally tall."

"How tall?"

"I'd say…about six foot four…or five."

"Clothes?" The Chief Superintendent was watching him closely as he answered. Any hesitation on his part would be construed as evasive or fabricating evidence.

"Dark clothes...maybe even a cape of some sort."

"A cape? Like Batman?" Cruickshank asked, his tone incredulous.

Clay met his gaze. "Something like that."

"Anything else?"

"Not that I can remember."

"You had better be telling me everything, sir, or there will be consequences. Dire consequences. Someone has just ripped the head off a young constable with a wife and two children. So let's hear it again. You came up here to see the murder scene *at night* and were attacked in your automobile. You gave chase, he fired at you and you came back to your companion here. Then you heard someone scream?"

"That's correct," Clay said. "It was a man's voice."

He sighed. "I've seen your car...with the bullet hole in the roof. Wouldn't the weapon be inside the automobile? If you had it in hand and then dropped it? Because it isn't there now; we checked."

"As I said, I lost control of it when we crashed."

"So you chased after this madman completely unarmed?" His tone clearly said he didn't believe him but Clay was determined to protect the possession of his own weapon. He didn't know if it would be seized as evidence of something if discovered. Or simply seized.

"Not the wisest course of action, I guess." Clay tried to look embarrassed.

"And he took two shots at you somewhere in the cemetery."

"That's when I decided discretion was the better part of valor and discontinued the chase."

"How did he do that, Mr. Montague? I mean, since you initially had control of his weapon? Do you think he carried two guns, possibly like some of your American cowboys?"

"Perhaps...or when we collided and I lost his weapon, he picked it up."

"Yes...how convenient," The Chief Superintendent scowled at Clay. "There is something rotten here, Mr. Montague, but I have enough to do tonight. The constable has your hotel address and will drive you and Miss Lapierre back to your suite and collect your passports while he's there. We shall send a car for you both about ten tomorrow. Please be ready."

He stared at them again for a moment and then spun on his heel and stalked off.

~ 10 ~

Cardinal Malachi stepped out of the Pope's office, his mind whirling. Behind him, the grinning Prefect Giuseppe Lopez retreated backwards pulling the double doors closed and bowing as he did so. As he looked back, Malachi thought Lopez was the perfect personification of a Cheshire Cat.

It was over, thought a stunned Malachi. Though he'd been allowed to give a shortened version of his presentation, he soon realized that his words were falling on deaf ears. It was obvious that His Holiness had already been thoroughly briefed by someone other than Malachi.

When the Cardinal finished, the Pope had simply said that there would be no more money expended on such a ridiculous venture. He briefly commiserated with Malachi about having inherited the *Hellspawn* dossier but ventured that this was plainly a holdover from the Middle-Ages that should have been discontinued centuries ago. And, certainly not pursued in the active sense. The Church could no longer afford to squander millions of dollars on an ecclesiastical ghost story. Not to mention the risk to the Vatican's reputation if word got out it was conducting a hunt for one of hell's demons, purportedly living on earth.

After carefully questioning Malachi about the various expenditures, and finding his team had a flying administration center and hospital aboard a leased A320, he ordered the aircraft lease terminated immediately. He also wanted *The Seven* disbanded forthwith, the *Crusaders* returned to their duties as soon as possible, and the *Watchers* reassigned. Malachi was to work with the Holy See Budget Committee to salvage what they could.

Now, as Malachi walked across Saint Peter's Square from the Papal Palace, storm clouds were gathering directly overhead; he felt a light but welcome sprinkling. How appropriate, he thought feeling the coolness of the rain on his face. There was little doubt he'd been set up. Someone had gotten to the Holy Father. Someone had made a point of deliberately undermining their work. But who? There had been little in the way of information from the tired looking Pontiff to give him any hint as to who had done the dirty deed; rather, it was plain he was extremely annoyed over the entire program and wanted it to cease. Based on the pointed and well-informed questions which His Holiness had so eloquently posed, one thing was obvious: there was a traitor in their group. Someone had passed on minute details and very complete information of the *Hellspawn* mission.

On exiting the Pope's chambers Malachi had immediately called Father Peter Austin via his cell phone. He told him what had happened and ordered an emergency meeting of *The Seven* in the *Chamber* for the next morning. Just what he was going to tell them, however, he wasn't quite sure. They were so damned close to finding their ancient quarry. And they seemed to have a weapon that might take care of it once and for all. His mind racing, he was already exploring possible options when his cell phone rang. It was more bad news.

~ 11 ~

After the constable had seen them to their room and secured both passports, he bid them a polite good evening and left Clay and Maria looking at each other. They said not a word but Clay could see Maria's lower lip beginning to tremble. "Maria…what is it?" he asked, as kindly as he could.

She didn't reply but instead gave a deep sigh and turned quickly away. She had wrapped her arms about her. After a moment he saw her shoulders heaving and deep sobs wracked her small frame. For a moment he stood there, unsure of what to do. Finally he allowed his natural feelings to overcome his awkwardness with her being a nun. He reached out, turned her slowly around and pulled her to his chest. She came willingly and cried for several minutes as he attempted to comfort her. Then, taking a deep breath, she eased out of his arms and sought to compose herself.

"T-Thank you….I'm sorry…so sorry," she said.

"For what?" asked Clay, somewhat bewildered. "For feeling human?"

"N-no…" she stuttered. "For-for being useless. For not anticipating or sensing anything until it was on top of the car. And then, for not being able to help that poor policeman." She pulled a tissue from her sleeve and mopped her eyes. "What good am I to you? What good am I to anyone in this-this…hunt…or whatever it is we're doing?"

"Maria, that wasn't your fault? We just happened to be there. That's all. He would have died if we were there or not."

"Y-you mean Adramelech wasn't following us?"

"Well, we have no way of knowing if that is true," Clay said, honestly. "But we don't even know if it was him. Unless he moved his hunting grounds to Highgate and we just happened to come along at the right time."

"Clay, he knew we were all coming to Rome. He knew what car we were in. And now he was able to know we were going to Highgate. Cardinal Malachi said he was knowing but not *all knowing*. And in all the teachings of Sister Raphael, she never once said that this thing was omnipotent. So how did he know?"

"I don't know," he answered.

"He already knows we're trying to find him," she reasoned, heading for her bathroom where she splashed some water on her face and returned with towel in hand.

They explored what happened for several more minutes and then Maria, eyes drooping, reluctantly yawned. "I'm exhausted. I'll call Cardinal Malachi and tell him what happened and then let's get to bed. The police will be here at ten tomorrow."

An hour later, despite Clay gently sawing logs in the other bed, Maria found it almost impossible to sleep. She tossed and turned, rearranged her pillows, got up for water and finally went to the window and looked out at the almost deserted London street.

It was raining and the only life below consisted of a man in a trench coat with umbrella in hand hurrying along the sidewalk. He turned into a doorway as a cab, its dome light on, splashed by and vanished leaving the street empty. It looked as lonely and forlorn as Maria felt. Doubts as to her abilities, psychic and otherwise, surfaced again. What if she no longer was able to sense evil or the Beast's impending arrival until it was at their throats? What if it was on top of them, like tonight, before she had a chance to warn Clay? From everything she'd learned, it could kill them both in an instant. And, despite the detective seeming to feel confident carrying his small cannon, she knew it wouldn't do much against a demon.

And there was something else bothering her. For the first time in many years, she was feeling a familiar stirring in her heart, much like when she first began dating as a teenager. She admitted to herself that she was finding Clay somewhat attractive. Not only was he inordinately handsome, but he presented qualities she found especially endearing: kindness, sensitivity and strength. At the same time his grey eyes conveyed a sense of vulnerability and deep loss that somehow made her want to help and protect him. Juxtaposed against this attraction was the guilt of knowing his true purpose on their mission. Finally, despite how wrong it was, deep in her heart she wished there might be more between them – an impossible dream. She had dedicated herself to God and there could be no turning back.

Or could there? Indeed, she could sense that he had some feelings for her. And despite her best efforts, she was beginning to feel the same way towards him. But even if he did care for her in that way, how could she suddenly choose a secular life after so many years dedicated to achieving a closer relationship with God?

She sighed and turned from the window. Anyhow, she thought, for any of this to be relevant, first they'd have to survive. Lately she found it strange that whenever she tried to speculate on the future and consider possibilities for herself, or even to think about what her life would be like in a convent, she saw little. It was as though someone had put up a wall between her and the future. Well, fate was fate she decided and if it was the Lord's will that they both survive and for her to cleave onto the man – she smiled at the biblical term that had swept into her mind – then it would happen. If it was His will that they give their lives for God, then so be it.

Being as quiet as possible, she crawled back into bed. There she lay until a growing blanket of weariness covered her worries and she fell fast asleep. The grandfather clock in the corner of their room labored on, slowly ticking away the seconds, turning them into minutes and then hours.

Maria didn't know how long she'd been asleep when she partially awoke and kicked off the covers. She felt incredibly warm, as though burning up with a fever. She rolled onto her stomach and draped her bare arm over the side of the mattress looking for any way to cool down. That felt good, she decided through a half stupor; she would leave off the covers.

As she began to slip back to sleep, something long and milky slowly snaked out from the darkness underneath the bed. Maria felt the cold clamminess of its grip and the wiry bristles of hair on its skin a fraction of a second before it clamped down on her arm with a vice-like hold.

She tried to scream, tried to pull back, but the grip was like iron. It began to pull her across the bed.

Paralyzed with terror, heart hammering in her ears, she yelled for Clay to help her. No words came out. Desperately she grabbed the bed sheets with her left hand and held on. It didn't work; inexorably she was slowly dragged towards the side of the bed. A fetid stench wafted upward and she retched. It was only through sheer will she didn't throw up. Whatever had hold of her continued to relentlessly pull her towards the edge!

Maria tried to scream again; still no sound came out. The tucked sheets she gripped for a purchase abruptly let go. She slid towards the side and what she instinctively knew was certain death.

CLAY…MY GOD…HELP ME…IT'S GOING TO KILL ME!

But the call was only in her mind; his unbroken breathing continued barely a few feet away. There was to be no reprieve. She was certain that this was the end. She could feel hate and anger transferred through its grip on her arm. She tried to free herself, to cry out again. Nothing. As the balance of her weight shifted, she slipped over the bedside and fell towards the floor and the monster that lurked beneath her bed. She summoned her last reserve of strength and silently screamed….

HEAVENLY FATHER…PLEASE…PLEASE HELP ME!

Maria thudded onto the carpet on her back. The grip suddenly loosened and slithered from her arm.

"What in the hell…?" The bedside lamp snapped on and Clay, hair rumpled and eyes confused, stared down at her between the beds. "Maria…are you okay? What are you doing there?"

She was panting like she'd just run a marathon. Sweat poured from her face and she quickly yanked her hand from under the bed and dived over Clay and onto his bed behind him, hitting the wall with a resounding thump. "Dear God…it's there…it's under the bed," she yelled, relieved to hear the sound of her voice. "Your gun…get your gun…!"

Clay's stared uncomprehendingly at Maria and now leaned down and looked under her bed. "There's nothing there," he said, turning awkwardly because her weight was pinning him down with his own bed covers. "What are you talking about?"

"It's under my bed," she gasped, unconvinced the shadows were empty.

Clay pulled free of the covers, his feet hit the floor and he dropped to a prone position supporting himself with his arms. "There's nothing under your bed except some pretty vicious dust bunnies," he said lightly, realizing what had happened. "It was a dream, Maria, a nightmare." He stood up.

She stared up at him, her eyes large and dark. Damp chestnut hair lay plastered by perspiration across her forehead. Her breathing gradually returned to normal.

"Nightmare?" she asked. "N-Nothing there? Are-are you sure?"

"Positive...look for yourself."

Hesitantly she approached the edge of his bed and leaned over. "But I felt it grab my hand. It dragged me onto the floor."

He sat down on the edge of the bed and gently grasped her trembling shoulders. "It was a nightmare; you rolled off your bed."

"B-But it felt so real," she said, fingering the silver Crucifix hanging from her neck for comfort. Suddenly aware of her baby doll pajamas, she drew his blanket across her bare thighs.

"Of course it felt real," he said gently, feeling a deep shudder run through her body as she remembered. "It's no wonder with all this stuff going on. I'm not sure that this is the best thing for you to be doing. For either of us." He wiped the sodden hair back from her forehead. "Are you okay now? Back into your own bed and catch a few winks...I mean before the 'fuzz' arrive in the morning?"

He smiled encouragingly at her, hoping to further relieve her tension.

She wasn't buying it and shook her head, large eyes begging him for an invitation.

"You want to stay right there?"

She nodded. "We-we can't...we mustn't...you know," She stammered, looking distressed and embarrassed. What exactly was she doing, she wondered, other than betraying her own thoughts?

Clay smiled again and got back into bed. "It's alright. I'm sure we're both too sleepy to consider anything untoward," he lied gently, letting her off any perceived hook as he switched off the light and turned outward. "Now go to sleep. Okay?"

"Thank you," she said simply and curled up as close to the wall as she could. But that lasted only for a moment. "God…I'm-I'm still so scared," she said, breaking the silence.

He turned toward here. "Come here, kiddo," he said. "No more bogeymen tonight."

She came to him without hesitation and he folded her into his arms. Within a few seconds she couldn't help burrowing her head into his shoulder and Clay felt her beginning to relax. Her breath and her hair both smelled as sweet as a summer flower.

Despite the terror she had felt moments before, somehow she now felt totally safe in his arms. She found herself smiling in relief and contentment. Exhausted, it wasn't long before she was snoring softly.

For Clay, however, sleep was not so easy. As the minutes passed, all inhibitions banished by sleep, she had instinctively moved closer seeking warmth and he could feel her small apple-like breasts against his chest and the Venus mound of her pelvis pressed lightly against his leg. Every breath she took sent electric tingles through his whole body and he groaned as he fought a physical desire for her. There was no doubt in his mind now; this small nun had truly captured his heart. But what were the options? Really there were none, he admitted to himself. She had already told him she hoped to take her final vows after this was over. Any feelings he might have for her were most certainly doomed. If only we could stay like this forever, he mused silently and finally slipped into the nether world of sleep.

* * * *

PART SIX

"WHEN NIGHT IS DARKEST"

God answers sharp and sudden on some
Prayers,
And thrusts, the thing we have prayed
For in our face,
A gauntlet with a gift in 'it.

Elizabeth Barrett Browning
AUROA LEIGH (1857)

~ 1 ~

Three cups of tea were set down along with milk and sweetener on Detective Chief Superintendent Cruickshank's desk. A female constable placed three spoons on his blotter, took her tray and began to exit. She stopped at the door and looked back. "Will that be all, Chief Superintendent," she asked, matter-of-factly.

Cruickshank nodded: "Yes…I shan't forget this, Constable."

"Always glad to 'serve', sir," she said, smiling. "Davidson will buy more coffee before lunch." She exited, humming softly.

"Good," Cruickshank said. He turned his attention to Clay and Maria "Very sorry about this. We each give a pound every fortnight into the kitty and we're supposed to have coffee on hand. So there'll be some jangled nerves this morning. Fortunately I'm a tea man, myself."

Maria smiled and Clay was happy she was regaining a semblance of normality. The morning had been awkward when they woke up, her body still nestled in his arms. As she stirred he could feel that her first instinct was to recoil like a jilted snake, however, his grip was such that it wasn't possible so she had settled for a sleepy good morning greeting. It had its intended effect and Clay immediately opened his arms and freed her.

It soon became obvious that both felt the awkwardness so he vanished into the bathroom to take a shower and shave. He met her once more as they simultaneously came into the bedroom to retrieve fresh clothes. Neither spoke but he tried to give her a friendly smile. He then worried for the next ten minutes as he shaved and brushed his teeth that it might have looked like a leer. A knock at their door announced a Metropolitan London Bobby, helmet in hand, who politely offered them a ride to Scotland Yard. On the trip, they exchanged conversation about the weather and little else.

"I'd like you to return to the crime scene this morning, in particular, where you crashed," Cruickshank said when they entered his office. "I would dearly love to find this chap's hiding place; if we can trace his path in daylight when he ran from you, we may have a spot of luck and find him."

Within the hour all three stood in front of the smashed Previa with police still busily milling about. The car was surrounded with blue police tape; the doors still stood open, and the bullet hole in the roof with protruding shards of metal plainly showing that a shot had come from the inside.

"That's an impressive bullet hole," Cruickshank said eyeing the roof. "What sort of weapon did you grab from this fellow?"

"I'm not sure," Clay said. "It all happened so fast."

The Chief Superintendent raised a hand and a short, heavyset plainclothes detective hurried forward and handed him a canvas sack. With his back to them, he extracted something, handed the sack back to the detective and turned. "Might this be yours, old chap?" he asked politely, holding the Ruger .44 cal. and holster in hand.

Clay sighed and slowly nodded. There had been no opportunity to retrieve his weapon under the watchful eyes of the constables the previous night and he was hoping they would miss it. "Yes...it's mine," he said, resolutely.

"We had to have protection," Maria protested, stepping forward.

The Chief Superintendent looked at her and pursed his lips. "I suppose that's what compromised the leak-proof guarantee on the Previa's roof?" he asked.

"Yes," Clay said simply. "He must have jumped from a tree onto our roof, smashed in the windshield and was trying to grab Maria when I lost control, went through the fence and we ended up here. I grabbed my gun and fired through the roof in case he was still there."

"But he obviously wasn't."

"No...but I caught a glimpse of something after I got out of the car. And, as I said, I chased him...that way," he said pointing towards some monuments.

"Why make up a story about grabbing his weapon?"

"To enable me to keep my own. I was afraid you might seize it."

"Quite," Cruickshank said. He shook his head. "You know you are wasting our time with evasions and half truths? We are on the same side, Mr. Montague. Or, at least I hope we are."

"I'm sorry," Clay said, digging out a card. "I have a permit for the revolver."

Cruickshank turned it slightly to catch the light and handed it back. "I know. Your cardinal has friends in powerful offices to get that permit." He abruptly shoved the holster and weapon at Clay.

"Put it away and do not…I say again…*do not* fire it in this city unless you are in mortal danger. Have I made myself clear?"

Clay nodded. "Yes. Thank you."

"There's another condition attached to keeping that," he said, pointing at the Ruger.

"Name it," Clay said.

"I want the truth from now on. First time…every time."

"Fair enough. But sometimes you may not like what we tell you."

"Very well. What I find strange is that, despite the fact we've been chasing this blighter for months, you are in the city one day and you have had the good fortune…or bad fortune, as it were…for him to immediately find you. Any comment on that?"

"Truthfully…no."

"I spoke to your 'employer' last night. He was his usually circumspect self, however, he did promise me you would cooperate."

"Of course," Maria said.

They attempted to retrace the path that Clay had taken the night before and found where he had fired at the shadow he'd been chasing. Cruickshank examined two pock marks in an Ivy-covered stone wall where Clay's bullets had struck. There was no sign of blood anywhere so it was pretty certain he'd missed both shots.

They returned to the Previa which was now being removed by what Cruickshank called a recovery vehicle. The Chief Superintendent advised Clay and Maria to let the rental agency know the status of their automobile as soon as possible. He told them that he was satisfied they couldn't help further with the investigation and returned their passports. However, he wanted them to keep in touch and let him know immediately if they uncovered anything or had contact with the killer. Clay agreed and they were offered a ride back to the hotel.

As they sat waiting in the back of a police cruiser with the window lowered, Clay looked between two police cars and nudged Maria. Off in the distance, Cruickshank was deep in conversation with two of the military-type men who had been in the car in Swain's Lane the previous night. The dark-haired man with the lantern jaw who had identified himself as Kit Nathaniel, and one of his accomplices was nodding slowly. They reached out and shook hands with the Chief Superintendent.

So Scotland Yard was working with some Americans trying to find the Millennium Ripper, Clay thought. He'd been right to be somewhat suspicious. They just didn't happen by. They must have had the cemetery under surveillance and responded to their situation. Still, he was puzzled. If they were responding to the car crash and the shots, why drive away and leave them? Why hadn't they become involved at that point rather than posing as people just passing by? Little was making sense. He looked up to see Cruickshank making his way to their police car.

Reaching them, he leaned on the window frame and looked inside. "Just one more thing, Mr. Montague. You said this blighter was off the roof when you fired at him last night. And yet we took some skin and tissue scrapings from around the bullet hole and other places off the roof of your car. We had them analyzed at the lab and the results came back this morning. Can you guess the details?"

Clay shook his head.

"Well they seemed somewhat normal, apart from the fact they were in an advanced state of decomposition and likely cadaveric."

"Cadaveric?" Clay asked, in surprise.

"Yes," Cruickshank said, "tissue straight from a corpse. I personally find it hard to believe that, being dead – and for some time by the looks of it – your assailant simply ran away. But then, I'm just a backward London flatfoot obviously out of his ever-loving depth. Have a nice day."

With that final comment, the Chief Superintendent banged the automobile roof twice with his palm and the driver turned the patrol car and pulled away, The Chief Superintendent looked after them with hands in his pockets.

As his image grew smaller, Maria turned to Clay and then whispered: "How come he's letting us go when he knows there is more here than meets the eye?" She spoke as quietly as possible since they were both well aware of the constable in the front seat.

Clay thought for a moment and then also leaned close to avoid the driver's ears. "I doubt it's benevolence on his part, Maria. I think it's called: Giving us enough rope to hang ourselves."

~ 2 ~

Counting himself, Malachi saw that five of *The Seven* were present and clustered around the formidable oak table in the *Chamber* as he lit up a Bances Habana Corona de luxe, and puffed furiously until he was sure he had an even burn. Comfort tobacco, he mused. He held a paper in his hands, the Vatican letterhead was plain enough for most to see as he flipped and scanned it once more vainly looking for any loophole of hope that might have been extended. There was none. Still, it couldn't end this way.

"Gentlemen," he said, addressing the group.

The conversation stopped and they gave him their full attention. For some reason Malachi found himself noting small and insignificant details about his band of merry men. For instance, Monsignor Heinz Rautenberg, who was in charge of the *Crusaders,* had a fresh haircut. Fred Gant, the *Keeper of the Relic*, and this was the most secret and significant relic the Catholic Church possessed, was madly chewing gum in his own continuing quest to quit smoking. Bishop Jean Castilloux, their PR man, seemed somewhat bleary eyed as though he hadn't gotten enough sleep. And finally, Father Peter Austin, their Provost Marshall, leader of the *Watchers,* and the only other man among them who knew what Malachi was about to say, had taken to shredding paper for amusement. A four inch yellow pile sat in front of him as he seized another 3M Post-It note and awkwardly began to tear it into even squares. His left hand, curled and stiff was barely able to grip the tiny pieces. Near the pile was a small, red leather notebook which he periodically moved as the pile got bigger.

"Gentlemen," Malachi began again, clearing his throat, "Last night I received two pieces of news. Sadly, both are extremely unfortunate." His congregation said not a word and he wondered idly in Prefect Lopez had already been busy stoking the fires of Vatican gossip. "I regret to tell you that our dear friend and confident, Bishop Flavious Aquila, died in his sleep last night."

"Oh my goodness," Rautenberg said. "How? I mean, do we know the cause of death?"

There were other murmurings around the table of shock and dismay.

"Not yet," Malachi answered. "But since he was blinded less than ten days ago in the most holy of causes, he has not been well.

He had virtually ceased to eat and he was battling a great depression that had settled over him. As you know, I visited him several times. Each time he was increasingly morose and appeared to lack any hope for the future. In fact, I personally wonder if his brief but intense proximity to the demon was the cause. Of course, we may never know. We can only be certain that it was a most difficult time for our brother in Christ and that God surely welcomed him home with open arms. In his honor, and to comfort his soul, I would like to lead you in a brief prayer.

All bowed their heads and blessed themselves. Malachi said the Our Father and then made a heartfelt request that the angels lead Bishop Aquila, a servant of the Lord, into the glory of Heaven. All joined him in the "Amen."

He looked up. Father Austin was fingering the leather book as though pondering what to do with it.

Malachi held up the letter. "My brothers, I am also sad to say that we have a crisis unlike any other. Last night, I had a brief audience with the Holy Father, and he has chosen to recognize our conversation in this letter which I received this morning. In it, he has officially ordered us to cease any operations regarding the *Hellspawn*. We are to surrender any assets acquired to a financial representative – to be appointed – cease accessing any previously allocated funds, and avoid the use of existing equipment. I imagine he means the aircraft which he knew all about. This is extremely grave gentlemen. It could be the end of the line."

There was a stunned silence and Malachi saw that there hadn't been enough time for the rumor mill to work. Father Gant sat back and shook his head but lost no time in getting down to business.

"We must retrieve the Relic right now," he said. "I am assuming it's still where I think it is, right?"

"Naturally," Monsignor Rautenberg answered. "It's aboard our A320 in a heavily secure area at Leonardo da Vinci Airport ready for shipping to London."

"Why?" Bishop Castilloux asked, somewhat impatient with Gant's constant and obsessive focus on the Relic as though that was their only priority. "Why would His Holiness stop us now?"

"Because someone got to him before I did," Malachi answered. "Someone with detailed knowledge of our operations. Someone who may have wanted us 'out-of-business'."

"A traitor to our cause?" Father Gant asked in disbelief. Then he looked around the table. "Where's Benito? Where's Father Gallo?"

"It wasn't Gallo," Father Austin said. He pushed the small red leather book towards Malachi. "I got hold of Flavius' calendar that was still being kept by Brother Rusty Swaga. Look at the entry for yesterday – the 13th before he died – a visit from the Holy Father."

Malachi scanned the page and sure enough, there was a notation that the Pontiff had made a hastily scheduled appointment to see Aquila in his quarters, likely to express condolences over his blindness. The visit had been allocated five minutes. Two other appointments, immediately following, were crossed out by the same red pen and showed that the Pope's visit had lasted one hour and thirty minutes in its entirety – not significant for the bishop but an enormous amount of time out of the Pope's calendar, considering his obligations.

"I also spoke directly to Brother Swaga, Mustavias," Father Austin continued. "I'm not sure if you know this but it appears our poor colleague may have died of a self-administered overdose of sleeping pills."

"Suicide!" Monsignor Rautenberg exclaimed. "He would never do that. He knows full well that he would risk spending eternity in Purgatory. Or worse."

Austin shrugged. "Maybe he felt he was already there...with his eyes and all."

"Flavius was a good man," Monsignor Rautenberg angrily shot back. "He wouldn't compromise us!"

"Understand, I'm not judging anyone, I'm merely looking at the facts," Austin returned. "And I may have a few more facts than you do, Heinz."

"Enough!" Malachi said, and all looked toward him. "There would be no reason for Flavius to skewer our operation. He very nearly gave his life in pursuit of Adramelech. Why would he try to sabotage us?"

Austin shrugged. "It was well known to all of us of your difficulty in getting to see the Holy Father regarding our financial crisis," he offered. "When he received the visit, Flavius may have seized the opportunity to try to help...to tell exactly how he was blinded and then to give details of the hunt. After all, the road to hell is paved with good intentions." He said the last bit with the hint of a crooked smile.

"Very funny," Monsignor Rautenberg muttered.

"And the Pontiff's reaction wasn't what he hoped for; in fact, he let Flavius know he intended to close us down," Father Gant finished. "You already said he was depressed, Mustavias. Perhaps the knowledge that rather than helping us, he had 'skewered' us, got to him?"

The five men were silent as they considered the possibility and then grudgingly accepted the possible theory.

"And hence my sudden summoning to see our most Holy Pontiff," Malachi said. "Makes sense."

"And so *The Seven* become six," Father Gant said. "And soon to be none. By the way, where is Father Gallo anyhow?"

"He is on his way to London to help our emissaries," Malachi said. "Sister Maria reported that she and Mr. Montague were attacked and nearly killed by Adramelech in Highgate Cemetery. Anyhow, despite this letter, I think we still have a chance to get the deed done." He sighed, puffed once more on the Havana and exhaled slowly looking at the smoke rising towards the ceiling. "As Sherlock Holmes used to say gentlemen: 'The game is afoot!' And I, for one, am *not* going to quit when we are breathing down Adramelech's neck."

~ 3 ~

Adramelech, clad in a blue-black cloak and dark suit over a black turtleneck, moved slowly through the swirls of midnight fog, stepping over stones and dead branches as he approached the Circle of Lebanon in Highgate Cemetery, a neo-Egyptian mausoleum complex.

This section of the post-Gothic Victorian necropolis was overrun by nature. Visitors were severely restricted except for timed tours during the morning and afternoon. Not that it was a problem for the Beast since he avoided the daytime. He did this simply because his work was best done under cover of darkness.

While there was a lingering anger over his failure to excise the soldier, he was ever confident in his ability to find him once again. Meanwhile, there were larger issues surfacing.

As mankind turned more and more away from the spiritual world, Adramelech could feel the time drawing ever nearer for his and his kind to come forth and seize power. While wars and atrocities around the world were nothing new, it was the increasing abandonment of religious belief in favor of a moral relativism that was creating a godless society, one that believed nothing was inherently good or evil. Increasingly, mankind as a whole seemed to feel that it was in charge of its own destiny, that it was no longer accountable to a higher power. As the church surrendered its traditions and office to corporatism, the edges of what constituted morality became more and more blurry.

The Beast chuckled to himself. The last time that strategy was adopted, Adam and Eve figuratively had their asses kicked out of Paradise on Earth and were left to fend for themselves. Surely their righteous God must be close to washing his hands of such sinners? Surely he must be ready to surrender to Satan what had been rightfully earned?

For instance, even in the Middle Ages, men and women would suffer for their faith for hours, sometimes for days, until madness from the pain of torture would bring about their capitulation. But, modern humans were willing to barter their souls just for a few moments of relief from pain. Their secularly focused lives of ease and comfort were obviously their undoing. They were weak and narcissistic. And, since they had the gift of *free will*, the Hated One seldom interfered.

It had been a good afternoon with news of the Relic's whereabouts. He knew through his network of unholy alliances and his insider that this was something to be feared indeed. If he could destroy it, humanity would have lost its chance to rid itself of him. His existence was particularly effective this time. He'd now had decades of life in which to work his deeds of horror as evidence that there was no God looking to save humanity. Still he yearned for the triumphs of yesteryears when he sat at the right hand of the powerful corrupting their intentions through devious suggestions and carefully fostered paranoia. And it would be so again.

Indeed, Adramelech, bred to bring misery to humanity, sensed that the Self Anointed One was well pleased in his work as the human race abandoned spiritual focus, saw greed, avarice and gluttony as evidences of success, and viewed integrity, honor and charity as holdovers from a darker age. A pursuit of Heaven had been replaced by the quest for the almighty dollar, and as business conglomerates maneuvered and manipulated their indentured servants, casting them aside when necessary and destroying families and livelihoods along the way, the very idea of a loving and tolerant God lost its luster and its credibility.

He stopped at the sound of a twig snapping in the distance and then decided it was likely an animal since few humans would venture here after his delightful young female meals of some nights ago. His thoughts of triumph continued. Suffer the little children to come unto me, indeed? Almost 30,000 children died every day in the third world from starvation and disease, their bellies distended, flies crawling on their faces and their hopes crushed. Meanwhile their sanctimonious earthly brothers and sisters engaged in halcyon days of makeovers, massages and McDonalds. And, what did the Church offer in the way of support? Promises of glory supported by benign platitudes issued from golden thrones.

He arrived at his destination. Across the entranceway to a tomb directly in front of him lay a rock barrier with a family inscription **MORGAN** chiseled into it. The carefully sculpted rock was obviously carved to approximate the Son's tomb but the family would whistle long and hard before that pile of dust inside resurrected itself, thought Adramelech. The barrier weighed almost a ton.

The Beast grasped the rock and easily pulled it aside. He entered the 12 X 12 foot room where a cement sarcophagus rested on a simple stone shelf.

Rosalita sat in a corner slowly rocking back and forth in a vain attempt to find comfort. He smiled at her, lips drawing back over carnivorous, dead white teeth. Over the years when he'd roamed the South American continent, his ability to shape shift from the grotesque to almost human form had served him well as it did now. In the dusk he had easily moved among humans without experiencing more than the occasional second look followed by a wave of confused revulsion on the looker's face. He could more than pass now and that was enough. Still, when there was the devil's work to be done, he happily resumed his natural shape and became the stuff of nightmares.

His small familiar continued to gaze at him trying to anticipate his needs; the dull lifeless look in her eyes said she awaited his pleasure.

"We leave soon to go elsewhere, Rosalita," he said aloud, his voice low and modulated.

She stared at him and nodded without ceasing her rocking. Finally she stopped for a few seconds. "Will it be warm?" she asked.

The Beast smiled at her and asked: "Why do you ask that? You feel neither heat nor cold. You are of the dead."

She nodded once more and began rocking again. "Will I ever be warm again?"

"Oh yes, my dear" he said with a horrible grin. "When our work is finished and we join the Anointed One I can promise you that you will be warm forever."

He loomed over her and then turned and stared at the darkness outside of the tomb. The girl tried to anticipate his needs.

"What is your will?" She prepared to rise.

"To sleep and then leave you for the night. I have much to do before we go to our home again."

Rosalita sat back down and with hollow eyes began her rocking once more. Deep in the recesses of her consciousness, far-off memories of belonging, of love and of security danced like will-o-wisps just beyond her grasp. But within her limited senses she knew any independent thought was forbidden and would be harshly dealt with if discovered. She would stay with her Master until his work was done. Then perhaps he would free her from her immortality and she could sleep.

~ 4 ~

Back at the hotel, Clay had arranged for Hertz Rental to deliver another car. It would arrive within an hour, a cheery attendant promised, but Clay said they were in no hurry; he was at a loss as to what they would do when it arrived anyhow. Obviously there would be no more trips to Highgate. Maria had informed Malachi the previous night of their adventure and his orders had been to stay away from the cemetery. It had been searched by their own team of assassins.

More and more questions arose in his mind: Why was Cruickshank being so generous? In particular, why had he returned the revolver? Who were the military types that he was talking with at the cemetery? Now that they knew this fiend was somewhere near Highgate Cemetery, was his job over?

So far he had let Maria handle any communications with Malachi but he did have his cell phone number and the cardinal had promised it would be answered at any time of the day or night. Right now, he was also worried about the dangers of trying to find this "thing" as far as Maria was concerned. His feelings for her were growing exponentially and he wasn't about to let her get hurt. Time to address that issue he decided. He would call the cardinal while she was downstairs picking up a newspaper. He dialed the number and waited as it rang. Abruptly a click launched a voice mail response but that was soon interrupted.

"Malachi...."

"It's Clay Montague, Your Eminence."

"Hello Clay," came back the voice, now slightly guarded. "How are you? By the way…this is not a secure line. How about I get to a land line and call you back. This is your cell line I presume?"

Clay said yes and within minutes his cell phone rang again. He punched the receive button.

"That's better," Malachi said. "Your cell also has a custom encryption device built in."

"You know what happened?" Clay asked.

"Of course…you met our friend."

"Only temporarily," answered Clay. "He left abruptly but a police officer was murdered along the way."

"Not your fault."

"Agreed, but what now? Is this over?"

"He hasn't been located yet."

"He's here in London somewhere around Highgate Cemetery."

"We need his lair…where he spends his time when he isn't terrorizing people."

"Is this wise?"

"Unfortunately, yes."

"Sir, I have a concern."

"I would be surprised if you hadn't," Malachi answered. And more kindly: "What is it?"

"Maria. I don't think she should be involved in this."

There was silence at the end of the phone. Finally he spoke: "She is there to help you, Clay."

"I don't need her help. I can find this guy on my own, thanks very much."

"You do need her help. As I told you, she senses the evil in this thing. Sometimes she sees the future. So she can give warning and you can call us and have time to escape."

"Well that didn't work out too well the other night."

"I understand that. It wasn't her fault; he arrived too soon."

"I'm worried and I don't want her harmed. Maria is just…baggage." He genuinely tried to make it sound as though she was getting in his way.

"Remember the protocols we developed?" Cardinal Malachi asked. "The ones where she will be able to contact us if you are injured. And vice versa. It's all about time…time to get our people to where it is to get a crack at this thing. Maria can buy us that time."

"At the expense of her life? I'm putting her on a plane back to Rome this evening."

Malachi laughed, but not too unkindly. "I'd like to see that. She has quite the spirit and is committed to helping us any way she can, Clay."

"Well as far as I'm concerned, Maria isn't risking her life anymore. I want you to call her off and I'll do whatever you need done."

There was silence at the other end of the phone again and Clay took that as a sign Malachi was considering his offer. He was wrong. "Clay, it's *Sister* Maria. You understand that? We really can't get into interpersonal relationships here. That isn't what's happening, is it?"

"All I want is for her to be away from this area, Your Eminence. If that guy, or thing, had grabbed her through the windshield last night, he'd have killed her."

"Look Clay, I understand your feelings. Nor am I without concern for *both* your safety. However, when you consider how close we are and what's at stake, we have to proceed. At any cost."

"Sir, you tell me that if we dial a certain number on our cell phone, this 'hit' team or whatever you call it…will come to where we are."

"The *Crusaders*…yes."

"So if I find it, I call. Why does Maria–?"

He was interrupted as the door opened and Maria stepped through with two cardboard coffee cups and a newspaper under her arm. Her eyebrows went up and she mouthed: "Who?"

"Clay…are you still there?"

"Yes sir."

"Is Sister Maria there?"

"Yes…right here."

"May I speak with her?"

"Certainly…but what about my concern?"

"I think we'll keep the status quo for now. Don't worry. Sister Maria can take care of herself."

Clay reluctantly handed the phone to Maria who had set the coffee down on the roll-top desk and was approaching, a quizzical look on her face.

"Cardinal Malachi," he said shortly, and stalked over to read the newspapers headlines as he half listened to the conversation.

"Yes, Your Eminence?" She listened for a few minutes nodding, occasionally glancing at Clay. Then she thanked the cardinal and hung up. "So you think you'd be better off alone?"

"That's not the point, Maria…"

"*Sister* Maria," she said pointedly, staring him down.

Oh no, he thought. What had Malachi said to her? Had he voiced his suspicions on Clay's feelings for Maria? He felt himself reddening. "I just don't want you hurt. And after what happened last night, I can see that we're chasing a very capable madman. Or maybe something worse."

She came over to him, placed a hand on his arm and gave him an earnest look. "I don't want you hurt neither, Clay. At the risk of sounding trite, this is something that is bigger than both of us. And, we were told it wasn't without risks."

"I know, but I can find this guy by myself. Why risk two lives?"

"Because I'm your support. That's why I'm here."

"Alright, they believe you can help but have you ever asked yourself why they would bring me half way round the world? None of it adds up. I don't buy the fact that I'm here simply because I saw something in Panama. Or, that the Vatican is giving me a chance to avenge Hitch and Jody. There are thousands of PIs or soldiers of fortune who would be just as capable of tracking this thing for a price." Clay paused, sighed and then sat down heavily on the bed.

"What is it?" Maria asked.

"Nothing," he said, the pieces finally falling into place. He felt sick to his stomach, not with fear but with disappointment.

"Look...." Maria began.

"Something is wrong with this picture," he interrupted and then stopped. He shook his head.

Maria suddenly looked embarrassed. Crestfallen she sat down beside him, her face ashen. She also looked sick.

"I'm here because I'm bait," Clay said. "That's it, isn't it?"

Maria shook her head in dismay and stared at the carpet. Finally she nodded. "One of the known characteristics of Adramelech is that he hunts down those who see him in his original form and eliminates them," she said in a small voice. "The greatest power for Satan is that people don't believe he exists. And, Adramelech maintains his anonymity by not leaving any witnesses, any loose ends." Her voice was trembling.

"And I'm a loose end," Clay agreed. "And, you've known all along."

She turned towards him, tried to take his hands in hers, her eyes pleading. He drew back and wouldn't let her say anything. Instead he stood up and headed for the door. He felt angry and hurt. It seemed that while he was deeply in love with Maria, to her and the rest of the cast in this lunatic play he was merely a means to an end. He was a pawn.

"At least I'm now clear on my value," he said, bitterly. "As a Judas Goat, I mean."

"Clay...I'm so sorry," Maria called desperately as he approached the door and yanked it open. "Wait, please!"

He turned his back on her but then paused and said: "No wonder he attacked us in the cemetery, *Sister* Maria. We're not hunting him. He's hunting me."

He exited, slamming the door.

Maria sunk down on the edge of the bed and began to cry.

~ 5 ~

"The inevitable end to a dream assignment," First Officer Gostini spoke as the aircraft stopped its backward motion and the pushback tractor was detached. He looked out at the rapidly setting sun. It was going to be a nice evening; stars were already appearing in the deep purple sky over a band of orange and gold on the western horizon over the Seven Hills of Rome. He double-checked that the start levers were at idle, the stabilizer trim was checked and set, and electrical, standby and galley power all checked out as normal. Engine number one was up and Bowden started engine number two. They droned on through the check list ensuring bleed valves were open, hydraulics were normal, the door lights were checked out, the APU was checked as stopped, and brake pressure was normal.

"Taxi instructions, please," Bowden asked, as he surveyed the instruments one last time.

"Charter 104, taxi clearance, over?" Gostini said, into his headset.

Ground control came back immediately: "Charter 104, taxi via Delta, hold short of Charlie. Give way to the Pan Am 747 on your left, follow him for runway thirty-four right."

"Roger, follow Pan Am and taxi via Delta to hold short of Charlie...thank you, sir."

As the Pan Am flight passed, Bowden released the brakes and advanced the throttles with his right hand while steering the aircraft with his left. The sound of the engines smoothly spooling up gave way as the aircraft began to sluggishly move forward and they bumped along the taxiway in their short journey towards runway 34 right. They continued calling out the before-takeoff check list to each other as they taxied.

"Takeoff flaps, two selected, two indicated ..." Bowden said.

"Affirmative...," Answered Gostini

"Speed brakes...Armed.

"Affirmative ..."

"Flight controls?"

"Checked...."

"Take-off Memo?"

"Go," responded Bowden confirming all checks had been completed as A-Okay.

Pressurization was checked and set, and they droned on through the checklist as though this was a first flight. Their routine was broken momentarily as Ground Control contacted them once more. "Charter 104, proceed and follow Pan Am and contact the tower at one eighteen point seven, holding short of taxiway Charlie."

Gostini keyed his microphone: "Roger, contact tower one eighteen point seven, holding short of Charlie...good day, sir." He selected the tower frequency and let them know they were with them. He was told they were number two, after Pan Am.

"So we turn this baby in at United at JFK and that's it?" asked Gostini with a lopsided smile. No thank you…no gold watch?"

"Apparently one of the New York dioceses has arranged for the aircraft to be stripped of its medical equipment and other stuff first," Bowden said. "And the cardinal also asked me to thank you and said there would be a letter of reference for each of us as well as a bonus check, and an open overseas ticket waiting for us in New York in three days. He examined the small clipboard in his hand. "We can pick them up at the Opus Dei building on Lexington Avenue in Manhattan any time after the 3rd."

"Great," Gostini said without much enthusiasm. "Two unemployed pilots."

"Not quite…."

"No?"

"No…the cardinal said he'd set up interviews for us both with Alitalia if we're interested. He said he was pretty certain we'd be taken on although we'll have zero seniority. What do you think?"

"Better than unemployment….I'm game. You?" Gostini sounded brighter.

"Thinking about it. It'll depend on convincing the wife to live in Rome. And I think I can. Susan is such a sport. Not many other wives would put up with their husbands being away so much."

"Charter 104, after departing Pan Am, line up and hold thirty-four right," the tower ordered with a burst of static.

Gostini acknowledged the instructions and within a few minutes, the 747 in front of them was rumbling down the runway and they moved into position on the threshold and held. They completed the takeoff check list.

"Charter 104, cleared for takeoff. Wind two five zero at fifteen."

Bowden and Gostini placed their hands on the throttles and advanced them both towards the stops. The aircraft began picking up speed at about 4 knots per second. The ASI became effective and the instrument needles on both Bowden and Gostini's panels jumped.

"Airspeed building," Gostini called.

As they hit 80 knots, the rudder took hold and Gostini called it out. Bowden transferred his left hand to the stick and continued steering with the rudders.

"I have control," Bowden said.

"Your column," Gostini acknowledged.

Their speed built until Gostini called out V-1. The aircraft was now committed to flight and Bowden moved his right hand from the throttles; Gostini assumed control of the engines. A moment later the co-pilot called out "rotate" and Bowden pulled gently back on the joystick and the aircraft lifted into the sky and climbed quickly.

"Gear up," Bowden ordered and Gostini reached for the lever in front of them and pulled it up to retract the wheels. They heard the whine and thumps as the nose wheels settled in the well and the doors closed. Three lights showed gear up.

"Charter 104 Heavy, call departure one three zero point nine," the tower radioed.

"Charter 104, good day," Gostini responded. "Departure, Charter 104 passing one thousand three hundred."

"Good evening, Charter 104, climb and maintain six thousand on reaching."

"Charter 104, maintain six thousand."

"Climb power," Bowden said, easing the nose down 10 degrees to allow for the power reduction and Gostini obliged by easing the throttles back to the climb power setting indicated on the EPR limit indicator. Bowden then lowered the nose a little further: "Flaps five degrees."

"Flaps five, set," Gostini said.

They were at 2,000 feet now, barely climbing but still accelerating. At **7 DME** on their assigned radial, Gostini called out the distance to Bowden and he turned the aircraft right to track using the automatic direction finding needles on the radio magnetic indicator pointing towards the beacon. When they hit 225 knots they retracted the flaps in two stages and continued climbing towards 6,000 feet. Gostini told departure they were out of five for six thousand and they were again asked to maintain six thousand. The three-dimensional chess game being played by the flight controllers necessitated that they control and move hundreds of other aircraft safely through the skies.

Next Rome departure asked them to turn right onto a new vector and cleared them to flight level one two zero and asked them to call Rome control with their heading.

That meant they were cleared for further climb and were being handed off to Rome control. They were soon cleared again to flight level one eight zero and climbed to 18,000 feet and then, as they approached it, were again cleared to 28,000 feet. After another few minutes Bowden had Gostini call for their oceanic clearance while he stayed with Rome on their second radio. They soon received their oceanic clearance.

"Rome clears Charter 104, track foxtrot to Heathrow, flight level three-three zero mach decimal eight four from five three north, one five west."

They climbed through 29,000 feet and within a half an hour they were out over the Mediterranean with the INS waypoints keyed in, at altitude, and settling back for a long cruise. Bowden asked Gostini to take control, took off his headset and headed back for a pit stop. Gostini's gaze swept the instruments. His experience enabled him to look at the panel and automatically see that everything was fine. If an instrument registered an anomaly, he would spot it right off.

After a few minutes, Bowden returned and made his way into his seat.

Gostini looked over. "Should we put on the Bishop's visibility lights?" he asked with a smile.

"Only if you feel a need to be closer to God," Bowden answered back in the same spirit. He then added in a southern preacher style: "Praise the Lord, y'all but first pass the bucks."

They had been flying for more than two hours, just approaching the English Channel when something hit the fuselage near the cockpit with a noticeable thud.

"What the hell," Bowden exclaimed, looking over at Gostini. "Did you hear that?"

Gostini nodded and again his eyes swept the instruments. Both pilots began checking their panels.

"Bird strike?" Gostini offered, without thinking but feeling his anxiety growing. This seemed like a repeat performance of their previous troubles.

"If so, our little feathered friend was wearing an oxygen mask," Bowden muttered moving the controls gently to ensure their operation. The aircraft tipped to the left and then the right. Next the nose rose and then dipped and the pilot brought them back to their assigned altitude of 33,000 feet and shook his head. "Controls unrestricted...don't know what it could have been."

Without warning, two lights on the annunciator panel lit up showing a cabin pressure problem and a door open.

"Jesus...door open...cabin pressure," Gostini said struggling to remain calm as the aircraft suddenly shook violently and Bowden fought to steady it.

Just as abruptly, both panel lights went out, and the aircraft steadied. The pilots looked at each other.

"We've got a situation," Bowden said, shaking his head. "Contact London, we may need an altitude tout suite."

"It's got to be a circuit breaker," Gostini ventured. "Want me to go back and do a visual on the doors."

"Alright...but make it quick and watch yourself. Hang on to something solid until you can confirm we don't have a defective door. I'll contact London, declare an emergency and get a descent to 10,000 feet or below in case it blows. Watch yourself. Understood?"

"Got it."

Gostini opened the cockpit door and moved through the pilot's rest compartment into the sick bay. He checked that the forward passenger entrance door was secure as he moved back towards the office, the sleeping quarters and the common area near the tail. Along the way he opened each door to the next section with caution. Between the sick bay and the office, the modifiers had left a large section of typical airline seating where 20 people could be accommodated. With only a few lights on and no passengers, the cabin had taken on that eerie, empty dancehall look. He carefully checked the overwing emergency exits. All appeared secure. There was only the passenger aft entrance and possibly the emergency jettison-cable tail cone to examine. He entered the common area and stopped dead.

Ahead he could see the passenger aft entrance. The handle to the door was bent inward at an odd angle and he could see evidence of torn metal and scraped paint on the inside frame of the door as well as on the flange of the door itself. He felt his pulse quicken as he turned to head back forward to tell Bowden. If the aft door suddenly opened, he could easily be sucked out when depressurization occurred. But instead of continuing his retreat, he stopped. Because the door opened inward and the cabin was pressurized, it would take tens of tons of pressure to pry open the door from the inside. His mind raced – he'd been back before takeoff ensuring any loose objects were secure and the door had not been damaged. What had happened? What could possibly account for what he was seeing?

He moved carefully towards the intercom keeping a cautious eye on the door as he felt the aircraft suddenly slow and begin a descent. Good, he thought as he picked up the telephone and pushed the cockpit button. They were getting down to a flight level where they could more effectively manage a sudden depressurization if it occurred. Also there'd be air to breathe.

"What did you find?" Bowden demanded, his voice tinny over the intercom.

"The aft passenger entrance door has damage to it."

"Get out of there, Danny," Bowden ordered. "Get out of there right now. We're descending to 9,000 feet, so get back up here."

There was no mistaking the tension in the pilot's voice but Gostini's attention was on something else. As though in a dream, he whispered to Bowden that he had to go. He hung up the handset and stared uncomprehendingly at the three-foot hole ripped in the floor of the cabin ten feet from him. The hole obviously led into the aft lower cargo compartment in the belly of the aircraft. It gaped open like a gutted fish daring him to come and look into it. Behind him he heard the buzzer for the intercom repeatedly calling to be answered but he paid it little heed.

Gostini moved towards the hole because he heard noise coming from the cargo hold. In the half light, he could sense more than see someone down below as he leaned slightly forward. Cables and wires running under the floor had been pried and pulled aside but seemed to be undamaged. A shadowy bulk moved and something was dropped below with a metal clang. Gostini jumped, turned and hurried forward to the cockpit not bothering to close any doors behind him.

As the co-pilot entered the cockpit, Bowden turned in his seat. Even with his emergency oxygen mask on, Gostini could see the concern etched on his face. "Why didn't you answer the intercom?" he barked, his annoyance evident.

"Wayne…there's someone else on board."

"What?" The pilot automatically checked his altimeter; they were descending through flight level two-two zero. "Are you sure?"

Gostini nodded and climbed into his seat. "There's a hole in the aft cabin floor and someone is down in the cargo hold." It was plain he was shaken and scared.

"Who's down there? What kind of hole?"

"A three-foot, rounded frigging hole that looks like it's been chopped or somehow ripped open in the floor. There are cables and wire bundles exposed but they seem intact."

"Jesus Christ! Stowaway?"

"You don't understand. I checked this aircraft before we left making sure everything was secure. Because we're turning the aircraft in, I looked in all storage compartments as well. There was no-one else aboard. Now it looks as though someone tried to pry open the aft door. And there's a hole in the cabin floor and someone rummaging around in the cargo bay."

Bowden glanced at the cockpit door. "We have to get him under control. Maybe he tried to open the door and when that failed, he got a fire axe and started chopping his way to China."

Gostini hesitated. "I checked the aircraft pretty thoroughly."

"Well he's in here, isn't he? Unless he just stopped in at 33,000 feet for a visit? Take control. We have clearance to 9,000 feet. Continue our descent and maintain the heading. I've got to get back there and stop this guy before he kills us all."

Bowden waited until Gostini was belted in, had donned his oxygen mask as required in a potential depressurization situation and nodded that he had control. Then he moved swiftly through the open doors until he came to the common area. He bent forward, looked through the door and quickly drew back his head. The damage to the passenger aft door was easily visible as well as the hole in the floor ahead. He decided that stealth might be a better initial approach. If he could see who he was dealing with, he might have a better chance of reasoning with his quarry.

The pilot quietly moved forward towards the hole. There was no sound from below. Gingerly he dropped to his knees and stretched out on the carpet to where he could just get his head through the hole to have a look. He could feel the vibration of the engines through the floor as he cautiously inched his body forward. His eyes approached the lip of the hole.

Nothing visible.

STOP!

An instinct, an inner voice screamed at him that all was not as it seemed. He found himself beginning to tremble as he heard a Velcro-like sound of tearing below and his nostrils detected a rotten smell that seemed to be coming from the cargo hold. He shifted forward. Then a little more…so he could get his entire head through the opening. He moved his shoulders through the jagged hole in the floor and dropped his head cautiously.

For a split second he didn't believe what he was seeing, convinced that the blood rushing to his head was causing him to hallucinate. He was staring upside down at a horned, reptilian head fronted by two smoldering eyes. The creature's teeth were bared as though in a smile. As Bowden desperately tried to draw back, two claws wrapped securely around his head and twisted. The last thing the pilot knew was the sound of cartilage tearing and the crunching of bone.

Blackness….

In the cockpit, Gostini began to ease out of the descent so the altimeter would read exactly 9,000 feet as they leveled out. He resisted buzzing the back cabin in case he interfered with Bowden negotiating with whoever was there. The man was berserk to have gone through the floor that way. He could have severed sensitive wires that might have mortally wounded the big jet and sent them all plunging down into the dark ocean below. He had manually flown the aircraft for another five minutes when he suddenly felt the aircraft shudder as though a great weight had been placed on it. What was going on? He felt an icy fear in his stomach. Enough was enough. He keyed the microphone….

"Pan, pan, pan…London Control, this is Charter 104."

"Charter 104 …London Heathrow…go ahead."

"London…Charter 104 declaring an emergency," he stated flatly.

"Charter 104…what is the nature of your emergency?"

"London…we have unauthorized personnel aboard and he appears to have chopped a hole in the floor of the aircraft. The Captain is back dealing with him."

A rattle at the cockpit door made him turn in his seat. The door opened and Bowden stood in the doorway; Gostini sighed, much relieved. He pulled the oxygen mask from his face. "Wayne…what happened?" He stared closer at the captain and realized with a sudden sinking feeling that he was staring into sightless eyes just as the body was dropped to the floor.

"Jesus, Mary and Joseph..." Gostini said, switching on the autopilot and pulling himself up from his seat to deal with the shadowy intruder looming in the doorway. Though he had never been a physical person, the adrenaline surged and he prepared to do battle.

The shadow moved into the light of the cockpit and taunted him in a rasping voice. "Do you renounce your heathen God and all He stands for throughout eternity?"

Gostini stared at the tall stranger standing before him. He was dressed in black from head to toe. Despite the situation Gostini thought that the man didn't look mad. In fact he was extremely handsome, his black hair combed straight back, his deep blue eyes sporting a slight twinkle in them. And yet, at his feet lay Gostini's obviously dead captain, his body a crumpled rag.

Suddenly the man's head physically transformed from human to a reptilian looking creature and then back to the handsome stranger again. The co-pilot stared in horror, not believing what he was seeing. The monstrous creature's head was suddenly back and it spoke again, this time through bladed teeth on which thick, green saliva glistened.

"If you wish to live, tell me where *it* is." The voice coming out of the thing was low, almost seductive.

"M-Mother of God...w-what are you...?" Gostini stammered, fear and loathing obvious in his quivering voice.

"I am the future of earth and the eclipse of humankind," the Beast answered.

"I-I..." Gostini stammered, lost for words.

"Your symbol...your *relic*...where is it?" pressed the creature, persuasively, almost gently. Its human-sounding voice was at odds with its terrifying form. It didn't advance past the cockpit door.

To try to reassert his world, to try to force a sense of reality over what he was seeing, for just a split second, Gostini glanced back towards the glass cockpit with its computer screens, and modern controls which reassuringly told him this couldn't be happening. There could not be a horned, prehistoric form standing in the middle of this high-tech imagery; it was impossible.

But when he turned back, it stood there still, yellow, half-hooded eyes fixed on him. It threw back its cape. Explosive energy and strength massed in muscles that rippled and flowed beneath a black leathery skin – a nightmare come to life.

"Not with us…" Gostini whispered, now understanding it was looking for the special package they were supposed to carry to London.

"Then renounce His teachings and you may live…." The lie dropped from curled lips and the co-pilot knew it immediately for what it was. But to Gostini, rather than continuing to feel fear, he suddenly felt hope. In fact, the world of which he and Bowden had been a part for the past two years suddenly made sense. The mysterious priests, the cardinal, the secret flights and meetings; the whisperings about a *demon from hell* had all been about this creature. That was the bad news. The good news was a new, stronger sense of his Catholic faith flowed into him. It gave him the hope and the strength he would need for his few remaining seconds on earth.

"Renounce him! Renounce him! RENOUNCE!" the Beast screamed at him.

But Gostini, good Catholic that he was, slowly shook his head. And with a certainty reserved for those who knew without question that they were about to die, he closed his eyes and carefully answered the demon.

"Our Father, who art in Heaven, hallowed be thy name…."

~ 6 ~

The telephone only rang twice before Malachi turned over in his bed and snatched it from the cradle. Even as he said hello, he was grabbing his alarm clock and peering at the blue green numerals: Midnight.

"Mustavias? Heinz here. The plane went down."

"Plane? Our plane?" Malachi asked, tossing back the covers and sitting up on the side of the bed feeling his feet hit the cold floor.

"Yes ….on its first leg to London. I just got a call from United. It happened about three hours ago. As aircraft owners United was notified first. Someone finally thought to inform us.

"Are they sure?"

"Yes...happened over the channel...the French Affaires Maritimes and Her Majesty's Coast Guard have conducted a joint search and already located wreckage."

"Who was on board?"

"Just the pilots."

"Mother of God." He sighed and ran a hand through his hair. "Alright...have their families been notified?"

"Not yet. We just found out. It's all over the late news."

"They're sure it's ours."

"They don't make mistakes about these things. We're trying to find out what happened but all we know so far is that they declared an emergency because they suspected a door was ajar in mid-flight. They were cleared to descend to 9,000 feet and a little later they declared an unauthorized passenger on board. Then they just kept descending until they vanished off radar."

"Well for God's sake find out where their families live and get the priest from the local dioceses to them right away. Or rather have Castilloux do it...he's our PR guy. Also, see if there is anything we can do for their families. We all need to meet in an hour. Or at least the five of us left. There's going to be a lot of questions from the press as to why the Catholic Church had an A320 on charter and we'd better cobble together a press release and a lot of answers to questions we'd rather not hear."

"Right."

"Alright...wait a minute. The Relic. It was to be dropped off in London. It was on board! And, so was Gant."

"No...! When the aircraft was ordered back to New York to the leaser, Gant was afraid of foul-ups and took himself off the manifest. He's still here in Rome with the Relic and plans to fly to London on a commercial carrier later this evening. Sorry about that, Chief; you should have been informed."

"Not to worry," Malachi said, in relief. For once Gant's obsession with the Relic had paid off. "Gallo was expecting the package to be delivered by Father Gant. Find him at his hotel and get him teleconferenced in to our meeting so we're all on the same page. I expect there will also be hell to pay coming from our Supreme Pontiff."

"I'll get on it. And Malachi?"

"What?"

"Good luck." It was a strange thing for Rautenberg to say since he was the most pragmatic of the group and seldom indulged in idle salutations. Still, at this time it seemed appropriate.

"Thanks," Malachi said. "We'll all need it."

They rang off and Malachi began to dress. Where was Gallo, he wondered? The man should have made contact with Maria and Clay yesterday, at the latest. And called in to report.

As he moved to the bathroom he made a mental note to call Maria and see if they'd heard from the old priest. It seemed things were coming apart faster than he could fix them.

~ 7 ~

The knock on the door was gentle but firm. Maria opened it to find the stooped figure of Father Gallo standing before her. He smiled wanly and raised a hand. "Good morning Sister Maria. I gather you've been expecting me?"

"Father Gallo…yes…the cardinal just called and asked if we'd heard from you yet," Maria said. "He was desperate to talk to you…." She trailed off remembering her manners and stepped back gesturing him to enter. "Please?"

He came in carrying a small briefcase and she immediately began straightening up the room. "That's Mustavias, alright…always impatient," he said, putting down the case and looking about the room. "Where is our detective?"

"Clay is downstairs getting coffee."

"Well I hope he brings three…"

"I'll call the front desk," Maria offered quickly, but he merely smiled and waved the idea away.

"That's fine," he answered. "I'd just as soon talk to you first. The cardinal wants a full report on what you saw…you know when, where and how. And the Relic was sent here on our aircraft last night."

"The plane?" Maria asked. "Your plane?"

"Yes," Gallo said, puzzled by her change in demeanor.

"You haven't heard!?"

"Heard what?" Gallo asked, his tone a little sharper.

"The plane …it crashed," she said. "Last night…it crashed into the English Channel."

"It crashed?" Gallo whispered, his eyes wide in surprise. He turned and sat down on Clay's bed looking somewhat dazed. "How did it happen?"

"I don't know any details," Maria said.

"Of course, forgive me," Father Gallo replied. "Poor Father Gant? Who else was on board?"

"Just the pilots were on board from what I understand."

"I'll miss him," he said, his tone regretful.

"Father Gant *wasn't* on board," Maria explained, now wondering if the shock had been too much for the old man. "Father Gant wasn't on board."

"Oh he was aboard all right. He's the Keeper of the Relic so he would have been on board as well. And now the Relic is at the bottom of the ocean." His tone conveyed a puzzling air of finality.

"Just the pilots were on board, Father. Cardinal Malachi said that they were the only ones aboard. Father Gant is flying in later today."

"Are you sure?"

"Positive."

The key turned in the door of the latch and Clay entered juggling two cardboard coffee cups in his hands as he pushed open the door with his foot. "Excuse me," he said, looking at Maria. "Father Gallo?" He put the coffee on the dresser.

"Mr. Montague," Gallo said, standing up and shaking Clay's hand. "You would not remember but we met in a hospital in upstate New York."

"I do remember," Clay said. "I understand something happened to you? You went missing."

"A long story with an appropriate ending yet to be written," Gallo said, somewhat dismissively.

"Clay...the Vatican's aircraft crashed in the channel last night," Maria interrupted. "Cardinal Malachi called just before Father Gallo arrived. They are sure the pilots were killed."

"What happened?" Clay asked.

"I don't know....but those poor men are gone."

"Tragic...tragic," Gallo muttered, shaking his head. "Can we get room service here...get another coffee?"

Clay, puzzled, looked from Gallo to Maria. "I suppose so. I just found it quicker to fetch one from the dining room."

"Then if you don't mind, I'll just trot down there and get one," Gallo said, excusing himself and opening the door. "Back in a jiffy."

As the door clicked shut, Clay looked Maria. "Well he's all broken up."

"He's an old man," Maria said, by way of explanation.

"He moved pretty fast for an old man," Clay said, handing Maria her coffee container. She thanked him and gently squeezed his arm affectionately.

They were friends again despite Clay having figured out his true role in the hunt and storming out the room the day before. Maria had followed him down to the hotel bar where he seemed about to order a drink, but then thought better of it and settled for a Perrier. She joined him at a black leather upholstered semi-booth and apologized over and over again. She explained she hated the deception but whether he knew it or not he was being hunted anyway. To be sure *The Seven* were aware of this fact and hoped to use him to attract and engage Adramelech, however, they were doing everything possible to keep him safe. In fact, that was her primary role – to keep him safe by forewarning him of danger. And they truly did need his skills to help find their quarry. The fact they found it so soon at Highgate Cemetery was entirely unexpected.

Finally, Maria had hesitantly admitted she was finding her task a trifle disconcerting because of something she had never expected. She confessed that she knew it was wrong but she had some feelings for him. She blushed crimson when she said this, keeping her eyes downcast. Her words had elicited a feeling of joy within Clay and he'd nodded his forgiveness, sighed and suggested they forget his little tantrum and go out for dinner. When, at dinner, he had tried to tell her that he was in love with her, she had placed her finger on his lips and begged him not to do so. Not just now, she had said. He'd understood he was placing her in an untenable situation and so he took her hand, held it for a moment and then placed it back on her side of the table, symbolizing he was leaving the ball in her court.

Today he sipped his coffee, looked at her and realized he was truly head-over-heels in love with a nun. *Just great*! He pushed his feelings aside. "So what happened to the aircraft?"

"I don't know," she said. "I just heard about it from the cardinal. He called looking for Father Gallo and said for us to just sit tight. This crash is going to occupy them for the next few days." Maria began placing some clothes in a drawer. "Father Gallo kept insisting he is going to miss Father Gant."

"But not as much as his coffee," Clay cracked, with a shake of his head.

Maria shot him a look. "I kept telling him Father Gant was safe but he wouldn't listen."

"Did he say where he was for the last day and a half?" Clay asked. "Cardinal Malachi said he'd contact us yesterday."

"No, he said nothing."

Clay lay sat down on the bed and shrugged. "Well, if this is going to occupy them for a few days, what do we do?"

Maria hesitated. "I-I don't know. Stay put, I supposed."

"Thousand bucks a day, eh?" Clay shook his head. "Want to take a tour of London?"

Maria shook her head and with a tiny smile to herself muttered: "I hardly think that's appropriate right now."

"Hey! The alternative is staying in this hotel room." The rejection stung but then he caught her smile and it suddenly made everything better.

"Let's see what Father Gallo has to say."

"Of course. Maybe he'll give us some direction…*after* he has his coffee."

Maria gave him another look that he didn't bother to decipher.

~ 8 ~

As Clay and Maria waited for Father Gallo's return, Malachi was calling Robert Monarch, his late Aunt Helen's barrister and investment counselor in Boston. When he had him on the line, he cut right to the chase: how much did he have in the trust fund his aunt had set up for him and how long would it take him to access it? When he heard the amount, he almost dropped the phone.

"Are you sure?"

"I just received the statement today," Monarch explained, and Malachi could hear the rustle of papers thousands of miles away. "We mail them to you but, of course, you never open them. Over the years our financial people have made some excellent investments for you and cashed in a lot of stocks before the dot.com bubble burst.

We made you as liquid as possible. Between mutual funds, money markets, some stocks and a lesser amount of bonds, you have $8 million and change."

"Jesus!" Malachi said.

"I beg your pardon?"

"I was just saying a brief prayer," Malachi answered, realizing for the first time that he was a multi-millionaire. He'd known that his aunt had left him quite a bit of money but he had no idea it had grown so large.

The topic changed to how quickly he could access the funds. When he said that, in view of the amount, he would like to have a half million dollars deposited in his personal account, it was Monarch's turn to almost drop the phone. "My God man, do you know that you'll lose more than half of that in taxes? Ten percent right off for withholding if we do it in small amounts."

"Doesn't matter Robert, I need it."

"Why? Are you funding a revolution in the Catholic Church?"

"You missed your calling," Malachi said. "You should have been a comedian,"

"Sorry Cardinal," Monarch apologized, suddenly remembering who he was talking to. "I just know that Helen would want me to do whatever was best for you and redeeming half a million dollars will open you up to all sorts of tax liabilities."

"Not doing this will open me to liabilities you would never believe," Malachi responded, cryptically.

"Cardinal, I'm a lawyer as well as a friend. Is there anything I can do to help?"

"Just show me the money."

"We could leave your accounts alone, arrange a short-term loan, if you'd like," he offered.

"Just cash what mutual funds or bonds we need and let's get it done," Malachi said.

"It'll take a few days at best," Monarch said, giving up in his gentle attempt to persuade Malachi to reconsider. "I can have it transferred to your account by Friday, I would expect. Instituo per le Opere di Religione...right?"

"Yes...the Vatican Bank. You have my account number?"

"Yes," Monarch said.

"And the bank identifier code?"

"Yes…IOPRVAVX. It's all here."
"Good. And, Robert?"
"Yes?"
"I may need more."
"Jesus!" the lawyer said.

~ 9 ~

Father Gallo sipped his coffee slowly, blowing on it every few moments while Clay and Maria looked on. The old man appeared to be in a daze and had barely spoken a word since he returned.

"Are you alright, Father?" Clay finally asked.

"Yes…quite alright," he answered, and then went back to staring into space and sipping his coffee.

"We expected you yesterday," Clay said.

"Yesterday?" Gallo responded. "What day is it?"

"Wednesday," Maria answered.

Gallo looked at her is surprise. "What happened to Tuesday?"

Maria and Clay exchanged looks. Gallo took another sip of coffee and then said, hesitantly: "I've been having these blackouts."

"Have you seen a doctor?" Maria asked.

"No…no doctor. I-I remember landing at Heathrow…and then…everything is a blank. I only remember standing on a road – Swain's Road I think it was called – and summoning a taxi to come here."

"Swain's Road?" Clay asked, in surprise. "Near Highgate Cemetery?"

"I-I don't know…I just saw a sign," Gallo said.

"That's it," Maria said, with finality. "You may have had a stroke. I'm calling the cardinal."

"No, I'll call him later and mention it, my child," Gallo answered. "These blackouts aren't new; I've been having them for years. Right now we have work to do." After a few more seconds, he looked at them both. "I may have a lead."

"A lead? What sort of lead?" Clay asked.

"I think I know where *it* is," the old priest whispered.

"The demon?" Clay asked, realizing that for the first time, he wasn't referring to their quarry as a mad man or some other generic entity. He'd actually used the word *demon*.

"Yes," Gallo responded. "But apprehending it means breaking a few of Malachi's rules. And we'll have to leave as soon as possible."

"*We* have to leave?" Maria moved forward and knelt in front of Gallo who continued to sit on the bed with his coffee. "Father, it's the *Crusaders* who must deal with it. If you know where it is, you must tell Cardinal Malachi at once."

"No child... it's up to us," the priest said, his voice rising slightly with excitement. "We have one chance and we have to take it now! There's no time to lose."

Confused, Maria stood up and looked over at Clay trying to read his thoughts.

"What are you proposing?" Clay asked.

"We can't let him put it off any more," the priest mused, ignoring his question.

"Who," Clay asked, now a trifle more impatient.

"Malachi," Father Gallo said and stared glassily into his eyes. "He's known where it is time and again, and he's put obstacles in our path for years. He doesn't act when he should. He's too cautious."

"Cardinal Malachi?" Maria exclaimed in disbelief, rising to the cardinal's defense. "How can you say that?"

"You said Gant wasn't on the plane. Where is the Relic?" Gallo asked.

"I don't know," Maria answered. "Maybe in Rome?"

"Of course," Gallo said. "And yet, we know Adramelech to be here. Malachi didn't order Gant to take the relic on the plane."

"It's a good thing he didn't."

"Fortuitous indeed, this time. But why not?"

"I don't know...perhaps—."

She was cut off by Gallo. "Perhaps...nothing. The reason it's in Rome is that once again *he* is too cautious. Listen to me, both of you. We must secure the Relic and move on Adramelech while there is still time. Mr. Montague, whether you know it or not...you have been the cheese in a trap; my good friend Mustavias is pragmatic but not always above board. I'll call him, find out exactly when the Relic is coming and we'll plan from there."

"Father Gallo...," Maria began, but he silenced her with a wave.

"I have taken you into my confidence," he said. "Don't fail me."

"We need the *Crusaders*," Maria protested.

"I'll take care of the details," Gallo promised. "However, Malachi must remain at arm's length until we are underway at least." The priest's frustration was evident as he rose, muttering to himself. "Too cautious...too worried about exposure to the public...too worried about danger to our people. We don't have the luxury of a guaranteed, fail-safe plan of attack. We need the flexibility to change course as we see fit, to strike on its home turf and put it down for eternity. Doesn't that make sense?"

Maria stared at Clay who turned and walked to the window and stared out at the London street below and muttered: "This is bizarre."

"Yes it is," Gallo said, overhearing him. "But remember, Malachi sent me here to help you find the Beast. I'm doing that and we have to act now...for everyone's sake. After all, would he object to our killing it?"

"Of course not," Maria said. "But how do you know where it is?"

"My child, you may know I was taken once. Much of the memory of my capture and imprisonment was wiped from my mind. But periodically, I remember things. And now I am sure I know the location of its lair, where it goes to rest or plan or whatever it does...from time to time. I am reasonably sure that since Adramelech is here in the UK, he's heading home."

"Where is this 'home'?" Clay demanded, turning to face Gallo.

"A Scottish baronial castle on a moor," answered Gallo. "It's been under the care of his familiars for years. *When* he needs it."

Clay shuddered at the word "familiars." But Maria was not so easily convinced. "We have to call Malachi."

"I will deal with Mustavias," Gallo said firmly

Maria turned to Clay, torn between the sincerity of the priest and her loyalty to Malachi. Instinctively she moved closer to the detective for comfort and, without thinking, he put his arm around her. Gallo raised his eyebrows momentarily, but said nothing.

"Is this what we are supposed to do? Are you sure ...?" she asked

"What harm are we doing other than ridding the world of the scourge of mankind? Our cardinal friend will thank us later for taking the initiative. Let us not disappoint our good friend."

"You're sure of where it is?" Clay asked.

"With more clarity each day," Gallo responded.

Clay shrugged. "Well Cardinal Malachi said he was sending you to provide us with guidance, didn't he? So he trusts you to make the right decisions. Go ahead. Make your plans. We'll not interfere."

"The logic and deductive reasoning of a good detective," Gallo said, rising and heading for the door. "My room is upstairs. I'll call him from there. Since Gant is on his way, as soon as we have the Relic, we'll leave for the highlands."

As the door closed, Maria threw up her hands. "What do you mean we'll not interfere?" she said, in exasperation. "A few hours ago you wouldn't even admit this thing existed and now suddenly you're an authority on what we should or should not do?"

"Maria, he's being straight with us. Lately I've had to face a few of my own issues. I can't fool myself any longer. I saw it in Panama. I admit it. And, I faced its' 'familiar' in Vermont. The little bitch killed my friend and perhaps my wife in an attempt to get to me. So if Father Gallo thinks he can stop it now, we should help him."

"I don't like it." She turned and sat down on the bed, her hands folded in her lap.

"Look, I'm sick of the convoluted agendas of these people. For God's sake, look at how they operate. They move across borders without reserve, kidnap people with impunity, and throw the bodies of murder victims in the trunks of their cars like so much flour with not a thought for the police. I want this to be over and I want to make sure you don't get hurt. I couldn't stand for anything to happen to you." He looked at Maria, his eyes revealing what his voice wasn't allowed to say. She met his gaze openly.

Maria moved to him as he moved to her; they met and embraced. An electric-like tingle surged through their bodies as an unfulfilled hunger and a moment of wantonness sparked by the ache of a forbidden love they shared moved through them. They kissed, at first softly, and then with more passion and strength holding each other tightly. He rubbed his hand up the length of her spine and she shuddered and pressed closer. "I love you Maria," he said softly.

"No," she said, but didn't move away. "I can't...we can't...I-I have something I must do. Something...I-I can't put my feelings ahead of my-my duty," she stammered, her voice trailing off.

"Duty? Don't you have some obligation to yourself, to your own happiness?"

"I'm promised to God," she said, holding him tighter.

Clay was breathing hard, his heart hammering in his chest. Finally he let his feelings spill out. There was no denying the reality of the moment. "I love you, Maria. I don't know how it happened or why it happened, but I love you more than life."

"My vows...." She protested weakly.

He held her tighter feeling her small breasts pressing into his chest and the warmth of her hips solidly against him; every possible inch of their bodies made contact. "Nothing matters except us," he said, his voice shaking. "I promise you that we'll see this through and after it is over—."

"After it's over, we'll talk," she said, reluctantly removing her head from where it was pressed against his chest and looking up at him with soft, brown, doe-like eyes.

"Do you love me?" he demanded, refusing to let her go.

"I love you in Christ," she whispered simply, but with heartfelt sincerity. "That's all I can say now Clay. I wish I could say more. I-I'm so confused. This isn't for me. It's cruel to give me these feelings."

She felt him tense and start to pull away. She held him tighter. "No... don't! Just hold me for a few more seconds."

He did.

~ 10 ~

Malachi put down the phone and threw his feet onto his office desk. He'd been suffering some swelling lately and they needed to be up for a time. The doctor had diagnosed his condition as Type II diabetes, not serious yet and controllable with diet. He knew he should lose about twenty pounds and he would have to give up his penchant for chocolate. Of course, sacrifice was something he was used to on a spiritual level. On the physical plane, he found it more challenging.

Still, he'd just transferred $50,000 into the personal accounts of the remaining team members for their use in the pursuit of the *Hellspawn* and he felt good. He'd done the same for the *Crusaders* and Murphy and Langevin. To hell with the official budget. He could personally fund this hunt for a time. He said a silent thank you to his late Aunt Helen. After a moment he pulled out a Cuban Romeo Y Julieta Churchill cigar straight from Havana and ran his tongue over its entire length. The words *Totalmente a mano* signified it was hand rolled. He bit the end off, lit it and luxuriated in the heavy, pungent tobacco flavor as he smoked. A small reward for a creative solution to their problems. Somehow his victory again mitigated his vow of abstinence from tobacco.

Gallo's telephone report had been brief but thorough. He reported he was sure it was Adramelech that had attacked Maria and Clay. The demon was likely in Highgate Cemetery, a historic and abandoned graveyard of considerable size with all kinds of growth and nooks and crannies in which to hide. In fact, it would be hard to find a place more appropriate, Gallo had said.

He then told Malachi that he needed to have the Relic in the hands of the *Crusaders* by midnight. Malachi informed him the Keeper of the Relic would arrive in London by 7:10 p.m. He had personally moved his flight up. He gave Gallo the airline and flight number and added that he would also be coming to London the following day. He cautioned Gallo not to move on Adramelech until he got there.

Malachi hung up and immediately picked up the phone again. He asked his secretary to get Father Gant on the line. The priest answered and said he planned to leave on a redeye flight and would arrive at Heathrow in the morning. Malachi told him to cancel it; he was booked on a late afternoon flight. He told him that Gallo was sure the demon was in Highgate Cemetery and they needed the Relic there as soon as possible. Gant agreed to make the earlier flight and began questioning him on what he knew about the plane crash. "Not much," Malachi said. "They declared an emergency, claimed to have an unauthorized passenger on board and pressurization problems. They were then cleared to descend to 9,000 feet but seemed to keep dropping and disappeared off the radar screens. Her Majesty's Coast Guard cutters have retrieved pieces of wreckage but the pilots' bodies are still missing."

"May God have mercy on their souls," Gant said.

"They were good and loyal men," Malachi agreed. "And they helped get us to this point in our hunt for this demon. I fear we can expect the death of more before this is over."

"We have to destroy it before it gets any stronger," Gant said. "Or we'll truly face hell on earth."

"We'll get it." Malachi's steely determination came through loud and clear to Gant.

Gant hesitated for a moment and finally said: "If the Relic works."

"We've seen its power for good," Malachi asserted. "It healed Father Murphy and the scroll said the *Wood of the Cross* would rid us of this scourge."

"Yes, we must have faith," Gant agreed.

"That shouldn't be hard for us…since our whole lives have been based on faith."

"Where are Benito and the *Crusaders* staying?" Gant pressed.

"My secretary has already emailed you your itinerary and you'll find their hotel address there. We've booked you in the Halkin for tonight. I'll be there tomorrow."

"Then there's nothing left for me to say."

"Godspeed Reverend Father Fred."

Gant chuckled at the familiarity from a man who claimed not to stand on ceremony but often did. "Thank you, Your Extravagance," he answered.

"Smart ass," Malachi said, and hung up.

-- 11 --

Father Gant breathed a sigh of relief as the wheels of the Alitalia jetliner touched down at Heathrow. He loosened his grip on his heavy, silver-plated Crucifix on the empty seat beside him. He had deliberately removed it from where he usually tucked it into his cummerbund at the beginning of the flight because of the discomfort when he was seated. But still, it was one of his most prized possessions having been personally taken in hand and blessed by Pope John Paul II. Though it hadn't been a particularly bumpy flight, the other passengers also expressed their collective relief at being back on terra firma through a round of spontaneous applause.

Now, hours later Father Gant still found himself smarting from his confrontation with an airline check-in clerk who had forced him to check the Relic case with his other piece of luggage. Though it did not fit in the stainless steel prefab baggage mold used to measure carry-on luggage, he had maintained that he would keep it in his lap. The attendant and his supervisor, citing safety and security concerns, insisted the metal luggage case with the yellow florescent tape be checked. Since it was a condition of boarding, he had ensured the two combination locks on the case were engaged and reluctantly complied. Their one concession had been to faithfully promise him it would be on the same flight and it would be handled with a special designation so he could pick it up at the reclaim baggage carousel as soon as they landed. He wondered if they would have been so quick or so callous to consign it to the baggage hold of the aircraft if they had known that it contained a petrified piece of the Holy Cross on which their savior had been mercilessly crucified.

Fearful that the Relic might somehow be stolen, he reinserted the heavy Crucifix into the waistband of his cassock and was on his feet and moving towards the front of the plane before the aircraft had ceased its taxi roll.

"Father, please sit down," called a pretty red-haired flight attendant spying him from her jump-seat as he neared the front entrance. The sincere look of concern in her bright green eyes brought him to a stop. Grumbling, but rows ahead of where he would have been if he hadn't bolted for the door, he sat down in a vacant seat. The plane braked and he was up like a jack rabbit. He made it to the door where two attendants were opening it with the help of an airline worker outside.

"Thank you, excellent flight," he mumbled hurriedly, squeezing between them and triumphantly exiting the aircraft. Moving swiftly and effortlessly through the terminal, he thanked God for the European Union that did away with Custom & Immigration checks. He had just located the luggage carousel for his flight when he spied Father Gallo hurrying towards him.

"Frederick…so wonderful to see you," Gallo called, as he arrived and pumped his confederate's hand.

"Benito…I didn't expect you here," Gant said, with a pleased smile. "I thought I was to see you at the hotel."

"The Relic," Gallo said, gulping air after his brief exertion. "Do you have it?"

"I was forced to check it," Gant said, the exasperation still in his voice. "It should come out of there as soon as they turn the damn thing on." He pointed at the dark mouth of the luggage tube and the barely visible and motionless conveyor belt at the top of the carousel. The other passengers still hadn't reached them so they were alone except for a security guard who passed through the room barely giving them a glance.

"I know how we can get it right away," Gallo said. "I have a friend here who can let us take it right off the luggage carrier."

"Truly?" Gant asked, in surprise.

"Yes…he's an old friend," Gallo said. "You can tell me what it looks like and we'll retrieve it. Come with me."

Father Gant hesitated. "But if they turn on the carousel and we're not here…"

"They won't…it takes at least ten-to-15 minutes to get the carrier over here from the plane. We can intercept it before they begin removing the baggage from the cart."

"Are you sure…?" Gant asked, uneasily.

"I know people; give me the claim check and come quickly!"

"Security…" Gant ventured, but Gallo waved his concerns aside.

The two old men in their black robes hurried to a side door which opened before they even reached it as though activated by a switch for people with disabilities; they exited the baggage area and the door closed silently behind them.

Ten minutes later, with the Alitalia passengers milling about near the carousel, the conveyor belt started up and pieces of luggage began to pop out onto the baggage chute and slide down onto the rotating carousel. A polished aluminum case, sporting three yellow pieces of reflective tape, had just dropped down to begin its cyclical journey when Father Gallo stepped out of the crowd and seized it. He compared the tag against his own claim check, nodded and moved swiftly away from the others.

Father Gallo had just exited the room when there was a collective intake of breathe from the crowd and several female passengers screamed.

Father Frederick Gant's body was slowly squeezing itself through the conveyor opening of the baggage chute. Freed of constraints, the Keeper of the Relic slid face-up and upside down onto the carousel. The crossbeam and head of his silver-plated

Crucifix was sticking out of his throat. Massive amounts of blood were coursing from the wound in aggressive spurts flecking several horrified bystanders. It had run over the mortally wounded priest's neck and face, and drenched his white collar and cassock even as it turned his bright red hair a darker, blood red; the arterial spray continued to soil the highly polished floors.

The glassy-eyed priest struggled to take a ragged, wet breath and tried to roll over while sprawled among the luggage. As bags continued to plummet onto the carousel he clawed at his throat and struggled valiantly to at least raise his head. Desperate to live, his eyes gradually dulling, he looked for help as he was carried in a circle by the carousel, a grotesque display of horror and gore.

People who, moments before, had been jostling for position to grab their bags had now leaped back in panic, stumbling and shrieking. They stared in shocked fascination at his bleeding body.

Trying to warn anyone who would listen of an omnipresent danger, Father Gant opened his mouth to speak. Instead, bloody foam spewed forth and ran over his lips, nose and forehead. He sighed, his eyes rolled back in his head and he died.

* * * *

PART SEVEN

"ADAM'S CURSE"

Love, like Death,
Levels all ranks, and lays the shepherd's
Crook
Beside the scepter

Edward Bulwer-Lytton
THE LADY OF LYONS (1838)

~ 1 ~

Detective Chief Superintendent Ian Cruickshank stood with Cardinal Malachi in a small back-up command and security control room at Heathrow Airport. In case an emergency rendered the main control room inoperative, redundancy offered a remote area where information could still be received, observations recorded and decisions made. The detective wore a three-piece, brown tweed suit complete with white shirt, woolen tie and vest. Beside him, devoid of any church trappings, Malachi wore a charcoal grey suit with an open-necked cobalt-blue, cotton shirt. The two men stared up at the wall. Cruickshank had met Malachi at the gate when he arrived; by this time the cardinal was barely off his plane a full hour.

Facing them was a bank of 16 monitor screens with only one lit; a black & white still picture flickered on it as they watched. The camera was pointed at a luggage carousel cordoned off by police tape and guarded by a helmeted London bobby. Off to the side, still within camera range, two British Army soldiers stood with submachine guns at the ready. The camera had paused, freezing them all in position.

"Heathrow's baggage system actually runs under the airfield and handles more than 100 million individual pieces of luggage each year," Cruickshank said. "The normal carousel is the conveyor belt type that brings bags out a door in the wall, circulates them on the belt and re-enters the wall. This is the reclaim carousel where they come out of the ceiling and drop onto the racetrack stainless steel carousel. That's where it happened." He pointed.

Malachi nodded curtly, his expression unfathomable.

"Whoever stabbed him with the Crucifix must have been extremely strong," the detective continued. "It wasn't sharpened or pointed in any way and so driving it that far into Father Gant's throat took quite an effort." He paused, shaking his head. "Ready?"

"Yes," Malachi said, his tone clipped and angry.

Cruickshank nodded to a young video engineer operating the control board. The detective had assured Malachi that the man was covertly "one of his" and was sworn to secrecy.

The engineer pushed a button and the image on the screen flickered and was replaced by another image of the same location.

This time, however, the carousel was not surrounded by police tape. Suddenly Father Gant appeared in the picture. He stood anxiously examining the carousel and then turned in surprise. Father Gallo entered the frame and Gant reached out and shook hands with him.

"That's Father Gallo," Malachi confirmed.

"Yes," Cruickshank answered. "But watch what happens a little later."

Gant continued talking to Gallo, gesturing, half turning and eventually he handed a small cardboard ticket to him. Abruptly both wheeled and quickly walked towards a side door.

"There," Cruickshank said. "Watch this. Did you see it?"

"See what?" Malachi asked.

"Run it back," the detective said to the operator who did so. The video showed the priests make for the door. As Malachi watched, the door opened wide a good three feet in front of them of its own accord, and a few second later both men exited the baggage area.

"What did you want me to see?" Malachi asked.

"The door," Cruickshank said. "That is a high security door that has an alarm on it, an electronic security connection that is triggered if the bolt and the latch lose contact, such as when it's opened. The only thing that suspends the alarm for 15 seconds is if you swipe your authorized security pass right there." He pointed to a small metal wall plate near the handle. "They had no passes and yet it opened in front of them without anyone even being there."

"So what are we looking at? H.G. Well's Invisible Man?" Malachi asked, dryly.

"You tell me, Mustavias. There is no disability apparatus on that door. It's reinforced steel weighting almost 20 stone, and you have to pull it hard to get it open. I tried it myself. And, there was no recorded alarm when they went through."

"Maybe it was faulty. What about other cameras…?"

"Oh we caught them inside a few times. Then they went into an area where there were no cameras and the next time we saw Father Gant …." He nodded at the engineer who pushed another button. A second screen flickered to life and Malachi watched from a different angle as a mortally wounded Father Gant came out the luggage chute and dropped upside down onto the carousel with people drawing back in horror. The priest struggled to right himself and managed to raise his head for a moment and then dropped it as he died. For a full two minutes his body continued to rotate on the carousel and luggage continued to plummet from the chute, until security officers appeared on the run.

Malachi sighed and shook his head. "That bloody butcher. What about Father Gallo?"

"We've no idea. But for some unexplained reason, we did lose some footage of before the body arrived. No idea why. About 30 seconds seemed to have been electronically…messed up. "

"No doubt you are searching for Father Gallo?" Malachi's tone was ripe with worry; he feared the worst.

"In every crook and cranny of the airport."

"Well, it's likely you may find a body, unless he managed to escape from whoever killed Father Gant."

"Could he have…?"

"Father Gallo didn't kill Father Gant," Malachi said, cutting him short. "That I can assure you. Something else did and we can only pray that Benito escaped with his life."

"So you have some idea of who the perpetrator might be I take it?"

"I'm sorry my friend. All I can tell you is that we are hunting an extremely dangerous and resourceful person. Perhaps, I can tell you more after I've met up with some of my colleagues here in London."

"You've kept me in the dark for some time, Cardinal Malachi," Cruickshank protested.

Malachi raised his eyebrows at the formality and motioned towards the video engineer operating the cameras. Again Cruickshank waved away his concern. "He's also my brother-in-law. He's the reason we're able to be in here."

"Alright, if you say so," the cardinal responded.

"Did I mention that Father Nathaniel, Father Oberon and Father Vandetti showed up at Highgate Cemetery the night of the shooting?"

"They should have," Malachi muttered, watching the runback of the tape again."

"They questioned me like some second class constable about what happened. I didn't appreciate it."

"They were just doing their job."

"Which is…?" the Chief Superintendent inquired, his head cocked to the side.

"We've been over this countless times, Ian. I'm sorry...I can't tell you more than I already have."

"I told you about the tissue samples taken from the glass and frame of the car in which Montague and Lapierre were attacked?"

"Yes," Malachi said, trying to appear remote and disinterested. "Apparently someone mixed them up with some cadaveric tissue or something?"

"There was no mix-up," Cruickshank said, watching the cardinal closely.

"Well, I certainly can't explain it."

"*Won't*...you mean," the Chief Superintendent said. "Mustavias, despite your claim this is a Church matter, there are laws we have to follow. For God's sake, I've had some of your people shooting up Highgate Cemetery...I've had a young constable murdered the same night...and now we have one of your priests butchered alive at Heathrow. Withholding pertinent information in a murder investigation is a punishable offense; I can only do so much. My superiors are already on my tail."

"Look Ian, I can say they were likely committed by the same individual. But if I told you who we were chasing, you'd laugh." Malachi said.

"I don't find murder amusing."

"I know that...and I'm grateful for all your help."

"Give me his name...I'll run it through Interpol and see what we come up with."

"Trust me, my friend," Malachi said, with a mirthless grin. "He won't be in any database. Just give me another day."

"Twenty-four hours," Cruickshank said. "That's it! Then I'll haul you and the others into the yard for a little talk. Understood?"

"Thank you. Now this is extremely important. Did you find a three-by-two foot, aluminum case with Father Gant's name on it and the Vatican address? It was fashioned from airline strength aluminum, had yellow, reflective tape, I'm told, and featured two heavy-duty combination locks."

"No, all we have for Father Gant is a single piece of luggage with his clothes in it. There was no aluminum case."

"We desperately need to find that case if it's here."

"And I desperately need to find a murderer."

"There are more things in Heaven and hell..." Malachi began, but Cruickshank waved his hand to stop him.

"Twenty-four hours and you start talking to me."

They shook hands and within minutes Malachi was in a London cab and on his way to the Halkin Hotel. At the front desk he waited for Jean Marie, a desk clerk he knew from other visits, to call the room for Clay and Maria. The hotel was a small, boutique-design establishment noted for exclusivity and boasting a five-star rating as well as proximity to Hyde Park Corner. Though of contemporary Italian design, there were subtle oriental influences throughout that balanced its modernity with a feeling of luxury without being stuffy. Featuring 30 rooms and 11 suites, it was a mere 40 minutes from Heathrow. In fact, one of the reasons Malachi liked it was because of its authentic Thai cooking in its on-site and unparalleled "nahm" restaurant. The other thing he valued more than anything else about the Halkin was its discretion, something he had often needed as the hunt for Adramelech had intensified.

Jean Marie returned and shook his head. "They checked out, Your Eminence."

"Who checked out?"

"All of them…Mr. & Mrs. Montague and Father Benito Gallo. They left last night."

"Did you actually *see* Father Gallo?"

"But of course. He paid zee bills."

"There must be some mistake…" Malachi began, but quickly rescinded his contention when Jean Marie shook his head sympathetically. Of course there was no mistake. They didn't make mistakes at the Halkin. Malachi's mind raced. Father Gallo was alive. Did he, in fact, know what had happened to Father Gant? "What about 210 and 211? Under the names of Father Nathaniel and Father Oberon?"

Jean Marie punched a few keys and nodded. "They are still checked in. As a matter of fact, I am sure I saw some of them going upstairs about an hour ago."

The desk phone rang and Jean Marie excused himself for a moment and answered it. He looked at Malachi and nodded. He moved the phone onto the counter and handed the receiver to the cardinal. "It's for you."

The cardinal took the receiver. "Malachi here."

"It's Ian. We were going through more tapes. You said you were looking for an aluminum case, quite a large one?"

"Yes."

"Well I think we've found it. Or at least we know roughly who took it."

"Who...?" Malachi asked, pretty sure he knew who it would be.

"It was on a corridor camera. There weren't many metal cases that size about. This camera shoots in color and you said the case had pieces of yellow reflective tape on it as identifying markers? We saw one that perfectly matched your description."

"That might be it," Malachi said hopefully, his heart beginning to race. "Who took it?"

"Elderly man wearing a cassock? We caught him from the back but I'm pretty sure it's your Father Gallo. Same chap we saw on the other video."

"Well I've also confirmed he's alive alright," Malachi said. "Checked out of the hotel last night. I'll get back to you, Ian. Thanks." He hung up.

Noting that the cardinal had gone white, the desk clerk was about to ask if he could help when Malachi abruptly headed across the lobby and, without waiting for the elevator, bounded up the steps to the second floor.

He reached 210 and rapped sharply on the door. There was no answer. Just as he was about to knock again, the door opened a half inch and he found himself staring at the dark eyes, crew cut and square jaw of Father Kit Nathaniel. When the priest saw Malachi, he jerked the door wide and stepped back.

"You Eminence," he said. "We didn't expect you. We were told you cancelled your flight here. Father Gallo said..."

"Where is Father Gallo and the others?" Malachi demanded, not wasting any time. I'm told they checked out." He surveyed the room. Father Nathaniel was flanked by Fathers Robert Oberon, Pasqual Vandetti, and Serge Lavoie – the entire *Crusader* team. The three others were seated on the twin beds watching TV and drinking sodas. *The Simpson's* danced on the screen as Homer tried his best to outwit Monty Burns.

"They left for Rome last night," Nathaniel said. "To see you, I believe."

"Like hell they did," Malachi responded, angrily. "Like hell they did.

~ 2 ~

The Scotrail passenger train clicked and clacked its way northward on the West Highland line in the waning twilight through a barren wasteland of moss, rocks and sheep. Father Gallo, Maria and Clay sat in a nearly deserted, older car populated with navy blue velveteen seats and wood trim. With fewer tourists about, the conductor had informed them that the late fall brought abnormally low ridership.

Grey skies delivered freezing rain that pounded against the windows and ran in large rivulets horizontally across the glass as the diesel locomotive labored to pull them through the countryside. Clay stared out at the unending moor devoid of trees; nothing higher than scrub grass lived here. The monotony of the high countryside was only punctuated by the occasional small village; brief clusters of cottages with yellow windows glowed warmly in the cool evening light as they sped by. As the train made its way to higher altitudes, Clay glimpsed occasional patches of snow lingering in the shadows of large, rounded boulders scattered haphazardly on the moor as though remnants from some giant's bowling game.

The old priest was lost in thought again and hadn't said a word after they'd come back from the lounge car with packets of fish and chips. Not having eaten since the night before, they devoured them fairly quickly, washing them it down with bottles of sugar-free Raspberry Jetpop.

The day before, Gallo had returned to their hotel room at the Halkin, and told them he'd called Cardinal Malachi, and bade them pack up; the cardinal would meet them at their destination along with the *Crusaders*. He also advised Clay to pack his weapon in a suitcase rather than carry it, just in case they were stopped by some policeman. Clay agreed.

Before they knew it, they were on a night train from London, England to Glasgow, Scotland, an exhausting six hour journey. Since they weren't in sleeper cars, Maria had curled up on the seat beside Clay and slept with her head on his thighs. With one arm and shoulder propped against the window frame, Clay dozed fitfully, rocking with the movement of the train. Occasionally he awoke and watched Father Gallo staring unblinking through the window as, outside, periodic mournful howls of the locomotive whistle wafted back to them on the night wind.

The following evening they boarded another train out of Glasgow with Father Gallo hurrying them along; they weren't even sure where they were going. In the station in Port Glasgow, he told them he had telephoned and received further instructions from Malachi.

As Clay watched, the priest occasionally reached below his seat and touched the aluminum case with the yellow reflective tape containing the famed Relic. Clay eased upright so as not to disturb Maria and nodded at Gallo.

"So how did Cardinal Malachi react when you told him you knew where Adramelech is hiding?" he asked, giving up trying to sleep.

"He said to proceed there as quickly as possible and they will fly ahead and meet us in a village nearby."

"And that would be…?" Clay asked.

"Inverness," the priest said shortly. Then he added for good measure. "If he hasn't arrived, we are to make the next leg of the journey via the ferry at Ullapool."

"Ullapool? Where are we going?" Clay demanded, irritably. "There's no need to keep us in the dark, for God's sake." His lack of sleep was beginning to show. Maria roused and sat up. Though surprised at his sudden sharpness, she agreed with him and nodded. "Yes, Father. Where are we headed?"

Gallo gave them both a long searching look and then said apologetically: "You aren't running this show, Mr. Montague. I'm afraid I am."

"Well I don't have to be part of any show; neither Maria nor I will be present for much longer unless you clear up a few things."

Gallo smiled slightly and nodded. "Very well. What do you want to know?"

"Where are we going?"

"The Outer Hebrides," Gallo answered. "More specifically, we are taking a car from Inverness to Ullapool and a ferry from Ullapool to Stornoway. From there we will take another car to the west coast of Lewis Island."

"That's where he is?"

"Yes …the culmination of an eight-hundred-year search."

"Adramelech…" Maria whispered, both fear and wonder in her voice.

"But he was in London a few nights ago," Clay persisted.

"Yes…and doubtlessly he was headed for his lair," Gallo answered. "There is nothing in London for him. No wars to start, genocides to manage. He must be heading home."

"If you know exactly where he is, why didn't you tell anyone before this," Clay asked.

"Because he wasn't there till now."

"Did he give you his itinerary?" Clay asked, sarcastically, unable to shake the feeling he was being played again. Father Gallo was being evasive and he didn't like it one bit. "Why are you so certain he's there now?"

"Quite frankly, I don't know one hundred percent. But when I awoke from my last blackout, I knew exactly where he was headed as sure as I know my own name. Now we have less than an hour of train time left before we reach Inverness. I suggest you and Sister Maria get some rest."

Gallo stood, pulled his raincoat from the overhead rack, balled it up as a pillow and made himself comfortable on the opposite seat. Within seconds, Clay and Maria heard him snoring softly.

"Maria, I want you to stay in Inverness," Clay said.

"And leave you to face this monster with the others while I hide?" she asked. "Sorry…no."

"There is no need for you to be there," he said. "We know where he is and we don't need you to warn us of anything."

Maria gave him a long, searching look. "Clay, we're in this together. I don't know what will happen there…but I want you to know something." She paused, sighed deeply and then added: "I do love you."

"You love me…brotherly love?"

She looked nervously at Father Gallo and finally said: "No, I love you with all my heart, mentally, physically and with my soul. I still have obligations but I've fallen deeply in love with you." She choked back emotions, failing to meet his eyes though he couldn't take his off her. "I want you to know that. In case…in case…." she finished lamely.

Clay felt his heart surge with an unfamiliar joy and smiled at her. "And if we get out of this…?" He let the question hang, the hope evident in his voice.

"I don't know about my vows any more," she said, her eyes suddenly welling with tears. "I love my God but I love you too. I hope I never have to choose."

"Maria, I can't believe that God wouldn't want you to be happy. And I promise, if you'll let me, I'll devote every waking moment to making you happy."

"I know you would Clay. But I also must see this through first." She looked at him, sighed and reached out and took his hand gently in hers. "I know I sound a little fanatical. Still, I can't help how I feel."

He thought about what she was feeling and what it must have cost her emotionally to confess that she loved him. In effect, she was admitting something that was at odds with her entire focus in life. Even if he won her over in the end, and she left the church, would she regret it? Would it ultimately impair or even doom their relationship? She looked up at him. A declaration of love should have been filled with joy. Instead, she looked worried as well as tired and somewhat harassed.

"Don't worry," she said. "God will make everything come out as it should."

"Maria…you have no doubts, do you? You believe in God. I mean…really…as a both a physical and a spiritual entity that gets involved in our lives and loves us unconditionally."

"Of course. This demon we're hunting proves there is a celestial evil that was spawned before creation, just as the scroll revealed. And its existence supports the scriptures. By default it proves there is a God who loves us."

"But what kind of God allows the slaughters we see on earth?" He wasn't sure it was fair to ask Maria to answer questions that even the best educated theologians on earth had trouble explaining.

Maria took his other hand. Certainly he was asking her to answer age-old questions that plagued mankind since the dawn of reason. In defense of her Heavenly Father, she was certainly willing to try. "Clay…I'll tell you what I believe. I believe God gave us the gift of free will because he loves us. But with freedom come risks, and rewards and penalties. If He ruled our lives, we would hate Him for it. We would be nothing but His pets. So He allows us to choose our paths…to make of our lives what we wish. And then He brings us home to His love and we see where we did well and where we erred. Life doesn't end when we die. I think it's an endless cycle of learning in which we are engaged until we learn perfect love."

"Are you telling me I'll have to go through another life?"

Maria laughed and her voice seemed to tinkle musically. "Of course, I have no more knowledge than anyone else; no one knows what happens after we die. But I believe we are on a journey. And remember, we have our life energy. According to the laws of physics, energy can neither be created nor destroyed. But it can be changed. When we die, we change. That's all. At least that's what I have come to believe. Can you understand this? Can you free yourself to have faith?"

He tried again. "I still want you to stay at Inverness."

"I can't."

"And if Cardinal Malachi ordered you to stay there?"

She shook her head. "We'll discuss it later."

Clay sighed and they embraced. He held her tightly. "I just love you so much. It's weird, I don't know how it happened…but I do love you. I didn't know I was capable of loving anyone again. After Jody, I mean."

"Oh Clay…!" She rested her head on his shoulder and they took comfort in their togetherness until they sank into fitful dozes.

On the bench opposite, Father Gallo opened his eyes for a moment and frowned. "Sorry people…no happy endings this time," he muttered quietly.

~ 3 ~

"What is he up to," Malachi grated, watching the screen and seeing the back of Father Gallo vanishing down a corridor carrying the case with the Relic in it.

"I'll ask again: Any chance at all he killed Father Gant?" Cruickshank queried.

"No, no…Father Gallo somehow managed to escape from the killer and he's trying to save the case."

They were in a video viewing room at Scotland Yard. One half-finished coffee and one fully drained cup of tea sat on the conference table before them. Cruickshank pressed a button on the remote and the screen went blank. His two feet rested, crossed, on the table. His coat was off and he'd rolled up his sleeves. The buttons on his vest strained from his ample girth as he took a deep breath.

"What's in the case?" Cruickshank asked. "We're approaching the 24 hours I gave you."

Malachi rolled his tired shoulders. "A weapon. A most formidable weapon."

The detective's feet came off the table with a bang and he sat up straight in alarm. "Tell me it's not nuclear," he said. "It's not one of those suitcase nukes, is it!? Because we'll have a real problem if it is? I mean it. This can't go on–."

Malachi couldn't help chuckling at his reaction. "Relax Ian…take a valium…it's a piece of wood."

"Wood?"

"Yes…wood. Petrified wood."

"Wood? That's some weapon, my friend."

"We think it is."

"You actually mean a piece of wood with Semtex or C-4 or some type of RDX explosive tied or wired or nailed to it, right?"

The cardinal looked over at him. "The *Wood of the Cross*."

"*The* cross? You're having me on."

Malachi looked at him again. "Do I look like I'm kidding?"

Cruickshank stood up, his expression doubtful. Finally he shrugged. "Whatever you say. So…what's next?"

"We have to find them. Photos of all three are being sent from the Vatican to your fax here as you suggested."

"Fine. I'll get all-points out and say they are wanted for questioning in the death of Father Gant. That isn't far from the truth."

"It's urgent that we find them."

"Do you think they left the city?"

Malachi shook his head. "I don't know."

"Credit cards?"

"Photos, credit card information, driver license numbers; every pertinent detail we have on them should all be in your fax room right now."

Cruickshank stood up. "I'll get some people on it. If they bought tickets anywhere using their credit cards, we'll soon have their destination."

He left the room and Malachi went to the window and looked out on Broadway running beside the New Scotland Yard sign. What was his old friend Benito up to, he wondered? What worried Malachi most was that the old man seemed to have taken matters into his own hands. Rather than providing guidance, he was taking initiative. To take the Relic and go after Adramelech, he must be spoiling for revenge. But then more troubling questions came to mind. If Adramelech had tried to intercept and seize the Relic at the airport, how had he known about it? How did Benito get away? What was his destination? What had he told Maria? What about Clay Montague?

Within less than half an hour, Cruickshank was back with some notes scribbled on a yellow legal pad. "I have it. Your Father Gallo bought three tickets via Network Rail. They booked themselves to Glasgow and then booked three more from Glasgow to Inverness on Scotrail."

"Inverness…where exactly is that?" Malachi asked.

"The Scottish Highlands," Cruickshank said. "It's a little over six hours to Glasgow and about three and a half to Inverness by rail…." He looked at his wristwatch. "So that means they are already there."

"Inverness…" the cardinal mused. "Could Benito have remembered where he was held and is bent on finishing the job himself?"

"If I knew what you were talking about, I might comment," the detective said, somewhat miffed.

"Sorry. In time…" Malachi said.

"Time? It's long overdue, Mustavias. So what is it? A renegade has stolen funds from the Catholic Church? Possibly someone of rank? And based on the happenings at Highgate, he is also criminally insane?" He paused, an idea occurred. "Now I see. Father Gant stole a relic from the Vatican…this-this…piece of the cross? And Father Gallo was sent to intercept him."

Malachi stared at the Chief Superintendent and shook his head. "Not even close."

Cruickshank sat down and grunted. "Huh! Worth a stab, anyhow. So tell me."

"We are hunting a demon that was sent from hell to torment the righteous and support sinners. An arch demon directly linked to Satan."

"Blimey…now pull the other one; it has bells on it," the Chief Superintendent said with a sardonic smile. He stared at the cardinal trying his best to catch a glimmer of amusement in the man's eyes. But Malachi just returned his gaze, his eyes deadly serious. Finally, Cruickshank chuckled. "You're serious? A *demon*? Here on earth?"

"That's right."

"A flesh and blood demon who buys newspapers and has milk delivered to his residence, or a ghostie, will'o'the wisp demon that we never see, but we hear rattling chains and such?"

"The kind who rips the hearts out of a pair of London Bobbies in Soho, takes the head off another in Highgate, and eviscerates streetwalkers for pleasure," Malachi said.

"The Ripper?"

"That's what you call him…but we know him as Adramelech."

The detective picked up his pencil. "Is that his first or last name?"

"That's the only name he's got. Listen to me, Ian. This is not a joke. We are *not* chasing a human fiend. This is a true demon from Genesis that has been here since time began. The Catholic Church first realized the veracity of the demon slightly more than 800 years ago. Since then, we have been hunting it and occasionally killing it throughout the ages."

"Then…why is it here now…if you killed it, I mean?"

"Because he's immortal, my friend. Each time we manage to kill him with a blessed pike or stake through his heart, or decapitation with a blessed sword, he has stayed down for years or even decades. But then, invariably, the murders start again and we soon find evidence that he's alive once more and wreaking havoc on earth. In fact, we believe he's aided some of the greatest mass murderers through the ages."

The Chief Superintendent sat back in his chair and absentmindedly began pulling at his mustache. Abruptly he sat forward. "Mustavias, if you are toying with me…?" he threatened.

"No joke, Ian. As an official of the Most Holy and Apostolic Catholic Church, I give you my word. We are hunting something supernatural. This being has plagued mankind since its inception. As to its final purpose, we can only speculate." Malachi watched the Chief Superintendent carefully to see if he was accepting the truth of the revelation or not.

"And it's *immortal*? Can't be killed?"

"Not permanently. At least so far. We know it has limitations but we know less than we'd like. The problem now is that Father Gallo has apparently convinced our private detective and Sister Maria – people we enlisted to help find it – that he can finish it off himself. And, I'm afraid he's not going to be successful."

"Out of curiosity, why do you think this 'piece of the cross' has any place in this drama?"

"One of the Dead Sea Scrolls, one that was never catalogued because we got to it first, hinted that if the *Hellspawn* was touched by the *Wood*–"

"*Hellspawn?*" Cruickshank asked, interrupting.

"Another name for the demon. Anyhow, the scroll told us that if the demon was touched by the *Wood* – and we are assuming it's the *Wood of the Cross* – then it would be forever vanquished. Killed once and for all."

"Look, old boy, I respect your beliefs…I most certainly do," Cruickshank said, stuffily. "But, really…I think we have to get a grip here."

"These aren't beliefs, Ian; these are facts, and you have the bodies to back them up."

"This Ripper is a madman, no doubt…but he is a human madman."

"Well you asked," Malachi said, shrugging. "It's really not important what you believe, Ian, but I need your help to find our people."

"You have that, Cardinal. I would say that your next move would be to fly to Inverness as soon as possible."

There was a knock at the door and Cruickshank hollered: "Enter."

A young constable stood in the doorway. "Chief Superintendent, there's a Father Murphy here to see you. Or rather to see your guest, Mr. Malachi?"

Malachi sighed. "Show him in, Constable."

~ 4 ~

When they reached Inverness, the weather was penetratingly chilly. A light fog rolled through the rental parking lot. Clay pulled Maria aside as Father Gallo went to rent a car for them. "I want you to stay here. We'll get you a room in a hotel and when it's over, we'll be back for you."

"I can't stay here, Clay," Maria insisted.

"Maria, I love you; I can't take a chance on losing you.'

She looked up at him, her eyes earnest and full of feelings. "This isn't about us. It's about something much bigger. Cardinal Malachi brought me halfway round the world to help. None of us know what we're facing and I can't let anyone down. Everyone is at risk. So hush. Please!"

Father Gallo returned from the Auto Europe desk with car keys in one hand and a map and a travel book in the other. He'd rented a blue Opel Vectra Wagon. Handing the keys to Clay, and the map and book to Maria, he said: "Clay, you'll drive and Maria will navigate."

"Fine," Clay said, his tone somewhat sullen. He was both disappointed and frustrated that Maria insisted on accompanying them. His instincts told him it wasn't a good idea.

"Smile...we may be moving towards a defining moment in our lives," the priest said, picking up his suitcase in one hand and the aluminum case in the other.

"I've had all the defining moments that I need in my life," Clay responded, trying not to sound bitter.

Maria and Clay had already checked their larger cases into lockers at the train station and transferred a few needed clothes into a single, smaller case belonging to Maria. The Ruger .44 and his ammunition and holster was also in their case wrapped in one of Clay's shirts. Unfortunately, neither had packed any warm clothing. The elderly priest didn't seem to be aware of the cold and dampness as they walked out to the automobile under grey clouds and stray wisps of fog; fortunately for him, he wore a raincoat.

"It's okay," Maria said to Clay who was now exceptionally quiet. "Father...where are we meeting Cardinal Malachi?"

"In Stornoway. We'll drive to Ullapool and take the ferry from there to Stornoway on Lewis Island."

"Why aren't we waiting for him here?" Maria persisted.

"Because there's no time to waste. Now, my dear...we'd better go."

A rental agent appeared and accompanied them to the automobile, helped place their bags in the car's "boot," and they were soon on their way. After a few minutes they were on the A9 on their way to Tore, a few miles north of Inverness. They would then turn onto the A835, a straighter, more open highway towards their final destination. They drove in silence.

The craggy and sometimes wooded land moved by more quickly as Clay increased their speed. The countryside changed slowly. Hugged by mists below the levels of the mountains, pale ghost clouds sifted through the valleys while the mountaintops, dark and soaked by freezing drizzle, poked through above like disembodied islands.

At a junction with A832 they came upon a magnificent waterfall plunging at least 150 feet into the chiseled, 200-foot deep Corrieshalloch Gorge. The road skirted the north edge of Loch Broom; Clay accelerated once more toward Ullapool.

"I figure it's still about 90 kilometers to Ullapool but we've been on the road for almost an hour," Maria said to Clay, holding a map and looking over the rims of a pair of drugstore reading glasses.

Clay felt his heart beat a little faster as he thought of how pretty she looked. "That's because I can't get any decent speed on these roads," he answered, by way of diversion. "Also, I have to keep re-adjusting my thinking on what side I should be driving." They drove for another 15 minutes.

"There's lots of time," Father Gallo said, finally. "The ferry doesn't leave for hours."

"Oh, we're getting closer," Maria said, looking at the map. We just have to go round this inlet."

Less than 25 minutes later they reached Ullapool, a compact seaside community surrounded by low hills covered by a light dusting of snow. As they came over the rise and approached the town, they could immediately see the *MV Isle of Lewis* ferry sitting at dock, dwarfing the town buildings around it. The harbor was grey and unfriendly. Clay noted a choppy sea spotted with plenty of white caps as the small car reacted to a sudden gust of wind, heading for the road's shoulder. He quickly regained control and straightened it.

They found it was easy enough to secure tickets thanks to the lateness of the season. As they lined up in the cueing area to board the ferry, Maria read a pamphlet saying that the vessel could take 970 passengers and 123 cars, and was the largest of the Caledonian MacBrayne fleet.

After being directed aboard the ferry, they had to leave their automobile for the duration of the journey. As the trio trudged from the B deck upstairs with hands in pockets, they could hear the clank of metal on metal and the hollow roars of the last few cars being driven onto the decks. The smell of oil and grease mixed with the sweet smell of gasoline, or petrol as the Brits called it, was everywhere. After the up and down ride in the automobile, Maria felt slightly nauseated and was glad to escape the smell by exiting the motor vehicle deck. Both Maria and Clay were shivering from the cold. Once on the passenger deck, they went in search of the ship's gift shop while Father Gallo headed for the passenger lounge. The old priest had asked them to buy a flashlight since they might have to travel in the dark at some point.

The shop was well stocked with souvenirs as well as heavy clothing including a selection of traditional knit Irish Aran sweaters and weather-proof anoraks. They purchased three sweaters and three anoraks and a long, black metal, halogen flashlight.

"Aye, these will keep ye warm," the lady sales clerk said. "It's getting a wee bit brisk out there. Going for a late holiday, are ye?"

"I'm not sure where the hell we're going," Clay grumbled, more to himself. He was still disturbed that Maria chose to accompany them.

The clerk looked at him and smiled: "If ye don't know where you're goin', how will ye know when ye get there."

"A good point," Clay answered, as he paid for their purchases with a Vatican Bank credit card issued in his name. The sale went through and Clay caught Maria looking at him.

"Oh Clay," she said, in a teasing voice trying to lighten his mood as she accepted a yellow anorak. "You've bought matching colors for us."

Clay realized she was right; no use trying to deny it. He'd bought a small and large yellow anorak for himself and Maria, and a medium in hunter green for Father Gallo. He mumbled something about visibility and made for the door with Maria following and the lady sales clerk grinning after them. "I'm sure you'll have a fine time lad…wherever ye wind up," she called

They carried the clothing back to the passenger lounge and found Father Gallo seated on a comfortable, upholstered vinyl bench seat with his bag beside him. He was carefully examining a map splayed out on a round coffee table secured to the floor in case of heavy weather. The priest nodded his thanks for the clothing that Clay put beside him on the bench seat.

"See where we're supposed to go?" Clay asked.

"Why don't you get something to eat," Gallo inquired, without answering his question or looking up; he then added that he wasn't hungry. They agreed to do so as the boat gave a blast of its horn and the deck vibrated ever so slightly with the throttling up of the engines. Through the window they could see the mountains surrounding the harbor sliding by and knew they were underway.

Though hungry, Maria and Clay decided to watch their departure before eating. They donned their new clothing and made their way to the aft upper deck where, outdoors, they discovered rows of red plastic seats in the open where they could watch the departure. They inhaled the bracing smell of the salt water and fought the wind to get to the seats, hanging on to each other and laughing, their concerns forgotten for the moment. As they sat down, a brilliant yellow, long-stemmed rose blew across the deck towards their feet and Clay snatched it up. "Where did this come from," he said aloud looking around in vain for someone with a bouquet of flowers that might be short a yellow rose.

"I don't know, but yellow roses are my favorite," Maria said. "They signify happiness, friendship and 'I care'." She looked directly at Clay. "Which I do." There was no coyness, no qualifications in her statement.

He stared back for a moment. Despite everything, he couldn't help feeling joy at the fact they had admitted of their feelings for each other. Clay presented the rose to her. "For her ladyship."

"Thank you, my knight," she answered in mock earnestness, feeling somewhat silly but not caring.

They both smiled, a stolen moment realized. Clay looked into her dark, earnest eyes and saw that she did, indeed, love him.

"Let's go up forward by the railing," Maria said, suddenly excited. Though they had barely sat down, they rose and lined up at the railing with a few other passengers to watch as their ship moved out and around Ullapool Point and headed for the mouth of Loch Broom. Next they worked their way up to the bow. They zipped up their anoraks and Clay pulled up Maria's hood and fastened it. Her dark eyes flashed at him and she smiled and nestled close.

As they got out into open water to cross The Minch, the larger swells caused the ship to noticeably rise and fall, hesitate, stagger, and surge forward again as the propellers dug in. The bow was now sending up great sheets of spray and a cutting wind made both Maria and Clay turn around whenever it dug into the sea. They took the spray on their backs.

After some time, with the mainland receding in the distance, and the smell of the salt air in their nostrils, they went below into the cafeteria and ordered bowls of steaming mutton stew. The ship was encountering heavier seas and they had to eat with one hand cupping their bowls to keep them from sliding off the table. Wisely the ship's fitters had incorporated a raised beveled edge around each table to help keep plates and coffee cups from sliding off.

Though the *MV Isle of Lewis* was the largest in the fleet, the seas were getting heavier and more than a few passengers had stopped eating. With serious looks on their faces, they began to look for the lavatories. Neither Clay nor Maria felt sick. They commandeered abandoned newspapers from deserted tables to read. Clay found himself looking at *The Hebridean* newspaper.

"Darn, I left my reading glasses in the car," Maria said.

Clay offered to get them and was soon down on a darkened deck dimly lit by security lights. He staggered among the parked cars as the ship pitched and rolled, staying erect by supporting himself with hands on different vehicles. He could see the Opel parked near the far bulkhead and holding on to other autos to steady himself, he made for it.

A shadow crossed one of the security lights flicking in and out in an instant.

Clay looked up. Nothing. Must be my imagination, he thought.

The ship rolled again. Bracing himself he started for their rental once more but caught a shadowy movement out of the corner of his eye. He stopped and stared towards where the movement had been. Again, zip. Still, as he squinted he found his heart beginning to pound a little harder. Visions of the witch-like little girl flooded his mind and he cursed himself for leaving the revolver in the carry-all with Maria. For a moment his thoughts turned to escape but, instead, he chastised himself for getting spooked. He started for their car again, but this time the heavy shadow moved directly in front of the security light and he saw the outline of something large, dark and menacing.

Abruptly the ship pitched and there was a rush of movement as the shadow charged him.

~ 5 ~

"Bishop Castilloux and I have been to Father Gallo's quarters as you requested Mustavias, but we found little," Monsignor Heinz Rautenberg said, speaking from his office in the Vatican. "Particularly since we didn't know what we were looking for other than 'something out of the ordinary.' What is going on? Has Father Gant reached you?"

"Father Gant is dead," Malachi said, flatly. He adjusted the phone to his ear. "And Father Gallo has the Relic and has set out for the Scottish Highlands."

"Frederick is dead? How?" Rautenberg asked, his voice catching.

"We think Adramelech somehow knew he was coming in at Heathrow and tried to steal the Relic. Benito went to meet Frederick; he was a little luckier and managed to escape with it. Unfortunately, Father Gant was stabbed in the neck with his own Crucifix."

"That depraved, sick, evil slimy bastard," Rautenberg cursed. "I wish I were there to personally send him back to hell where he belongs."

Malachi sighed heavily. "I know. Frederick was a good man."

"And a devoted brother of the church. May God rest his soul." Rautenberg was silent for a moment. He then brushed aside his sadness and his professionalism took hold; he got back to business. "Did you say Benito was on his way to Scotland?"

"As near as I can figure, he's remembered where he was held captive and is bent on trying to put an end to Adramelech himself."

"Is he totally addled?" Concern was evident in Rautenberg's voice. "How does he expect to do that?"

"He has Sister Maria and the detective with him."

"That should slow the Beast down for a full second or two. Lot of good they'll do in a fight with an emissary from hell who eats people like breakfast cereal."

"Father Gallo also has the Relic. Superintendent Cruickshank is trying to get a police helicopter to fly us to Inverness now. My only problem is to track him once we get there."

"Who is with you? Should Austin and I come?"

"No time...you hold the fort. I have the *Crusaders*...and a late arrival...Father Murphy."

"I've had several calls asking if I knew where Dermott Murphy was...now I do."

"He said he felt he owed it to us to help since we saved his life."

"I'm getting on a plane," Rautenberg said.

"It's too late, Heinz. Wait a minute, please!"

The Monsignor waited impatiently while Malachi held a side conversation and then he came back on the line. "Never mind, we have a copter...but it will only take six of us including the pilot and his police observer, so I will take two of the *Crusaders* – Fathers Oberon and Nathaniel – and Inspector Cruickshank."

"What about Murphy? He's a pretty tough hombre."

"No...I have no idea what I'm going to find in Inverness but I think Ian Cruickshank, a Detective Chief Superintendent of Scotland Yard, will likely be more useful – able to grease some wheels there if we need cooperation or additional help. Oh, by the way, I have a satellite phone and will call you as needed."

"Mustavias? For God's sake...be careful."

"John 5:1...*We are of God...but the whole world lies under the sway of the wicked one*. Careful is out the window, my friend. This may be our last go at this bugger."

"Cardinal, it should be me there instead of you. You are worth far more to our cause. It doesn't make sense to risk you."

"Heinz, if it gets us, we need committed soldiers in the Vatican to carry on the good fight. And you, Jean and Peter must be ready to find others of suitable intellect, as well as the will to re-form *The Seven* and start again. I have left a letter on my desk in which I appoint you as leader should I...be incapacitated."

"Cardinal, you do me a great honor but I doubt I can fill your shoes."

"You are well qualified to lead *The Seven*, my friend. If we don't kill it, then I have every confidence you will find this dark seed and put an end to it one day."

"Are you saying good-bye, old friend? It sure sounds like it." There was a catch in his voice and he covered it by clearing his throat.

"Who knows? Without meaning to be overly dramatic, we each go to our destiny and do our duty." Malachi paused. "I'm beginning to sound like a rerun of an old war movie, am I not?"

"A little," Rautenberg answered with a smile in his voice in spite of himself. "Still, they never faced a battle such as you are about to face."

"Maybe not...but dead is dead. And that's pretty much an iron-clad guarantee if we loose this one."

~ 6 ~

With the shadow racing towards him at almost superhuman speed, Clay didn't waste any time. He hoisted himself onto the hood of the nearest car and readied himself for a kick at his adversary.

"What do you think you are doing, lad? Get down from there!" came a voice out of the darkness as a rotund, grey-haired sailor clad in an oversized goose-down parka and watch cap slid to a stop in front of him. "That last wave almost sent me right through that kraut wagon there, thanks to you." The man, obviously too well fed, gasped for breath after his unexpected "downhill" run.

"I-I'm sorry," Clay said, the relief evident in his voice. "I thought you were someone else."

"There's someone else down here?" the crewman asked.

"No, I thought my friend had followed me down here."

"Well, off the automobile please; the owner wouldn't be very appreciative."

"Right. Sorry about this," Clay said, climbing down off the Volkswagen. "I just need some reading glasses from my car over there."

Clay opened the Opel, grabbed the glasses and quickly made his way back to Maria, pushing himself off steel walls in the corridors as the seas became rougher. As it turned out, she wasn't in the cafeteria and their table was empty. He made for the passenger lounge where he found Maria and Father Gallo arguing in low voices.

"What am I interrupting?"

"He hasn't called Cardinal Malachi."

"What?" Clay was both shocked and dismayed. "Why not?"

"Let me explain if I can," Father Gallo said, wearily. "Many years ago, when I left your hospital room in New York, Adramelech was waiting in the shadows with the Little Witch. He took me and when I awoke, I was being held captive in some sort of medieval-style castle; I didn't know where I was. He kept me for almost six months exposing me to the most horrible of sights, sights of hell and damnation. For some reason I was then set free and made my way to civilization. Some Good Samaritan took me to a hospital and word got to Cardinal Malachi who had me brought to the Vatican. Because of Mustavias, I am alive. And now, I am going to finish off this demon once and for all. When we dock, we'll wait until dark. I will only need your help until I'm inside his domicile; then you may leave and I will do what is necessary."

"With the Relic?" Maria asked, nodding towards the aluminum case half under the bench and guarded by his legs and feet.

"Yes…with the Relic," Father Gallo answered. "Cardinal Malachi told us of your first encounter with the Relic in the garden. Do you sense anything now, Maria?"

"Yes. I sense confusion. I sense anger. I sense betrayal."

"From the Relic?"

"No, from you Father. You must feel betrayed by God to have let you suffer as you did but you must not let this feeling for vengeance impair your judgment."

Gallo smiled. "God had nothing to do with it, my child. That demon is all powerful here on earth. And now, I must end its reign of darkness. So don't impede me. Let me get on with my revenge."

~ 7 ~

The wash from the Eurocopter EC 145 helicopter rotor blades beat down on Cardinal Malachi and Father Murphy as the men stood beside it, instinctively hunched over to avoid the blades. Off to the west, the sun, a gold ball, dropped steadily towards the horizon. Heavy clouds were already moving in and reducing the ambient light though it was just past six o'clock. The late autumn air was chilly but neither of the two men seemed to notice as they argued. They were standing at the heliport portion of the airport in Lippitts Hill, Loughton, where three Metropolitan Police Helicopters were based; two were now out on patrol and Chief Superintendent Cruickshank had called in a lot of favors to secure a third for the next 24 hours.

Murphy, dressed in a dark suit and long dark cape, held his broad-brimmed dark hat secure as Malachi, bareheaded, but sporting a borrowed police parka, shook his head emphatically.

"You must take me," Father Murphy shouted at the cardinal.

"There is no room, Dermott. It's been configured for four passengers and police cargo."

"Leave the police observer."

"We can't. At least one police officer from the Air Support Unit must be aboard for us to fly. I'll call you."

"Call me?" Father Murphy said, his anxiety showing on his face. "You aren't going to a dinner party, man." He regretted his tone and words the moment they were out of his mouth. "Sorry, Your Eminence...I didn't mean--!"

"Never mind Dermott," Malachi said, with a smile. "It's fine. Now, we have no time to waste. We have tracked them to Inverness so far. After that we have no idea where they are headed and no way of finding out, so it's going to be a catch-as-catch-can. If you happen to find out anything or they get in contact with Heinz or Jean or yourself, call me. This is the number for my global satellite phone." Malachi put a hand on Father Murphy's shoulder. "Thank you for the offer."

Fathers Robert Oberon and Kit Nathaniel, and Inspector Ian Cruickshank watched from inside the copter as Malachi finally jumped aboard and slammed the door. The police constable in the co-pilot's seat made a pushing motion with his hand and Malachi locked down the handle to secure it as they rose into the air. At 100 feet, they saw Murphy looking up from the tarmac as the pilot advanced the throttle. The twin engines whistled and they were on their way through the evening sky towards Inverness. Though a carpet of London's multi-colored, jeweled lights seemed to stretch forever in every direction, it wasn't long until they were over-flying the dark countryside.

"The pilot says we have a good tail wind so we should make it in about three hours – ETA about 9:00 P.M.," Cruickshank said to the cardinal. "And this craft's top range is about 700 kilometers so, with a little luck we won't have to refuel."

The pilot turned in his seat and shouted: "Myles Frazer." He extended his hand backward and Malachi clasped it for a moment. "My observer, Police Constable Arthur Cockerill." Both the pilot and the observer wore helmets sporting night vision goggles tipped up out of their way but ready to be lowered to eye level for night landings.

Malachi nodded and waved towards the two *Crusaders*. "Fathers Kit Nathaniel and Robert Oberon." Both men waved and then decided to wile away the time by checking the heavy navy blue canvas bags of equipment they had brought on board. Both priests were wearing their white clerical collars again, he noted.

As they flew, Fathers Oberon and Nathaniel pulled their bags from the back, opened them and began to prepare. They used speedloaders to punch .50 caliber bullets into their revolvers and then reloaded the speed loaders, thumbed 9 mm Parabellum shells into their submachine gun clips, and counted their comprehensive supply of concussion, incendiary, stun and fragmentation grenades. Next they broke out six-inch square blocks of C-4 explosives, taped a few together and stored them back in their bags. Finally each pulled out a modified M16A2 rifle with a cut-down barrel for close-combat and then clipped PAQ-4 infrared scopes to them. Squeezing oil from time to time into appropriate spots and then wiping it off, they worked the actions to ensure the weapons would perform flawlessly. Next they pulled out carbon steel commando knifes, tested the blades with their thumbs and pushed them into sheaths which they strapped to the calves of their legs.

In the front, Constable Cockerill's eyes became big as marbles as he stared at the priests and saw the arsenal they carried. He started to say something to the grim, unsmiling men but caught Cruickshank's eye; the Chief Superintendent gave a barely perceptible shake of his head and the young policeman turned and assumed the eyes-front position. What he didn't see was probably a lot better than what he was seeing, he decided.

The two priests, absorbed totally in their work, didn't seem to notice. They continued checking equipment that included ropes, web harnesses, crossbows and bolts as well as mallets, stakes, Crucifixes, and plastic bottles of holy water. Each one took out and hung a cloth Immaculate Heart scapular around his neck and offered one each to the pilots, Malachi and Cruickshank. Malachi accepted his, hung it round his neck and tucked it under his turtle neck. The Chief Superintendent examined the green cloth with the image of the Sacred Heart on it and looked at the cardinal. Malachi held out his hands, palms up and said nothing. The superintendent decided that there was nothing to lose so he placed it carefully around his neck. The pilot and observer exchanged questioning glances but did likewise.

With that, Cruickshank and Malachi let their heads rest back against the seat cushions and were soon fast asleep.

~ 8 ~

Father Dermott Murphy pulled up to the ramp at Stapleford Aerodrome in Essex. The daylight was almost gone. Among the many parked private aircraft, one over to his left blinked its landing lights on and off. He spun the rented Volkswagen and drove over to meet the pilot disembarking from his yellow Cessna 210 Centurion. The man motioned for him to park his automobile beside a small, half-moon, steel Quonset hut off to the right. The hut had a sign on top that was almost larger than the facility itself. It read: *Grantham Air Charter Services*.

Murphy parked the small car, took his heavy, oversize, canvas soft-sided suitcase, and lugged it over to the man. The pilot was wearing a ball cap, blue jeans, aviator sun glasses and a battered bomber jacket with pens and pencils sticking out of various sleeve pockets. The priest handed him an envelope with his left hand. "Dermott Murphy," he said extending his other hand which the pilot shook. "One thousand pounds, sir. As agreed."

The pilot accepted the money. "Colin Grantham," he answered and was about to open the envelope and then gawked at Father Murphy's white collar. "You're a minister?"

"Catholic priest," Murphy said, changing his grip on the heavy suitcase. The two *Crusaders* who had been left behind had been most generous with their wares. "Can we get started?"

"Quite," Grantham said, in his proper-sounding, matter-of-fact English accent; he went to check the envelope, regarded Murphy's collar once again, and pocketed it without bothering. He looked at the twilight, took off his sun glasses and stored them in a case which he had clipped to his belt. "As I said, she'll cruise at a little over 300 kilometers an hour and we do have a tailwind so we should land in Inverness around 21:30 hours."

"Nine-thirty?"

"Yes. Barring weather changes."

"Is there a spot in Inverness where helicopters land?"

"I'd guess the heliport is also at the airport but I can check my Chart Supplement after take off."

Murphy nodded. "Can I use a cell phone once we're in the air?"

"Depends on your service. But I have a Globalstar satellite phone if you need to use one. It'll work just about anywhere on earth. Now this is a night flight and we'll be flying IFR, so if I tell you to hang up because it's screwing up my navigation equipment or instruments, do it immediately."

"Aye, no problem."

They boarded the aircraft and taxied to the end of the partially paved landing strip. There the pilot advanced the throttles with brakes on, ran up the engines and checked the magnetos and oil pressure. As it was an uncontrolled airport, he broadcast his intention to take off into the ether. Satisfied, he craned his neck to look around as much as possible out the Plexiglas cockpit windshield, released the brakes and eased the throttle to the wall. The aircraft responded and within seconds they were in the air. He banked at 1,000 feet and rolled it out perfectly onto his first heading for Inverness. They continued to climb for a few minutes but then quickly leveled off as the pilot explained he wanted to avoid having to get clearance from London ATC to enter the TMA zone.

Murphy pulled out his cell phone, dialed numbers to access the local London service and then shook his head. The pilot reached down and passed over his own Global Satellite telephone. Murphy listened as the service connected him and Malachi answered.

"It's Father Murphy, Cardinal."

"Dermott, I hope you're not holding onto the tail of this helicopter," Malachi said trying to stifle a yawn. Murphy could hear the beat of the rotors in the background.

"Something you said bothered me, sir."

"What was that?"

"Catch-as-catch-can. I'm assuming you meant you weren't sure how to track Father Gallo once you reached Inverness. How did you track them there?"

"Credit cards," Malachi answered. "Ian Cruickshank checked their credit card records and found they'd bought tickets to Glasgow and then on to Inverness. Why?"

"Father Gallo has the Relic with him, does he not?"

"Yes. At least we believe so."

"Surely you know, Cardinal, that there is a GPS transmitting device inside with a battery that lasts up to fifteen days and an antenna wired to the outside of the case?"

"Are you serious, Dermott?"

"I heard Father Gant telling Monsignor Rautenberg about it last year. He was always worried about losing the *Wood of the Cross* and so, when the technology came along, he forked over the dough himself and had a small transmitter installed. As long as the Relic is in the case, he could go on any computer and know its exact whereabouts – within about ten feet. And if the Relic now remains with Father Gallo, well…you get the picture."

"My God…how do we find out where they are?"

"It's a matter of accessing the service on the Internet and using his tracker software. Monsignor Rautenberg could probably tell you how, or he could do it for you."

"Do you mean we could tap in from here? From the helicopter?"

"If you have a wireless card and service, I'm don't see why not. That's how GM's OnStar service works. They know where your car is, they can do a diagnostic on your engine as you drive or open your car if you lock it…all from a satellite."

"Dermott, I don't know how to thank you but I have to call Heinz so I'm going to hang up."

"Glad to be of service."

"By the way…where are you? It's awful noisy at your end."

"Let's just say I'm taking a little initiative."

Malachi was too excited by the news to read anything into his statement, thanked him again and pushed the end button.

Murphy already had Heinz Rautenberg's Vatican number in hand and he quickly dialed him.

After a moment, the Monsignor answered. "Rautenberg."

"It's Dermott Murphy."

"Late of *The Watchers*, I take it," Rautenberg said, dryly. "Father Langevin has been asking where you are. So where are you?"

"On an aircraft on my way to Scotland. This is urgent. I am trying to help Cardinal Malachi who is headed with two of the *Crusaders* to Inverness, Scotland."

"I know. To intercept Father Gallo before he tries something foolish."

"Yes…but he didn't know about the GPS transmitter inside the Relic's case," Murphy said.

"He must know; he tracked them to Inverness."

"Using credit card information gleaned when they bought train tickets. Are you near a PC?"

"Yes…right here on my desk."

"You know the URL for the tracking service and the password to track the Relic, right?"

"Certainly…I have them preset into my laptop. Father Castilloux and I were Father Gant's backup."

Murphy could hear the rattle of keys. "Can you see where it is?"

"Just a minute," Rautenberg said. There were a few more tapings on keys and then: "There…I see it. It's in…wait a minute…it's in Stornoway, not Inverness."

"Stornoway? Where's that?" Murphy asked, one finger now plugged in his open ear to hear better over the aircraft engine.

The pilot, obviously listening, spoke up: "On Lewis Island, across the Minch – in the Outer Hebrides."

"Lewis Island…the Outer Hebrides of Scotland," Rautenberg said, repeating the pilot's words. "Why is it so noisy on your end? Where are you?"

"Monsignor…Cardinal Malachi will call you as soon as I hang up. Please have the coordinates ready for him as he's headed to the wrong location. If he doesn't call, then call him; we're going to have to know the minute the Relic moves. I'm going to give you the number of my satellite phone." He looked at Grantham who called out the number and he relayed it to Rautenberg. The Monsignor repeated it back to make sure it was correct and then said good-bye.

"Course if you're not with me later…I'll be getting all your calls," the pilot said.

"One thousand pounds," Murphy offered.

"Sold," Grantham intoned, with a grin. "I'll give you the charger, the case and my wife for that."

"Marriage is a sacred union," the priest admonished, and then grinned at the pilot's embarrassment. "But God will forgive you if you forget Inverness and take me to Stornoway."

"What's all this?" Grantham asked, suspiciously. "There's nothing illegal about, is there?"

"Illegal? The Catholic Church? Bite your tongue, lad!" Murphy said, his hand hanging over the seat back touching his suitcase containing an assortment of grenades, 75 pounds of high explosive TNT, blasting caps, detonators and a Stoner 96 Knights 5.56 mm belt feed Light Machine Gun with a 200-round belt container; it was capable of spitting out 550 bullets per minute. "The Catholic Church is the ethical seat of morality, the heart of our collective soul, and a model of peace and forgiveness in the free and not so free world. Remember that, my boy." He shifted to make his snub-nosed .45 Police Special sit more comfortably in the inside pocket of his heavy cape. "Illegal indeed!" he sniffed.

"Sorry," the pilot said quickly. "Well...I can radio an amendment to my flight plan and figure a new heading for Stornoway. If the weather isn't cooperating, Inverness is our alternate."

"Surely it can't be that bad."

"No offence, Father, but though I learned to fly in hours... it's taken me years to learn when *not* to fly. And that experience makes me a good and a safe pilot."

"One thou–," Murphy began.

"I know, I know," pilot said, with good humor. "One thousand pounds. But we still fly safe." He shook his head, chuckling to himself as he rolled the aircraft to the left and picked up the VHF microphone to get a weather update and file a new flight plan. Business was booming.

* * * *

PART EIGHT

"HOUR OF THE WOLF"

It draws nigh, silent as night
Fangs agleam, eyes pits of fire
Promises broken, spirits conspire
Hearts beat wildly, sobbing in fright

J. Richard Wright
HOUR OF THE WOLF (1989)

Into the eternal darkness into fire
And into ice....

Dante Alighieri
THE DIVINE COMEDY – INFERNO

~ 1 ~

"Stornoway? What in the deuce is he doing up there," Cruickshank asked, as Malachi ended the call from Rautenberg.

"He obviously has a specific destination in mind, whatever it might be," Malachi said. "Can we alter our course?"

They were almost a half hour into their flight. Father Nathaniel and Father Oberon dozed in their seats now, their faces barely lit by the red night lights shining from the front of the cockpit where they illuminated the instrument panel. The priests seemed used to sleeping in odd places, and neither the buffeting of the craft by the wind nor the periodic crackle of cross-talk on the VHF radio appeared to bother them.

Cruickshank took down a headset and boom-microphone hanging on the bulkhead and plugged it into a receptacle. "Sergeant Frazer, we need to go to Stornoway on Lewis Island. Yes…alright, I understand. Quite right…yes. Check and see. That's a good chap." He hung the headset back up and leaned over to Malachi as the radio in the cockpit crackled and the pilot asked for a heading to Glasgow Port Airport. "He says we'll have to set down at Glasgow, take on more fuel and then fly to Ullapool first," the detective shouted over the noise of the engines. "He also said that during his preflight he noticed that there were high winds over The North Minch, gusting to 45 knots with even more heavy weather expected. It wouldn't be a nice night to fly over it. If we got lost and wandered from the channel over the North Atlantic and had to ditch in the ocean, we'd freeze to death within five minutes of being in the water."

"Charming," Malachi shouted back. "But it's no use going to Inverness if Father Gallo is in Stornoway."

The helicopter banked and the pilot gave them a thumbs up signaling they were on their way to Glasgow. He then motioned for Cruickshank and Malachi to put on their headsets.

"Sir, we're cleared all the way to Ullapool once we take on more fuel," the pilot said. "Now there's no airport in the town but we can set down there if we have to, or divert over to Inverness. Control tells me the weather over The Minch is deteriorating rapidly. I grew up in Ullapool and the strait can get pretty nasty. It's about 75 kilometers across and I don't know that it would be wise to cross it tonight."

"Can we take a boat?" Malachi asked.

"Almost more risky," the pilot answered. "Though it's sheltered water, this time of the year you could get waves five to ten meters high. I doubt anybody would take you in bad weather."

"We must reach Stornoway tonight," Malachi insisted.

"Ullapool is near the maximum wind velocity for safe flight for this helicopter but we'll head up there and make a decision as to whether we cross when we arrive."

Cruickshank cut in: "Mustavias, we can only do what we can do."

Malachi shrugged: "We're going to find a way across that strait even if we have to swim."

Both men removed their headsets and settled back in their seats, each lost in his own thoughts as the engines droned and winds began to buffet the helicopter.

Unaware of the quickening drama around them, the *Crusaders* continued to sleep peacefully as the tiny craft flew on, discernible only by its red and green navigation lights, and a powerful strobe sending blue-white flashes into the inky blackness of the night.

~ 2 ~

Seven hundred kilometers to the northeast, the heavy beat of huge, bat-like wings slowed in the night sky as Adramelech wound his flight over the forbidding landscape of Lewis Island and looked down on the dark stone turrets of his earthly home; a mere few hundred yards away was a two-hundred-foot cliff ending at the boiling Atlantic ocean below. Rain mixed with sleet peppered the air. As he watched from on high above the stone castle, plumes of white spray exploded upward from fierce, rolling waves hitting the jagged rocks as gale force winds drove the sea into the cliffs in a relentless assault as old as the ocean itself.

Clutched tightly to his belly with one of the demon's muscular arms, Rosalita used her own two hands to cling to the bluish-black skin of the demon monstrosity as it wielded itself over the fortress and began to drop to the ground in a dizzying circular dive.

Even this horned aberration, in its purest hellish form, was glad to be home again. At the last possible moment, the creature extended its ribbed, leathery wings out fully and landed lightly on the wooden drawbridge over a water-filled moat. It's familiar, used to the drill, dropped onto her tiny feet and made her way forward to the heavy oak doors. Rosalita pulled the round, wrought iron handle, and the door of the edifice swung open to receive its shadowy lord of the manor.

As the creature stalked inside, it began to morph into a more pleasing human form until it reached the Great Room. There it now stood tall, naked and darkly handsome, surveying its surroundings. Though immensely tired from the flight, Adramelech summoned his remaining strength and stood upright. "We must put on a fire for our impending guests, Rosalita," Adramelech said, his voice ripe with black humor. "We wouldn't want them to catch their death from a chill."

The Great Room was rectangle-shaped, and had a palladium-style, arched entranceway at one end and a wall-size stained glass window at the other. The glass featured a scene of a pentagram surrounding a figure being crucified upside down while a Roman soldier gleefully carved out the victim's innards with a long, sharp lance. Various stained glass-constructed demons rejoiced at the travesty.

The other two walls were hung with various medieval weapons and ancient renderings as befitted a castle. Gleaming brass trumpets stood out from one wall showcasing multi-colored banners hanging from them. A huge oil painting depicted scenes of torture including: naked humans being drawn and quartered; screaming victims being roasted over fires; and, rows of praying women awaiting their decapitation before a busy guillotine. Hanging alongside the painting was a tapestry ripe with demons madly fornicating before manic cheering crowds of devils. An array of ancient medieval broadswords, pikes, longbows, daggers and arrows lined the other wall completing the gruesome décor.

At floor level, lined along both walls were full-sized suits of armor standing mutely at attention holding pikes, broadswords and maces in their hollow, metal gloves. In the center of the room were three separate islands containing couches and chairs as well as end and coffee tables and reading lamps, somewhat reminiscent of a grand old hotel. Twelve-foot square carpets were scattered about covering the stone floors to lend a little warmth.

Between the rows of armored knights, on opposite walls, stood two walk-in sized fireplaces complete with logs piled high, ready for lighting. Rosalita now approached one of the fireplaces and reached high above her head to the mantle for some long matches.

Adramelech covered the distance to her in half a dozen strides and touched the logs that immediately burst into full flame. He grinned at her as she cowered before him, afraid of his displeasure. "Fear not, my faithful," he said with a grin that bared sparkling white, razor-sharp teeth. "After all, am I not the Prince of Fire?" As she began to rise, no longer fearful, Adramelech's arm snaked out and seized her; she screamed as he hurled her against the stone wall where she hit with tremendous force and slid down, her shift bunching under her arms leaving her naked. On the wall was a trail of tissue, mucus and blood. Though the pain of the wounds caused her to gasp, she was already healing as she scrambled to her feet.

Adramelech laughed and said: "Soon my little friend, I will be more invulnerable and powerful than I have ever been. Tonight I will crush the power of the church; I will vanquish these cheating champions of the most holy, and I will begin to prepare for *our* Master to ascend to his rightful place on earth and rule it as his dominion."

Rosalita stood waiting for more orders but the demon ignored her. Instead he crossed the room and sat on a couch facing the fire. He watched as, within it, tiny human figures materialized, screamed and tried to run as they were captured by small crab-like figures and dragged back to be tortured and burned in the brilliant yellow and red flames.

"By the way, *that* was your last healing, Rosalita," he called out. "I've decided you've become tiresome and I no longer have any need for you. I shall take a new familiar, one that is somewhat more nubile…and eligible." He laughed harshly and waved his hand. "Sleep tight."

With that pronouncement, Adramelech went back to watching the scenes play out in the fire. He began to quietly chuckle which quickly build to unrestrained mirth and soon became a hysterical shriek of maniacal laugher echoing off the cavernous walls of the castle. Rosalita fearfully scurried away.

~ 3 ~

Father Gallo arose from his bed in Stornaway's Cabarfeidh Hotel where he had not been sleeping. Maria and Clay, exhausted from the journey, had begged for a few hours rest and remained asleep in an adjoining room connected to his by an open doorway; each was flaked out on a queen bed fully clothed. He looked at his watch and saw that it was nearing 11 p.m. They had to be going soon; he estimated the drive would take about an hour. Then they would proceed on foot through open countryside for another half an hour. The advantage was that in the wee hours of the morning, they wouldn't arouse any curiosity. The priest tiptoed into their room, quietly reached into Maria's single piece of luggage and removed a Crucifix which he deposited out of sight under her bed. They could sleep another ten minutes, he decided.

Unknown to Gallo, before sleeping, Maria had placed a call to Cardinal Malachi in the Vatican. Unable to reach him, she had tried several other members of *The Seven* and finally settled for Monsignor Heinz Rautenberg's voicemail. She left a terse message saying she was trying to get in touch with Cardinal Malachi, and they were in Stornoway, Scotland. Gallo insisted he knew where Adramelech's lair was and they were going after him without any further delay; he was determined to end the demon's existence now. Maria and Clay didn't know what to do. Maria then ran out of change for the payphone and the call was cut off. The two soon fell asleep.

In his room next door, Gallo cautiously opened the combination locks on the case containing the Relic. He gazed in awe at the long dark piece of wood as it sat encased in a blue velvet notch custom shaped for it. However, he soon felt his pulse quicken and his head begin to swim. Sweat broke out on his brow and ran into his eyes and he became nauseous. Managing to stagger to the bathroom, he threw up repeatedly before finally returning and slamming the case shut. He locked it again and set it in the farthest corner of the room away from him. Nerves!

A half hour later, feeling better, he knocked softly on the doorjamb of Maria and Clay's room. He looked at his watch: 11:30 p.m. Few people would be about to see them now. He held a map of

Lewis Island in his hand. Neither stirred. "Sister Maria, Clay...we have to go."

When they awoke, however, a major argument erupted with Clay and Maria saying it was foolish to proceed without help.

"I have what I need to kill him," Gallo asserted. "If you don't wish to come, then I will face him alone. Abandon me if you wish. I'm an old man but I seem to have more courage than some."

"You can't face him alone," Clay said. "Where are these *Crusaders*? Have you called them? If so, why aren't they here? Aren't they the ones trained to deal with this...*thing*?"

"Yes, they've been trained. But they've also failed repeatedly and gotten themselves killed more than once in the bargain. All I need to do is get close enough to him and he's finished. The scroll said that if he is touched by the *Wood*, mankind would no longer suffer this plague."

"Wait for Cardinal Malachi and we'll all go," Maria said, taking hold of the old man's hand.

Father Gallo withdrew his hand and shook his head. "The cardinal saved my life and I owe it to him to bring this wretched monster to its end."

"And you know exactly where it is?" Clay asked.

"Precisely," Gallo responded, waving the map on which they could plainly see an **X** marked in black ink.

"How can you be sure the demon will be there?"

"If he isn't, it's simply a matter of waiting for him. And, that's where you'll come in, Maria, to give us warning. But eventually he will be there. That's why he's in the British Isles." He looked them both in the eyes and continued. "He's going home because even an emissary of hell doesn't have unlimited strength. Now is the time to get him – when he's weakened."

"How do you know this, Father?" Maria asked.

"I spent half a year in his tender care."

Clay and Maria exchanged glances.

"Are you with me or am I off to fight it alone," Gallo asked. When neither replied, he turned and went back into his own room, quietly closing the connecting door.

"What do we do?" Maria asked. "We can't allow him to go alone."

"And we can't convince him to stay. Shall we try Malachi again? If we could get him on the line, he might be able to convince Father Gallo to wait."

"I left the hotel number with his answering service. He must be as desperate to find us as we are to find him. He would have called back if he'd called into his service."

"Well there seems to be little choice," Clay said. "You remain here and wait for the Cardinal to get in touch with you. I'll accompany Father Gallo and try to get him to hold off as long as possible."

"Clay, I am not *staying* anywhere. I may be his best chance of anticipating if Adramelech is there…or to alert him if he is returning."

Both heard the door of the other room slamming loudly. "He's leaving," Maria said, opening their room door and looking out down the hall. "Father, wait! We're coming with you."

~ 4 ~

The Metropolitan Police Air Support helicopter bucked, twisted and then abruptly dropped 200 feet toward the churning ocean a mere 800 feet below; the pilot used his collective and throttle to bring them back to altitude. Sleet and hail pounded against the windscreen as he fought the controls, working the cyclic and anti-torque pedals to maintain their desired heading and keep the craft from yawing or even turning turtle. He had his helmet on with night vision goggles down seeking some measure of sight in the darkness. The conditions were, by far the worst in which he had ever flown. Sweat gleamed on his forehead as he yelled back without benefit of radio: "Bad idea, Chief."

Cruickshank, clutching an air sickness bag and looking very green, nodded his agreement with Frazer.

Beside Frazer, Constable Cockerill held onto the edges of his seat; for him too this was an unusual ride. By now, everyone on board was awake.

A half hour before, they had landed in Ullapool and found a formidable storm growing in intensity over The Minch. Still, at Malachi's insistence that this was a matter of life and death, the pilot had reluctantly agreed to try the crossing. Whose death wasn't discussed, but more and more it began to look like it now involved the six men in the chopper.

"How long to Stornoway?" Malachi shouted above the beat of the rotors and the screaming of the wind penetrating the cabin.

"No-no idea..." the pilot said through gritted teeth. "We're fighting a 40 knot headwind and we've passed the point of no return. This is suicide."

The police observer beside him hung on for dear life as, more and more, the chopper resembled a rodeo bronco rather than a million dollar piece of high technology. At times it seemed to pause in the air and was almost blown backwards. The two *Crusaders*, while fully aware of the danger, merely watched Cruickshank hovering over his sick bag in amusement. Father Oberon looked at his watch and then passed Father Nathaniel a five-pound note since the detective had not used the bag as yet. The priest grinned and accepted the money from his colleague.

The pilot slapped his goggles attached to his helmet up out of his sight line and said tersely to his observer, Arthur Cockerill: "Nightsun." It was critical neither the pilot nor the observer had on their night vision goggles when they turned on any other light. The night vision goggles worked by gathering and amplifying any ambient light present as well as leveraging the lower portion of the infrared light spectrum invisible to the naked eye. Turning on the NIGHTSUN while wearing night vision goggles would blind them both for some time.

Malachi stood and hung on for dear life as he peered anxiously over the pilot's shoulder trying to see land as the spot of the "NIGHTSUN", a 30-million candlepower spotlight mounted under the tail of the helicopter, turned on and pointed down and forward. All he saw was a sheet of rain and sleet being driven horizontally through the blue-white light beam by heavy winds. The copter continued to roller coaster with its human riders being jerked against their seat belts. Suddenly the craft yawed wildly and dropped at the same time.

"We're going down," Constable Cockerill yelled, obviously frightened as the craft continued its wild dive.

"No...we're...not!" Frazer said, fighting the controls and stopping their descent.

All aboard let out a collective sigh of relief as the chopper gained altitude again.

"Why don't we go higher," Malachi yelled above the roaring of the engine and the wind and rain buffeting the craft.

"Because those are cumulonimbus clouds over us and the ceiling is a thousand feet," Frazer yelled back. "If we get into them, we'll be nothing but metal confetti."

"Who...is...the idiot who suggested we...cross tonight?" Malachi shouted in an effort to break the fear and tension. It worked. All eyes turned towards him. He made an elaborate gesture of pointing at himself in mock surprise. "Moi??"

Cruickshank and the two *Crusaders* couldn't help but laugh and even the police constable cracked a tentative but nervous smile. The pilot was too busy to allow any distractions.

Suddenly, Malachi became serious and slapped his hand down on his thigh.

"What's wrong," Cruickshank yelled.

"Damnit...how could I miss that?" He sat down and buckled his seat belt.

"Miss what?"

Malachi leaned close to Cruickshank. "Father Gant was stabbed with his own crucifix."

"We know that," Cruickshank replied.

"It couldn't have been Adramelech. He couldn't handle the crucifix. Nor can any of his familiars."

"Then if not that chap...who?"

"Who wound up with the case...the Relic?"

"Your friend, Father Gallo. But Why? What would be his motive?"

"I don't know. He's never been the same since he was taken. I put it down to trauma but maybe Adramelech has somehow managed to...subvert him?"

Cruickshank shook his head. "Well, if he's changed sides, why are we risking life and limb to save him?"

"Because there is more at stake than Father Gallo," Malachi said. "It would mean Sister Maria and Clay Montague are being led into a trap. And, the Relic might be lost forever; in fact, a clear priority of Adramelech would be to destroy it."

"I-I see breakers," the pilot yelled, interrupting them.

Sure enough, far below, the sea was breaking over a long beach. The police constable worked the NIGHTSUN'S remote control and scanned back and forth on the beach, recognizable only as a mass of water that surged white against the land and then retreated in a foaming cauldron of bubbles. Within five minutes of making landfall, while still rough, the ride in the helicopter improved considerably. Ten minutes later, the pilot was on the radio to Stornoway Control trying to advise them of their ETA. The pilot finally called Her Majesty's Coastguard operations based at the airport and found the airport was closed and transportation was limited. They could still land if required at the heliport. The pilot shrugged and half turned to his passengers: "Airport's closed but that's not a problem for us. I'd say this would be the least of our problems tonight, right chaps?"

In fact, he was dead right.

~ 5 ~

Grantham told Murphy that Stornoway Airport did not keep its landing lights on all night but there was a 24-hour On Call system for emergencies or Air Ambulance flights. The pilot called for help, declaring a fuel emergency and a controller was at the airport and responding within fifteen minutes.

"Stornoway Control, this is golf, x-ray, tango, foxtrot, golf, Cessna two one zero en route Stornoway, over," Grantham said into his microphone.

"Cessna two one zero, this is Stornoway Control," came back an immediate reply. "Stornoway Airport is closed until 0730 hours tomorrow; however, I understand you've declared a fuel emergency, over."

"Roger Stornoway. Are your runway lights active yet, over?"

"Roger, Cessna, we have LIRL; you are cleared for runway two-five, winds at two-eight-five at forty gusting to fifty knots. Must have been a right nightmare of a flight, old chap; be a rough landing."

"Thank you, sir." The pilot hung up the microphone. "There's the beacon...and the strip."

"What's LIRL?" Murphy asked, hanging on as the plane bucked and rolled.

"Low intensity runway lights; and there they are – dead ahead," Grantham said, tersely.

Within five minutes, despite gale force winds, the pilot had skillfully landed the aircraft and they were taxing towards the single-story terminal building lit only by outside lights. Above them the airport beacon rotated, its beam swinging endlessly through the wild night sky. The wind sent leaves and bits of brambles scuttling across the tarmac in front of them in the glare of the plane's landing light. They could see a small Austin painted in a Union Jack motif parked by the tower, and some low level lighting in the tower windows. Likely the controller was watching them.

Murphy's new satellite phone rang. It was Rautenberg. "Father Murphy, I've just got off the line with Cardinal Malachi; he was wondering where the dickens you are?"

"I'm at Stornoway Airport."

"How did you get there?"

"On the wings of angels."

"Well...however...," Rautenberg answered, sounding a little grumpy. "They've just diverted from Stornoway."

"Diverted? Why?"

"The Relic has been on the move."

"Where?"

"As near as I can tell from the signal, Father Gallo and his entourage traveled northwest from Stornoway, up A857, turned west on A858 and then into a small hamlet called Arbor. I 'Googled' the area and tapped into some satellite photos of Arbor and the coast. I see a road out of the hamlet going northwest to the coast. They reached the end of that, and from the speed they are now making, I'm guessing they're out of the car and proceeding directly north on foot towards the ocean...some miles away."

"But Cardinal Malachi and the others will still have to land here," Murphy exclaimed.

"They're in a *helicopter*, Einstein" Rautenberg exclaimed. "They can land virtually anywhere they'd like."

"I knew that," Murphy responded quickly, trying to cover.

"Sure you did," Rautenberg answered, his dry humor returning. "From what I can see on the Google satellite photo, it's pretty desolate up there. I just see one major structure – sort of looks like an old stone castle with a moat – and they seem to be heading directly for it. Based on the topography, it's right beside some fairly high cliffs overlooking the ocean."

"So I'd have no hope of finding it in the dark?"

"Father, no offense, but what are you up to?" Rautenberg asked.

"I was hoping to help."

"Very noble, and I mean that sincerely, but Malachi and the others can't wait, Father. They are proceeding towards the Relic's signal in the helicopter."

Colin Grantham, with one ear cocked, leaned over to Murphy. "Get the longitude and latitude of whatever you're looking for and I can find it for you in a pea soup fog with a set of knickers tied over me eyes."

"What?" Murphy asked, staring at the pilot.

"Just get the coordinates and I'll tell you later," Grantham stage whispered over the noise of the idling engine as they sat on the apron in front of the tower.

"Monsignor, is there any way you can give me the coordinates for this castle?"

"Just a minute," Rautenberg said. He was back momentarily. "Love this Google. Just put the cursor over the structure on the satellite photo and click the mouse and presto: 58.35894 North–."

"Just a minute," Murphy said, snatching a pen out of the sleeve pocket on the pilot's bomber jacket and a map out of a door pocket beside him. "Go ahead."

"Ready? The coordinates are 58.35894 North and 6.59017 West. Got that?"

"Yes," Murphy answered, scrawling the numbers on the edge of the map.

"As I mentioned, they are not landing at Stornoway but going directly after Father Gallo."

"I know but I'm in Stornoway. How far away am I from Arbor?"

"From what I can see, it's about 20 kilometers north and then five kilometers west. Then maybe five or six kilometers from the end of the road to this structure."

"So maybe a half hour or so driving?"

"At best," Rautenberg answered, hesitantly.

Murphy thought for a moment and then asked: "What's their ETA?"

"From what they said five minutes ago…about 40 to 50 minutes I believe. They are bucking some terrible headwinds."

"Then I may make it with bells on," Murphy said. "I'm going to have to go."

"Well...watch yourself." Rautenberg's tone was one of resignation. "They are heavily armed and don't know you are anywhere near. You don't want to be taken out by friendly fire that wouldn't be so friendly. I'll call you on your phone if there's any change in direction."

"Right, thank you," Murphy said, pushing the *end* button.

The pilot looked at Murphy and handed him a small device with a screen. "You are holding a portable GPS unit," Grantham said. "Day or night it can guide you to within ten feet of those coordinates you have. I'll put them in and explain how it works."

"I love technology," Murphy answered. "But before you do that, can you get the control tower on the radio? I need an automobile and assuming the controller drove here in that mini I'm seeing, I'm going to make him an offer he can't refuse."

~ 6 ~

Clay stood in the pounding rain and wild wind looking in awe at an immense, perfectly-preserved, black, gothic-looking stone structure in front of him.

It was a full-sized castle all right, complete with corner towers, a keep, a chemise and a 40-foot wide moat filled with water. The wall of the castle was easily 100 feet high topped by what appeared to be a parapet walk and battlements from which soldiers could rain arrows down at their enemies in days of old. As he stared, thunder exploded almost directly above him; multiple forks of lightning split the night sky rendering brilliant daylight on his surroundings. The strobe lasted for a full five seconds before the sapphire-colored flash winked out and the gloom returned. In that time he was able to see a lowered drawbridge at the end of which were twin doors set in an arch frame. Clay had passed a half-dozen *No Trespassing, Private Property* and *Trespassers will be Forcefully Prosecuted* signs a half-mile from the perimeter of the castle.

They had run well off the road, gotten lost and run out of gasoline a few miles back. Gathering their gear, they had hiked onward and been surprised to find a brightly painted, wrecked and abandoned Austin Mini over hill and dale less than a mile from where they now stood. There was no sign of any driver.

He heard the labored breathing of Father Gallo as Maria and the priest approached behind him; Maria had volunteered to stay back with the old man as Clay had forged ahead at first sight of the amazing edifice.

The priest still stubbornly clutched the handle of the aluminum case despite Clay's offer to carry it. Maria's yellow anorak made her visible as she moved forward holding the halogen security flashlight that emitted a brilliant swath of bluish light; she kept it pointed at the ground with one hand while she held Father Gallo's arm with the other.

"Not...through...there," Gallo said, trying to catch his breath as he noticed Clay looking at the drawbridge. "There's a better way."

Maria now stood transfixed by the sight of the castle. Suddenly she shuddered and the blood drained from her face, evident even in the limited light. "It's in there," she whispered, her words lost on the wailing wind, her countenance ghostlike.

"What did you say?" Gallo asked.

"He's is in there somewhere," she shouted forcefully. "I sense blackness...an overbearing and suffocating evil. Something this strong could only be Adramelech."

Clay reached under his anorak and pulled the Ruger from the holster set on his waist belt for a Texas John Slaughter cross-draw. He flipped the weapon open and checked the loads. Six brass cartridge heads gleamed in the cylinder. He gave it a flip and the cylinder snapped closed.

"It's time," Gallo said. "Come with me." Surprisingly, he led them away from the castle and to the right over increasingly rough and rocky ground towards the ocean cliffs.

Shivering from the cold and dampness, they soon found themselves traversing a carpet of smooth, rounded stones on what seemed to be a dried up creek bed; it deepened and twisted and turned as it led them down towards the sea cliffs. With both sides of the channel in which they trekked now higher than their heads, they gave thanks they were partially sheltered from the wind. Within minutes, however, they stood at the edge of a cliff where the creek had once emptied into the ocean. The wind shrieked like a banshee as a maelstrom of water and foam seethed below them, the hollow boom of the waves almost deafening as they exploded against the sharp rocks.

"Where are we going?" Clay yelled, but his words were whipped away by the wind as Maria clasped his hand tightly and looked at him for reassurance. For the first time he saw fear in her eyes.

Gallo motioned and then moved to the side. Carefully he led them onto a barely discernible, narrow, earthen path which led sideways along the cliff face and gradually sloped downward. Two hundred feet below, a single misstep away, the ocean boiled.

They moved across the cliff for a hundred yards, all the way fighting the wind that threatened to pluck them off the face; they were now forced to tread on a broken rocky shelf no wider than a foot. It led to another rock shelf and another. Clay put the flashlight in his pocket and used one hand to grasp rocks that jutted out overhead and the other to hang on to Maria who often couldn't reach the viable handholds. After five minutes, the biting cold wind and the wetness were beginning to take a toll as his fingers gradually lost their feeling.

Father Gallo seemed to have discovered a renewed energy and was moving across the rock face with the agility of a mountain goat – one hand grabbing the rocks and the other securing the aluminum case with the Relic inside. Maria and Clay exchanged glances. They cautiously moved forward again towards the priest and started in shock; Father Gallo had vanished.

"Oh my God," Maria yelled, straining to be heard above the shriek of the wind. "Where is he?"

Both looked down towards the raging ocean below but the mist and spray prevented them from seeing anything.

"Father Gallo!" Maria screamed.

Nothing.

"He's gone," Clay replied, his voice shaking. He felt himself sag with a mixture of despair, grief and some relief since there was no longer any question of going on to face whatever lived in the castle. But his relief was, in fact, short-lived.

"I'm here," Gallo called, his voice seemingly distant and distorted by the roar of the wind and water. "In here."

Clay and Maria looked at each other in surprise. "Where?" Clay hollered back. "We can't see you."

"Keep coming. I'm in an opening."

They resumed their forward trek, Clay still holding onto Maria with one hand. He squeezed around an outcrop with the bulge of flashlight in his pocket and the holstered revolver forcing him to lean farther out over the ledge than he wished. Just as he got set to push off again, he felt the outer rock crumbling under his forward foot. Instinctively he kicked off with his secure foot to land on another ledge a foot away where he seized a firm handhold. In doing so, however, he also violently yanked Maria's arm. She stumbled forward, managed to get one foot on another ledge and then swung out into thin air. With a shriek, she began to drop like a stone.

Without hesitation Clay tightened his grip on her hand to a vise-like hold and bent double as her weight almost dragged him over. Desperation sent a surge of adrenaline through him and he summoned every ounce of his remaining strength. With an energy reserved for those in mortal danger, he pulled and she came up like a cork popping out of a bottle and was secure in his arms within a second.

"Oh my God," she cried into his ear. "I-I thought I was a dead …thank you. Thank you."

"I'm sorry, Maria…my fault," he said, panting with the effort.

"In here…get in here," Gallo shouted, standing safely on the edge of a large round passageway cut in the rock; it was so perfect it looked like it had been quarried.

"You don't have to ask us twice," Clay said, anxious not to become a casualty of the wild and broken coastline.

They took a few more steps and were able to attain the safety of the passage. Clay felt Maria trembling uncontrollably; he suspected it was from far more than the cold.

"Where are we?" he asked, as they worked to catch their breaths. The wind roared into the opening around them and howled its way down the rock corridor for some distance.

"It's a tunnel under the castle," Gallo said.

"How-how did you know it was here?" Maria asked, the full realization of just how close to death she had been moments before sinking in. She continued to shake and Clay drew her to him.

"I escaped through here," Gallo explained. Without another word, he picked up the case and started to lead them deeper into the depths of the tunnel.

"Wait," Clay said, his voice sounding hollow in the round enclosure. "Do you have a plan? Is there something we should be doing?"

"Yes," Gallo said. "Pray." With that he reached under his coat, removed his Crucifix from his cummerbund and flung it backwards over the lip of the tunnel and into the abyss.

"Why did you do that?"

"This is no place for holy objects," the priest said shortly. "He senses these things. No use telegraphing our presence. Use the light." He moved on.

Clay and Maria followed with Clay snapping on the flashlight. As they moved through the tunnel, the shriek of the wind gradually faded until it became a distant, undulating moan. It was soon replaced by an uneasy stillness that was punctuated only by the hollow sound of dripping water as they moved ever deeper. Following the pathway, they soon encountered a number of small and large caves, some featuring the mouths of other tunnels. Gallo seemed to know exactly where he was going and confidently selected each new entrance, leading them deeper into the recesses. Clay played the flashlight over the rocky walls of the tunnels that seemed to be uniformly the same size and devoid of any stones or other debris on the paths they followed.

They had just reached the third series of new tunnel entrances and Gallo had chosen one to the right when they heard a far-off shriek of human pain that rose in intensity, faded to a moan and finally disappeared altogether. It was soon followed by further keening, the words indistinguishable but definitely echoing confusion, sorrow and desperation; Gallo turned suddenly in a panic and quickly pushed them back out of the tunnel and into another entrance.

"What was that?" Maria asked, her eyes wide.

"You don't want to know," Gallo said, with a shudder and strode forward into the darkness of the middle tunnel. Clay and Maria hurried to catch up as Clay tried to shine the light ahead to illuminate Gallo's path. Water continued to drip from the rocks and the light bounced off the moisture creating strange shadows that twisted and jumped from wall to floor to ceiling.

Within a few minutes they reached a squared-off, man-made passageway that was built of stone. Along the walls were flaming torches set in metal sconces angled at 45-degree angles.

"Christ, it looks like we're in Dracula's castle," Clay said, attempting to lighten his own mood that was stuck somewhere between fear and despair.

"We should be so lucky," Maria answered, continually scanning ahead and behind. Clutching Clay's hand tighter and tighter, she now seemed to be walking ever more slowly; Clay began to feel like he was dragging her.

"Do you want to stay here, Maria?" he asked.

"N-Not on your life," she stammered, weakly.

Now Clay also felt it increasingly difficult to advance. He lifted each foot with great effort. Father Gallo, however, seemed to be pulling away from them while they felt like they were struggling to walk through a vat of molasses. Their feet dragged and an omnipotent sense of a thick, phantasmal evil seemed to envelope both making it almost impossible to proceed. Clay held Maria's hand trying to help. He would swear the air was growing thicker and thicker.

"M-My God...are...you having trouble breathing?" Clay asked, gasping.

Maria met his eyes and nodded as she took ever deeper breaths to compensate for the lack of oxygen in a normal breath. Gallo looked back and motioned them forward with his head. "Quickly, we must not delay." He came back and seized Maria's other hand. With Father Gallo's help, they were released from that mysterious rendition of virtual "quicksand" in which they had become mired; they were able to walk normally again.

"What happened?" Clay asked in surprise, moving forward and finding he could also breathe normally.

"The power of Christ and his goodness is helping us," Maria mused softly. With those words, her eyes glazed over and she ceased to speak. Her feet began to drag again.

To Clay, she exhibited every sign of being lost in a trance with a wide range of emotions playing over her features as they walked. She stumbled several times and then suddenly collapsed. Frightened, Clay stopped and tended to her. She was breathing quickly, her eyelids jumping as though experiencing REM sleep. His battlefield first-aid training clicked in. He took her pulse. It was rapid but strong. To his great relief, after some seconds, she opened her eyes. They were large and liquid, and she looked at Clay with pity and despair.

"Oh Clay," she said, sorrow in her voice. "I'm so sorry...so sorry...! I never wanted anything like this to happen to you. It's not fair."

"What do you mean?" he asked in alarm. "What is it?"

She stared at him for a moment and then looked around at her surroundings. She took a deep breath and gathered herself together. "I-It's okay," she stammered.

"Did you have a premonition?" Father Gallo asked, staring at her strangely.

"Let-let's move on," she said, struggling to her feet and leaning on him.

"You did...you saw the future?" the old priest exclaimed. "You saw what's going to happen."

Maria turned to Clay. "Clay...I'm sorry...I didn't want you hurt..." She trailed off, her voice trembling and uneven.

The detective looked at her with the sudden realization that unfolding events had become transparent to Maria. Somehow she had seen their destiny. And, it didn't look like there was a happy outcome for him.

"I want you to go back," he said, his voice hardening. "Now! I want you out of here *now!*"

Maria shook her head as she sought to regain her balance. "Not possible. What will happen, will happen. There's no changing it."

"What did you see, Maria?" he pleaded.

"Come...hurry," Father Gallo interrupted perfunctorily from ahead. He beckoned them with urgent waves.

Moving forward with reluctance, Clay decided that as long as Maria would be alright, he could accept his fate. He held her hand a little tighter and realized that he would gladly go to his death if it meant protecting her.

The stone passageway gradually curved to the left. As they rounded a corner, they came to a stone, circular staircase leading upward, seemingly forever. In the shadow of the staircase Clay saw a pile of abnormally large humanoid skulls and a heap of bleached, yellow bones. "What in the hell are those?" he whispered to Gallo.

"Familiars who displeased him," Father Gallo answered, and then suddenly snatched Maria's hand and ran up the stairs, pulling her behind him. Gallo paused halfway up, turned and smiled down at Clay. It certainly wasn't a benevolent smile. Nor was it one touched by any modicum of humor. Rather it was a venomous, sadistic grin, with lips stretched wide and nostrils flared – a look of triumphant glee. A sudden chill washed over Clay.

"Maria had a little lamb, whose fleece was white as snow," the old priest chanted in a singsong fashion. "And, everywhere Maria went, Clay was sure to go." He then screamed out a laugh and increased his speed up the stairs, his cassock billowing as he dragged Maria.

Clay felt his stomach sink and goose-bumps rise on his arms. Whatever had happened to Father Gallo, he no longer was the kindly old priest they had come to know. He raced after the pair of them. They were virtually running full tilt up the long winding stairs now and Clay knew he and Maria were in far more trouble than they could have ever imagined. "Stop…Father Gallo…stop!" he shouted.

The priest continued the climb until they reached the top of the stairs where there was another stone hallway. He paused with an iron grip on Maria's arm as Clay reached them, revolver in hand. Maria was now struggling to free herself from his grasp, terror on her face. Gallo's eyes were alert and bright, his age seeming to have dropped off. He stood taller and more robust, his stance suddenly threatening.

"Let her go!" Clay said, pointing the weapon at the priest's head.

Gallo looked at him in amusement. "Or what? You'll shoot me? You can't hurt me, Clay. Don't you get it? I'm under *his* protection."

"Whose protection?" Clay asked, already knowing the answer. They'd been had.

"You'll find out soon enough. Now let's stop this game shall we?" He grabbed Maria by the back of the neck with one hand; she froze, afraid to move. Next, he gently put the case with the Relic down and placed his free hand on the top of Maria's head, his long and now powerful fingers extending over the crown and around her forehead.

She stared helplessly back at Clay, paralyzed by the neck hold, unable to move or speak. Father Gallo relentlessly began squeezing, his fingers putting increased pressure on her skull. Maria's eyes widened at the sudden pain and she choked back a whimper.

"If you want to see her live for a few more minutes, you'll put that gun back in its holster where it belongs," Gallo said. He smiled as Maria began to moan.

Clay quickly pushed the Ruger into his pocket and held up his empty hands. "What's the matter with you? Stop…please stop," he implored the priest.

"That's much better." Gallo released his grip.

Maria sank toward the floor in a dead faint. Clay moved forward quickly and caught her.

"What are you doing, Gallo?" Clay demanded angrily. "Have you lost your mind?"

"Apparently so," Gallo said, with a shrug. "I suppose you might say I lost it while I was here for six months abandoned by the church and God and everyone else in the world. Left for dead…or worse." The light of madness gleamed in his eyes.

"So that's what this is about? Revenge?"

"Revenge? Hardly. This is about loyalty to one that is greater than our so called Trinity. This is about a power that isn't afraid to get down deep and dirty, and work with humankind. This is about a force that vets the people of earth and actively works to eradicate the useless baggage in humanity. Much better than a benign Being that professes love while watching His beloved people get slaughtered by the millions, surrender to disease, and destroy their own planet without a thought for the next generation. Humankind is one big thieving ball of greed, avarice, and gluttony. And those are the *nice* people. Am I coming through? Hello? Getting the picture, *Mister Montague?*"

"You're crazy," Clay cried. "Whatever is here will be defeated. You'll be arrested –!" He stopped in mid-sentence and felt a sudden terror welling up inside himself. Still holding Maria, who was slowly regaining her senses and trying to stand, he turned halfway around to face a new danger. The Little Witch, Rosalita, was walking slowly towards him from twenty feet away. Her red-rimmed eyes glared at him and a snarl spilled from her lips.

"No!" Maria whispered pulling a Crucifix from her anorak pocket and extending it towards the little girl; she stopped dead in her tracks.

"Where the hell did you get that?" Gallo demanded, angrily. "I got rid of them this afternoon."

Maria then spun towards the priest. "Stay back, Father."

"Oh don't be silly. That can't hurt me. I'm no demon. At least, not yet. I haven't taken the exam, chewed the gum OR bought the T-Shirt." Rosalita remained at bay watching them with interest.

"Father, why are you doing this?" Maria cried. "What about God? What about your eternal soul?"

"Haven't you been listening, you little bitch. Or are you still so fixated on becoming Christ's whore that you can't see past your holy hormones? Your God is a frightened turtle. We can do what we want down here on terra firma and He's not going to care squat. It's time for the real lord and master to see what kind of world he can create amongst this rabble, don't you think?" His voice suddenly changed into a deep rasping whisper. "Satan, through his exalted disciple Adramelech, the *King of Fire*, has earned a divine right to rule."

Clay grabbed Maria's hand. "C'mon...we're getting out of here." He started for the stairs.

"Stop them!" Gallo shouted at the familiar and the little girl instinctively moved between them and the stairs.

In one fluid motion Clay dropped Maria's hand, snatched out his gun and was thumbing back the hammer as it came up. When it reached eye-level, he didn't hesitate but drew a quick bead on Rosalita and fired five times. Flame belched from the muzzle but only two of the heavy slugs hit her in the right side of her chest punching through her dress and blowing blood, cloth and tissue out her back. She jerked violently at the head of the stairs, swayed for a moment, and finally fell face forward at the head of the stairs. She didn't move.

They all waited for what seemed an eternity but the child did not rise.

"Well, that's a surprise," Gallo said, with all the emotion of one reading the Sunday newspaper.

Clay quickly moved to the little girl, a rising tide of bile in his throat.

"No Clay...don't go near her," Maria begged, but Clay was already rolling her over.

He steeled himself against what might happen next if she awoke, but she remained mute, her eyes closed. "She's dead," Clay said aloud. And then he surprised himself by saying: "May God have mercy on her soul."

With those words Rosalita's hand snaked out and seized his wrist; he couldn't help yelling in fright. However, the grip was weak as her eyes slowly fluttered open. This time they were not the eyes of an animal but the eyes of a tired and frightened little girl. In fact, her eyes, dark as almonds, were quite beautiful.

"G-Gracias s-senor," she managed to say, bright human arterial blood from a lung wound spotting her lips. "Thank you…now I c-can be w-warm…and sleep." She sighed once and closed her eyes forever.

~ 7 ~

Out of the night the EC 145 copter swept like an avenging angel, a mere 200 feet over the small hamlet of Arbor. Its rotor blades whipped through the rain and sleet as it sped at more than 160 knots towards its destination; the countryside was a dark blur under its fuselage. With Rautenberg's longitude and latitude punched into the flight computer, Malachi and his crew were headed directly towards where the Relic was located. Whether they would find Father Gallo, Clay, and Maria there or not, was still to be determined.

Thirty minutes before, Monsignor Rautenberg had called to say he'd lost the signal at the coordinates he had previously given them. Within a few minutes he'd called back to say he'd regained it and it seemed the Relic was in the structure on the satellite photograph.

"Our DME says we're about three minutes out," the pilot shouted, over the howling of the outside wind competing for supremacy with the engine roar. Having already exceeded maximum limits for flight he was constantly fighting the controls as they neared the seaward side of the island and the wind increased in intensity. "We should see this building soon."

Beside him, the police constable was working the remote control for the NIGHTSUN and the spotlight was cutting a swathe through the sheets of sleet, back and forth across the rocky and uneven, moss-covered ground. The chopper began to buck more; Frazer was surprised to spot the moon through a break in the clouds as its pale light glinted off the nose of his craft. Still, rolling dark clouds continued to spawn gale force winds and the sleet was turning to snow before his eyes.

Cardinal Malachi looked at Cruickshank who had an old Webley top-break .455 caliber Mark IV revolver in hand and was inserting cartridges. Fathers Oberon and Nathaniel stared at him in disbelief, their own sub machines guns strapped across their chests and their heavy caliber side-arms secured in belt holsters. They now had grenades clipped to a bandolier that each wore, as well as machetes in sheaths strapped to their backs. Each priest had a hand looped through a duffle bag containing other assorted toys.

"What the heck is that?" Father Nathaniel yelled to Cruickshank.

"It was my father's," Cruickshank responded loudly. "And, his father's before him."

"Does it work?" Father Oberon asked, mouthing the words to help the Chief Superintendent understand what he was saying.

"Work? I once downed a charging rhino in Africa with it," Cruickshank yelled back, indignantly.

"Really?" Father Nathaniel exclaimed, somewhat in awe.

"No," Cruickshank said, grinning at him. "Good God man, surely you know you can't kill a rhino with a pistol. Unless you're Jungle Jim or some other Hollywood blighter." He'd seen their little wager when he was on the verge of filling his airsick bag; in typical British fashion he showed them they could be had too. "But *you* wouldn't want to be on the business end of it."

The two priests nodded with sheepish smiles. They turned their attention to the pilot.

"Will we rappel down from the chopper," Father Nathaniel shouted, to the pilot, holding up a rope and tether for him to see.

"You can," Frazer yelled back, with a quick glance. He adjusted his heading a few degrees and finished: "The rest of us will probably just land."

Despite the tenseness they were all feeling, Malachi and Cruickshank couldn't help smiling and the two priests collectively shook their heads and grinned at being skewered twice in as many minutes.

The humor and ability to joke and smile in the face of possible death was a typical bravado that warriors exhibited since time immemorial before going into battle – a deliberate defiance of their own mortality, but one chosen carefully not to break any superstitions or tread on personal fears or beliefs. Too many times men had been jinxed by predictions one way or the other, and so discussions of outcomes were usually scrupulously avoided by combat veterans.

"You will make it a priority to secure and use the Relic?" Malachi said to the two *Crusaders*.

"Of course," Father Nathaniel replied. Then he added is a firm voice: "At any cost."

Malachi nodded. They knew their priorities well, having trained for almost every scenario and situation possible. This particular scenario he knew was listed as a D-4/BLD, *Battle in a Large Building*, in the training manual that had been developed and continually updated over hundreds of years. Their MO was simple: secure entry, find the target or associates of the target causing maximum destruction along the way, and hit the Beast with as much firepower as possible to weaken him and get close enough to drive a blessed stake into his heart. If they were unable to secure the Relic, they planned to return to their traditional stakes though they also carried a special "stake" that could be used from a distance.

Father Oberon was skilled in the use of this one: a custom, powder charged, shot-gun looking weapon containing a bolt fashioned from ironwood taken from a Caribbean tree called *lignum vitae* meaning somewhat ironically, the *Wood of Life*. Recognized as the hardest and heaviest wood in the world, it had a specific gravity of 1.37 and under most conditions would wear better than iron. Just in front of the bolt's nock, the fletching was fashioned from aluminum, hinged and slanted forward so that it would open in flight and on impact become an effective barb preventing the arrow from passing through the heart. Secure in place, it would prevent Adramelech's powers from healing the wound and seal his fate. At least, for a time. This bolt had been blessed by three successive popes and, according to everything they had learned, if it entered his heart, it should put the Beast down. Unfortunately, it was a one-shot deal.

"I see something," the police observer shouted. The pilot slowed the helicopter until it hovered over the object held in the spotlight. It was an Austin Mini with its right front end in the ditch; snow was rapidly gathering on most of the automobile and the ground around it.

Cruickshank and Malachi had taken off their seat belts and crammed forward to see out the front window. Frazer obligingly tilted the copter forward, the NIGHTSUN illuminating the custom paint job on the automobile; a British Union Jack flag motif encompassed the entire vehicle.

"Father Gallo?" Cruickshank guessed.

"Who else would be out here at this hour?" Malachi asked.

"Hasn't been there that long," Cruickshank said, as the copter rotated above and around the Mini and Cockerill kept the NIGHTSUN illuminating the vehicle. The intense downdraft from their rotor blades whipped up twigs and grass and bits of ice and snow throwing them into the air and, at times, fully obscuring their view of the vehicle.

"How can you tell?" Malachi asked squinting at the vehicle through the sleet and debris.

"Snow on the roof and on the door...none on the bonnet. It's melting too rapidly to stay. Means the engine is still warm."

"Oh you Brits," Malachi muttered at the detective who simply smiled. "Let's go."

The helicopter swung to the right, its nose came up and it quickly accelerated. It moved over the ground again at about 50 feet and at a more cautious speed. Within a few minutes the pilot muttered an epitaph and brought the craft to a jarring and complete stop in the air, slamming all the occupants against their seat belts. It hovered there for a moment as all stared out the front windscreen. No more than 100 meters in front of them, the NIGHTSUN swung up to reveal a charcoal grey, round, stone corner tower, with a row of square windows immediately under its rounded peaked roof. The windows spilled yellow light.

"Arthur, didn't you see it?" Frazer asked, annoyance in his tone.

"No, I had the light pointed down," Constable Cockerill replied. "I was looking at the ground."

"We almost hit that bloody wall. You're the observer – observe!"

"Sorry Myles...sorry," Cockerill said contritely, though they both knew the pilot's annoyance was more with himself since he was flying the craft.

"Righto...and so will I," the pilot finished lamely by way of apology.

Constable Cockerill moved the light from the base of the tower and brought the beam slowly up the wall illuminating most of its 150-foot-plus height. They hovered in front of it like a mosquito eyeing a fencepost. "Shades of Frankenstein, it's massive," he said.

Frazer moved his controls and the helicopter rose straight up 200 feet and above the structure. He brought it over the wall and pivoted on its own axis as the NIGHTSUN revealed an inner courtyard surrounded by 100-foot walls with four corner towers half again as tall. A flanking tower stood on the side of the east wall, and there was a smaller lookout tower at the rear near the ocean cliffs. Yellow light spilled from windows in the rectangular courtyard and from some in the corner towers.

The castle was monstrous and the pilot immediately wondered two things: how his passengers intended to gain entrance, and if they were going to ask him to set his craft down in the courtyard. He hoped not as the shrieking wind was continuing to rock the copter. It was flowing over the ramparts likely creating a partial vacuum inside the courtyard. He was sure he'd encounter a nasty downdraft if he tried to land within the walls.

"Right, let's get down there and get to work," Malachi said, brusquely. "Land this thing somewhere in front of the castle." Though he tried to sound confident, the longer he looked at the fortress, the more trepidation Malachi felt. He wished they had been more circumspect in their approach, but what was done was done. There would be no element of surprise unless they were extremely lucky. Monsignor Rautenberg had pinpointed the Relic as being within the structure. He wondered how Father Gallo had managed to get in there. Was there another entrance? If so, where was it?

The EC 145 spun about, accelerated away from the castle over the edge of the cliff and over the black raging sea for a few moments and then swung back in a tight 180 degree arc. The NIGHTSUN illuminated a fairly level patch of dead grass below in front of the castle and they curved down and hovered ten feet above the ground. They were about 120 feet out in front of what looked like a drawbridge and a set of huge wooden doors inset in the stone face.

"How the deuce are we ever going to break in there?" Cruickshank asked, looking up at the immensity of the stronghold from a bygone age. "I don't imagine he has a doorbell." No-one laughed, no-one commented.

As though to answer Cruickshank's question, a huge cloud of black-tinged, yellow fire suddenly mushroomed from the entrance doors at the end of the drawbridge. A blast of hot air hit the helicopter at about the same time a deafening crack sounded and the chopper reeled backwards.

Frazer slammed the throttle to max and the engine whined as they tried to escape by gaining altitude. Instead, they spun out of control. "We're going down …we're crashing…brace, brace!" he yelled in frustration. The laws of aerodynamics now assumed control and the pilot became nothing more than a passenger as cockpit alarms screamed in protest and the chopper began to spin on its own axis. With a stomach clenching motion the helicopter abruptly ceased flying and pan-caked into the hard earth.

The tail hit first and immediately bent sideways with the anti-torque tail rotor chewing into the rocks, dirt and grass. Within a split second the rest of the chopper dropped the remaining few feet to earth. Tilting sideway as it impacted, the main rotor blades wind-milled into the ground. Their composite materials bent, splintered and shattered sending a hail of dirt and plastic-like debris exploding into the air. Within a few seconds it dropped back to the earth, rattling like buckshot against the skin of the helicopter.

Silence!

Inside the cockpit Frazer coughed as the first hint of burning electrics wafted into his nostrils. He called out: "Everyone okay? Everyone out!"

The only response was the wind howling anew outside and the distant roar of crackling flames from the burning drawbridge in front of the fortress.

~ 8 ~

At the base of the stone stairs was a growing chorus of chattering and clicking sounds much like a nest of angry hornets. Clay looked from Rosalita's body down to the lower level and his heart sank. Primal fear overwhelmed him as hundreds of reddish orange creatures with large heads and protuberances from their temples gathered at the base of the stairs. Their watery eyes were larger than humans but their bodies were small and misshapen – barely three feet high. Many carried small, hand-held scythes in claw-like appendages as they scuttled rather than walked and jockeyed for position below; some gestured angrily upward at Clay. Though they milled about, a teaming mass of nightmarish freaks, something seemed to be holding them back from climbing the staircase.

Gallo stood back, looking down at them with revulsion on his face. Quickly, however, it was replaced by a business-like look, that of a man with places to go and things to do. Remarkably his movements and gestures seemed to be in keeping with a young man rather than one of his actual age. Clay quickly moved to Maria and pulled her to him while he covered Gallo with the revolver. Gallo looked at him and picked up the aluminum case.

"Still think I can't hurt you?" Clay asked a certain unholy satisfaction in his voice.

"Obviously she had outlived her usefulness but I have the healing," Gallo replied. He began to move towards them holding out his free hand.

"Don't..." Maria cried, pulling Clay backward.

With no other recourse, Clay fired at Gallo but shot to wound him. His aim was true and the aluminum case dropped to the floor. Maria made a small cry and turned away as blood flowed freely from the priest's ruined hand. Then, both watched in shock as the hand reformed itself in seconds and Gallo used it to brush flecks of blood and bone off his cassock.

Maria seized the moment, fearlessly stepped forward and snatched up the aluminum case with one hand and her nearby Crucifix with the other. Immediately she could sense warmth and calm radiating from the Relic inside; it also gave her strength.

Gallo looked at her with an amused smile. "Fine, you carry it. You can't open it anyway. Now, if you don't mind, *he's* waiting." He turned to walk away and then said without looking back: "Don't bother trying to escape; there's no way out. And if you go back down there, those little monsters will dice and slice you into party-sized snacks and suck up the pieces. If you're lucky. Now come, or it will be the worse for you."

He strode off and Clay and Maria looked at each other.

"I love you Clay...with all my heart," she said, looking deep into his eyes. "Remember that, no matter what happens. Come, it's time; don't be afraid – God will protect us for now."

Carrying the Relic case in one hand, Maria led him down the hall after Gallo. On their way, they passed a long corridor. Halfway down its length Clay saw an opening to a large foyer. He wondered if the two oak doors with the iron stays he had seen from outside were down that corridor. If so, the doors led to the drawbridge, a possible escape route.

They soon entered the Great Room behind Gallo where they could see a single, solitary figure seated on a couch in front of an impressively large open-hearth fireplace.

Adramelech stared into the fire where tiny renditions of human figures writhed and threw themselves left and right trying to escape the hot coals. Gallo said nothing but merely watched as though waiting to be noticed; they could see him trembling. Clay looked down the long room and noted the assortment of weapons on the walls, the lined up suits of armor, and the huge stained glass window at the end. Maria took an involuntary step backwards, almost overcome by a contagion of evil emanating from the figure.

"Lord and Master…" Gallo finally began, in a halting voice.

Adramelech eased to his feet without surprise and spun towards them. "Speak," the Arch Demon ordered in a baritone that seemed just a little off key, a curious harmonic of double notes sounding as though they had been run through a series of electronic reverberations with nanosecond delays.

Clay and Maria stared in awe at the man who seemed to tower above them although standing almost twenty feet away. His features were perfect and Maria couldn't help thinking he was the handsomest man she had ever seen. His coal-black hair was swept straight back from his wide forehead set over a strong, perfectly proportioned nose, and midnight blue eyes. His broad shoulders were covered in a black cape lined with purple and his entire being was clad in a tight-fitting black body suit of some substance that showed a well-muscled form. He ignored them and kept his gaze on Gallo.

"Y-Yes…" Gallo said. "I have the-the soldier and the girl….and the Relic."

"And, you also bring me barbarians at my gate?"

"I-I don't understand," Gallo protested, fearfully.

"Of course you don't," he answered. "Your limited intellect barely allows you to see beyond your own nose." His gaze shifted towards Clay and Maria. He smiled this time, his eyes twinkling with good humor. "Well, well…what have we here?" His voice had now become clear, strong and deep; in fact, it seemed to have a largeness and richness that reached out to caress and nurture them. "It's been a long time, Lieutenant Montague; Panama wasn't it?" He didn't move from where he stood but merely cocked his head in a questioning manner. "Though we almost met in Vermont."

Clay stood there with the Ruger in his hand feeling somewhat foolish. He didn't know whether to point it or holster it. Adramelech made the choice for him.

"That's a dangerous weapon, my friend," he purred, as he beckoned them to advance. "Why don't you put it away until you *need* it? It can't hurt me but your pretty companion could wind up begging you to blow her brains out. And you might do it, if it amused me."

Obediently Clay pulled the yellow anorak back and holstered the revolver. He could feel Maria trembling beside him. She was shaking so hard he thought her teeth were going to chatter aloud. Desperately he wished she'd get hold of herself and not embarrass them both in front of this amazing gentleman. After all, charm and charisma fairly oozed from him and he seemed so delighted to see them. The least they could do was guard their manners and afford him a hearing. Indeed, how could anyone blessed with such a perfect countenance be as bad as they had made him out to be? He graciously beckoned them forward.

Adramelech continued as they all stopped a few feet from him: "Yes, it was Panama, that tropical armpit of the world where those fucking monks got their hands on me decades ago. I must remember later to go back there and turn it into one great smoking hole in the ground, a stinking hemorrhoid to all those who would defy the true power."

His words hit Clay like being dowsed with ice water. He berated himself for his thoughts of a few moments before. What had he been thinking? This was a living manifestation of evil, the Beast itself, an arch enemy of all that was good and pure. So why was he having to fight rising feelings of love and charity towards the man.

"Steady Clay," Maria warned, feeling him relax beside her and guessing why he showed no concern. "Don't fall under his spell. He is evil…he is a devil. Pray for strength …pray…pray." Clay could hear her whispering the *Our Father* again and again as they stood.

The detective felt as though two halves of him were fighting for supremacy, one yearning to surrender to the charms of this handsome and friendly stranger, the other urging him to loath and distrust it. Still, his manner was so warm and inviting that Clay was actually beginning to feel affection for him. He took a deep breath, recited a silent Hail Mary and asked for the strength to resist. He felt the demon's hold on him begin to wane.

"There, there," Adramelech said. "Relax. We're all old friends here, though I think our esteemed Father Gallo may carry a grudge based on his time as my house guest. Still, he did come round. See, if you promise a mortal immortality, few will refuse, no matter what the price. And, we all know that Father Gallo was perilously close to going to that big reward in the sky. Or, was it to eternal damnation for his sins against the church. Can't remember – must be something in the water."

He laughed and fixed the old priest with a wicked stare as he swept back his cloak over one shoulder. "He was some firebrand when he was younger though; before he decided to settle, that is. Always questioning dogma, always lobbying for revisions in an organization that resists change like a bad smell. Yes, he was a thorn in the side of the Catholic Church for some time." He laughed out loud and then resumed his speech. "But if you think he spoke ill of his God and his church because of his inherent inability to harbor faith, you should have been privy to his other inner thoughts as well. I was...after a fashion."

Gallo stood limply in front of Adramelech like a deactivated puppet, not reacting to anything said.

Adramelech now turned slightly and faced Clay. "Man, remember that nurse that looked after you in the veteran's hospital in New York? The one with the ass. Well he wanted nothing more than to ram his pickle into her and watch her eyes light up. And, his housekeeper? Many a night he dreamed of her in his bed, I tell you. He was certainly a randy old fart. But like all old guys when they have little left to offer, he resumed his desire for his religion."

Gallo still stood mute in front of the demon, eyes downcast, posture wilting the longer he stood erect.

Adramelech advanced and waved his hand in front of the priest's face. "Holy boy...still got doubts about the Church? About your God? About those mongrels in the Vatican? Let's hear from you. Oh, I forgot." He looked up at Clay and Maria with a tiny apologetic smile. "He's still *mine*; perhaps I'll give him back his mind and we'll see what he thinks. Look...hocus pocus! *I release you from my will.*"

Father Gallo staggered, caught himself and slowly shook his head. He looked up at Adramelech. "You!" he whispered in anger, as though seeing Adramelech for the first time. The old priest spit at the demon, his hatred as plain as an immediate and evident deterioration in his physical condition. His shoulders lumped into their usual rounded condition, his frame bent forward and his stance became that of an arthritic-laced 75-year-old. Pain flashed across his face as he stiffly sought to move a few steps.

"You see," Adramelech said. "I take him in, nurture him and make him one of us and what thanks do I get. Nada. As soon as I remove my influence, he reverts back to type. See, he's a priest again…but only because I no longer want control of him. Because I no longer need him. He fulfilled his purpose, to deliver you two and your precious little case there. Now he has outlived his usefulness. Hey, holy boy. Face it, my dear Father Gallo; you're a professional fuck-up."

Summoning his remaining energy, Father Gallo suddenly leaped at the demon, his hands going for his throat. Adramelech smashed him flat with a backhand that rendered the priest senseless and sent him sprawling, rag-doll-like, to the floor.

Forgetting her fear, Maria hurried forward, knelt beside the old man and looked at Adramelech with contempt. "You are doomed, Beast…God knows it, we know it and *you* should know it," she called out in a surprisingly firm voice. She confirmed Father Gallo was breathing normally and, clutching the aluminum case to her breast, retreated back to Clay. There was nothing more she could do.

The demon grinned maliciously. "Oh, there you go. Spoiling the party with your God things. Look little girl, your God…actually…*our* God… doesn't really meddle down here anymore, does He? After all, He sent you His Son with the intention of saving mankind and how did you humans repay Him? By whipping the shit out of His boy, jamming a crown of thorns on His head and nailing the little bastard to a cross – thank you very much. Wow…no reception, no cake and no parade.

"So even you can understand why He was pissed with you. I mean, *really* pissed." He chuckled again. "No more leading His chosen people to glory; no more redemption for the Jews. And no more free manna from Heaven. No sirree Bob…after that little debacle, you may have noticed that he let a lot of bad things happen here. Genocides, plagues, fires, floods, earthquakes, wars and even…corporate malfeasance. Now that last one is a real shitter isn't it? All those captains of industry going to jail? What? About five out of five thousand who deserve it? Boy when I'm king, I'm going to recruit those good ole corporate types since they know how to slip it to the public without them even feeling it. Long as they get their stock options and obscene bonuses, fuck the shareholders and the rest of the world. They happily sell both their humanity and morals for pieces of paper. But you know when they see the light? When they're gasping for their last fucking breath. Then they expect to be forgiven." He laughed shrilly. "But by that time they discover that they've been abandoned and nobody in hell really gives a shit about a few pieces of paper with pictures of dead presidents on them."

"G-God has not abandoned us," Maria responded, though shakily.

"SHUT THE FUCK UP," Adramelech screamed, his voice booming off the walls and echoing down the corridors. Panicked squeaking and clicking could be heard from afar.

Clay and Maria visibly wilted and held each other tight, the case between them. The air had grown darker and thicker; once again they began to gasp for breath.

The Arch Demon seemed to regain his composure and the twinkle was back in his eye as he manipulated his own shoulders as though slipping back into a more comfortable role. "You're right Maria, He hasn't abandoned you. He's just forgotten about you and the Catholic Church and every other godforsaken religion in this world. That's where the term comes from – God-for-saken – means He's left on the last train to Clarkston…hopped a slow boat to China…took a powder…punched His ticket and is *outta* here."

"You will never defeat the Lord."

"Defeat Him? He won't even come out and play. Where is He, pray tell?" He reached down with a single hand and lifted up the end of the couch on which he'd been sitting moments before. "Is He here…under the couch? Nope." He dropped it with a loud crash that echoed in the hall.

"Is He in my pocket?" He dug a hand into a side pocket. "Nope. Not there neither. Where is He? It's a fair question, isn't it? Do you see His handiwork in the diseases, famines or pestilence? Nope. But you see my boss's handiwork everywhere. Why just yesterday we wiped out a whole busload of those Holy Rollers on

US I-95." He chuckled again. "Get this. They were all still singing hymns when they went over the cliff in their new, Sunday go-to-meeting van. Course I can't mention the brand name of the vehicle whose brakes failed, but let's just say it wasn't Japanese. If those Nips know one thing, its quality; got to give them that."

Adramelech stretched and yawned showing perfectly white teeth in a wide handsome mouth. "Now I suppose you think because I'm all dressed up here and look pretty good for a human, that we're going to all sit down at a Last Supper or something, but the truth is I'm tired. Yes, even demons in human form need their sleep. So I'll just take that case of which you seem so fond, Sister Maria. Or have you abandoned all that malarkey because you have the 'hots' for Lieutenant Montague here? Sorry, that should be Detective Montague, right?"

Maria reached down and tried to open the snaps of the case but they held fast. She nodded to herself and abandoned any further attempts. "His will be done," she said simply.

"You bet, *his* will is to be done," Adramelech said. "Of course, we aren't thinking of the same party, I'm sure. Now look. We can do this the easy way or the hard way. The easy way is to give me the Relic and I'll smite you and you'll be history and the world will live happily ever after. Or *unhappily* ever after, as it were. Or, I can chase you round trying to get my hand up your skirt and eventually you'll falter and I'll have my way with you AND get the case. Truth is, I'm tired and I have some of your hangers-on to deal with outside. So let's make a deal. Give it to me or I'll kill you both…slowly." He grinned. "Now you make a counter-offer…and we'll see what happens." The last sentence came out as nothing more than a malicious threat.

Clay and Maria watched in fascinated horror as Adramelech began to morph into an alternate humanoid form. His shoulders and arm and leg muscles grew more pronounced; his head became triangular in shape, his nose lengthened and lips stretched wide accompanied by sickening wet snapping sounds. His eyes had changed from an attractive blue to a black shiny obsidian obscuring the whites entirely. If the eyes were the windows to the soul, Clay and Maria were looking into turpitude of depravity, wickedness and hopelessness. The transformation complete, the Beast grinned.

Father Gallo had regained consciousness and was trying to rise. He held up one hand. "Sister...Maria, don't let him get the Relic," he implored. "God forgive me for what I've done."

"Oh don't get sanctimonious on us, Father," Adramelech said sarcastically. "You really didn't have any control, so why should anything have to be forgiven? If you'd like, old man, I'll write a letter to your boss telling him how I corrupted you and used some magic to get you to betray your friends, your church and everything you tried to believe in all your life —."

At that precise moment a clap of thunder split the air and the oak doors in the foyer blew inward sending splintered pieces of wood, chunks of stone and shards of fire ricocheting into the Great Room.

~ 9 ~

The pilot busily shut down systems, turning knobs, flipping switches and punching buttons until all power and fuel flow was cut. "We've got to get out," Frazer shouted to his passengers as he freed himself from his restraining harness. He grabbed his observer by the shoulder: "Arthur, wake up! Are you hurt?"

"N-No...I don't think so," Cockerill replied, recovering from shock and also undoing his harness.

"Cardinal...Chief Superintendent...everyone back there...is anyone injured?"

After a stunned silence, all four passengers leaped into action and unbuckled their seat belts as smoke began to fill the helicopter. Frazer heard a chorus of voices claiming they were unhurt.

While the rotor, and tail had pretty much disintegrated, the main body of the helicopter remained twisted and dented but in one piece.

"But that was a piss poor landing, old chap," Cruickshank grumbled, forcing open the door with a squeal of metal on metal.

The six men tumbled out the door to the ground, the *Crusaders* hauling huge, navy blue duffle bags emblazoned with gold, templar-style crosses. Frazer looked at the wreckage and shook his head. "What a bloody shame! I just couldn't hold her. There'll be right hell to pay for this."

"Nobody could have controlled it totally in that blast," Constable Cockerill said, laying a sympathetic hand on his shoulder. "You did a jolly good job in saving our lives, Myles."

The pilot reluctantly nodded.

Malachi, Cruickshank, and the two priests came round the wreckage and gathered together looking at the drawbridge. In fact, it wasn't the bridge on fire at all, but one of the oak doors. The other was partially blown off its hinges with pieces of it lying on the bridge blazing away. The opening itself was a sheet of flames licking hungrily at the remaining door, the assorted framing and the twisted steel staves effectively blocking the half entrance.

"Any idea who blew the doors?" Father Nathaniel demanded, as he and Father Oberon pulled on black leather gloves, extracted M-16s from their equipment bags, busily slapped 30-shot box clips into them and chambered initial rounds. They were ready to fire at the first pull of the trigger. A lethal-looking shotgun was slung over the shoulder of Father Oberon. Each man now reached into his personal duffle bag and selected three blessed hardwood stakes which were quickly fitted into their cartridge-like bandoliers.

"Father Gallo, perhaps?" Malachi ventured.

"No matter sir, we've somewhat lost the element of surprise." Father Nathaniel said. "Time to get in there before they regroup or whatever."

"We're coming," Malachi added, as the priests blessed themselves and began to move out.

Both priests stopped dead and Father Nathaniel held up a hand as his companion also turned back to the group.

"It would be better to wait until we clear the *immediate* area, Your Eminence," Father Oberon said, looking back at the huge fortress before them.

"Afraid not, my friends," Malachi insisted. "You'll need all the help you can get." He looked at Frazer and Cockerill. It wasn't going to be pleasant inside. If they failed, there was little use in more dying. Also, the two men brought little added value to the equation so he quickly found a way to spare them and their self esteem. "We need you two to guard the wreckage or even better…get the hell out of here and get us some help. I'm sure we'll need a doctor before this is done. Also, see if the village has any sort of ambulance."

The pilot and police observer looked at the size of the castle, the roaring fire in front and the weaponry of the priests. Trying not to appear too eager, they said in chorus: "If you're sure, sir…very good, sir…!" and immediately headed off across the boggy land.

"I'll go along with you Mustavias and arrest this blighter," Cruickshank insisted.

The two priests raised their eyebrows at Cruickshank and gave a questioning look to Malachi.

"He's a pragmatist," Malachi said, shortly.

The priests gave rueful grins and shrugged. Father Oberon brought his M-16 up, sighed and said: "Well…time to slay the dragon."

~ 10 ~

Clay and Maria scrambled to their feet, yards from where they had been standing after being hit by the concussion of the blast. Stunned for a moment by the explosion, they stared around at the smoke and wreckage. The main force of the blast had been deflected off an inner wall facing the doors and directed down the corridor they passed and into the Great Room where a previously pristine setting had been turned into a melee of overturned couches and chairs, smashed lamps and burning carpets on the floor. There were banners aflame on the walls and an assortment of medieval weapons and pieces of metal armor scattered everywhere. The suits of armor lay in precise rows along the walls like dead medieval soldiers.

Adramelech was nowhere to be seen and Father Gallo was picking himself off the floor. "What happened?" he asked, blankly looking around in a daze. His forehead was bleeding from a three-inch gash. "Oh…my Lord, I remember. Come, we can escape through the tunnel."

"Why should we listen to you," Clay said, still angry over his betrayal.

"It-It wasn't me…he-he had some sort of control," Father Gallo stammered. Clearly confused, and yet with memories rushing back, the old priest could barely maintain his balance. His previous strength and agility was long gone and he was breathing hard with the effort of merely standing. "I don't know what happened to me. He took me when I got off the plane in London and brought me to some cemetery." More memories followed and the sudden despair was evident on his face. "Oh my Heaven, he sent me to meet Father Gant. He made me..." Tears flooded his eyes and he sank to his knees. "No...no...Frederick," he kept saying over and over as memories of what he had done returned.

Though not understanding his lament, Maria stepped forward. "Father Gallo, please get hold of yourself! Nothing was your fault. But we must leave here at once."

"Go-go without me...I deserve to die for what I've done," Father Gallo said, down on one knee now and trying to catch his breath. "I remember...I was to bring you here." He looked around and slowly shook his head in amazement. "I betrayed you. What on earth have I done?"

Clay dragged out his revolver, flipped the cylinder open, and dropped the spent shells with a clatter onto the stone floor. He used a speedloader to punch six more rounds into the chambers.

"You have done nothing wrong, Father...come with us," Maria persisted.

"Leave...save the Relic...save yourselves," he answered. "With me along, you will never make it. I'll try and delay him. Go...go *now*! I beg you!"

"He's right Maria...come on," Clay said, grabbing her by the hand and heading through the smoke for the foyer. She still clutched the Relic in its case and together they ran towards the burning entranceway. Within seconds they skidded to a stop as they looked at the huge doorway which was now a solid mass of roaring flames. Only one door was partially down. Still, what remained was a burning and twisted mass of metal and wood that formed an impenetrable barrier.

"We can't get out," Maria cried. "We'll burn to death if we try."

"We have to make it back to the tunnel," Clay said, pulling her towards the Great Room and then around and down the corridor towards the steps to the lower level from where they had entered through the tunnel.

As they ran, Clay separated from Maria for a moment and scooped up a sword that had been blown off a wall. Ruger in one hand and sword in the other, he raced to the head of the stairs; they had just started down when they heard the clicking noises and the squat, freakish familiars ran en mass towards the base of the stairs. Their reddish orange figures appeared by the hundreds from down a hallway scrambling, slipping and falling in a mad haste to reach their quarry.

Five scuttled up the stairs and met Clay and Maria halfway; he fired five times in quick success knocking them backwards to be quickly replaced by ten more. He fired his last bullet, jammed the Ruger into his belt and pushed Maria behind him as he wielded the sword cutting into the small mutants with devastating results. Guts, brains, blood and tissue flooded the staircase in a bloody carnage causing those trying to run up the stairs to slip in the gore and fall back into others. But, as he hacked away at the drone-like figures, he realized that there was no winning this battle; two dead ones were quickly replaced by two others and five wounded were replaced by 10 others trying to crowd onto the steps.

"Back up the stairs," he shouted. As soon as Maria had made it to the top, he flung the sword at the small freaks and ran back up to join her.

The familiars followed but surprisingly slammed to a stop at the head of the stairs, obviously afraid to come any farther. They squeaked and clicked at each other, their eyes rolling and pincher claws snapping but none seemed to have the courage to trespass into what must be their Master's domain.

Clay pulled out the revolver again, spilled the empty shells, and punched six more rounds into the weapon via another speedloader. He had two speedloaders left still secure on his gun belt. Both he and Maria were panting from the tension and exertion. Clay desperately looked backwards down the corridor towards the Great Room. They had to pass through it to try the foyer again.

"C'mon," he said, less sure now they would ever make it out.

"Where's Adramelech?" Maria cried, franticly.

"I don't know but pray he's busy," Clay answered. "Let's go."

They ran full tilt back down the hall, their shoes clattering on the stone floor, only to almost run into Father Gallo who was heading towards them. "Maria, give me your Crucifix. I'll hold him off if he comes back. You save the Relic." She passed him the cross and he seemed to gain strength from it. "Try the front doors."

"They're in flames, we can't get through," Clay said.

"Try again," Father Gallo yelled. "You'll never get by those things downstairs."

The doorway in the foyer was still burning though less ferociously. Clay estimated that within a minute or two, there might be a space clear enough for them to jump through. Facing the inferno he heard some clatter and could make out movements outside on the drawbridge.

"Jesus, Adramelech's waiting for us out there," he guessed, gasping for air. "Come Maria, Father…back to the Great Room…maybe there's another way out." Gasping desperately for air they all ran back. Father Gallo brought up the rear. They had barely entered the Great Room when there was another explosion from the foyer behind them followed by the sound of machine-gun fire ricocheting off the stone walls. At that moment, Adramelech in his full and true demonic form strode into the Great Room, took two steps to clear the stone archway and leaped upward spreading his wings and rising thirty feet in the air to glare down at them from near the ceiling.

He was a ferocious sight, indeed. Long gone were the smiling midnight blue eyes and the handsome face, replaced by yellow catlike orbs set in a triangular head with arched cheekbones. A slanted mouth revealed razor sharp teeth glinting between thin lips drawn back in a perpetual snarl. He was entirely naked and his blue-black hairless skin was taunt and sickly shiny, stretched over a muscular frame. Two formidable horns protruded from his forehead, and pointed ears were set flat to his head. Surrounding him were large, angry blue-bottle flies buzzing and swarming.

With arms out, as though in supplication, he hovered on two ribbed, bat-like wings that slowly moved keeping him aloft. His arms ended in talon-like claws which now opened and closed in eager anticipation of what he would do to those staring up at him in dread.

As shouts sounded in the background, Clay felt an unquenchable fear; he was looking into the face of a terrible death. He was certain that he and the woman he loved were about to be killed.

Unless…!

There was one last desperate chance, one possibility that might let them live a few minutes longer and he took it. He held the revolver with one hand and grabbed the Relic's case from Maria with the other.

~ 11 ~

As Malachi and his men raced towards the yellow glow of the burning drawbridge, a stronger wind had suddenly begun to blow sending the heavy cloud cover racing across the night sky away from the castle. In fact, it came not from any point of the compass but from on high – it was blowing straight down. As the clouds cleared away in all directions simultaneously, cascading carpets of millions of stars appeared against a deep purple backdrop; the brilliant points of the various constellations gleamed overhead. The full moon had also emerged once more, and flooded the area with a pale white light allowing the men to see their way as they advanced.

They reached the drawbridge and the two priests began picking up flaming boards and throwing them left and right, some falling into the moat where they struck the water with a hiss and were doused. Protected by their gloves, the *Crusaders* worked to clear a path for Malachi and Cruickshank; the latter now wondering what the hell he had gotten himself into.

"Who *is* this chap?" the detective asked. "How in bloody hell could he live up here in such a place and not be inundated with tourists, or at least questioned by the local constabulary?"

"For Heaven's sake…I told you that he's not a man, Ian." Malachi yelled irritably as they moved forward.

Malachi's satellite phone suddenly rang and all action stopped. Cruickshank raised his eyebrows and the two priests looked at him incredulously, their expressions imaginable but indiscernible since they were silhouetted against the burning entranceway.

"I know, I know…" the cardinal grumbled at the others, punching the receive button.

"It's Heinz," Rautenberg said, from afar.

"Not now," Malachi replied shortly. "We're storming the ramparts, Heinz. And, I *mean* just that."

"That's just it," the Monsignor said. "I was looking at a satellite photo of the area from last month. It wasn't there."

"What wasn't where?"

"The building wasn't there. The structure just appeared in the last month. A physical impossibility based on its size–."

"Noted," Malachi responded, perfunctorily. "Thank you, my friend. Must go." He punched the end button and said to the others: "Ask and ye shall receive. This entire structure wasn't on a satellite photo taken last month. Small wonder that over the years we couldn't find it. It's only here when he needs it. Still think we're dealing with a mere *madman*, Chief Superintendent?"

Cruickshank spread his hands in ignorance and remained mute, wondering what sort of illusory world he had entered. Was he really trying to break into a castle on the moors in the middle of the night with demons afoot, or was it all a bizarre dream? The answer came all too soon in the voice of one of the priests.

"We'll have to blow the other door and get some of the wreckage away at the same time," Father Nathaniel explained. Father Oberon was working in the background setting C-4 explosive charges at just the right locations. Nathaniel joined Oberon at the wrecked doors.

The two *Crusaders* worked quickly pushing the electronic fuses into the cakes of putty-like material and placing them around the door avoiding the blackened and twisted metal stays from the first door which formed an effective barrier to their entry. They soon ran back to Malachi and Cruickshank holding a small transmitter. Its electronic numerals glowed red as Oberon flipped a button cover up on the remote control. "I'll set them all off simultaneously and blow the other door into the moat," he said. "We'll have to retreat a good few hundred yards."

If any of the four men had not been concentrating on the expected explosion and happened to look up, they might have seen a star slowly descending from the night sky until it resolved itself into a glowing, pulsing ball of white translucence Light that stationed itself over the castle. The Light expanded and contracted like a living mini star, but one that sent out waves of energy signifying peace, love, morality…and justice.

~ 12 ~

"Maria," Clay said tightly, ignoring the shouting that was growing in intensity outside the hall. He heard shooting begin again. He had no idea if the shooters were friends or foes and there wasn't time to find out. He held the case up as a shield against Adramelech who hovered above them, a wicked smile twisting his already mutated features. The gleam of intelligence was gone from the demon's eyes replaced by the fixed stare of a cunning predator. Clay said to Maria: "When I say 'go,' we run for the window with you behind me. Stay close!" he looked at the old priest. "Father Gallo, I'm sorry."

"Never mind, I now have the answer to so many of my questions, my young friends. Our Lord is alive and engaged as this heathen Beast will soon find out. Please forgive me as I did not know what I was doing. I love you both in Christ."

"Forgiven," Clay and Maria said, simultaneously.

As more shouts erupted and machine gun fire intensified, the demon was momentarily distracted and spun slightly in the air to face new enemies at the entrance to the Great Hall. Clay raised the revolver and fired four times into Adramelech watching the demon take the hits. He slapped his revolver back into its holster. Father Gallo wound up like a starting baseball pitcher and, with all his might, threw the Crucifix hitting the demon in the chest; the Beast bellowed and reared back in the air as though stung.

Fathers Oberon and Nathaniel were first into the hall just as the orange familiars poured from another entranceway to engage them. Their weapons chattered on full auto as they raked the squat gargoyles with withering fire. Body parts exploded quickly covering the floor with red mucus and shiny hunks of yellow and orange flesh and guts. Empty brass cartridge cases exploded from the priest's weapons as they advanced and dropped to the floor to mix with the offal.

Oberon slapped a fresh clip into his weapon and opened up again quickly tearing up another twenty small bodies which tumbled, slipped and fell backwards. The familiars were beginning to thin out as both Oberon and Nathaniel dropped their M-16s, whipped the Brugger & Thomet's off their chests and put an end to the remaining few. The Beast in the air screamed in fury and turned its full attention to the attackers.

From somewhere behind the *Crusaders* came the disbelieving voice of Chief Superintendent Cruickshank: "My sainted aunt ...what the hell is *that*??"

Father Nathaniel shoved his sub machine gun into Oberon's arms, pulled the custom shotgun with the blessed bolt forward from where it was hung behind his back, and pointed it towards Adramelech now descending towards them.

The priest cocked it, aimed dead center at the Beast's chest and fired. The bolt exploded from the weapon towards the demon's heart. A fraction of a second before it reached him, Adramelech pivoted in the air with a smile and the bolt flew harmlessly down the hall.

Clay saw the men out of the corner of his eye and seized the moment. "Go!" he cried to Maria, as Oberon and Nathaniel both opened up with their sub machine guns again and dozens of rounds whistled overhead striking the demon. "Follow me!"

Clay and Maria turned as one and ran for their lives, their feet pounding on the stone floor, both sucking air desperately into their lungs. As ricochets and pieces of chipped stone peppered where they had been moments before, they flew towards the huge stained glass window at the end of the hall. Their open anoraks flapped straight out behind them like yellow wings.

Adramelech, hit by more slugs, screamed in rage as he continued to rain down a form of blood that hit the stone floor and sizzled like bacon fat, its natural acidity immediately eating holes in the rock. But it wasn't doing much good for the *Crusaders* as the healing instantly renewed each wound. Suddenly he folded his wings, dropped like a stone, seized the terrified but resigned Father Gallo in his claws, and dragged him heavenward. When the Beast reached the Great Hall ceiling, he grinned wickedly and opened his arms. The old priest didn't yell or fight; he merely fell silently towards the stone floor, all doubts about his holy calling fully resolved at the moment of his execution.

Panting like racehorses as they neared the window, Clay saw the lip of the frame was a few dozen inches off the floor and at least a yard wide; thinking fast, he realized it would give them a good base on which to launch themselves. With Maria close behind, he picked out the spot he would hit on the window.

At the same time he desperately tried to place the location of the window in the castle; likely the north east side. But how high and what lay beneath? If they were lucky, the moat would extend all the way around the castle. Being unlucky meant they would suffer grave injury or fall to their deaths. Still, there was no choice. They had to try it.

They reached the lip, Clay aimed the Relic case towards the point he'd selected and kicked off with all his strength straight for the spot in the stained glass with the criss-crossed leading that he surmised would be its weakest point. Holding the case close, he suddenly jabbed it in front of him with all his strength. It broke through the glass weakening it and allowing Clay's body to explode through punching a much larger hole as it shattered and clattered around him.

Glass shards burst outward....

...Clay shot into nothingness...

...And, Maria followed!

Together, they plummeted towards their fate.

They hit the cold, black water and plunged straight down submerging a good fifteen feet before their bodies slowed and they hung suspended in an inky darkness surrounded by an eerie silence. Neither could see the other, but both felt the freezing water flooding into their clothes and overwhelming all other senses. Within seconds, the need to take a breath became urgent. They had used up all their oxygen in their run and their lungs screamed for more.

Panicking, Maria tried to thrash upward. She had never been a good swimmer and she wasn't making any headway. Weighed down by the heavy wool sweater, her boots and her outer covering, she began to sink. Oh no, she thought, she couldn't die here; it wasn't to be.

Twenty feet away, Clay clawed his way to the surface and gulped a lungful of air, his legs working hard to tread water. "Maria?!" He twisted desperately left and right in the water.

Nothing.

"Maria...where are you?" Clay cried again, his voice urgent. "Maria!"

Almost twenty feet down, Maria struggled valiantly to pull herself from the muddy bottom of the moat. Numbed by the freezing water, exhausted by her efforts, her movements were sluggish and ineffective. As her strength ebbed, a comforting detachment and acceptance was already rising from the deeper recesses of her mind.

Dear Clay, she thought. How she loved him. How she had hoped against hope for a reprieve from the inevitability of her vision. How she wished desperately for him to escape what was to come and, instead, find the happiness that had eluded him for so long. But, at the same time, she also felt anger and betrayal; this wasn't what she had foreseen. How could this have happened? Jesus help me, she prayed.

As the need for air became all encompassing, she desperately shook her head, trying to force her body to wait; she yelled a muffled cry for help through closed lips.

Taking a breath meant certain death.

No, she cried in her mind. I can't!

But finally Maria's hypoxic drive pushed aside her brain's logic. Her physiology demanded oxygen and reflexively sought it; she could no longer control the signals coming from her brain. She opened her mouth and tried to breath.

As she inhaled, cold, slimy water poured into the small creature of God, flooding her lungs and squeezing out the last traces of oxygen she needed to live. She flung herself left and right, body convulsing in terror, eyes straining to catch a final glimmer of light. Within a few seconds her sight faded to a red smear and her movements weakened. After a few more moments, her body went limp. With eyes still wide and questioning, she sank onto the dark muck of the bottom.

~ 13 ~

The demon peeled away from the relentless weapons' fire. Though they couldn't kill him, the necessary healings consumed energy and prevented him from immediately dealing with the intruders. As he flew at speed around the hall, the *Crusaders* temporarily lost track of him near the broken window; they dropped their empty guns and yanked grenades from their belts. Within seconds, Adramelech flew back down the hall towards them. They both pulled pins on their black, rock-like missiles and drew back their arms waiting for just the right moment.

Cardinal Malachi and Chief Superintendent Cruickshank stared in awe and revulsion at the sight of the demon in full flight.

Adramelech now recognized Malachi from information he had extracted from Gallo. So we finally meet, Prince of Rome, he thought, his powerful wings carrying him towards the tiny group. Payback time.

The grenades exploded almost simultaneously just in front of him sending multiple shards of steel into his body. He roared in anger, indignation and frustration, faltering in flight. He beseeched Satan for more strength. He had to deal with these heathen quickly and find the others with the Relic; it must be destroyed. Adramelech's supplication was answered and a new power surged into him, a burst of strength and malice.

"Still coming," Father Oberon said tersely, as the demon flew on towards them.

"Doesn't look good," Nathaniel agreed.

"Hate being bested by this asshole."

"Likewise," Nathaniel answered, drawing his sidearm. "See you in a better place, my friend." He opened fire but it was in vain.

Within seconds, the demon swept down on the two *Crusaders* and his huge leathery wings collided with both at once and sent them exploding backwards, end-over-end to smash into the stone wall with bone crunching finality. They lay in crumbled heaps, bleeding and twisted in ways that could only signify death. Their weapons lay scattered about them on the floor.

Adramelech turned toward Malachi who held his ground in front of the awful apparition. The cardinal snatched up one of several wooden stakes from where the two *Crusaders* fell and, extending a metal Crucifix before him, advanced towards the demon now standing on the stone in front of the dead priests. The Beast felt his bowels turning to jelly. Still, determined not to show weakness, he laughed a deep guttural bellow that halted the cardinal in his tracks.

Meanwhile, another man was running to the side to take Malachi out of the line of fire; he raised a weapon and fired six shots towards Adramelech. All connected and the demon could see the fright on Cruickshank's face when he failed to react to the bullets hitting him.

"Bloody hell…what kind of creature are you?" the detective shouted.

Adramelech ignored him and slashed one wing outward sweeping Malachi off his feet. The Crucifix and the stake went spinning away across the floor.

"We will defeat you, Son of Satan," Malachi gasped, from his prone position, trying vainly to stand. His legs, badly bruised and leg muscles contracting in angry spasms, refused to cooperate.

"How flowery," Adramelech commented in a relatively normal voice, a frightful contrast to his other-worldly appearance. "I like that. Son of Satan. Sort of like Son of Sam, one of my better pupils. Ready to die?"

"As a satanic being Adramelech, you know there is no death," Malachi said, looking desperately to see if he could reach any sort of weapon. Father Nathaniel and Father Oberon, lying against the wall, would not be of help anymore, God rest their souls.

"God looks after those who do not forsake Him as you and your evil master did so long ago."

"Forsake Him?" Adramelech crowed. "We very nearly vanquished Him and banished Him from His own Kingdom. And, I'll let you in on a little secret; we are getting stronger all the time. Hopefully, you've been astute enough to have figured out that earth is merely a battleground for good and evil? And, that each soul that comes to Satan is another arrow in our quiver. At the end of this apostasy, there will be a totaling up of those souls already burning in hell without redemption, and a total rendering of His souls...doing whatever they do *up there*. Then we'll see who won and who finally presides over this human zoo."

Adramelech paused for a moment and chuckled. "The way you have turned from Him on earth is even shameful to the inhabitants of hell. Where is your charity and kindness towards one another? Where is your intolerance for blasphemy and cruelty? Where is your righteousness? Indeed, how can earth's inhabitants have hope when they have lost their spirituality, their morality and their ethics? Instead you have appointed money as your God; why don't you just get rid of those infernal Crucifixes and put up a dollar bill...or better yet...a euro in your churches?"

Malachi, wincing at the pain, matched him: "There are people on earth who may fall prey to your evil manipulations, Beast, but mankind is inherently good. There is recognition and atonement from the faithful. There is acknowledgement of our God, people doing good works, and hope for a better world."

"Well, that's what this is all about...*isn't it?*" Adramelech agreed. "Who will triumph? As for seeing through our *evil* manipulations, what of your own machinations to create saints and heroes out of a bunch of poor, miserable, dead pawns? Good works indeed!" He shook his head and laughed. "Well forgive *me*! Mother Theresa and her hospitals? Unsanitary places, fronts to solicit donations where people died alright...needlessly. But when it came to herself, she made sure she was treated at the best hospitals in the world. Her institute's account had more than $40 million in it when she finally cashed in her chips. Give me a break. Poverty was just her shtik.

"Saint Jude, the Patron Saint of travelers? I hear he bails at the first sign of danger. Get a speeding ticket and he drops you like an insurance company. And, I *love* your Saint Francis of Assisi, the

Patron Saint of Animals. That's a hot one. He liked animals alright; he liked them boiled, fried and stewed. You all make me wretch thinking about your poster children, your self-serving rituals and your baseless and flawed doctrine."

Malachi tried to rise once more but fell back. "I am not here to debate you, heathen…I am here to stop you preying on the souls of our Mother the Church. You are not of this earth. Go back to hell!"

"Dear, dear Cardinal…how can you be so self-deluded? You're in no position to stop anything lying there like a beaten cur. But enough pleasantries dear prince of the oh-so-holy Catholic Church – now is your time."

"Our father, who art in Heaven, hallowed be thy name…." Malachi said, gallantly struggling to rise even though prepared for death. Adramelech raised himself to his full height and made ready to tear the life from the cardinal. To the side, Cruickshank suddenly emptied his Webley into the Beast again, the six shots echoing off the walls.

Adramelech staggered from the impact of the slugs and looked over at the Chief Superintendent in annoyance. "Now you've made me angry you annoying little ant," he screamed. "Prepare to meet your absentee maker." And then to Malachi: "Rest well in the knowledge that, Satan Most High, will fight to claim your soul for one of our own, even if it's on the basis of ineptitude."

"We have more Relics, monster. You will not destroy them all…and one day we will put one in your heart that will finish you for good." Malachi again tried to rise to fight but his bruised leg muscles simply refused to hold him and he collapsed.

At the mention of the word Relic, Adramelech abruptly backed up and then spun about and took wing towards the broken window at the end of the hall leaving a shaken and surprised Malachi, and an equally shaken Cruickshank. They looked at each other as the beast paused only briefly on the lip of the broken window and then vanished outside. The Scotland Yard detective let out a long sigh of relief and made his way over to the wounded Malachi. He surveyed the carnage, shaking his head. In the understatement of his career he said shakily: "Rather nasty chap isn't he?"

~ 14 ~

A strong arm suddenly encircled Maria and squeezed her sternum expelling water from her lungs. Clay dragged her upwards with powerful kicks of his legs. A second later they broke the surface. He squeezed her to him, expelling more water.

He managed to keep their heads up and desperately blew air into Maria's lungs several times as he tread water. He tightened his hold on her forcing more water from her mouth and she finally coughed and took a small breath. On exhale, another brackish discharge spewed from her nose and mouth. She gasped once more, coughed several times, discharged more water, and finally welcomed pure, sweet air back into her lungs. After another minute of alternately coughing and gasping, she was finally able to breathe semi-normally. Clay swam with one hand pulling Maria to the outer edge of the moat where an earthen wall with old roots sticking out of it went straight up. A faint light from the broken window spilled down and shimmered on the water.

"God, God…oh-my…God," Maria cried, when she had her breathing under control. "Clay, t-thank you." She hung onto a root with both hands, the occasional cough still wracking her frame. Finally she shook water from her face and looked about: "The-the Relic…where is the Relic?"

Two explosions rocked the inside of the castle. A pressure wave blew out more of the now weakened window and both instinctively ducked as huge shards of glass and pieces of broken leading splashed down around them. The light from the explosions, flickering through the window, enabled Clay to spot the aluminum case bobbing about twenty feet away.

He floated Maria around him and eased her against the moat wall so she could continue hanging onto the exposed roots. Reaching the case in a few powerful strokes, he grabbed the handle and arrived back with it just as a root broke off and Maria started to sink. She grabbed another one. It broke too. Clay began treading water again trying to keep them both afloat. Neither could find a secure handhold. Exhausted, their efforts became weaker by the second. Every time they managed to grab any purchase at all, it broke away. Though using the aluminum case as a floatation device, the weight of their soaked clothes dragged them progressively lower in the water with each passing second.

Maria tried to kick to help hold them up, but her legs were now numbed by the freezing water. Her brain shunted blood to her vital organs depriving her limb muscles of the oxygen they needed to keep functioning; they began to cramp.

How ironic, Clay thought, to have somehow made it out of that hell hole alive and to drown in the very water that had saved them when they fell. "I-I don't know how long…we can do this," he stammered, the cold becoming paralytic. Already he was also having difficulty feeling his legs as he strove to keep them pumping.

"Reach up."

"What?" Clay said.

"I-I didn't say anything," she gasped.

"Reach up, fer Jesus' sake!" The command came again in a deep, strong voice, but this time with the attached Irish lilt slightly more pronounced; Father Murphy was reaching a strong hand down towards them.

"Father Murphy!" Maria exclaimed, gratefully. "Thank the Lord."

Clay immediately extended his hand and felt Murphy's strong grip secure him. Clay held on to Maria as Murphy began hauling him upward.

"I-I can't raise you both," Murphy said. "One at a time."

Clay let go and pushed Maria and the case up with his last bit of energy. He completely submerging himself in the process as the priest grabbed her. He came back to the surface sputtering and shaking from the cold. Within seconds both of them were laying full length on the grass panting and shivering violently.

"Where-where did you come from?" Clay gasped, remaining prone as pins and needles attacked his legs and feet, and the feelings reluctantly returned.

"There's donnybrook going on inside," Murphy said, ignoring the question. "I blew the first door partly off for them when I saw their helicopter landing. Apparently I used a wee bit too much of a charge and set the chopper back on its arse. Knocked me into next week too. I was down for the count and woke up in a gulley over there just as they blew off the second door to get in. I was trying to find which way was up and you two come blasting through the window. We don't have much time. Both of you have to get as far away from here as possible."

"W-Who is in there," Clay asked, as the sound of six revolver shots echoed from the hall.

"Cardinal Malachi himself…and the *Crusaders*," Murphy answered. "And that Scotland Yard detective is there as well but surely wishing to God he was home in front of the telly."

"Adramelech is too strong now," Maria interrupted, her tone brooking no argument. "Without the Relic they can't possibly kill him."

"I think it's a little late for any of that Sister. But if you really want me to do it, I will try to get the Relic back inside and in the cardinal's hands," Murphy offered.

"No Father, I must –!" She stopped and stared back at the shattered, stained glass window. Clay and Murphy followed her gaze and their hearts sank.

Silhouetted against the light from within, standing on the edge of the broken sill with wings extended, Adramelech waited like a huge bird of prey.

"Shush!" Murphy whispered quietly. "For the love of God, be still." Slowly, cautiously, he opened his long, dark cape and quietly slid between Clay and Maria on the ground, extending it to cover their yellow anoraks and the aluminum case; their only hope was a measure of camouflage. The priest also lowered his head, his broad-brimmed black hat shielding his face. They were nothing but a black lump on the black earth.

The demon stood on the shattered window's ledge for a full minute, twisting his head from left to right to listen and then, finally with a heavy beat of his wings, took to the sky. His dark shadow soon crossed the face of the moon – a devil incarnate on a mission of death.

There were no more sounds coming from within the castle.

"He'll be back," Murphy said. "Give me your jackets. And, take off those bright sweaters; they make you stand out in the dark; they're sodden anyway."

They complied and he held a sweater and anorak in each hand. "Listen to me carefully," the priest said. "The demon is out here now. I've no idea if there is anyone inside alive so we'll assume they're dead. He'll be scanning the moor for warm bodies. Everything has gone badly and it's unlikely the Relic could be used effectively anyhow. I am going to take your yellow jackets and try and draw him off by crossing the moor. You must save the Relic for another time. Head for the cliff edge; I saw a pathway a few feet down when I was casing the joint earlier. It will take you away along the cliff towards the east. Stay below the level of the ground as long as you can and then come up and get back to Stornoway. Take refuge in any church and call Monsignor Rautenberg. He will make arrangements to get you and the Relic back to Rome. Live to fight another day." He handed his satellite phone to Clay who stored it in his pocket.

"What about you?" Clay asked.

"I will do what I was meant to do. I'm an old man and I'll make him mad so it will be quick. Later…I hope many years later…we'll all meet in Heaven for an ale. Oh…tell Ronny…."

Clay looked at him. "Ronny?"

"Father Langevin," Murphy said. "Tell him-tell…just tell him there's no 'doubting Dermott' any longer." He raised his hand and made the sign of the cross over Maria and Clay, giving them his blessing. "In the name of the Father, the Son and the Holy Ghost…Amen. Now, both of you…be off! Run!"

Without further ado, he rose and set off across the moor directly away from the cliffs. Soon he began to run. When the priest was tired, he walked. He did this for ten minutes until he sensed, rather than saw, a black shadow in the clear sky behind him. He glanced over his shoulder and the shadow blotted out the stars to his right; it could only be the Beast. He raised the yellow anoraks high over his head with each hand to simulate the presence of two people and began to run.

Father Dermott Murphy ran before the wind. His age seemed to drop off as he pounded across the grass and leaped over rocks like a seventeen-year-old. He held the garments high and drove himself faster and faster, away from the edge of the cliff, away from Maria and Clay. He ran, not to save his life but to fulfill a destiny that had been his since he was born.

Far above, Satan's emissary prowled the night sky determined to find and seize a holy weapon that could surely defeat him.

Below, as he ran, Father Murphy noticed a larger-than-normal ball of light hovering in the sky. In front of him now, it flared and pulsed as though powered from within and he found it impossible to look away from it. Strangely, as he flew over the rough ground, rather than experiencing terror at what he knew was to come, a feeling of contentment and calmness washed over him. In fact, for the first time in his life, he realized that he now understood the true meaning of the word grace. A wonderfully warm feeling of deliberate sacrifice, of boundless charity and limitless forgiveness filled his body and soul.

Indeed, he never even felt Adramelech fly up behind him and drive a claw through his spine to seize and rip out his heart in a bloody extraction. Father Murphy was still smiling when he hit the ground. Moments later, when he stood up, he realized he was formless, but that didn't stop him from directing his smile up towards the Light.

~ 15 ~

Clay and Maria raced like spooked deer. The wind was dampening slightly and now blowing from the northwest as they reached the cliffs.

"Are you alright," he called to her, between painful gasps as they ran.

"Yes," Maria answered in a somewhat detached manner, slowing as they neared the cliff edge. She had stubbornly refused to allow Clay to carry the Relic.

They made the edge of the precipice and looked over at the jagged rocks and at the oversized breakers falling on them with thunderous booms far below. Maria shuddered. Then she summoned her strength for what was to come and turned to Clay with a gentle smile.

"We have to find the path down the cliff," he said, urgently, looking left and right.

Maria didn't answer.

For a moment, time seemed to stand still. The two of them looked up at the endless night sky filled with the milky wash of stars and a bloated full moon riding low in the heavens over the moor. When they turned and dropped their gaze, it was to the immense sea where a river of reflected moonlight from behind bisected it extending as far as they could see. Both vistas seemed to signify a new beginning, an endless and mysterious journey stretching far into the future. The wind even seemed warmer and more comforting now.

"Let's get going," he said, trying again.

Maria pulled him away from the edge and turned her back to the ocean. She stared over Clay's shoulder.

He turned.

About a mile away, an unnaturally large Light pulsed in the night sky. Star-like, it was too low to be a natural heavenly body. As they watched, a smaller but equally intense ball of light moved slowly up from the moor and headed towards the Light on high where it merged making the original flare brighter for a brief second.

"Father Murphy," Maria breathed.

Before Clay could comment, two other equally intense globes of Light moved away from the castle and also headed upward towards the larger Light. For some reason, Clay felt a profound sadness and loss; a lump began to grow in his throat. "W-what are they?" he asked, barely able to speak. Deep down, however, he already knew the answer.

"Souls," Maria said quietly. She placed an arm around Clay as they watched the remaining two merge with the others. "Father Nathaniel and Father Oberon."

"How-how do you know?" he asked, his voice catching.

"I know," she said simply, looking at him with a mixture of warmth and profound sadness.

Finally, another small, single ball of light made its way slowly up from the castle and then suddenly accelerated, did a joyful loop and merged.

"Father Gallo," Maria said with a tender laugh. "Now all his questions have been answered and he has his proof of God's pure love."

Clay leaned towards her, both a longing and a sense of fear clouding his handsome, grey eyes. Something compelled him to again tell her how he felt towards her. "Maria, I love you…more than life itself. I want this nightmare to end…to spend my life with you. I want to watch you go to sleep at night and wake up with you in the morning. I want to be one with you and to live our lives for each other, to have a family and be happy. Surely we have earned the right to be happy –?"

Ever so lightly she pressed a warm finger to his lips, silencing his outburst. Her eyes were shiny in the moonlight as she pressed her body against his; he could feel her warmth through their cold, wet clothes. She raised her lips, closed her eyes and they met in a tender, lengthy kiss that stretched on as they entered a place where human hearts are fortunate to go even once in a lifetime. He felt her kindness, her dedication and her inherent goodness in her kiss. He felt her strength, her faith and her devotion in her kiss. And, he felt her yearning, her surrender and her undying and eternal love for him in her kiss.

They broke away, breathless. He pulled her close again, never wanting to let her go. But something drew his eyes upward and he found himself looking back at the Light pulsing in the air. Suddenly he was afraid. In fact, he was more afraid than he'd ever been in his life. He watched it, growing and receding in intensity but all the while moving inevitably closer. He didn't want it to come closer. He wanted it to go away. He wanted it to disappear. It had taken enough.

"Why is it moving this way?" Clay asked, his question almost choking in his throat. "What does it want? What is it waiting for?"

Maria took his hand and looked up at him with love in her eyes. In a small, calm voice she gently said: "It's waiting for me, Clay."

He stared at her, this woman who – in such a short time – had given new meaning to his life, this woman who somehow reawakened emotions within him and one who he would love forever.

"N-No," he said. "I won't let you go. I love you so much." He pulled her close.

Again she placed a small finger against his lips to quiet his protests. "I'm so sorry; if I could spare you this pain, I would. I never wanted you to be hurt."

Maria, don't leave me...," he said, his throat swelling as he realized the full implications of her prior premonition. *He* was not the one in danger. But he would be the one who was hurt.

She looked at him sadly and slowly nodded. "Remember my love...."

The shrieking screech from above heralded the arrival of Adramelech as he thundered down on a violent, cold wind and landed with a dull thud on the edge of the cliff sending clumps of earth and rocks sliding over the side. The Great Carrion grinned wickedly. The Light was forgotten for the moment. They both spun about and stared at the mutation from hell that had grown larger and more powerful.

"Get back, Maria," Clay shouted, pushing her behind him.

Adramelech spread his arms while his wings moved slowly, keeping him poised at the exact edge of the cliff where any attack would be suicidal; there was no way to go after him without falling over the precipice.

Maria pulled Clay around and thrust the case at him. "It's locked, open it!" She commanded, her tone brooking no argument. They both bent over it shielding their actions.

He snatched his weapon from its holster. With four shots fired at the Beast in the castle, two remained. He aimed at the first lock and flames roared out of the barrel; the right side of the metal case sprung open. A second shot followed almost on top of the first. The top popped open. Inside the Relic suddenly pulsed with a radiant blue energy outlining its form. It snapped and hissed like a live electric wire.

Without hesitation, Maria pulled the dagger-like piece of petrified wood from the case. She held it behind her back. She moved out from behind Clay who tried to keep himself between her and the demon. He needed to intervene. He needed to get back between her and Adramelech. He needed to stop her. He faced the demon. Then, inexplicably he couldn't move an inch. He was frozen.

Maria walked purposely forward, around him.

"No Maria...*DON'T!*" Clay screamed.

As she faced the demon, he felt both desperation and helplessness. But mostly, once again...fear! Not for himself, but for Maria. It clutched at his heart and moved into his throat, an invisible hand squeezing his chest in a paralytic pincer hold that weakened his knees.

For a brief moment Adramelech smiled at her boldness as he purred empty words of encouragement and challenge, and beckoned her forward with one claw. When she reached him, he would simply retreat and she would plunge over the edge to her death below. With her, would go the cursed Relic thus assuring his sovereignty for all time.

But Maria knew she now possessed a God-given weapon...and she was going to use it. This was her destiny, the reason she had been brought into this world. She would not disappoint the Father. She would not flinch nor fail in her duty. With a cry she charged forward, pulling the Relic from behind her back.

The Beast grinned and sifted back from the edge, creating the opening where she would plunge to her death.

But her small figure didn't hesitate, teeter and fall as he'd planned. She didn't let her fear of death interfere with her purpose. Rather, her courage was such that she ran as hard and fast as she could, and leaped fearlessly across the impossibly wide void ignoring the 200-foot drop below. She slammed into Adramelech's body and with all her remaining strength, supplemented with the anger and righteousness of all of earth's creatures, she stabbed downward driving the blessed *Wood of the Cross* deep into his heart.

Adramelech screamed. Instinctively he grabbed and pulled her to him as the pain exploded in his chest. For a moment the two were frozen, hanging in the air near the edge of the cliff. A blue fire radiated outward from where the Relic protruded from his body; instantly the blue fire spread and totally covered the demon who writhed and jerked in agony as the power fried, sizzled and crackled within him. His malevolent energy was turned inward draining his physical force while pulverizing his already dried and wizened soul. He wailed in rage, a sound that began as a base roar and climbed higher and higher in pitch till it was so penetrating Clay thought his head would burst.

The exact moment the instrument of Christ's death pierced Adramelech's chest, Clay had been freed from his paralysis. He staggered back momentarily, found his balance and raced forward towards Maria to snatch her back from disaster. His heart sank as, locked in Adramelech's grip, she cast a frightened glance back at him. The deed was done and now her human instinct for survival took over.

"No!" Clay screamed hard and long as Adramelech struggled in vain to keep them both afloat in the air. They were a mere few feet below the level of the cliff. If he could just reach her…! Desperately he threw himself flat and stretched his arm over the precipice.

The demon's wings were beating frantically now, the blue fire gradually dissipating. Together Adramelech and Maria ascended a few feet, almost coming parallel with the edge. New hope surged in Clay's heart and he desperately shoved his hand out towards Maria.

She also reached for him and their fingers touched. He surged forward, grabbed her wrist and locked his grip. But the demon still had the presence of mind to see what was happening. Even in his death throes, he seized a small moment of triumph. Crushing Maria closer, he ripped her hand from Clay, and gave him a wicked smile as he pulled her out of reach. Mortally wounded, the beat of his wings began to weaken; the light of evil slowly died in his eyes.

Adramelech trilled weakly in defeat. He continued to hold Maria close as she struggled, reaching desperately out to Clay. It was not to be. They began to spiral slowly downward. As they dropped, his dead talons finally freed her; she separated from him and floated away in the air.

The Beast's body, on its back, with wings spread wide, whirled faster and faster towards the ocean accelerating away from Maria who seemed to actually slow in her descent. Adramelech slammed into the jagged rocks and shattered into thousands of pieces that immediately ignited into small fireballs. One-by-one the fireballs, shrieking madly in multiple disembodied voices, smashed insanely into the rocks of the cliff, shot up in the sky to fade into nothing, or dropped down to hiss out in the roaring surf.

Maria, also falling on her back, looked upward at Clay. The distance between them seemed to dissolve and they looked directly into each other's souls. Her eyes told him to have faith and be calm and strong. His eyes – already brimming with tears of pain and loss – were simply telling her that he loved her.

Later, Clay would question what he saw next.

He would questioned it over and over in his mind, never sure of its validity, afraid to believe, and even more afraid *not* to believe.

For some seconds, ones that confirmed a holy power's eternal commitment to humankind, he was allowed to see what few humans have ever been privileged to see. Perhaps, he reasoned later, it was God's way of making it less painful for him; possibly it was his own psyche furnishing an ending that he could live with more easily. Still, despite the doubts that regularly tested his faith for many years thereafter, he knew that to his dying day, he would be certain that he saw...what he saw.

Before Maria could plummet into the rocks and waves below, a star-bright beam of light shot down from on high and enveloped her entire body, freezing her motionless in mid-air. The beam then slowly retracted, raising her back up the face to about twenty feet below where Clay lay on edge of the grassy cliff. She seemed to hang there in limbo for a few seconds surrounded by a growing halo of magnificent radiance.

    Its brilliance was such that Clay was forced to close his eyes against the glare. Gradually, unable to resist, he opened them again. As his sight adjusted to the shining, he made out a beautiful, snow-white, winged Being, at least twice Maria's size, holding her tenderly like a babe in its arms. The Being, human looking and yet possessing a benign alien quality, gazed lovingly at Clay with large limpid blue eyes mirroring tenderness tempered with sadness, perhaps, at what was to come. Its garments were also luminous, flowing like wisps of silver mist about its body as it balanced in the night air casting brilliant reflections on the cliff and grasses surrounding Clay. Giant wings of snow white, gossamer-like feathers throbbed slowly in powerful strokes. A cobalt blue girdle that appeared and disappeared into its animated, flowing garments showed a golden sword attached to it.

    An immense positive energy surged towards Clay. No longer was he saddled with feelings of despair and sadness. Instead he felt warmth and awe. Maria, her face also enraptured, and with a peaceful smile on her delicate features, looked deep into his eyes and deeper into his heart. Her features seemed to have grown more beautiful as her tiny lips mouthed a final good-bye....

    Then her gaze shifted towards the heavens.

    And, in an instant...

    ...Maria and the Being were gone.

    They had simply vanished leaving behind the empty darkness, the howl of the wind and the massive waves of a thick, oily black ocean breaking relentlessly on the rocks below.

    Clay desperately rolled on his back and watched as the small orb of Maria's body and soul, held in the tender care of God's angel, climbed towards the ball of Light in the sky. It paused for a moment as though reluctant to leave him, but then merged.

    Its holy mission accomplished, the pulsing light became stronger and brighter and slowly moved away. Finally, its magnificence taking on the power of a super nova, it exploded and accelerated sharply upward until it became one with the stars.

    It was too much for any mortal. Clay's head spun and he passed out.

A short time later, a limping Cardinal Malachi, supported by Detective Chief Superintendent Cruickshank, found him sitting by the edge of the cliff, his shoulders occasionally wracked and quivering. As Malachi separated from Cruickshank, the Scotland Yard man looked back towards where the castle had been. "Bloody hell," he said. "It's gone. The bloody castle has disappeared."

"Back to hell, I hope," Malachi said, moving forward. "Clay…where is he…where's Adramelech?"

Clay managed to regain his self control and said simply: "Dead."

Malachi hesitated and then more gently asked: "Maria?"

"Gone…," Clay said, looking up. Tears shimmered in his eyes and he drew a ragged breath, and stared at the night sky. After a moment, he added the word: "…home."

Malachi exchanged glances with Cruickshank, waved him away, and lowered his frame to the ground beside Clay. He sat silently and patiently with his arm around the trembling man.

Later, just before dawn when the pilot, observer and police arrived, Cruickshank met them, presented his credentials and moved them away trying to explain that they all must have suffered from some sort of hallucination since there was obviously no castle or any other structure about. He began a long litany of explanations and a cover story that he would perfect over time. With no bodies and no crime scene other than a crashed helicopter, he was taken at face value.

A half-hour later, Clay and Malachi sat together at the edge of the cliff and felt the warmth of the sun as it rose to cast its golden glow over a calm, turquoise sea rolling languidly onto the rocks below under a blue sky. Clay took a deep breath, sighed, and looked up searching for the star that mattered most to him. Of course, with the sunlight now flooding the countryside, the star was nowhere to be seen.

With the torture of his terrible loss mirrored in his eyes, he looked at Malachi seeking an explanation for this final cruelty. The cardinal merely shook his head, his compassion, understanding and empathy evident but in no way an elixir for this loss. With one hand, he softly brushed Clay's hair back from his forehead as a loving father would do for a son.

It was a new day for those that had been left behind…

…And a new era for mankind.

~ 16 ~

Maria ran into the garden towards Clay and he met her halfway, seized her in his arms and spun her around in a big circle as she wailed in delight. "My God, I love you so much," she said, laughing gaily.

He put her down, looked into her sparkling dark eyes and kissed her heart-shaped ruby-red lips gently but with such enthusiasm that it turned it into a lengthy kiss of exploration and happiness. They were standing in the garden where she had once met Malachi and had been touched by the holiness of the Relic.

"You let me think I had lost you forever," he said, accusingly.

"We have to do what we have to do," she responded impishly and smoothed down her red sweater and grey wool skirt, the same outfit she'd worn the first time he'd laid eyes on her. Her hair, freshly cut, was bobbed at the front and hung in a bang over her mischievous eyes, also the exact style she had been sporting when he first saw her on the aircraft. She grinned and her little pink tongue peaked between her lips teasingly at him.

"Boy, if we weren't on Vatican grounds, you'd be in trouble young lady," he said, sternly.

"Promises, promises." She laughed. "Now we do have to display some decorum for Cardinal Malachi when he arrives."

"Oh I'm sure he'll just be happy to see us together," Clay said.

"Nevertheless, I can't turn from a novice into a tease in a few weeks."

"It didn't take a few weeks," Clay responded. "You were sending me signals the moment you met me."

"Was not."

"Was too."

They looked at each other grinning. Life was good and they were going to be married in the spring. They were there to ask for Cardinal Malachi's blessing and if he would do the honor of marrying them. Maria had told Clay that the cardinal had assured her that if she undertook the mission, whatever path in life she chose afterward would have the blessing of the church. And, she had chosen Clay.

But then, as it had so many times before, the moment arrived.

Maria took his hand and her expression became serious. "I love you Clay and I love to bring you these small moments of happiness that you seem to need so much, but it's time to get on with life. If you truly love me, you will do this."

He always hated this moment and the cruel finality it brought because it was always followed by the blackness of reality that invaded and smothered any goodness left in his heart.

"Clay?"

He didn't respond.

"Clay," Cardinal Malachi said again, as he shook the former detective's shoulder.

Clay sat up straight in the noonday sun and looked around. He was sitting on a bench in a small Vatican garden. "W-What? Maria?" he asked, and then shook his head. A sad and embarrassed smile finally played on his lips.

Malachi looked at him sympathetically. He placed a hand on his shoulder. "It's alright."

"Oh...how silly of me," Clay said, standing up. "I fell asleep for a bit. I-I seem to be doing that lately. I can't sleep at night but I fall asleep at the drop of a hat during the day." He dropped back to a sitting position on the bench, spent and disappointed.

"And you've lost more weight, both signs of clinical depression, my friend. It's been over a year now. Have you been seeing Doctor Couture regularly, as I asked?" The cardinal sat beside him on the bench.

Clay knew that the cardinal realized full well that he hadn't been seeing the doctor. "Oh, I saw her for a bit, but she kept probing for details. You know, stuff I couldn't very well tell her. At least, without being locked away in a rubber room."

"But I said that you could be completely candid with Sandra. She has treated legions of priests who have been either physically or mentally damaged from performing exorcisms, or simply worn out from hearing about sin and evil day-after-day. The job of savings souls takes a terrible toll on mere mortals." He smiled and continued. "She is also a believer in evil being able to manifest itself here on earth."

"Well, that's good," Clay responded, somewhat bitterly. "We can both say an Amen to that one, can't we?"

Malachi nodded slowly. "You know she knew Maria as a teen-ager? Both lived in the Eastern Townships in Quebec and went to school together for a short time."

Clay nodded. "She told me." He raised his eyebrows and with a half-hearted attempt at humor did an imitation of William Shatner: "Weird or what?"

Malachi looked at him seriously. "Clay, after writing my report for the archives last year I realized a few things; things I should probably share with you."

Clay was only mildly interested. "Such as?"

"Over the years, from 1989 onward, what seemed like random happenings weren't random at all. As near as I could piece things together, there must have been a plan."

"A plan? Whose plan?"

"I know you don't feel very charitable right now towards anyone or anything…so I'll simply say it was a Heavenly plan."

"A plan to kill Hitch? To kill Jody? To ultimately kill…Maria." His tone fell somewhere between bitterness and sarcasm.

Malachi felt empathy for his charge, so he gently continued: "Unfortunately they were some of the casualties of a battle that started eons ago, give or take some billions of years. The enemy makes one move and the opposing force makes a countermove just as in a physical battle here on earth. And we all played a role in it. Our brethren, like dear Father Murphy, Frederick, Benito, and the rest of our holy warriors made the ultimate sacrifice while others survived. In hindsight, your role seemed to be to get Maria to where she could fulfill her destiny, a not insignificant one, I might add. That's why you survived repeated attempts by the demon to destroy you. And Maria bested Adramelech. She sent him back to hell. And whether you want to accept what you saw on that cliff and in the sky that night…or not…deep down you know she is not dead. She is alive in Heaven as is your friend Hitch and your wife Jody."

"None of this makes sense," Clay responded, quickly. "If God is all knowing and all seeing and all powerful, why didn't He just destroy this thing …and leave the rest of us alone?"

Malachi shrugged. "Perhaps because of Original Sin. Perhaps because we initially blew it in the garden. Figuratively, of course.

We can only make a guess. Perhaps He played by the rules because He created us, gave us free will and a conscience. Then He showed His faith in our goodness and fairness and our desire to do the right thing by accepting the challenge from the darker beings. And once He accepted the challenge, no turning back. But...He didn't forsake us. First he sent His son. And when we blew that, He came up with another plan. *The Plan,* so to speak."

"And we're all cogs in the holy wheel?" Clay half-smiled, briefly.

Malachi chuckled. "Something like that, I suppose. My guess is as good as yours. Still, Adramelech got extra help. And so did we along the way." He decided to change the subject and leaned back on the bench. "I bumped into Monsignor Rautenberg, Fathers Austin and Langevin, and Bishop Castilloux at a café the other day; they said hello and promised to drop in to visit you more often."

Clay said nothing.

"Also Ian Cruickshank."

"The Chief Superintendent is here? In Italy?" Clay asked, a little curious.

"It's Brother Cruickshank now," Malachi responded, with a smile.

"He got religion?"

"That he did." Malachi paused and then said quietly: "You need help, Clay."

"I know. But I keep having these dreams. Dreams where everything is all right."

"That's because it's supposed to be all right."

"But it isn't. I lost someone that I loved dearly. We all did."

Malachi sat down on the bench and looked earnestly at Clay. "Listen to me, my friend. Do you realize the full extent of what happened out there?"

"Vaguely, I suppose. Sometimes it all seems like a bad dream, and at other times, it's so real I can't keep my hands from shaking."

"You are one of the few people on earth who has ever faced a true demon and was instrumental in its defeat. You helped send him back to hell where he belongs. I fully believe that you...all of us...had a hand in changing the course of this world. There were terrible sacrifices made by so many good people. I know Maria has received her reward and someday you will too. Not necessarily on earth."

"Well, I don't notice things getting any better, sans our demon."

"But they are. In the past year I've seen subtle but unmistakable shifts in the way everything operates. In fact, more evidence of cooperation, charity and concern for the human condition than I've seen in the past quarter century. For instance, some political leaders are looking out for the welfare of their people rather than trying to serve themselves and exploit their positions. On the private front, we have pharmaceutical companies announcing new strategies to research and develop drugs to eradicate disease rather than just developing treatments that enable them to profit from human misery."

Clay smiled in spite of himself. "Really? What about the oil companies?"

Malachi gave him a look and said: "They still don't get it."

"Insurance companies?"

The cardinal shrugged and sighed: "Get real. Still it's a beginning, Clay."

They both had a rare, quiet chuckle. Malachi then added: "The families of the pilots finally received full payouts of $2 million each on insurance policies we had on them. Tragic affair! Their local dioceses have instructions to keep an eye on the families; stay close and assist in any and every matter. The least we can do."

Clay nodded and then seemed to be trying to make a decision about something. Finally he blurted out: "Do you believe in dreams, Mustavias? That they may be a medium for the subconscious to influence our conscious existence?"

"Of course," Malachi responded, without hesitation. "*Not* to believe in dreams, is to silence prophesy. Think of the Bible. How many times were prophetic revelations made to people through dreams?"

"Well, Maria keeps coming to me in dreams."

"You've mentioned this before."

Clay knew that he hadn't mentioned it directly to Malachi but he never expected his communications with his therapist to be kept totally private. The cardinal looked at him with sadness. "And...?" he prompted.

"They're usually the same dream: we meet, flirt a little and then she tells me that if I love her, I will get on with my life."

"So what's wrong with that?"

Clay looked at him closely, trying to read his eyes. "She's telling me this in a *dream*?"

"What? She should use Western Union?"

"You're incorrigible."

"Clay, from what you've said, I believe that she is contacting you as best she can. And, obviously, because she loves you, she has your welfare at heart. You have been given a life to live on earth and it would be wasteful and ungrateful not to live it to its fullest."

Clay sighed and thought of his present existence. He lived in a small pensión Malachi had rented for him in the hills just outside of Rome where he had spent the last year doing little other than devouring books on science, philosophy and religion in a search for answers to what he had seen and experienced. The cardinal had explained to him again and again that he had to take time to recover from a profound spiritual and mental shock. Each month they met and Malachi would try to nurture Clay's spirit, even as a Vatican consulting psychiatrist worked to treat his emotional and mental well being in weekly sessions. According to the doctor, he was a prime example of Post Traumatic Stress Disorder. A diagnosis telling him he was broken didn't help much since he always had a pioneer attitude towards injuries that weren't physically evident: pull up your socks and tough it out. So he waited to get better. And impatiently waited some more. He asked to be left alone even as he hated the loneliness. Granted, the nightmares, terrible sorrow and his depression had lessened, but of late, he had missed a number of therapy sessions and hence his summons to the garden.

"There-there's another reason I haven't been seeing Sandra...I mean Dr. Couture...lately."

Malachi nodded seriously and yet knowingly, almost as though he was privy to Clay's innermost thoughts. "And, why is that?"

Clay sighed and took the plunge. "Because I'm starting to like her a little. Just a little! Very unprofessional, wouldn't you say? Not to mention, inappropriate. I never saw myself as a two-timer. And..."

"....and you feel guilty? You feel you're betraying Maria?"

"Of course." He breathed a sigh of relief. There it was out.

"Clay," Malachi said, shaking his head as though trying to straighten out an errant son for the umpteenth time. "As I said, it's more than a year since we lost our wonderful friends and colleagues. I mourn and miss them too. But Dr. Couture wants you to come back for treatment. I couldn't break the sacrament of the confessional by telling you that she...well... regards you as a *personal* special project. So just go back and see her. She'll help you work through these things."

"But Maria?"

"Surely there is no exclusivity of love in Heaven, Clay," Cardinal Malachi insisted, patiently. "I can guarantee you that if you find happiness, Maria will be able to rest knowing you're well looked after." He stood up. "Sorry but I have a meeting that I can't miss. Another one of those budget things. Let's meet for lunch next Wednesday. I've already penciled you in and I'll want to hear about your latest session with our esteemed doctor. Make an appointment with her. That's an order."

They shook hands as usual.

Malachi went to leave but then suddenly turned back, reached forward and embraced Clay, held him for a moment and said earnestly into his ear: "It's time, Clay...time to let her go."

Clay noticed that the man's eyes were uncharacteristically moist.

"Damn allergies," Malachi muttered as he hurriedly strode off.

Alone again, Clay sighed and looked around at the gardens; he found himself staring at a bed of red roses in full bloom. His mother's last words came back to him: *All that matters in life is love and that never dies; it only changes.*

Slowly he walked over and looked down. Surprisingly, amid the splash of scarlet, was a single, small yellow rose. Unlike the others, it was closed tight, even in the bright sunshine. He stared at it. Then, impulsively, he leaned forward and said aloud: "Maria, I'll never forget you but if you really want me to move on with my life, I-I need...need some sign...something." His voice trailed off.

He waited for a moment, feeling slightly foolish.

Nothing happened. Indeed, he needed psychiatric help.

Chagrined, he straightened up...

...and watched as the petals slowly opened and revealed the splendid beauty of a glorious yellow rose in full bloom. He stared at it for a full minute. It remained open, drinking in the sunshine. A feeling of great calm slowly suffused his body; he could only equate it to a blanket of love and comfort being wrapped around his soul.

"I will always love you," he said aloud, his voice breaking, his eyes welling.

Petal-by-petal the rose slowly and painstakingly closed, and immediately opened again. From somewhere a latent drop of late morning dew slowly trickled from the bud and ran down the stem.

Clay Montague stood silently for a moment, a huge lump in his throat, his own tears running unheeded down his cheeks. In his heart he knew this was a final good-bye. There would be no more dreams of happiness, no more pleas from Maria to get on with life. When he finally had his voice back, he opened his cell phone before he changed his mind. He pushed a speed dial button and was rewarded by the voice of Doctor Couture.

"Doctor Couture?" he asked, hesitantly.

"Clay," she said in surprise. "This is so amazing. I *never* personally answer my general office phone but something…just something made me do it. And, for some reason I knew it was going to be you on the other end."

"That's because I have an angel in my corner," Clay said, in all seriousness.

"Perhaps you do," she answered, with an easy laugh. "I expect I'll be seeing you again?"

"Count on it," he promised, taking another deep breath. "It's time I started rebuilding my life."

"Good," she replied. For a moment she hesitated and then said "You're a good person, Clay, and we aren't going to let that go to waste."

They exchanged a few more pleasantries and hung up.

He looked back down at the small yellow rose.

It was closed tight.

╬

Dear Readers:

Thank you for reading *The Plan*. If you enjoyed it, I would be grateful if you would tell your friends. Also please consider visiting my web site **jrichardwright.com** and then reading my next novel entitled ***Torngat.***

I am targeting its launch for the fall of 2014 and it will be available as an eBook or as a paper version on Amazon.com and other popular eBook sites. It will also be available in selected bookstores and through my web site. On the following two pages is a brief description of ***Torngat***.

Happy reading....

J. Richard Wright

TORNGAT
By
J. Richard Wright

October 1962: *Two CF-100 Long Range Interceptors scramble out of Goose Bay, Labrador, to intercept and identify a bogey coming into Canadian airspace across the Labrador Sea. Tracking the target descending from Greenland, NORAD has two concerns. The first is the target's unannounced intrusion into Canadian airspace. The second is an airspeed exceeding an impossible 1,800 knots. After the intercept, only one of two jets returns. The official Royal Canadian Air Force Air Crash Investigation Report is declared **Top Secret** and has never been released to this day.*

Geologist Matthew Corrigan is suddenly summoned to Old World Montreal by Andre Jacquard, his firm's CEO. *Labrador & Ungava Diamonds* is failing fast with a cancelled IPO and exploration capital dwindling. As legions of financial backers pull out, a chance to save the company appears in the form of Jerome St. Onge, a First Nations' medicine man who drops a 25-karat, uncut, fire-white diamond on the CEO's desk. The old native says that if Jacquard wants to know where the diamond originated, he will send Matthew Corrigan to Labrador to meet with him. Matthew's search takes him to Nain, Labrador, where he finds the diamond likely came from deep in the *Torngat Mountains* – an inhospitable and extremely dangerous wilderness also know as The Devil Mountains. Superstition and tales of strangeness and vanishing trespassers keep most natives away. His only hope of finding the diamond's source is in the form of the beautiful and mysterious grand daughter of the medicine man. Sky St. Onge reluctantly agrees to act as his guide but only if he promises to obey her commands without question; one false move in these mountains can send them both to their deaths.

Tracked by what they think is a competing prospecting company, and covert drone-like aircraft, and complicated by arctic winter weather moving in, Matthew and Sky have just weeks to find the kimberlitic pipes and prove to his company's investors that there are diamonds in Labrador. In the mountains, he and his fatalistic guide soon find that their competitors will apparently stop at nothing, including murder, to stake their own claim to the diamond field. With the *Land God Gave to Cain* as a forbidding and hostile backdrop for intrigue, Matthew finds three things he never set out to look for in the Torngats: the truth about his long dead father's disappearance; a wild and tempestuous love affair; and, an alternate reality that is completely out of this world.

* * * *

498

Made in the USA
Lexington, KY
08 May 2014